Chicago, 1930-70

CHICAGO
1930-70
Building, Planning, and Urban Technology

Carl W. Condit

The University of Chicago Press Chicago and London

The University of Chicago Press, Chicago 60637
The University of Chicago Press, Ltd., London
© 1974 by The University of Chicago
All rights reserved. Published 1974
Printed in the United States of America
International Standard Book Number: 0–226–11457–0
Library of Congress Catalog Card Number: 73–79996

Carl W. Condit is professor of history, urban affairs, and art history at Northwestern University. He is an acknowledged authority on urban architecture and has published many books and articles on the subject.

1974

Contents

Illustrations

Preface

My original plan was to regard this history as a single unified work, and the corresponding intention of the University of Chicago Press was to publish it in a single volume under the title *Chicago since 1910*. A number of factors, however, suggested that there would be advantages to both reader and publisher in splitting the book into two separate parts. The long text, the total of 176 plates and line cuts, the extensive tables and index, and the formidable bibliography would together have resulted in a book of nearly unmanageable size and discouraging price to the reader, and of prohibitive cost, in this age of tight budgets, to the publisher. Publication in two volumes, though it would mean no saving in total expense, at least had the merit of spreading it over a longer period of time. I doubt that the division adversely affects the continuity of the text—indeed, it throws into sharper relief the drastic discontinuity in urban development that came with the long hiatus in building caused by the depression of the thirties and the war that followed it. Those years marked the turning point for the American city—from expansion, confidence, and civic resurgence to economic and cultural decline. The two volumes thus treat two markedly different manifestations of the modern urban world.

An undertaking of this magnitude always involves the assistance of many individuals and institutions, and now that I have assembled what I hope is the complete roster, I am surprised at how many friends, associates, and students I have depended on. The gathering and tabulation of statistical data, the most tedious and exacting task in the preparation of the book, was almost entirely the work of Patricia Wishart. Some of the bibliographical material and tabular details were assembled by Marilyn Mollman, Sandra Page, Elizabeth Dull, Rosanne Maine, Susan Hull, and Lucy Shaffer. Among the librarians to whose patience and willing cooperation I am indebted are the following: Joseph Benson, former director of the Municipal Reference Library of Chicago; Joyce Malden, the present acting director; Candace Morgan, a staff member of the same library; Pauline Steffens, former director of the Chicago Park District Library; Benjamin Jacobson, director of the Transportation Library of Northwestern University; Mary Roy, his assistant librarian; and Janet Ayers of the library of the Northwestern Technological Institute. For answers to numerous and varied questions about the architectural history of Chicago, along with many conversations as useful as they were pleasant, I could always count on Wilbert Hasbrouck, executive director of the Chicago chapter of the American Institute of Architects, editor of the *Prairie School Review*, and director of the Prairie School Press. Information on rail traffic at Union Station was made available to me by Robert E. Clarkson of the Burlington Railroad's Industrial Engineering Department, and much valuable material on the Chicago Transit Authority and its predecessors was provided by George Krambles, director of the CTA's Research and Planning Department. Architectural plans and voluminous tabular data on Chicago schools were placed at my disposal by Francis Lederer, superintendent of physical plant and equipment, and Saul Samuels, chief architect, both of the Chicago Board of Education. Among those who provided photographs and drawings, I must single out for special thanks Richard Nickel, who gave his life for the preservation of Chicago's architectural heritage, Betty Ritter of the Perkins and Will Partnership, Jack Schaffer of Skidmore, Owings and Merrill, and Ben Weese of Harry Weese and Associates. Photographers, architects, libraries, and other institutions that provided photographs, drawings, and various prints are indicated in the list of credits for illustrations, and all sources of quotations are given in the notes.

The considerable expenses of fieldwork, travel, research assistance, and the assembly of illustrative material were borne by a number of organizations. I am indebted to Professor Scott Greer and the Center for Metropolitan Studies (now the Center for Urban Affairs) of Northwestern University for the largest single grant made in support of this work. Next in generosity was the Committee on Research Funds of the university, which provided me with annual grants over a period of five years. Finally, parts of recent grants from the American Philosophical Society and the National Science Foundation covered a share of the costs, chiefly of travel for comparative study in the field.

I think that anyone who labors in his home at what we are pleased to call scholarly work owes a special kind of continuing seven-day-a-week gratitude to the members of his family—in my case to my children, as much for their intermittent but apparently genuine expressions of interest in the uninteresting activity of authorship as for their willingness to forego conversation when it would be an unwanted interruption, and to my wife Isabel for patience, good humor, much useful criticism, and that belief in the validity of one's work that a man's ego can seldom survive without.

The City at a Standstill: Depression and War

1. The Century of Progress Exposition

The depression that began in 1930 and was ended ten years later only by a massive program of military procurement was a disaster for the nation as a whole but an absolute and unmitigated calamity for Chicago. It was not only the collapse of the public and private economy; it was also the Sophoclean reversal of fortune, from the expansive forces of the twenties that seemed to have no limit to the impotence and hopelessness of the thirties. The building industry, which had always been characterized by extreme swings of the business pendulum, was nearly struck dead by the depression, with the further consequence that real estate values in Chicago and the return on real estate investments both experienced an appalling attrition. By February 1932 Chicago had suffered the worst drop in property values of any major city in the United States, a decline of 50 percent from the high point of 1926 that was accompanied by a record number of defaults, foreclosures, and tax arrears.[1]

This grim prospect was both cause and consequence of the paralysis that afflicted the Chicago building industry. The value of new construction reached $366,586,400 in 1926 (about $1,906,000,000 at 1972 prices), a record the city was never to regain; from this peak the total dollar volume shrank to little more than one-one-hundredth of this figure, or $3,824,500 in 1932. Commercial building fared worst of all: the total expansion of office space in ten years of depression (1931–40) was 161,150 square feet, the demolition of existing space being offset mainly by the opening of the Field Building in 1934. Office construction during the five war years (1941–45), as we might expect, was nonexistent. Housing construction fell to a low point of 137 units in 1933, after which the public works and public housing programs of the New Deal added a sufficient volume to bring the total for the depression decade to 23,659 units, equal to about 7 percent of the total for the previous ten years. School construction virtually ceased in the two years preceding the inauguration of President Franklin Roosevelt in 1933, when the flow of public works grants from Washington made it possible to add thirty-four new schools by 1940, a total equal to less than 40 percent of those built by the city alone during the decade of the twenties.[2]

The immediate human consequence of these disasters was extensive unemployment, which not only precipitated thousands of families into desperate poverty, but what was sometimes worse for the wage earner, placed workers in the frightening psychological state of being arbitrarily denied an active and productive life when they were perfectly capable of both. But under the irrationality and the moral indifference of the American economic system, the wheel of the depression, once it began to turn, could only gather momentum. As the paralysis of business deepened, the tax revenues of the city fell, and by 1933 it could no longer pay its schoolteachers. The decline in real estate earnings led to the massive demolition of buildings in favor of parking lots or in some cases empty space simply to escape taxes. The worst example of this kind of vandalism was the destruction in 1930 of Richardson's Marshall Field Wholesale Store and the sale of the land to the R. G. Lydy Company for a generous parking area. The skyscraper boom of the twenties turned into an epidemic of receiverships in the thirties, and the vast program of public works undertaken to implement the Burnham Plan reached a dead end in 1930 when the city exhausted its bonding power and declining taxes left no funds for further construction. Vigorous commercial development in intermediate and peripheral areas of the city, such as the neighborhoods of Wilson Avenue (4600N) at Broadway, Howard Street (7600N) between Rogers and Ridge Avenue, and the Halsted–63rd Street center of Englewood, led to the usual land speculation followed by collapse, poverty, and blight. Meanwhile, vultures in the form of speculators hidden by dummy corporations and anonymous bank trusts, working in bad times as well as good, manipulated land values, acquired derelict property for a missed tax return, spread panic among racist whites with tales of ghetto onslaughts, and in general made handsome profits while contributing to the fear and chaos from which everyone suffered.

Before this sea of troubles nothing seemed more incongruous than the notion that Chicago should create a second world's fair forty years after the first to commemorate a hundred years of urban growth.[3] But like many ventures that were physically realized in the early years of the depression, the Century of Progress Exposition was planned in the twenties by a group of big-time financial operators who had gone too far by 1930 to pull back. Chicago had much to recommend it as the site for a national celebration of industrial progress by virtue of its geographical location, its position as a transportation hub, its unrivaled hotel accommodations, and its successes of happier years; but the choice also rested on a psychological state, a kind of bravado that managed to survive the troubles of the time at least until 1934. It was nicely described by the editors of *Architectural Forum* in a Monday-morning assessment of the two-year show.

Chicago is a good place to hold a fair. Sprawling like an alligator along the lakefront, it supplies its 3,500,000 head of more or less employed citizenry with every convenience—from swimming water to beaches to golf courses; from parks to highways to hot dog stands; from a river that flows the wrong way to industry galore; from a wheat pit to cattle on the hoof.

But those are physical aspects. Chicago also has a temperament ideally suited to tom-tom beating and fireworks and hurrah showmanship. It bursts to the buttons with a civic pride that built operas, Negro tenements and street corner waste containers significantly marked HELP KEEP OUR CITY CLEAN. It is as self-conscious as a Saturday afternoon window-dresser, as naïve as a schoolboy's conception of George Washington, as noisy as an evangelist. It gets good advertising by being the butt of more—and worse—jokes than the Model T Ford or Aimee Semple McPherson or Mae West or all three together could ever boast.

The sum total of its widely heralded gangsterism has been to lodge in the breasts of the country's honest travelers a curiosity to see what was inside the place. Indeed, against Chicago hardly a criticism could be launched which would be a satisfactory reason why a fair should not be held there.[4]

There were others who shared the view that Chicago was beyond question as a world's fair site, and the proposal for a new variant on the Columbian Exposition had come as early as 1924, the original author apparently having been the industrialist W. E. Clow. The possibility of realizing this dream at least suggested itself in 1927, when the brothers Charles Gates Dawes and Rufus C. Dawes, owners of various utilities and the Pure Oil Company, took the first steps leading to the necessary financial and organizational arrangements. With their advisers, they fixed the theme as a century of progress in science and its effect on industry and life, organized an exposition corporation, and appointed a board of trustees under the chairmanship of Rufus Dawes in the spring of the following year.[5] Money, of course, was the first necessity. Magnates like the Dawes brothers were naturally opposed to a government subsidy and sought to raise private capital from as large a group as possible in order to broaden personal and financial interest in the enterprise. They offered a $10,000,000 bond issue at 6 percent interest in January 1929; by May they had received a total of $12,176,000 in guarantees that were rapidly honored through the purchase of bonds or by direct loans. The chief guarantors were men on the highest financial plateau: various officers of the Dawes's utility and oil group, Julius Rosenwald of Sears, Roebuck and Company, Philip K. Wrigley of the chewing-gum empire, and Robert R. McCormick of the *Chicago Tribune*. A stroke of genius on the part of Charles and Rufus Dawes was the appointment of Major Lenox Riley Lohr, a military officer, editor, and administrator in the grand style of the twenties, as director of the exposition. Thus the fair was conceived in a time of prosperity and unlimited optimism, but it was to be opened at the very bottom of the worst depression, an unfortunate circumstance that failed to daunt the intrepid Lohr, who discovered among other things that economic disaster turned architects into energetic salesmen.

Even before money was in hand the trustees authorized Rufus Dawes to meet with Raymond Hood of New York and Paul Cret of Philadelphia to select five architects who possessed three qualifications stipulated by the board—reputation as architects, capacity as revealed by existing buildings designed in their offices, and ability to cooperate with others. In a striking parallel to the 1893 fair the trustees went far outside Chicago to choose the talented five: Harvey Wiley Corbett, Raymond Hood, and Ralph T. Walker of New York, Paul Philippe Cret of Philadelphia, and Arthur Brown, Jr., of San Francisco. The slight to Chicago was partly offset when the five unanimously chose Edward H. Bennett, Hubert Burnham, and John A. Holabird to serve on the architectural commission. Younger and little-known men of the city were also included, among them Nathaniel Owings and Louis Skidmore, who quickly proved to be remarkably skillful architectural entrepreneurs. The first meeting of the commission was held in May 1928, at which time the members issued their manifesto on the architectural theme of the fair.

The architecture of the buildings and grounds of the Exposition of 1933 will illustrate . . . the art of architecture since the great Fair of 1893, not only as in America but the world at large. New elements of construction, products of modern invention and science, will be the factors of the architectural composition. Artificial light, the tremendous progress of which has astonished all designers in recent years, will become an inherent component of the architectural composition. The extraordinary opportunities of the site for the use of water as an intrinsic element of the composition will be developed to the maximum.

The architecture of the world is undergoing a great change. It has shown those signs that indicate the birth of a great fresh impulse. The architects of the Chicago World's Fair of 1933 intend that the buildings of the Fair shall express the beauty of form and detail of both the national and the international aspects of this creative movement.[6]

The commission continued to meet throughout 1929, preparing and rejecting various site plans, although hard cash had yet to flow into the treasury. The site, which differed from that of any previous exposition, offered the architects a challenge while at the same time it presented them with the builder's equivalent of a tabula rasa. It was to comprise that portion of the new fill for Burnham Park and Northerly Island that extended southward from the line of Roosevelt Road (1200S) to 39th Street for a length of 3½ miles and was divided among the so-called island on the east, the connecting causeway, and the narrow mainland strip that varied in width from 300 to 440 yards. The planning program that the commission eventually adopted in the summer of 1929 rested on four principles: the site plan was to be two parallel, irregular, and asymmetrical strips; the buildings were to be kept low, with a maximum of three circulation levels; people were to be brought directly to the upper levels by ramps, then allowed to "filter down inside";[7] the buildings were to be connected as extensively as possible by means of outside ramps and passerelles. With a general plan broadly established, organizing and designing activities gained momentum. The commission established a Department of Works in the late summer of 1929, charging it with the preparation of working drawings and the fabrication of a thirty-two-foot-long model of the fairgrounds. The director of this department was Daniel H. Burnham, Jr., whose presence thus provided another link to the 1893 fair; his assistant was Clarence W. Farrier, the chief of design was Louis Skidmore, the chief engineer was Bert M. Thorud, and the supervisor of development was Nathaniel A. Owings. As design and construction progressed, the architectural commission and the Department of Works were expanded in size and responsibilities: the commission added separate designing staffs for landscape, color, and illumination; subdepartments of exhibits and concessions organized their own design divisions to advise exhibitors and concessionaires on problems of design; a part of the original Department of Works was reorganized as a Department of Operations and Maintenance to supervise the operation and maintenance of finished buildings, grounds, continuing programs, and special events.[8]

Before design had progressed very far the stock market crash of October 1929 ushered in the depression that began the following year. With more than $12,000,000 in hand or pledged, it was possible for the trustees to make a good start, but the forbidding economic climate made the whole enterprise seem hazardous, and it was probably Lohr's energy and promotional daring that were chiefly responsible for its ultimate success. As money came in, he boldly authorized construction of the major buildings, and he turned unemployed architects into salesmen who persuaded potential exhibitors and concessionaires to join what might be a promising venture. By 1932 the Administration Building and some exhibition space had been completed, and their presence encouraged additional exhibitors, who invested money or constructed their own exhibition buildings. When there was no cash in the till Lohr paid contractors in unsold bonds. It was a risky business, but the gamble paid off. Who, after all, had anything to lose? When the fair opened in May 1933, $1,000,000 in cash still remained in the bank, $25,000,000 had been invested in grounds and structures by the fair corporation, by numerous exhibitors, concessionaires, states, and the federal government, and—most gratifying of all—119,675 visitors came through the gates to look upon this rainbow city stretched along the blue and shining lake. The real city, the beaten, hungry, impotent Chicago behind them, was forgotten for the day at least (fig. 1).

The depression and the absence of any government subsidy proved to be blessings for the architects of the fair because the financial stringency compelled them to adopt a spirit of innovation and experiment in planning, construction, and materials that was to leave lasting benefits for the building arts. The informal site plan offered immediate practical advantages to offset an undoubted aesthetic poverty: it allowed a flexibility of design and construction that made it possible to meet any contingency, to expand or contract the area, to add or take away buildings large or small, as the flow of money dictated. The architects were forced to eliminate what they called the "grandiose effects" of earlier fairs and to develop the utmost economy of construction consistent with safety, utility, and the intended formal effects. The first group of buildings, those that were designed in 1929–30 by the members of the architectural commission, provided the major body of exhibition space and set the standard for all subsequent additions.[9] The aesthetic and structural character of these buildings, although it immediately became controversial and was ultimately regarded with contempt by the apostles of the new postwar fashions, did in fact represent a new if somewhat conservative architectural style drawn chiefly from the massing, the inflectional lines, and the moldings of the 1929 skyscraper, and in small part from the new forms developed by Le Corbusier, Mendelsohn, and Mies van der Rohe in Europe. What separated it from all previous work was the bold, vivid, and often astonishing use of color, employed along with illumination in wholly unprecedented ways. Louis Skidmore's original evaluation of what came to be called World's Fair Modern is still a just and even a prophetic estimate.

Certainly this architecture is free from the shackles of the past. It has brought the building and the exhibits it is to house into a close and sensible relationship with each other. The economy of construction, the use of new materials or the new uses of traditional materials, the departures in illumination, the use of colors in ways hardly imagined before may forecast a new era in building, an era that lays stress not so much on permanence as on the functioning of a building during its actual life, a building era that forgets the limitations of the past and designs buildings that are basically honest, which express the task they are performing, and which actually perform that task.[10]

The fair represented a second renaissance of modern architecture in the United States, in the city of its original birth, and a new consciousness of its character and meaning.

Since financial exigencies compelled the architects and engineers to abandon standard construction practices, they were in a position to adopt innovations of lasting value, chief of which was the use of manufactured components that could be

9

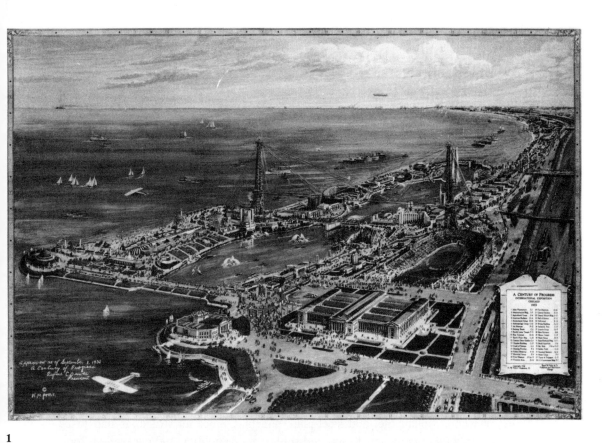

1

2

placed by hand, allowing the rapid assembly of building elements with a minimum of fieldwork. In this respect the designers enjoyed subsidiary advantages that also pointed to future possibilities in structural technology. First of all, both designers and exhibitors received extensive cooperation from manufacturing associations and manufacturers' laboratories, this generous cooperative spirit being another of the dividends arising from the depressed state of the economy. Second, because of the lakefront setting and because of partial state financing in the preparation of the fill, the city building code did not apply, and the appropriate state office drew up a special code to satisfy the safety requirements of the underwriters and to make possible the rapid removal of all structures at the close of the fair, which was a requirement of the contract between the corporation and the city and state.

The result of all these restrictions and opportunities was a model performance code that allowed the use of novel temporary materials and higher than standard working stresses in meeting the criteria of loading, fire resistance, exit capacity, light, ventilation, sanitation, and behavior of materials. Further, in spite of the limitations of time, new materials could be adopted after experimental demonstrations of their load-bearing capacity, salvage value, and resistance to fire and wear, a practice which alone offered the builder far more flexible standards than were provided in the permanent city code. The chief areas of research were those involving the choice of materials for decking and wall sheathing. The buildings of the fair accordingly were constructed of light steel or timber framing sheathed in prefabricated units of wall and deck materials, chiefly gypsum and other plasterboard, masonite, magnesite, plywood, asphalt tile, and steel-plate paneling. Since all structures had to be erected on a fill of compacted sand and spoil from demolition and excavation, footings and foundations were carried on piling, which was reduced to the minimum of one pile for each exterior column and two for each interior column. In the few places where eccentricities existed between columns and piles, wall beams and cantilevers of concrete were employed to avoid irregular settlement and consequent secondary stresses. The steel frames were required not only by the large open interiors like those of the Travel and Transport group (p. 11) but also by the numerous two-story buildings that formed a unique feature of the Century of Progress that was made feasible by the widespread use of ramps and passerelles. All two-story frames were designed on a twenty-foot bay span for exhibition space and constructed of steel columns and open-web joists, and all small one-story frames were timber with spans up to sixteen feet.[11]

In the vast agglomeration of buildings and other structures at the Century of Progress, designed by architects and engineers from Europe and Asia as well as

North America, four commanded special attention for intrinsic characteristics of design or for their subsequent importance to the building arts. Foremost of these was the Travel and Transport Building, the main enclosure of which was the first suspended structure in the United States, opened eighty years after James Bogardus and Hamilton Hoppin made the initial American proposal for such construction in a project for the New York Exhibition of 1853. The architects of the Chicago work were Bennett, Burnham, and Holabird, and the engineer was B. M. Thorud, for whom the celebrated bridge engineer Leon Moisseiff acted as consultant. The circular domed roof of the Transport building was supported by a network of steel cables descending from a ring of twelve steel towers that were braced laterally and radially by portal trusses and pyramidal space trusses (fig. 2). Since this was in essence suspension-bridge construction, it was necessary to anchor the carrying cables by means of backstays fixed to twelve reinforced concrete anchor blocks deeply imbedded in the ground outside the building wall. The reasons for adopting this innovation sprang from considerations of economy and structural efficiency: the heavy steel ribs or trusses by which domes were usually supported and the associated costly centering could be eliminated; the dome frame could then be reduced to relatively small radial I-beams, which could be carried most economically by means of direct tension in the cables and direct compression in the columns. The subsidiary rectangular enclosure of the Transport group was carried on three-hinged arched trusses that were less a novelty than the suspension system but were more elegant in form than the rather crude forerunner of the later cable-supported roofs.

The largest and most spectacular structure at the fair was the Sky Ride, designed by the bridge engineers David B. Steinman and Holton D. Robinson, with whom Joshua d'Esposito was associated as a consultant. This impressive work, proposed as the modern counterpart of the great Ferris wheel at the 1893 fair, was in basic form a long-span suspension bridge without a deck and without side or anchor spans. The two towers, 628 feet high and anchored by a network of radiating backstays, supported a double system of parallel stayed cables across a span of 1,850 feet at a clear height of 218 feet above grade. Each set of cables carried two double-deck observation cars with a capacity of thirty-six passengers, the cars being drawn along the fixed cables by a motor-driven set of moving cables. Although this extraordinary work was more prominent than any of the Chicago skyscrapers, it was erected at a cost of only $1,000,000.

There were many houses constructed of prefabricated units and designed as low-cost homes at the middle-income level, but they were generally undistinguished as works of architecture. The striking exception was the House of Tomorrow, designed by George Fred Keck under the sponsorship of the Century Homes Company. Dodecagonal in plan, with three levels contracting successively in area, the structure consisted essentially of a light steel frame carrying a wall paneling of molded fire-proof plastic at the ground floor and of glass in floor-to-ceiling sash at the second and third floors. A central heating and air-conditioning unit allowed the use of fixed sash, sunlight control being provided by aluminum-coated Venetian blinds. Movable wardrobes took the place of the customary built-in closets, and fixed partitions were frosted Carrara glass in a light metal framework. An all-electric kitchen and the central air-conditioning system constituted the chief innovations among interior utilities. The house was strictly experimental, and many of its features were at the time little known, but all of them except for the plastic wall panels became commonplace in later years.

Although 12,000,000 workers were totally unemployed at the end of 1933, the fair was such an astounding success that the directors quickly decided to repeat the show in the appropriate season of 1934. Among the new additions and changes the one perhaps most conducive to the festive spirit was the appearance of alcoholic beverages, following the repeal of the Prohibition amendment in April 1933. A new and simpler color scheme, involving a reduction of the number of tones from twenty-five to twelve, new buildings, better facilities for resting and strolling, and free toilets with "no tipping" signs were the chief improvements. The most prominent of the 1934 buildings was the Ford Exposition Center, the exterior design and the interior planning of which were the work of the Albert Kahn firm, the landscaping of Jens Jensen, and the photomural displays of Walter Dorwin Teague. There was a great proliferation of phony "villages"—Dutch, Spanish, Swiss, and the like—all of them designed as something of a depression joke by leading Chicago architects, among whom Holabird, Root, T. E. Tallmadge, and Hugh Garden were particularly distinguished. The most important of all the new buildings with respect to structural character was the modest and unspectacular enclosure of the Brook Hill Farm Dairy Company's exhibit, for it was this work that introduced concrete-shell construction to the United States, twenty-four years after the pioneer essay appeared in Europe. Designed by the architect Robert Philipp and the engineering firm of Roberts and Schaefer, the little building was roofed by a multilobe shell in the form of five trans-verse elliptical vaults supported only at their ends and hence providing a clear span over the 72-foot length of the enclosure. The shell thickness of three inches (in-creased to 6½ inches at the valley rib between adjacent shells) was greater than structurally necessary but was adopted to provide solar insulation.

As valuable for the subsequent development of architecture as the structural

innovations at the Century of Progress was the development of color as a fundamental element of the whole architectural composition. Color planning was carried
out under the direction of Joseph Urban and his assistants, Shepard Vogelgesang
and William Muschenheim, the latter of whom provided the best statement of the
principles of color design and their application to specific enclosures.

The first large scale application of color in this country with an entirely new purpose, a new realization of its potentialities as an architectural medium, has been
attempted at A Century of Progress Exposition. The problem was to coordinate and
give vitality to a huge group of buildings of widely varying use and design, and it
became the function of color to unify the whole scheme and articulate it to the best
advantage. But to achieve this effect the treatment of color as decoration superimposed upon the architectural form was inadequate. In this case, the effort was made
rather to employ color as a positive force, not as a trimming. . . . First of all, the
main buildings were studied in their spatial relations and a scheme was developed
which accentuated their relative positions, the color being designed to emphasize
both unity and contrast as given. Since the buildings were completed before any
color was planned the color was consistently used to heighten and enliven the effects
already achieved. . . . Since . . . the color was intended to make a positive contribution to the significance of the whole, it seemed necessary to employ a palette made
up of the strongest, clearest, purest, most direct pigments available.[12]

In more concrete terms, color was used to delineate the main functional spaces
and the formal or geometric volumes of particular buildings, to separate the masses
of a given structure, to distinguish structural elements from enclosing curtains, to
intensify structural articulation, to relate, separate, or contrast the main buildings
and groups, and to provide visual transitions among them. In the case of the palette
for a particular building—Paul Cret's very conspicuous Hall of Science, for example
—Muschenheim provided a more concrete analysis.

The main mass of deep orange with its wings of lighter orange rests on a series of
blue and white horizontally striped terraces stretching out toward the water, and is
pinned to earth by the main tower which picks up the blue of the terraces and whose
perpendicular function is emphasized by a vertical strip of the deep blue already
encountered in the avenue of approach.[13]

Lighting at the exposition was less marked by innovation than color and structure
and was inferior to that of the Paris Exposition of 1925, which considerably influenced the site planning and the architectural design of the Chicago fair, but it was a
product of scientific analysis aimed at good functional illumination as well as visual
impact. Street, walkway, and bridge lighting was fixed to high standards in order to

minimize direct glare to the eyes, except for the bridge to Northerly Island, which was lighted indirectly by lamps in the parapet. The exterior surfaces of buildings were illuminated by fixed floodlights to define volumes and to bring out the color at night. Luminous outlines of buildings and other decorative features were accomplished mainly by neon tubing that could be readily shaped into a lively abstract sculpture like the fifty-five-foot "cascade" of blue neon tubes at the Electric Building. Light in association with water displays was little used because of high cost, so that very few of the fountains were illuminated by colored underwater floodlights. Spectacular light patterns on the large scale were confined to the aurora borealis at the southern end of the fairgrounds, which was composed of moving beams of colored light, but scattered throughout the area there were many fans, plumes, clouds, pinwheels, and other vaporous shapes illuminated by colored beams. Interior lighting was almost entirely indirect, achieved again to a great extent by the use of neon tubing.

As a financial enterprise the fair was a success greater than anyone dared predict or even hope for on its opening day. The total attendance exceeded 36,000,000 for the two seasons, divided between 22,320,000 in 1933 and 14,000,000 in 1934, and the revenues were sufficient to meet all expenses and to pay the bondholders the full principal sum of their investment plus about $1,500,000 in interest. Few concessions lost money, and many were highly profitable, including the bitterly criticized pay toilets of the first season. The temporary economic benefits to bankrupt Chicago must have seemed like the difference between life and death. Money spent in the city by fair visitors during the two May–November seasons was estimated to be $700,000,000, but this sum was considerably augmented in 1933, when the city attracted 71 percent of all conventions held in the United States. The combined effects of the fair and the conventions on rail passenger traffic were impressive: 4,000,000 persons traveled to Chicago by rail in the 1933 season and another 2,700,000 in the 1934, the totals in both cases being equal to the number arriving from out of town by family car and about four times the number traveling by bus.

There can be no question that just as the Columbian Exposition gave rise to the City Beautiful movement, which left a permanent residue in the philosophy of American planning, so the Century of Progress played a major role in the rapid acceptance of modern architecture in the thirties and forties. The cultivated reactions to the fair at the time were as numerous and irreconcilable as the architects who delivered opinions, but there was a particular irony in the parallel attacks leveled by the two who stood at opposite ends of the architectural spectrum, Ralph Adams Cram and Frank Lloyd Wright. Cram, a medievalist permanently alienated from everything that had occurred since the fifteenth century, saw only horror.

The "progress" indicated by the architecture is solely that along technological and scientific lines. . . . It may be admitted that this architecture we now see, which, to put it baldly, seems to me a casual association of the gasometer, the freight yard and the grain elevator, is an appropriate manifestation of technological civilization, but in my opinion this places the emphasis where it does not belong. Moreover, I claim that there is a difference between beauty and ugliness, that personal inclination and the ephemeral fashions of the time change neither the one nor the other, . . . so I maintain the present showing is one of incorrigible ugliness. Finally, I am persuaded that the "style" adopted for the present buildings is already old-fashioned and outmoded. It is already being abandoned in Europe. . . . For these reasons I deplore what has been done at this Exposition. I consider that it represents not real "progress" but definite retrogression, even degeneration. . . . Even as Rockefeller Center in New York is the *reductio ad absurdum* of technocratic principles, so these buildings at Chicago will prove not only a revelation but a warning. It is the end of an era.[14]

Given his premises, it would have to be argued that Cram was at least logical in his deductions: he looked for an architecture that might stand as the symbol of a cosmos, preferably divine, which modern architecture could not be; but even he must have had misgivings that Gothic and other medieval forms could not endlessly be applied to the diverse requirements of modern building.

Wright, on the other hand, saw the ugliness in a kind of fraudulence, a feeble but showy copying of a forgotten reality.

No synthesis is involved in this Fair except wholesale imitation, hit or miss, of the genuine new forms that occurred in our country in out of the way places many years ago. A formula has now been deduced from that which may be made to pass for a new style for a while. The "public," whatever that is, may be partially weaned from pseudo-classic only to find another "pseudo" thrust into its arms. How stale it all is where the spirit is hungry for reality. . . . To me, of course, the whole performance is petty, strident and base. Great repose, belonging by nature to the spontaneous, genuine originality which almost all of the superficial forms helplessly or craftily resemble, is nowhere. Genuine art must come from the inside. . . . And here is no inside, only an "I will," or an empty artifice. . . . I feel all these ignoble satisfactions to be contemptible waste. . . . Nothing has happened except gesture and gaudy—sometimes bawdy—self-indulgence.[15]

And a great deal more in a similar vein. It is difficult to see in this contemptuous, romantic, and possibly vindictive denunciation what the basis of Wright's criticism is, except that the buildings are not like those that Wright and his fellow architects of the Chicago school had created at the turn of the century. The fair should have included work of this mode, but to cite its absence constitutes neither a moral nor an aesthetic judgment.

Buckminster Fuller, whose prose as well as his thought was less tortured than in later years, also attacked the fair, but on the basis of social principles derived from some kind of populist-technocratic doctrines that he espoused during the depression.

It is true that the most successful bank-era architects have "composed" as a painter to a certain degree, but only when they have shrewdly learned to realize that the psychology of the patron, and the graft system of the city involved, and the underground economic control of the banking fraternities, and the labor racketeers' interest must be considered as of 95 percent important, against 1 percent for the visual design. (The physical requirements approximated 4 per cent.) . . . The desperate yet futile plagiarisms, pseudo-scientific wonders, and garish advertising-mania architecture of the '33 World's Fair, designed to restimulate business for the "good old" [business circles], rather than serving as a copyable composition for the current generations, may be analyzed as symbolizing the kaleidoscopic environment of the present world revolution out of which will grow an architecture typified by no one form but whose single characteristic will be continuity of growthfulness and adaptability.[16]

More genuinely critical and hence more positive assessments could come only from men closer to the architectural realities of the late twenties than Cram, Wright, or Fuller. Ely Jacques Kahn, who had designed the Home Planning Hall, regarded the fair as architecturally inferior to recent expositions in France and Germany, especially in the poor quality of its landscaping and in its miserly and uninviting entrances, but he understood what the architects were trying to do in their dissection of volumes into parallel and intersecting planes of color and luminosity. It was precisely the absence of sham along with the almost palpable color that gave the buildings their vivid quality.

It would seem to me that this color statement is by all odds the most vital contribution to a new architecture. We have been so subservient to a literary version of what classic architecture might have been that a sense of color has almost left us. . . . The struggles to break back into color are oases in history.

With the color as an outstanding accomplishment, one must bow to the splendid handling of the exhibits themselves, the interiors of the various buildings, the lighting, general color schemes and lettering. If anyone doubts that this work will not have a great influence on American architecture of the immediate future, he must question the judgment of the average American citizen.[17]

Corbett himself may claim the last word, for he was by necessity most thoroughly imbued with the functional, organic, and yet festive spirit that the architects tried to embody in the ephemeral materials of an exposition.

The all-important thing . . . which A Century of Progress architecture presents to the American public is the thoroughly rational exposition plan in which the design expresses the new construction. . . . Windowless buildings of two or more stories, interconnected at both levels and tied to the ground by broad, easy ramps, provide exhibitors with permanent and dependable artificial light and visitors with ease and comfort of movement. Symmetry and balance, except in a minor degree, are seldom suitable to the practical phases of the problem. . . . None of the old-fashioned, established principles of composition was applicable to the exposition plan. Certainly the buildings could not simulate masonry. Ornament, which had had its origin in masonry, could not be appropriately used. Color, brilliantly handled, was the logical substitute.[18]

It is another irony in the history of modern architecture that both the doctrine and its embodiment in an executed work were prefigured forty years earlier in Louis Sullivan's Transportation Building at the World's Columbian Exposition.

NOTES TO CHAPTER 1

1. The total assessed value of real estate in Chicago has been wildly erratic, marked by disastrous deflations that interrupted the overall upward rise in the curve of averages, as the accompanying list of extreme values shows.

1833	$ 168,000
1836	10,000,000
1842	1,400,000
1856	125,000,000
1861	60,000,000
1873	575,000,000
1879	250,000,000
1885	550,000,000
1892	1,500,000,000
1897	1,000,000,000
1910	1,500,000,000
1920	2,000,000,000
1926	5,000,000,000
1933	2,500,000,000

These cycles were accompanied by extreme fluctuations in the rate of return, from a minimum of 2.5 percent to a maximum of 12 percent. (Source: Chicago Title and

Trust Company; quoted in "The Ups and Downs of Chicago Real Estate . . . ," *Architectural Forum* 59[August 1933]:141.)

2. For statistical details of new office construction, housing, dollar volume of all construction, and school building, see tables 2, 3, 4, and 5 (all tables are at the end of the text).

3. The choice of 1933 as some kind of centennial year was rather arbitrary. Chicago was legally recognized as a town on 4 August 1830, incorporated as such in 1833, reincorporated within somewhat larger limits in 1835, and incorporated as a city under an Illinois charter on 4 March 1837.

4. "A Century of Progress Paradox," *Architectural Forum* 61(November 1934):374.

   Aimee Semple McPherson was a popular female evangelist who flourished in Los Angeles during the twenties and thirties. She never preached in Chicago, but the devastating impersonation of her by Fanny Brice in the Ziegfeld Follies of 1933 was one of the few cheerful interludes in the city's dismal depression winters. Mae West, a marvelously durable comedienne of burlesque, nightclubs, vaudeville, and the movies, was approaching the triumphant point of her career in a starring role opposite W. C. Fields in the movie *My Little Chickadee* (1940).

5. The board consisted of the following members: Rufus C. Dawes, chairman of the board and president of the corporation; Daniel H. Burnham, Jr., secretary; George Woodruff, treasurer; C. S. Peterson, vice-president; Lenox R. Lohr, general manager of the fair; Britton I. Budd, Francis X. Busch, Abel Davis, Mrs. Kellogg Fairbank, Amos C. Miller, F. R. Moulton, and William Allen Pusey.

   The thematic concept of the fair involved the usual popular confusion between science and technology.

6. Quoted in Louis Skidmore, "Planning and Planners," *Architectural Forum* 59(July 1933):30 (the entire issue was devoted to the exposition).

7. Ibid., p. 31.

8. The organization of the designing and supervising staff was developed in a highly pragmatic way—first, to provide practical as well as aesthetically satisfying designs and, second, to work out the means by which such designs could be translated into physical reality as rapidly and economically as possible. In the fall of 1930 the landscape architect Ferruccio Vitale was added to the architectural commission as chief landscape designer, and shortly thereafter Alfred Geiffert was appointed as his assistant. Joseph Urban was appointed director of color in the spring of 1932, Otto Teegen was named as his assistant, William Muschenheim as consultant, and Shepard Vogelgesang as supervisor of interior color. By the fall of 1932 Lee Lawrie had been retained as sculptural consultant and Walter D'Arcy Ryan as director of illumination. The architectural commission and its various consultants theoretically had no jurisdiction over the design of buildings erected by private exhibitors, but such designs were subject to commission review and approval. The respective design divisions of the exhibits and concessions departments worked closely with the individual exhibitors, and it was here that Louis Skidmore demonstrated his capacity for administering the complex activities of design teams: his advisory group in the Exhibits Department guided over five hundred exhibitors in the design of displays as well as of special exhibition buildings, in the process requiring that all designs be submitted for criticism, revision, and final approval.

   In addition to supervising the construction of buildings, special structures, walks, drives, and bridges, and the installation of landscaping, the Department of Works was also responsible for laying water, gas, electric, and sewer lines equivalent to those necessary to serve 1,000,000 persons. Bert Thorud was chiefly responsible for the supervision of this activity.

9. The main buildings of this initial group and their architects were the following: electrical exhibits complex on Northerly Island, Raymond Hood; General Exhibits Building (in part) and Hall of Science, Paul Cret; General Exhibits Building, Harvey Corbett; entrances, Administration and Travel and Transport buildings, Edward Bennett, D. H. Burnham, Jr., and John Holabird; Dairy, Agricultural, States, and United States Government buildings, Bennett and Arthur Brown, Jr. All buildings designed in 1929–30 were erected except for the Tower of Water and Light, which was replaced by the Sky Ride (see p. 11).

The subject of architectural design inevitably raises the question why Frank Lloyd Wright was not selected as one of the architects. He had been in Japan and California after leaving Chicago in 1916, so that he was virtually forgotten in the city of his first and most numerous triumphs. There were several proposals to invite him to design one or more of the fair buildings, but he appears to have rejected them, in spite of the fact that he was hard hit by the depression. Although the proposed association proved unsuccessful, however, it marked Wright's return to the Chicago region, and the largest of all his commissions (Administration Building, S. C. Johnson and Company, Racine, Wisconsin) was to come in two years from an area in which he had early demonstrated his power. (Wright's comments on the fair are given later in this chapter.)

10. Louis Skidmore, "Planning and Planners," *Architectural Forum* 59(July 1933):32.

11. Because of the importance of the exposition to the slow and frequently abortive process of the industrialization of building, I have summarized the data on materials, their properties, methods of testing and selection, and structural elements and techniques in the following outline:

Floor Materials

 I. Criteria of selection
  1. Minimum cost of material, manufacture, fabrication, and installation
  2. Strength, elasticity, and durability
  3. Fire resistance
  4. Ease of joining to columns and posts
  5. Minimum density
  6. Ease of applying insulation, finished flooring, and wearing surfaces
  7. Ease of demolition
  8. Salvage value
 II. Materials rejected because of high cost
  1. Precast reinforced gypsum slabs with interlocking joints
  2. Precast reinforced magnesite composition slabs with interlocking joints
  3. Matched wood planking with finished wearing surface in single-deck thickness
 III. Materials selected on basis of acceptable costs and laboratory and field tests
  1. Ribbed metal deck (light-gauge metal formed into long channel sections with flush top surfaces and interlocking edge ribs)
  2. Corrugated metal deck with various kinds of lightweight fire-resistant filling over corrugations

3. Precast reinforced lightweight concrete slabs with special wearing surface and interlocking joints (limited to ramps because of high cost)
4. Five-ply Douglas fir plywood with matched longitudinal joints, in 3 × 8 ft. or 3 × 12 ft. units.
5. Battle-deck steel-plate floor with interlocking joints, spanning up to 20 feet.

Wall Materials

I. Criteria of selection
  1–8. Same as those for flooring
  9. Sufficient strength to bear wind loads
  10. Joint construction adequate to maintain weather tightness
  11. Interior wall surfaces fully noncombustible
  12. Exterior surfaces slow-burning (twenty-minute fire resistance)
II. Materials rejected because of high cost
  1. Precast gypsum units extending from floor to floor with interlocking joints, forming finished interior surface; exterior surface glued canvas with overlapping joints
  2. Prefabricated laminated insulation boards covered on the exterior and interior with various kinds of sheet metal or asbestos cement board with interlocking joints, coverings glued with insoluble adhesives, in thicknesses strong enough to span from floor to intermediate girts
  3. Pressed-steel plate sections with flush exterior surfaces, interlocking joints, floor-to-floor lengths, formed for application of wallboard interior finish (equivalent to railroad boxcar construction)
III. Materials and wall and ceiling construction selected on basis of cost and laboratory and field tests
  1. Unit wall construction: ribbed metal siding set vertically with interlocking and weathertight joints, flush exterior surfaces, units clipped to horizontal girts, interior wallboard attached to metal or wood furring (equivalent of ribbed metal-deck flooring)
  2. Exterior wallboard: ½-inch asbestos cement wallboard set 24 inches center to center, with metal weatherstripping (limited use)
  3. Same: ½-inch five-ply Douglas fir plywood, mill-primed, in 4 × 8 ft. or 4 × 12 ft. sheets (limited use)
  4. Same: ½-inch gypsum board with tongue-and-groove joints, in 4 × 8 ft. or 4 × 12 ft. sheets, mill-primed and painted in situ (general use)
  5. Interior wallboard: ⅜-inch gypsum board, sheets fastened with cement-coated nails or galvanized screws; butt joints laid close without filler except where necessary for appearance
  6. Ceilings: ⅜-inch gypsum board on metal or wood furring suspended from open-web (steel) joists; in some cases fireproof cloth ceilings used for decorative effect; in a few cases ceiling omitted, roof joists providing architectural effect

(Note on framing: commercial metal I-section studs generally proved inadequate for wind resistance; forms adopted were either conventional timber studs or patented metal truss studs with grooved runners on the flanges to hold wallboard sheets.)

Wearing Surfaces, Roofs, Floors

I. Criteria of selection
    1. Minimum cost of material and application
    2. Durability and resistance to wear
    3. Low density
    4. Color and general appearance
II. Materials tested in laboratory and field
    1. Linoleum
    2. Precast composition tiles on mastic
    3. Asphalt-coated laminated felts
    4. Wood-finish floorings cemented to subfloor
    5. Same secured with lugs to channel runners on subfloor
    6. Masonite (wood-fiber composition sheet) flooring on mastic bed
    7. Cement finish reinforced with metal bars secured to subfloor
    8. Emulsified asphalt composition
    9. Magnesite composition
    10. Gypsum composition
III. Materials selected after testing under actual conditions
    1. Magnesite composition finish (for general exhibition buildings)
    2. Wood finish cemented down (for general exhibition buildings)
    3. Masonite sheets on mastic (for general exhibition buildings)
    4. Asphalt composition plank tile laid in hot asphalt mopping (for exterior terraces)
    5. Hot asphalt mastic finish laid over membrane (for exterior terraces where very light weight was desirable)
    6. Three-ply composition roofing felt with asphalt mopping, over various kinds of board-form insulation, secured to wood decks by nailing and to metal decks by mopped-on hot asphalts (all roofs)
    7. Plank laid on sleepers bedded in fill (light-duty floors on fill)
    8. Reinforced concrete slab (heavy-duty floors on fill)

Loading Factors

Roofs	25	pounds per square foot
Framed floors, exhibition	100	” ” ” ”
Framed floors, storage	150	” ” ” ”
Framed floors, office	50	” ” ” ”
Ground floors on fill	450	” ” ” ”
Horizontal wind on structure	20	” ” ” ”
Horizontal wind on wall	25	” ” ” ”
Deflection, maximum allowable	1/360 of span	

The chief determinants in framing for general exhibition buildings were long spans and noncombustibility, so that steel was chosen as the most economical material for exhibition space with maximum bay spans and wood for the smaller single-story buildings where short spans presented no obstacle to the arrangement of exhibits. In a typical wide-span frame bents of steel girders spanning up to 30 feet for floors and 50 feet for roofs extended across the shorter transverse dimension of the building for rigidity and were carried on columns usually set 20 feet center to center along the longitudinal line. Floors and roofs were supported by steel truss joists. Girders were bolted to columns through a shelf angle at the bottom flange and a plate at the top to provide a simple form of portal bracing very much like the pioneer installation at the Crystal Palace in London (1851).

(Source of the foregoing data: Bert M. Thorud, "Engineering Research and Building Construction," *Architectural Forum* 59[July 1933]:65–69.)

12. William Muschenheim, "The Color of the Exposition," *Architectural Forum* 59(July 1933):2–3.
13. Ibid., p. 3.
14. Ralph Adams Cram, "Retrogression, Ugliness," *Architectural Forum* 59(July 1933): 24–25.
15. Frank Lloyd Wright, "Another 'Pseudo,'" *Architectural Forum* 59(July 1933):25.
16. R. Buckminster Fuller, "Profit-Control and the Pseudo-Scientific," *Architectural Forum* 59(July 1933):27.
17. Ely Jacques Kahn, "Close-up Comments on the Fair," *Architectural Forum* 59(July 1933):23.
18. Harvey Wiley Corbett, "The Significance of the Exposition," *Architectural Forum* 59(July 1933):1.

2. Building under the New Deal

When the happy months of the exposition had ended, the continuing reality of the depression seemed more painful than ever. It was like a medieval plague whose origin could not be traced and whose cure could not be discovered. By 1934 even the comfortable middle class was beginning to suffer as the flow of income along its usual channels ceased: the city could not pay its teachers, who subsisted on a kind of scrip; landlords could not collect rents, and evictions were barred by law to prevent universal misery; stores gave up attempts to demand the payment of bills due under their charge accounts. The urban economy came perilously close to total collapse, a fate from which it was ultimately saved not by the fair but by the massive program of public works initiated by President Franklin Roosevelt's first New Deal administration in March 1933. A minor rescue operation was undertaken by the State of Illinois in 1930, but this proved to be a mere palliative that had to be abandoned at the very time the depression reached its lowest depth. When the federal government began its own program the concepts of slum clearance, low-cost housing, and building as an answer to pressing social needs were still in an embryonic stage in the United States, so that for the first half of the depression decade public expenditures were devoted mainly to traditional civic works such as boulevards, bridges, public transportation, and hydraulic and sanitary installations. In these areas Chicago was treated more generously than any other city for two very good reasons, namely, its well-established and extensively implemented plan and the huge Democratic majorities that Mayor Edward J. Kelley's powerful machine could regularly guarantee.[1]

The first group of public projects that formed the largest body of interrelated works were those having to do with the continuing expansion of Lincoln Park and the associated improvement of North Lake Shore Drive. The continuation of this vast enterprise immediately after the onset of the depression was the work of the state government. The fill which had been completed to Montrose Avenue (4400N) in 1929 was extended to Foster Avenue (5200N) in 1930–32, and the length of the present Lake Shore Drive between Belmont (3200N) and Foster, with its landscaped dividing strip and cloverleaf intersections, was constructed at about the same time, reaching completion in 1933.[2] In the following year a much more important work in the lakeshore program was undertaken when the city resumed construction of the Link Bridge over the Chicago River after a delay of nearly five years. The steady expansion of parks and drives north and south along the lakefront during the two decades following the adoption of the Burnham Plan made it essential to join the two halves if the system was to be used to its full potential and if Michigan Avenue was to be spared the intolerable volume of through traffic that was already being generated on the North Side and Grant Park boulevards. But since the undertaking involved the erection of an eight-lane movable bridge at an elevation sufficient for two levels, it required the simultaneous construction of two long approach viaducts, one extending north from the bridge to Ohio Street (600N), and the other south to Monroe (100S), for a total length of slightly less than one mile.[3] The Chicago Plan Commission in 1926 authorized its engineer, Hugh E. Young, to develop preliminary plans and cost estimates for the connection and in the following year began the process of land acquisition and the necessary legal and financial operations. The contract for the design of the bridge was awarded to the Strauss Engineering Company in 1929, but before actual construction could begin the city's economic collapse put an end to all further activity. The vital work was resumed in 1934 as Chicago's first project under the Public Works Administration and brought to completion in October 1937. If the lower deck had been added to the 264-foot long double-leaf bascule bridge, it would have been the heaviest structure of its kind ever built.

The opening of Link Bridge provided a continuous eight-lane high-speed boulevard from Jackson Park to Ohio Street, but between the latter point and the newly completed segment north of Belmont Avenue the increasingly heavy traffic was thrown onto the old four-lane drives bordering the Gold Coast and extending through the south third of Lincoln Park. The construction of the Gold Coast segment of the new drive (Ohio Street to North Avenue), which was placed immediately alongside the original artery on a broadened fill, was begun shortly before Link Bridge was completed and opened in 1939, again with a substantial Public Works Administration grant to bear the cost (fig. 3). The construction of the last remaining segment, North to Belmont, was part of an immense shoreline development that Burnham would have been proud of (fig. 4). With the Public Works Administration paying most of the cost, the city began in 1938 the simultaneous construction of the beach house, the curving concrete groin at North Avenue, and the two-mile length of Lake Shore Drive north to Belmont, opening the whole project to public use in 1942. Seldom have urban technology and civic art been combined to better recreational and aesthetic ends: the massive semicircular groin worked perfectly to trap the sand and allow hydrodynamic action to build up the broad sweep of North Avenue Beach, along which later extensions of the promenade provided a mile-long walkway to Fullerton Avenue; the three-hinged steel arch that carries the pedestrian passerelle over the drive is an elegant little classic of the bridge-building art; under-

Fig. 3. North Lake Shore Drive, from Oak Street Beach northward, as it appeared from 1939 up to the building of the Oak Street–Michigan Avenue Interchange, 1963–65.

Fig. 4. North Lake Shore Drive along the south portion of Lincoln Park, from Diversey Harbor southward. The length of the drive from Belmont to North Avenue was built in 1939–42.

3

4

neath it the busy artery possesses the unique feature of movable dividers that provide a six-lane inbound or outbound traffic flow during the rush hours and the customary balanced pattern between them. The grand scheme provides another of those stunning urban vistas that only Chicago offers: south of the Fullerton Avenue overpass the meadows, lagoons, and wooded areas of Lincoln Park lie to the west, the beach and the unbounded lake stretch to the east, and the extravagant skyscrapers of the Gold Coast constitute the city's flamboyant backdrop. The whole scene is composed like a work of art, balanced and harmonious, forming a seamless unity of water, land, and buildings.

Other park and shore projects served to round out the South Side development, the largest among them being associated with the expansion of the city's water supply system. The numerous separate park districts—a total of twenty-two at one time—were finally merged into a single Chicago Park District in 1934, an event that was celebrated by the completion of the district's administrative center, an uninspired work of what was once known as PWA modern that stands on 14th Boulevard directly opposite the rear elevation of the Field Museum. Far to the south, at 79th Street, a new recreational area and beach later designated Rainbow Park were beginning to take shape in 1938 as an integral part of the Water Department's huge South District Filtration Plant, which was itself the culmination of a continuing enlargement through the thirties and forties of the whole water supply system of tunnels, intake cribs, and pumping stations (fig. 5).[4]

The filtration plant, at 3300 East Cheltenham Avenue, was the first structure of its kind in Chicago, since the drinking water had not previously been filtered, although this had been recommended as early as 1910. Built in two separate phases, 1938–42 and 1945–47, as the result of wartime interruptions, the extensive complex of buildings and hydraulic equipment was the product of several talents: architectural design was carried out under the direction of Paul Gerhardt, Jr., the city architect, and the engineering work was chiefly the responsibility of W. W. De Berard, the city engineer, and John R. Baylis, the water filtration engineer (figs. 6–8). Filtration engineering was a well-established branch of technology, but the Chicago plant offered unique challenges because of its size and capacity, both of which considerably exceeded those of any previous installation, and because of its interaction with the surrounding urban ecology. The overall length of the site of about 2,000 feet consists essentially of the 1,400-foot long enclosure housing the filtration basins, the intake basins at the lake end, and the office, laboratory, and lobby building, V-shaped in plan, at the shore end.

The site in its original condition was a narrow strip of park and eroded beach bordered by a street of small houses (fig. 7). After the necessary demolition the first step in constructing the plant was filling a broad trapezoidal peninsula bounded by a bedrock cofferdam on three sides and by a beach in the form of a quarter-circle along the north side, the curving profile giving the new and much enlarged park its name. Within this enclosure, extending outward 2,000 feet from the original shore-line and embracing an area of thirty-eight acres, the huge filtration and pumping complex was built up, but more than half of its total area of twenty acres lies invisible below the grade level. The main elements of this complex, from lake to shore, are the pumping station, the chemical building, which stands above the mixing basins, the settling basins, which lie entirely below ground, the filter building, the adminis-tration and laboratory building, and the filtered water reservoir, which lies partly under the administrative area (fig. 8). The combined capacity of all pumps is 840,000,000 gallons per day, equivalent to about 75 percent of the city's average daily consumption of water but only a little more than half the maximum consump-tion that occurs in prolonged periods of hot, dry weather in the summer.[5]

Except for the chemical building, which is framed in reinforced concrete, and the filter tanks of monolithic reinforced concrete, the various structures are carried on steel frames supported by piers, footings, walls, and caissons of concrete. An unusual feature of the foundation system is that the caissons are anchored to bed-rock by means of steel dowels to prevent the uplifting of the plant by hydrostatic pressure when the internal enclosures are empty of water. The external curtain walls are thin slabs of fine-grained oolitic limestone with a greenstone trim; interior parti-tions and wall facings are plaster, terra-cotta, glazed tile, and marble, the dominant colors being marine blue and green, and the flooring is chiefly composed of various kinds of asphalt and ceramic tile.[6] In their formal character the visible buildings are severely simple blocklike masses, their smooth planes interrupted only by the ribbon windows of the administration building, the clock on its central tower, and the greenstone map of the Great Lakes in a recessed panel above the door of the low-lift pumping station at the lake end of the group. The sharp-edged volumes, the precise detailing, and the interior surfaces of single colors strongly suggest the architecture of the Tennessee Valley Authority as its design unfolded under the direction of Roland Anthony Wank during the great period of hydroelectric construction (1933–45). The excellence of the Chicago plant, like that of TVA, arises from the engineering necessities. As the commentator in *Progressive Architecture* observed, "It demonstrates again . . . the design satisfaction that results from intelligent engi-

Fig. 5. Map showing the intake cribs, tunnels, and pumping stations of the Chicago Water System.

Fig. 6. South District Filtration Plant, Chicago Water System, 3300 East Cheltenham Avenue, 1938–42, 1945–47. Paul Gerhardt, Jr., architect.

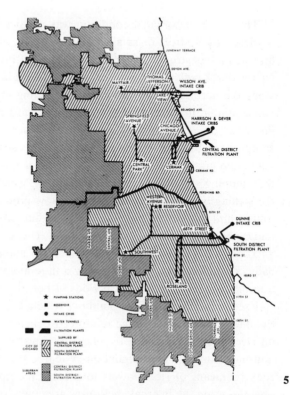

5

6

Fig. 7. South District Filtration Plant.
Site plan superimposed on an aerial
photograph of the original area.

Fig. 8. South District Filtration Plant.
Longitudinal section.

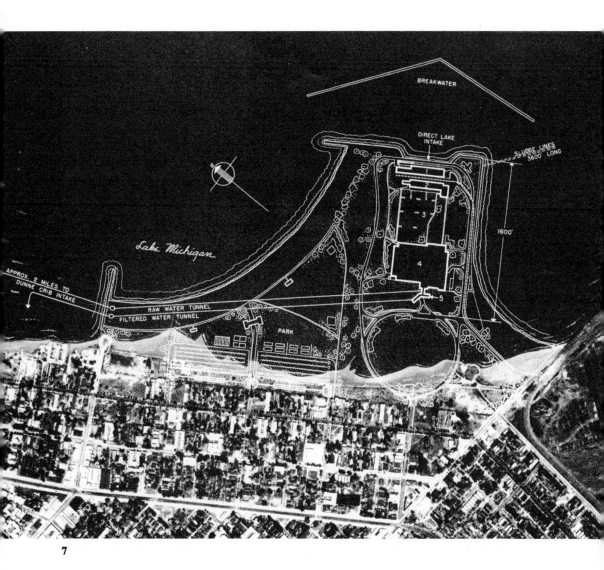

7

neering. In expression, the design as a whole rides triumphant, clean and fine, depending on its own integrity for effect."[7]

As modern architecture moved into the ascendant during the thirties and as architects progressively mastered its forms, a few schools and other public buildings comparable to the filtration plant began to appear, but the best of these lay outside the corporate limits of the city. The entire volume of construction for public purposes, of course, fell to a small fraction of the total in the preceding decade. The city erected thirty-four schools during the ten-year period of 1931–40, seemingly an impressive total for the economic conditions, but only four of them were opened before 1933, the remaining thirty having been built under substantial appropriations of the PWA. When the Second World War brought an end to the New Deal's public works program the volume of school construction fell even further, to a total of twenty buildings completed during the decade of 1941–50.[8] The foremost achievement of the depression period, the largest of all Chicago's public schools, and the one that very nearly brought derivative architecture to its end is the Albert G. Lane Technical High School, planned in part as early as 1930 and erected in 1932–34 at 2501 West Addison Street (3600N) from the plans of John C. Christensen, the board of education's staff architect. The big building, standing on a site of thirty acres, with overall dimensions of 562 × 600 feet on the ground, and designed for a total enrollment of 9,500 students, is characterized by an odd multiwing plan in which two wings at the front and three at the rear spread out from a central block surrounding an enclosed light court. The underlying idea of the plan was to provide an outer exposure for all of the school's multitude of classrooms and shops. The distribution of facilities throughout the four floors, the steel and reinforced concrete framing, and the Tudor forms of the elevations all represent minor variations on the principles of school design that Christensen had developed in the latter part of the twenties. After the Lane high school the new simplified verticalism derived from the 1929 skyscraper and the Century of Progress began to appear in the schools, first in Oakenwald and Sauganash elementary schools (respectively 1935 and 1936), eventually reaching emancipated modern forms in the Chicago Vocational High School of 1941.[9]

The revolution in scholastic design that had been initiated by Dwight Perkins in 1905 reached a new fulfillment in the Crow Island School on Willow Road in Winnetka, a wealthy North Shore suburb that disdained such radical heresies as the PWA (figs. 9 and 10). Designed by the office of Perkins, Wheeler and Will (founded by Dwight Perkins's son Lawrence) in collaboration with Eliel and Eero Saarinen and built in 1939–40, the school was the first outside Richard Neutra's work in

Fig. 9. Crow Island School, Willow
Road, Winnetka, Illinois, 1939–40.
Eliel and Eero Saarinen and Perkins,
Wheeler and Will, architects.

Fig. 10. Crow Island School.
Basement and main-floor plans.

9

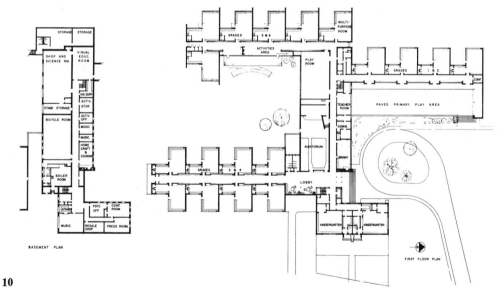

10

California to represent a direct architectural response to the principles of progressive education, as the local superintendent of schools himself pointed out. The design sprang from the "philosophy of progressive education . . . [which] recognizes the child's need for physical health, emotional and social adjustment, self-expression and the development of special aptitudes, and the mastery of the useful parts of reading, writing, arithmetic, history, geography and science."[10] After weeks spent in schools studying teachers, children, and physical arrangements, Lawrence Perkins made a model of a classroom unit, submitted it for comment and criticism to the board of education, the teachers, and the custodial staff, and when it was finally approved, made it the fundamental unit in the school's linear, spread-wing plan (fig. 10). The common space—lobby, auditorium, playroom, library—forms a central area from which the wing for the first and second grades extends to the north, that for the kindergarten and nursery to the west, and for the third through the sixth grades to the south. The most revolutionary features, however, are, first, the treatment of each classroom as a separate enclosure extending outward from a common access corridor, and second, the careful preservation of the child's scale throughout all spaces and details. It marked the beginning of a triumphant career for Perkins and Will, whose rapidly expanding firm became the leading school architects of metropolitan Chicago and eventually of the United States.

The largest quasi-public building erected in the city as a private investment is the International Amphitheatre, constructed by the Union Stock Yards and Transit Company at 43rd and Halsted streets in 1934–35 and designed by the architectural firm of A. Epstein and Sons. Owner of the stockyards and the railroads serving them, the company had built an exhibition hall before the turn of the century for livestock shows and other presentations of animals associated with the activities of the yards. This structure was destroyed in the disastrous fire of May 1934, which killed hundreds of head of cattle and wiped out many acres of pens, runs, buildings, freight cars, and various subsidiary structures, including the Stock Yards Branch of the Chicago Rapid Transit. The new Amphitheatre consists of three major parts: the most prominent is the Central Arena, its net floor area of 29,000 square feet covered by a gable roof supported by a series of huge rigid frames of steel; flanking it on both sides are the North and South wings, framed in reinforced concrete and each containing a floor area nearly four times that of the central enclosure. The building was twice expanded in the postwar years: the Exposition Hall was added in 1954, and a similar though smaller facility known as Donovan Hall was opened in 1956. The additions gave the entire group a total floor area of 585,000 square feet, sufficient to make it the largest exposition and convention facility in the United States until Chicago opened the state-sponsored McCormick Place in 1960.[11]

When the meat packing companies decentralized their operations following World War II, Chicago's capacity to attract conventions, trade shows, and popular entertainments soon made the activities at the Amphitheatre a perfect cross section of the business, political, recreational, and organizational life of the country. Livestock and poultry shows remain common features, but these have been greatly outnumbered by every kind of activity in which people, animals, plants, and objects are collected together—horse, dog, cat, flower, and garden shows; industrial, engineering, science, and design exhibitions; printing and typographical displays; ethnic dance festivals; conventions of political parties and of business, trade, professional, and labor organizations; religious convocations, or what passes for them in the land of Billy Sunday and Billy Graham; championship indoor sports events; Boy Scout and Junior Achievement fairs; Israel bond rallies; rodeos, circuses, banquets, and big-time comic acts. To serve this organized and compulsive gregariousness, annually worth hundreds of millions of dollars to Chicago, the Amphitheatre was planned on an immense scale and provided with rail and truck access facilities adequate to minister to the needs of a major city.

Among the few structures of transportation placed in operation during the depression and wartime years, two involved major changes in the movement of people within the city and between the city and other metropolitan areas. Most profound in its effect on intercity travel was the appearance of air transportation and the concomitant necessity of providing terminal facilities at a reasonable distance from the central business district, a problem rendered especially difficult by the airline's need for very extensive areas of flat, unobstructed ground space. Chicago's initial solution was to make use of an open area one mile square in the southwest corner of the city which is bounded by 55th and 63rd streets on the north and south and by Cicero (4800W) and Central Avenue (5600W) on the east and west. Designated as a school section under the Northwest Territories Ordinance of 1787 and still owned by the Chicago Board of Education, the level field provided so much space in the early days of air transport that the city in 1927 was able to tuck an adequate municipal airport into the southeast corner near the intersection of Cicero Avenue and 63rd Street. Thus at the very beginning the practice arose of municipal and federal subsidization of air transport, a policy that freed the airlines from the necessity of making the immense investment of the railroads in terminal facilities and traffic control devices.

Air mail service, the only kind in existence at the time, was moved from the old Maywood Airport in 1928, but the introduction of passenger flights during the following year eventually compelled the city to expand the little field. The major step came in 1937, when Chicago extended the runway space to the entire south half of the square mile area and built a much larger terminal building along Cicero Avenue in a horizontally elongated world's fair style. The preparation of the plans was again under the direction of the city architect, Paul Gerhardt, Jr. Although traffic grew rapidly before the war, the northward expansion of the field was blocked by the tracks of the Belt Railway, which cut across the open space on the east-west median line. The tracks were relocated north of 55th Street in 1940, and the entire area of 620 acres was opened to runways, hangars, and subsidiary structures in the following year. It served the city well enough in the days of propeller-driven planes, having become the world's busiest airport in the decade of the fifties, but the sheer density of traffic and the advent of jet propulsion compelled the opening of O'Hare Field in 1962.[12]

A long-delayed and desperately needed first step in the improvement of public transit came with the construction of the State Street subway line in 1938–43 as the initial implementation of a major proposal in every transit plan of the Burnham period. Of the total cost of $35,000,000 the PWA bore 76 percent through the last appropriation granted before Congress dropped public works in favor of military expenditures. The 4.8-mile subway, designed by the engineering staff of the Department of Public Works under the general direction of Joshua d'Esposito and extending southeastward and southward from Armitage Avenue (2000N) to 15th Street on the South Side, consists of two tracks laid in separate cylindrical tubes of reinforced concrete constructed by mining behind a shield through clay and sand. These tubes are widely separated and opened along their inner elements by means of steel-column supports to provide space for the broad center platforms of the stations. Part of the length under State Street was built by enlarging an unused streetcar tunnel which in turn had been made by widening the old narrow-gauge freight tunnel of the Chicago Tunnel Company. The electrically lighted subway, its traffic controlled by automatic block signals, is a well-designed artery from a strictly technological standpoint, but it suffers from two defects: the stations are depressingly ugly in a way that indicates a total absence of architectural imagination in their design, and the overall length is restricted to a relatively short segment of the main north-south elevated line, which was everywhere retained in its original character to carry about one-third of the total traffic on the route. One might very well argue, in addition, that a double-track subway line in a city of 3,500,000 is an anachronism since it prevents the simultaneous operation of local and express trains.

Other forms of mass transportation that experienced their major stimulus from the public works programs of the New Deal as well as from factors peculiar to the depression itself were the intercity bus and truck lines. The transportation of passengers by common-carrier motor coaches began nearly simultaneously in the Duluth region of Minnesota and betwen Los Angeles and Santa Barbara, California, in 1916. Five years later, in 1921, Frank Fageol of Muskegon, Michigan, manufactured the first vehicle claimed to be designed specifically as an intercity motor bus and established the Safety Motor Coach Lines, and in the following year he began transporting passengers under the slogan "Ride the Greyhounds." Various entrepreneurs, chiefly Carl E. Wickman and Orville S. Caesar of the early Minnesota project, began the merger of numerous little bus companies in 1925 and incorporated the new organization under the name of the Motor Transit Corporation in 1926. This company, with its system hub and its headquarters at Chicago, was destined to become the largest motor coach carrier and the first national transportation system in the United States; it reorganized itself in 1930 and went back to Fageol's old advertising rubric when it took the name Greyhound Corporation. Possessing five thousand route miles assembled from its numerous predecessors and provided with massive infusions of new capital, most ironically from several large railroad companies, notably the New York Central, the Pennsylvania, and the Southern Pacific, Greyhound was prepared to weather the economic storms. What in fact occurred was precisely opposite to expectations. A rare combination of contradictory factors led to depression-born prosperity: economic stagnation that made the rock-bottom fares a potent attraction, flexibility of operation that bordered on informality, a good safety record, the introduction of baggage and express handling facilities in 1936, the traffic generated by the Century of Progress Exposition—all these came together to place the bus company in the happy position of seeing revenues rise as the depression extended itself. The rapid increase in traffic meant that by the end of World War II a unified Chicago terminal was well overdue, but it was not to appear until 1950 (p. 233).

Following an exact parallel of fortune was the intercity motor truck system, but its origins are obscure because of the difficulty of determining when metropolitan delivery systems expanded to intercity status and when captive lines were transformed into common carriers. These events occurred piecemeal during World War I, and by 1920 the various forms of truck transportation had generated four billion ton-miles of traffic, or slightly less than 1 percent of the railroad total. In the coming decade that volume was to expand five times, and the sudden reversal of fortune that struck the railroads in the late months of 1929 had the effect of raising the truck lines' proportion to 5.2 percent of the rail freight traffic. Another set of factors peculiar to the depression decade brought about a 90 percent increase in tonnage by 1940: the low rates that appealed to hard-pressed shippers, the inexpensive packaging requirements, the door-to-door pickup and delivery, the low damage losses, and the sharply accelerated highway-building program of the New Deal contributed to the exact opposite of the attrition suffered by the staggering railroads. It was natural for Chicago to be the national focal point of the trucking industry, as it was of the railroad, and the chief federal highways leading into the city even before the Second World War were being pushed to the limit of both physical and traffic capacity by the roadway carriers. They had no need to construct their own right-of-way, and they took full advantage of the lavish subsidy that the railroads never enjoyed. In the city itself the flexibility of the truck system was offset by the chaos and congestion resulting from the multiplicity of separate companies and their numerous makeshift terminal facilities, the two together providing an exact reenactment of the rail expansion of the nineteenth century, from which business establishments and municipalities have still to learn the proper lessons.

Industrial building in the Chicago metropolitan area, as in the country as a whole, began to emerge from its moribund state in the mid-thirties, but it was arrested in 1938 by the second economic relapse. The brief recovery in local business activity was architecturally significant for bringing the firm of Albert Kahn to Chicago. The Electro-Motive Division of the General Motors Corporation was the pioneer mass-producer of diesel-electric locomotives. Its new and much enlarged factory was erected on 55th Street in suburban McCook in 1935–36 from the designs of the Austin Engineering Company, but the additions of 1937 and subsequent years were the work of the Kahn firm. The factory buildings are typical of the forms that Kahn had perfected in thirty years of service to the automotive industry: the long walls, equivalent to a three-story height, are opened to unbroken sweeps of glass in factory sash; the immense flat roof with its parallel light monitors is carried on truss frames or continuous girders in turn supported by H-columns, the entire frame having welded connections throughout. The success of the Burlington's Pioneer Zephyr and the Union Pacific's equivalent in 1934 and the introduction of diesel-electric locomotives for road freight service before the end of the decade assured the new company's prosperity, with the consequence that its plant at McCook was steadily expanded year by year up to 1966, by which date it had gained a monopoly in its field of manufacture.

The only industrial buildings comparable in size to the Electro-Motive factory were the wartime facilities constructed by the Defense Plant Corporation of the federal government, of which the most conspicuous in Chicago was the huge Dodge Aircraft Engine Plant, opened in 1942 at 73rd Street and Cicero Avenue (4800W). At the end of World War II it became the property of the abortive Tucker Automobile Company, only to revert to its original status under the operation of the Ford Motor Company during the Korean War of 1950–53. After being empty for ten years, the widely ramifying system of factories was converted in 1963–65 to the Ford City Industrial District and Shopping Center, which now flourishes.

In the depression the need for housing was as acute as the need for work, since evictions, foreclosures, abandonments, the nomadic life of jobless men, and outright physical decay, added to the collapse of the housing industry, brought the shortage of dwelling space to a desperate pass. This very obvious fact was bitterly underscored by the Hoovervilles of temporary shacks that sprang up across the nation along the railroad yards and on the ragged edges of the cities. The first Roosevelt administration sought to deal with the problem with the establishment in 1933–34 of three federal agencies designed to provide funds for lending institutions and for insuring loans against default, namely, the Federal Home Loan Bank, the Home Owners Loan Corporation, and the Home Credit Insurance Corporation; but it quickly became clear that more far-reaching legislation was necessary. The next step, accordingly, was the passage in June 1934 of the National Housing Act, which was initially drafted to provide credit through the federal insurance of loans granted for the construction of new housing and the modernization, renovation, and repair of the existing supply. The most controversial and vehemently contested part of the act was Title II, under the terms of which Congress for the first time placed the federal government in the business of lending money by permitting it to establish the National Mortgage Association, with authority to finance low-cost housing, to provide credit where no local supply was available, and to assume the partially amortized mortgages of other agencies in order to issue mortgage bonds against them.

The various New Deal programs and the slow improvement of business restored some circulation to the dormant housing industry, and the results gradually became visible as the annual total of new dwelling units erected within the city increased irregularly from a low point of 137 in 1933 to nearly 4,800 in 1939.[13] Standing out here and there in the slowly expanding volume were a few achievements that deserved attention for their architectural or urbanistic character. Julius Rosenwald made the first attempt to provide middle-income rental housing in the black ghetto when he built the Michigan Boulevard Garden Apartments along Michigan Avenue between 46th Street and 47th Street in 1933–34. Containing a total of 452 units, the group of five-story buildings disposed around a central landscaped court was designed by Ernest Grunsfeld, Jr., whose simple but nicely scaled prismatic forms combined with responsible maintenance gave them a human quality that later projects usually lacked. Farther south, in the comfortable academic ghetto surrounding the University of Chicago, George Fred and William Keck introduced the modern style to apartment buildings in their design of the block at 5551 South University Avenue, erected in 1936–37. The end of the depression brought the return of Frank Lloyd Wright to the Chicago area after an absence of twenty-five years. The Lloyd Lewis house, built in 1940–41 on Little Saint Mary's Road in Libertyville, was the first local work from the architect's hand since the Emil Bach house was completed in 1915 at 7415 Sheridan Road, where it still stands fully occupied and well maintained. At the same time a Taliesin Fellow, William Deknatel, brought the Wrightian spirit back to Evanston in his design of the Lambert Ennis house, constructed on Dempster Street near the lake in 1940.

But however welcome the return of Frank Lloyd Wright to Chicago might have been, houses such as those in Libertyville and Evanston seemed irrelevant to the overwhelming social need that had always existed but was now obvious even to the most indifferent politicians. The successive waves of immigration preceding the First World War left behind them a large segment of the urban population, as high as 40 percent in the major metropolitan areas, living either in outright poverty or in such straitened circumstances that existence was a precarious day-to-day gamble. The visible manifestation of this was the inner-city slum, which had its rural counterpart in the shacks of migrant workers and sharecroppers who were particularly concentrated in the South. The problem had grown steadily under a century's neglect, and, since it was clear that local government and private investment were incapable of doing anything about it, President Roosevelt made it a matter of federal concern as early as the summer of 1933. The result was that the construction of low-rent housing by the government—a revolutionary phenomenon in America's capitalist tradition—was included from the very beginning in the activities of the Public Works Administration. As with many New Deal programs, the aim was unemployment relief as well as the long-term social gain attendant upon material improvements in living conditions. The manifesto of the housing program, eventually reduced to the slogan "One-third of a nation," offered a kind of battle cry for many New Deal agencies. "Surveys indicate that one-third of the population of the cities and towns in all parts of our country are housed in substandard dwellings and that this condition contributes a menace to health, morals, comfort, and the happiness of this considerable part of our population. It is further shown that wherever these slum areas occur, the municipal costs of police and fire protection, the courts, and health and hospital services are excessive."[14]

Between 1933 and 1939 the Housing Division of the PWA financed and built fifty-two demonstration projects throughout the United States and financed seven privately owned limited-dividend ventures, to provide new housing for a total of about 24,000 persons. The program was not intended as the final answer. On the basis of this experience Congress passed the Wagner-Steagall Bill in 1937, which authorized the establishment of the Public Housing Authority to make available long-range financial aid to state, county, and municipal governments for housing and slum-clearance programs. The federal authority was to set the standards of design, site planning, and construction and to provide the funds, but in the interests of decentralization and local control, municipal and county governments were to carry out the planning, construction, maintenance, and operation of the individual projects. The whole program rested on three socioarchitectural principles that revealed a questionable dilution of initially laudable concepts. First, it was held that public housing should be available to all slum-dwellers and should be based on minimum criteria of health and safety, which were to be progressively improved as the income of tenants increased up to the point where the private housing industry could supersede the government program. This doctrine, of course, was to prove a prime factor in the failure of public housing, since it should have been steadily expanded in quantity, built immediately to the highest standards of design and construction, and permanently maintained by the municipalities at the highest standards of maintenance. Second, all facilities necessary for cleanliness, health, and the amenities of family life were to be provided, but they were to be granted condescendingly, without superfluous luxuries. Third, the standards of materials, structure, and utilities were to be equivalent to those used by builders of privately owned and sponsored housing but no higher.

The reason for this no-nonsense attitude was apparent to all those who understood how public programs take shape under what are called the political and economic realities of the United States. When a permanent public housing agency was first proposed in 1937 the idea was attacked by the real estate and building organizations, whose lobbyists threatened to block the necessary legislation unless public housing was built to such low standards of livability that it could not compete with privately built dwellings, even the well-worn odds and ends that were allowed to "trickle down" to the lower classes. The consequence was that the overwhelming bulk of public housing possesses a rude, Spartan, and even inhuman quality, carefully built in ways that guarantee a barely tolerable life for the inhabitants and insure that they will stand out as social misfits. As Albert Mayer wrote, "[Public housing officials] have sought to escape attack by being undeniably virtuous, and penurious, and inoffensive, practicing stark economies, squeezing down space, minimizing community facilities, eliminating anything that could be thought of as 'glamorizing,' squeezing down architects' fees."[15]

Yet the public housing program of the thirties and the wartime years, here and there attracting talented architects like Richard Neutra and Walter Gropius, was marked by a brave pioneering spirit and by valid and generous ends—a great and hopefully permanent improvement in the physical quality of dwelling units; adequate space, sanitary facilities, and utilities for every family; maximum light and air, outdoor space, and provision for recreational and community activities; the training of management personnel to organize tenants, act in their interest, and eventually enter the local housing administration. When the fifty-two projects of the PWA, all of which were completed by 31 December 1938, were turned over to the local housing authorities in the following year, the administrators of the program felt that they had reason to congratulate themselves. The demonstration groups possessed a modest human scale and revealed a nice balance of building and open space that could be pleasantly landscaped where some attention was paid to its maintenance. Rent arrears at the end of 1938 came to an average of 0.16 percent, among families with the lowest income and in the second-worst year of the depression. Like so many New Deal programs, the public housing enterprise was full of hope and promise for the future. "It is now a proved fact that public housing can be produced cheaply and can be brought within the reach of the under-privileged who now live in slum areas, and that its cost to the Federal Government, States, and cities is perhaps less than for any comparable economic and social improvement."[16]

In Chicago the three PWA projects, Addams, Lathrop, and Trumbull Park, are among the best of the local housing authority's vast and increasingly inhuman empire. The Jane Addams Houses were constructed in 1935–38 along Loomis Street (1400W) from Cabrini (828S) to Jane Addams Park, which serves as a buffer of green space between the buildings and the numerous contiguous tracks of the Burlington, Baltimore and Ohio Chicago Terminal, and North Western railroads (fig. 11). The original group, designed by a temporary association of ten architects, consists of three-story apartment buildings and two-story row houses containing a total of 304 units ranging in size from two to five rooms.[17] In its well-maintained grounds and buildings, its warmth and modest scale, the Addams group is the best that the Chicago housing program can show, in spite of the monastic severity of the unrelieved rectangular blocks. The landscaping on the spacious grounds is well grown; the generous recreation areas include play sculpture for the younger children as well as the usual facilities for the athletic activities of the older; the red-brick walls have weathered to a soft dark color in the heavily polluted air of the neighborhood.

41 Fig. 11. Chicago Housing Authority. Jane Addams Houses, Loomis Street from Cabrini to Jane Addams Park, 1935–38. Architects: John A. Armstrong, Melville C. Chatton, Ernest A. Grunsfeld, Jr., Frederick Hodgdon, John A. Holabird, Ralph D. Huszagh, Elmer C. Jensen, Philip B. Maher, John O. Merrill, and Chester U. Wolcott.

11

There was at least the promise of decent human possibilities, which were steadily eroded away as the Chicago Housing Authority poured its resources into huge ghetto-concentrated blocks, and Edith Abbott's almost idyllic description carries some conviction by contrast with the later reality.

The buildings themselves will cover only about 25 per cent of the six-acre tract. . . . The rest of the area will be left open; a part of it will be planted in trees, shrubbery, and grass; and parts will be reserved for playgrounds and gardens. The buildings will be of the most modern construction, fireproof and sanitary. They will have ample light and air. All rooms will be outside rooms. . . . In addition to this development . . . , the government purchased some fifteen acres of adjoining property to insure proper surroundings for the new project. Here the old buildings are being demolished and the land will be used for additional housing.[18]

The Julia Lathrop Homes were erected in 1936–38 on the Northwest Side from the designs of another architectural consortium, the Diversey Housing Project Associated Architects, under the direction of Robert S. De Golyer. The 923 dwelling units are distributed among twenty-nine two-, three-, and four-story buildings that occupy a V-shaped site bounded by the North Branch of the river on the west side and by Clybourne (diagonal) and Damen Avenue (2000W) on the east, and split in the middle by Diversey Parkway (2800N). The river setting (the industrially polluted water is attractive only at a distance of one hundred feet or more) and the extensive area give the Lathrop group some urbanity, but the minimal planting and the blocklike buildings of red brick relieved only by brick quoins and stringcourses at the third floor reveal the usual institutional monotony.[19]

As long as the PWA and its successor of 1939, the Chicago Housing Authority, followed the practice of building walk-up apartments with a maximum height of four stories, keeping the individual buildings small in area, and making some attempt to relate the site plans to the surrounding streets and services, there was some ground for believing that public housing might eventually become a racially integrated, stabilizing, and humanizing replacement of the blighted and ghettoized areas. The CHA made a modest attempt to adhere to the prescription throughout the thirties and early forties, when the unifying effects of depression and world war helped to preserve an uneasy community spirit. All the projects up to the postwar years consisted of two- to four-story buildings, but the architectural design was depressingly monotonous and the site planning was unimaginative. The largest of the groups, the Ida B. Wells Homes, erected in 1938–41 on the two-block area bounded by 37th and 39th streets and by South Parkway (now Martin Luther King, Jr., Drive) and Cottage Grove Avenue, embraces 1,652 units, for which there were

18,000 applicants when the project opened. Trumbull Park Homes (1936–38), at 105th Street and Oglesby Avenue, and Altgeld Gardens (1943–44), at 130th Street and Langley Avenue, had the merit of being far outside the ghetto area at the time, but the extensive postwar movement of black families into the two groups led to violent racial conflict that continued sporadically for years. All the other projects were situated within the ghetto and hence proved to be the most potent form of racial segregation.[20]

The ultimate failure of public housing in both quantity and quality can be traced to two primary and complex causes, of which one began to operate as soon as the military program brought prosperity and hence solved the hitherto insoluble problem of the depression, whereas the other lay hidden in the New Deal theory of public works from the very beginning. Both lay deep in what might be most simply called the human failure of the technologically oriented culture of the United States. As the historians Burchard and Bush-Brown wrote,

In quantity all the public housing efforts together did not scratch the surface if . . . one-third of the nation was ill-housed. As soon as there were harbingers of prosperity they dispelled the vision of extensive well-ordered American public housing comparable to the communities of Sweden, Denmark, Holland, Switzerland, or Germany. . . . It was clear the American people did not covet the planned way of life, was unwilling to make its own plans and did not trust anyone else with them either.[21]

The other cause was implied in the very philosophy of public works as this found convenient expression in manifestos that began with such statistical abstractions as "one-third of a nation." The Philadelphia planner Edmund Bacon saw the failure most acutely.

One concrete expression of the categorization of the "ill-housed, low-income group," both as an intellectual model and a legal entity, has been the construction of vast institutionalized public housing projects to replace the "slums." Individual families are uprooted from the individual and unique positions that they occupy in the complex of their social community, however undesirable some of these positions may be. They become one of a series of families on an essentially uniform basis. It is very much easier intellectually to categorize areas as "unsafe and unsanitary," to recommend their destruction and replacement by "safe and sanitary dwelling units," than it is to deal with the reality of the problem on an individual basis for each individual family where it exists. . . . The intellectual has failed both to structure [this latter approach] into a viable and communicable conceptual model and to suggest possible action programs geared to its basic tenets.

Another inhibition to clear thinking about the plight of cities is the habit of thinking of "housing" in discrete quantitative terms as though "dwelling units" have their existence as manipulable numbers rather than simply as fragments of an environment. . . . This type of thinking has led to the absurd situation where we think of family problems in terms of buildings, and we demolish the buildings and move the families to suit the convenience of the social and financial programs, rather than moving the abstract social and financial programs to accord with a logical treatment of buildings and a rational and humane treatment of the individual families. . . . [Our practice] is in contrast to the simple idea of adjusting aid programs to the needs of the people where they are, rather than moving people to the convenience of bureaucratic programs.

Thousands of vacant lots and derelict abandoned houses spread through hundreds of blocks of residential areas, crying out for new structures that would eliminate ghastly neighborhood hazards, that would infuse new life into neighborhood after neighborhood.

We must see the public housing program not narrowly from the viewpoint of the minority of the ill-housed, who are its tenants, but rather as an instrument for getting at the root of the housing problem for everyone. This purpose can be furthered and strengthened by a shift from thinking based on housing units as abstract, placeless, mathematical entities to that concerned about the real and total environment of every underprivileged citizen in the entire city.[22]

The only useful idea that Chicago appears to have derived from the planning experiments of the New Deal is the concept of a land-use survey, which was initiated in 1939 and the results published in 1943. It represented the first attempt in thirty years to reexamine the basis of and to revise the Burnham Plan. Otherwise the potentially valuable lessons of the Roosevelt administrations went unheeded, while the defects of an immature liberalism were retained. The tragic consequences might have been predicted: the enormous backlog of needs that accumulated during the twenty-year hiatus of depression, war, and readjustment went unmet, to bear the fruit of fear and violence and decay.

NOTES TO CHAPTER 2

1. The administration of Mayor Anton J. Cermak was cut short by his death from a wound received in Miami, Florida, at the hands of a presumed anarchist who was attempting to assassinate President-elect Franklin D. Roosevelt. Under Mayor Edward Kelly's long tenure (1933–47) the Chicago machine achieved the most potent influence in national politics of any municipal organization. The most awesome demonstration of his power came in 1944, when he single-handedly prevented the

nomination of Henry A. Wallace as vice-president under the fourth Roosevelt administration.

2. The first cloverleaf intersection was built at Woodbridge, New Jersey, in 1928, but the three along Lake Shore Drive, at Montrose, Wilson (4600N), and Lawrence (4800N) avenues, constitute the first multiple installation.

3. The Burnham Plan proposed that the double-level Wacker Drive be built along the entire south bank of the main river, from the confluence of the North and South branches to the lake, and that it intersect the shoreline drive near the east side of the Illinois Central yard lying between Randolph Street and the river. This plan carried with it two consequences: first, the elevation of the upper level of Wacker Drive was one determinant in fixing the elevation of the new bridge, and, second, the south approach viaduct would have to cross the eastward extension of Wacker Drive at ninety-degree intersections. This necessity accounts for the seemingly arbitrary right-angle turns immediately south of Link Bridge: the east-west segment of Lake Shore Drive at this point is actually an isolated length of Wacker Drive, from which Lake Shore extends to the north and south on a displaced alignment.

4. The expansion in the physical plant of the water supply system, 1930–45, comprehended the following elements, divided by type of facility, with dates of completion:
    I. Water tunnels
        1. Harrison Street cross-connection, 1932. Length 0.24 mile; interior diameter 7 feet.
        2. Chicago Avenue Lake and Land, 1935. Length 11.50 miles; interior diameters 10, 13, and 16 feet; maximum depth 190 feet below mean lake level (the longest tunnel of the Chicago system, the largest in cross-sectional area, and the deepest in its subaqueous length).
        3. Des Plaines Street, 1940. Length 1.60 miles; interior diameter 13 feet.
        4. Stewart Avenue, 1943. Length 4.28 miles; interior diameter 10 feet.
        5. Connection to South District Filtration Plant, 1945. Length 2.80 miles; interior diameters 9, 13, and 16 feet.
    The supply tunnels carrying water directly from the intake stations are reinforced concrete and are so located and pitched as to provide a gravity flow of water from the intake to the pumping plant and a flow by siphon action into the pump chamber.
    II. Pumping station: Anton W. Cermak, 735 West Harrison Street, 1936. Six electrically driven centrifugal pumps; capacity 300 mgd.
    III. Intake crib: William E. Dever, 2.65 miles off shore end of Chicago Avenue, 1934–35.

5. The South District Filtration Plant is supplied by the Edward F. Dunne intake crib, situated 3.2 miles from the lake end of the plant. Raw water flows from the supply tunnel to the intake basins, from which it is pumped upward at a maximum head of 25 feet to the raw water conduits. The water is discharged from the conduits into the mixing basins, where chemicals necessary to purify and fluoridate the water and to increase the coagulation rate of silt and organic materials are dissolved in the water after being diffused throughout the liquid volume by mechanical agitation. The chemically treated water then passes successively through 501 lineal feet of settling basins, eighty filters composed of a 46½ inch depth of gravel and sand graded progressively downward from a 3½ inch maximum size to a 0.62-millimeter minimum, and into the filtered-water reservoir.

6. Greenstone is a dark green diorite, an igneous rock whose complex mineral con-

stituents are compounds formed from oxides and hyroxides of calcium, iron, sodium, magnesium, titanium, and silicon.

7. "Water Filtration Plant: Chicago, Illinois," *Progressive Architecture* 31(March 1950):75.

8. See table 5.

9. Among public buildings other than schools constructed under PWA appropriations the most important were two additions to the hospital and medical school enclave known as the West Side Medical Center, which eventually expanded to fill a trapezoidal area bounded by Congress Street (500S) and Roosevelt Road (1200S) on the north and south, and by Paulina Street (1700W) and the diagonal Ogden Boulevard on the east and west. Cook County, Chicago State Tuberculosis, and the University of Illinois hospitals had long been established in the area when the PWA added the Cook County Hospital Nurses' Home (1934–35) and the University of Illinois Dental College (1936–37). A constant stream of postwar additions and ex-expansions produced a vast conglomeration of unattractive and ill-assorted buildings forming what is claimed to be the largest medical concentration in the world. The West Side Medical Center is an essential element of the city's life, but it is also a prime demonstration of the assertion that hospital design invariably stifles the architectural imagination.

A prize exception to this doctrine is the Lake County Tuberculosis Sanatorium, constructed in 1938–39 on Belvedere Road in Waukegan from the plans of William A. Ganster and William L. Pereira. Set in a pleasant twenty-two-acre site of meadow and woodland, the hospital constitutes the main structure in a group that includes a nurses' home and a supervising physician's residence. It is an impressive example of the intelligent use of glazed south wall areas and outdoor terraces connecting directly to the individual rooms. The entire work was the product of an exhaustive analysis of the problems peculiar to this type of building and an imaginative adaptation of the forms of the International Style to their solution.

10. Carleton Washburne, Winnetka superintendent of schools, quoted in "Crow Island School, Winnetka, Ill.," *Architectural Forum* 75(August 1941):80.

11. Long the convention and exhibition center of the United States, Chicago made good use of the Amphitheatre's generous space, which was increasingly available as live-animal traffic declined at the stockyards. The Central Arena measures 123 × 238 feet in plan, most of its 29,274 square feet of clear space lying under the roof frames, and can provide a total seating capacity of 12,250 on the ground floor and in boxes. The floor was designed for the extremely high unit load of 1,000 pounds per square foot. The North Wing measures 184 × 310 feet on the ground floor, giving it an area of 57,040 square feet, and 164 × 310 feet on the upper level, for an area of 50,840 square feet. The ground floor was designed for the 1,000-pound loading, the upper area for the more conventional 150 pounds. Exposition Hall measures 310 × 600 feet, for an area of 186,000 square feet, and was again designed for the high floor load; Donovan Hall extends 273 × 410 feet, or 111,930 square feet in area. (For McCormick Place, see pp. 141–46.)

12. For O'Hare Field and the subsequent renovation of Midway, see pp. 258–63.

13. See table 3.

14. C. W. Short and R. Stanley Brown, *Public Buildings: A Survey of Architecture of Projects Constructed by Federal and Other Governmental Bodies . . .* (Washington: U.S. Government Printing Office, 1939), p. 654.

15. Albert Mayer, "Public Housing Architecture," *Journal of Housing* 19(15 October 1962):449.
16. Short and Brown, *Public Buildings*, p. 655.
17. The associated architects of the Addams project were John A. Armstrong, Melville C. Chatton, Ernest A. Grunsfeld, Jr., Frederick Hodgdon, John A. Holabird, Ralph D. Huszagh, Elmer C. Jensen, Philip B. Maher, John O. Merrill, and Chester U. Wolcott. The original group of apartments was later expanded to 1,027 units distributed among thirty-two buildings covering twenty-six acres.
18. Edith Abbott, *The Tenements of Chicago, 1908–1935* (Chicago: University of Chicago Press, 1936); quoted in Harold M. Mayer and Richard C. Wade, *Chicago: Growth of a Metropolis* (Chicago: University of Chicago Press, 1969), pp. 366–67, caption to fig. 2.
19. The data on cost, size, and land usage for the Julia Lathrop Homes are typical of the large depression projects:

Total area of site	35 acres
Land cost	$599,989
Unit land cost	$0.39 per square foot
Percentage of land area covered	19%
Number of dwelling units	923
Number of rooms	3,313
Rooms per acre	94
Distribution of apartments by size	
two-room	5%
three-room	46%
four-room	42%
five-room	7%
Shelter rent	$5.39 per room
Shelter-plus-utilities rent	$7.25 per room
Total building volume	8,740,700 cubic feet
Construction cost	$4,609,514
Unit construction cost	$0.53 per cubic foot
Construction cost per room	$1,391
Construction cost per dwelling unit	$4,983
Total cost including land and fees	$5,556,900
Gross cost per room	$1,678
Gross cost per dwelling unit	$6,007

(Source: Short and Brown, *Public Buildings*, p. 657. There are slight and unaccountable discrepancies among these figures: the quotient of total cost and number of dwelling units, e.g., should be $13 higher, or $6,020.)
20. The final PWA projects and the CHA projects erected up to 1945 are the following:

Trumbull Park Homes; 452 units in 55 two- and four-story buildings. John A. Armstrong, Ernest A. Grunsfeld, Jr., John A. Holabird, Elmer C. Jensen, and Philip B. Maher, associated architects.

Ida B. Wells Homes; ultimate total 2,293 units in 124 two-, three-, and four-story buildings. South Park Housing Architects: Shaw, Naess and Murphy; Thielbar and Fugard; Nimmons, Carr and Wright; Metz and Gunderson.

Frances Cabrini Homes (original group), vicinity of Hudson Avenue (432W) and Oak Street (1000N), 1941–42; 586 units in 55 two-story row houses and three-story apartments. Associated Housing Architects: George E. Burmeister, Ernest A. Grunsfeld, Jr., Henry K. Holsman, George M. Jones, I. S. Loewenberg, Frank A. McNally, Maurice B. Rissman, Louis R. Solomon, and Karl M. Vitzthum. The 700 dwelling units—if they can be called that—replaced by the Cabrini Homes were typical of the city's inner slums: 43 had no toilets, 433 had no bathing facilities, and 480 had no hot water.

Bridgeport Homes, 31st Street and Lituanica Avenue (900W), 1942–43; 141 units in 18 two-story buildings. Burnham and Hammond, architects.

Lawndale Homes, 25th Street and California Avenue (2800W), 1942–43; 128 units in 16 two-story buildings. Eric E. Hall and Frank A. McNally, architects.

Brooks Homes, Roosevelt Road (1200S) and Loomis Street (1400W), 1942–44; 834 units in 89 two-story buildings. Associated Housing Architects (see under Cabrini Homes, above).

Altgeld Gardens (original group), 1943–45; 1,498 units in 162 two-story buildings. Shaw, Naess and Murphy, architects. This development, built to accommodate part of the immense influx of workers who poured into the Calumet rail and industrial district during the war, was unique in that it included schools and a shopping center.

21. John E. Burchard and Albert Bush-Brown, *Architecture in America: A Social and Cultural History* (Boston: Little, Brown and Company, 1961), p. 400.
22. Edmund N. Bacon, "Urban Process: Planning with and for the Community," *Architectural Record* 145(May 1969):130, 133.

Urban Problems and Urban Renewal

3. Residential and Commercial Building after World War II

Apartments

The mood of the nation after the defeat of Germany and Japan in August 1945 was a paradoxical mixture of feelings impossible to characterize in a word. On the one hand, there were relief and jubilation that American arms had triumphed once again, presumably in the cause of righteousness, and with these went a sense of expectancy and hope; on the other hand, there was an inescapable feeling of anticlimax intensified by uneasy fears that the heady prosperity of the wartime years could not be sustained through the conversion to what was expected to be peace. This assortment of conflicting emotions postponed the rush to large-scale building and industrial expansion, although rationing and the nearly complete prohibition on the manufacture of "hard" consumer goods left accumulating unsatisfied demands of enormous proportions. In Chicago the revival of commercial and industrial construction was slow in coming: in the case of office building, for example, it was ten years after the war before a new structure appeared in the central business district, and twelve before one opened within the Loop. Since there was little interest in any other kind of construction, the wry comment among the real estate men as late as 1947 was that the Loop might as well be returned to the Indians. The consequence of this attitude was that the post–World War II building boom was largely confined to high-rise apartment towers for the first decade following the surrender of the axis powers.

The annual construction of single-family residences often exceeded that of apartment units up to 1960, but after that date the relationship of the two totals was always reversed, with the proportion of individual houses constantly decreasing. Even the highest totals in both categories, however, fell far short of the equivalent volumes in the decade of the twenties, in spite of the existence of substantial public housing construction throughout the fifties and sixties. The total number of new dwelling units reached nearly 7,000 for 1955, and, although the annual volume fluctuated extremely, the total was to come close to 11,000 in 1961 and to exceed 14,000 in 1968.[1] The overwhelming majority of the new apartment towers were built along the various local streets and boulevards that lie at the west edge of Lincoln Park, for the obvious reason that the park and the lake offered a foreground matched in only a few cities of the world. The process had been under way, as we have seen, since the building up of the Gold Coast began in 1905. There was nothing comparable to this high-rise wall along the south lakeshore except in the Hyde Park area above Jackson Park, for equally compelling though negative factors: until Burnham Park and South Lake Shore Drive were completed in 1932, the shoreline was wholly preempted by the Illinois Central Railroad's ten-track main line, which not only brought the intrusion of some eight hundred trains per day into the lake view but effectively blocked access to the shore until the new viaducts were opened during the twenties. A group of widely spaced apartment towers had been erected in 1925–30 east of the tracks between 50th and 56th streets, where the shore curves out toward Promontory Point and where most of the South Side building continued to be concentrated in the postwar years. Expansion south of Jackson Park did not come until the decade of the sixties was well advanced.

It was in this earlier enclave of high-rise construction that Ludwig Mies van der Rohe was to find his first opportunity as an architect of privately sponsored dwelling and office skyscrapers, and the event marked the beginning of a new career that was to have a profound influence on urban building in Europe as well as North America. At the suggestion of John A. Holabird, Mies had been invited by President Henry T. Heald in 1938 to assume the chairmanship of the Department of Architecture at Armour Institute, which was to be merged with Lewis Institute two years later to form the present Illinois Institute of Technology. Mies began his American activity by creating the campus plan for the institute, but the inhibitions imposed by depression and war allowed him to design only two campus buildings up to 1945.[2] In the following year a young real estate entrepreneur named Herbert Greenwald, educated at the University of Chicago and possessed of a measure of civic idealism, offered the famous but seldom employed German architect the commission for an apartment tower to be erected on South Lake Shore Drive between 56th and 57th streets, at the base of Promontory Point. Mies drew two preliminary plans, one for a steel-framed structure covered with the fine vertical tracery that distinguished most of his subsequent designs, and the other for a work of reinforced concrete framing that was to be exposed in all elevations. The latter was chosen and took form in 1948–49 as the Promontory Apartments, the final working drawings of which were produced in collaboration with the large offices of Holsman, Klekamp and Holsman and Pace Associates (fig. 12). The building launched Mies on a career that was literally to transform the skyline of Chicago and to inaugurate what the editors of *Architectural Forum* were to call the second Chicago school. Given the architect's reputation and the fact that he had already trained several classes of students at IIT, Promontory was sufficiently influential to produce a steady stream of derivatives, of which the best is the L-shaped apartment block erected in 1951–52 at the southeast corner of

Sheridan Road and Oakdale Avenue (2932N) from the designs of Mies's collaborators, the firm of Pace Associates (fig. 13).

While the new buildings were multiplying on the IIT campus and the Promontory tower was beginning to rise, Mies undertook the design of the most famous of all his high-rise buildings, for which the details of working plans were again handled by the same collaborative group. The two apartment buildings at 860–80 North Lake Shore Drive, sponsored by Herbert Greenwald and the Robert Hall McCormicks, Sr. and Jr., were erected in 1949–52 and immediately gained such worldwide attention as to make them the Chicago equivalent of the Woolworth Tower or the Empire State Building in earlier architectural modes (figs. 14, 15). The two identical buildings, supported by welded steel frames and set with their long horizontal axes at right angles to each other, are distinguished by structural and formal characteristics that placed them in a unique class—first and most obvious, the clear glass walls set in the rectangular cells defined by the steel plates over the fireproof cladding of the columns and spandrel girders; second, the vertical tracery formed by I-section mullions welded to this covering; and finally, a refinement and exactitude of detail calculated to express an abstract mathematical impeccability (fig. 16). Since the vertical steel sections appear on the column coverings, where they cannot function as mullions, and since their eight-inch depth is more than is necessary for this minor structural role, it is clear that they are as much formal elements as they are functional. In reply to questions about their arbitrary character Mies had two good answers.

It was very important to preserve and extend the rhythm which the mullions set up on the rest of the building. We looked at it on the model without the steel section attached to the corner column and it did not look right. Now, the other reason is that this steel section was needed to stiffen the plate which covers the corner column so this plate would not ripple, and also we needed it for strength when the sections were hoisted into place. Now, of course, that's a very good reason, but the other reason is the real reason.[3]

The full visual and formal role of the mullions, however, is more complex than this spare assertion implies. The narrow rectangle defined by pairs of adjacent mullions and spandrel panels very nearly duplicates in its proportions those of the entire bay and thus repeats at the human scale the fundamental unit of the structural system. In this way the form becomes a restatement of the underlying geometry of the welded steel frame that symbolizes the mathematical rigor inherent in its structural

Fig. 12. Promontory Apartments, South Lake Shore Drive near 56th Street, 1948–49. Ludwig Mies van der Rohe, Pace Associates, and Holsman, Klekamp and Taylor, architects.

12

Fig. 13. Apartments, Sheridan Road and Oakdale Avenue, 1951–52. Pace Associates, architects.

Fig. 14. Apartments, 860–80 North Lake Shore Drive, 1949–52. Ludwig Mies van der Rohe, Pace Associates, and Holsman, Klekamp and Taylor, architects.

13

14

Fig. 15. 860–80 North Lake Shore
Drive. Site and ground-floor plan.

Fig. 16. 860–80 North Lake Shore
Drive. Interior of the entrance lobby.

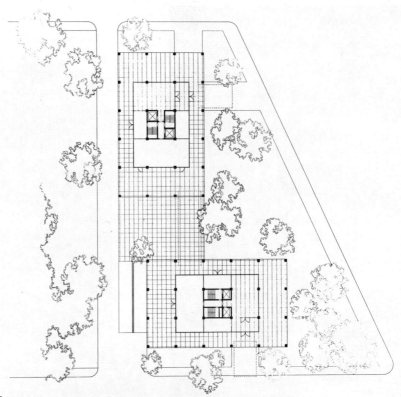

16

analysis. Further, the simple device of placing the mullions wholly outside the frame made possible a constant change in the pattern of light and shadow on the brittle glass walls and in the visual "weight" of the walls: seen head-on the elevation reveals maximum lightness and openness; as the angle of vision sharpens, the density and opacity of the wall increase until the transparency disappears into the overlapping bands of black-painted steel. Mies was searching for a perfectly generalized or Platonic form that would fit the requirements of the multistory building. "We reverse [form follows function]," he said, "and make a practical and satisfying shape, and then fit the functions into it. Today this is the only practical way to build because the functions of most buildings are continually changing, but economically the buildings cannot change."[4] He created a classic form, like the mature Doric temple, and it could neither be altered nor subjected to further refinement. There was nothing to do but repeat it with subtle variations in proportions and dimensions, and that is exactly what he and many of his students went on doing down through the years.[5]

Mies carried the principles underlying the 860–80 group to their ultimate perfection in the floating glass prism of the Farnsworth house, built in 1950 along the bottomland of the Fox River near Plano, Illinois (figs. 17, 18). In the purity, exactitude, and delicacy of the welded and sand-blasted steel frame and the transparent walls the house stands as close to abstract geometric form as it is possible to come with the hard materials of structure. The dense vertical tracery of the 860–80 apartments reappeared in black anodized aluminum for the two buildings built in 1955–58 on the adjacent block at 900 North Lake Shore Drive (fig. 19). The greater simplicity of the later group arises from the flat-slab concrete frame, which reveals itself in the elevations only as thin black bands marking the outer edges of the floor slabs. A similar structural system as well as formal treatment, except that the aluminum tracery is anodized to its natural color, appears in the single tower erected in 1961–62 at 2400 Lake View Avenue, where it faces Lincoln Park at the Fullerton intersection (figs. 20, 21).[6] It proved to be the last apartment building in the United States to emerge from the Mies firm, which was occupied mainly with the design of large office buildings in Chicago and Toronto and a variety of planned developments in Montreal during the architect's remaining active years (pp. 125, 129–34).

Beside these buildings most of the apartment blocks of the North Side and the Hyde Park area are conventional works, depressing in their heavy-handed monotony. This is especially true of the high-rise canyon that has taken the place of the handsome single-family residences that once lined both sides of Sheridan Road where it lies closest to the lake, between Hollywood Avenue (5700N) and Devon (6400N). Here, for the most part, vulgarity and big money have replaced a genuine

elegance and good taste, while the street staggers under a traffic it was never designed to handle. In a few places along Lincoln Park the exceptions stand out either
for novelty of treatment or straightforward good design. Louis R. Solomon and
J. Marion Gutnayer attempted a lively association of colors, textures, and rectangular forms in the L-shaped apartment building erected in 1950–51 at 3410 North
Lake Shore Drive (fig. 22). If the recessed and projecting areas of red brick, gray-
enameled brick, and gray white limestone form a rather inharmonious composition,
they at least add a welcome color to the excessive sobriety of modern design. The
neighboring apartment at 3440, also from the hand of Louis Solomon, is a more
restrained work in the International mode, with continuous windows and white brick
spandrels (fig. 22). J. M. Gutnayer added one of the few attractive works to the
Sheridan Road canyon in his design of the apartment building constructed in
1961–62 at 5740, which has the familiar cellular or articulated walls of the Chicago
style (figs. 23, 24). The building is most important, however, because it marked the
introduction of slip-form construction to the city: the solid-wall core in the shape of
a square prism, which acts to resist wind forces as well as to sustain part of the gravity load, was poured in a single operation by means of a form that was jacked upward at a continuous rate of one foot per hour, the 170-foot height requiring seven
days and sixteen hours to complete the pour and to strip the forms. The engineer
responsible for the structural design and for proposing the method of construction
was Frank J. Kornacker.[7]

The two buildings of the University Garden Apartments, erected in 1959–61 at
1451 East 55th Street, constitute one of the first two projects to embody the load-
bearing screen wall in concrete construction. The apartments were designed by the
office of I. M. Pei of New York in collaboration with the Chicago firm of Loewenberg and Loewenberg, and the screen wall was developed jointly by members of Pei's
staff and the engineer August E. Kommendant (fig. 25). The load-bearing screen is
a bearing wall of reinforced concrete that is divided into a large number of slender
columns and shallow spandrel beams, adjacent pairs of each forming the supporting frame for a single window. The technique offers several advantages: the rigid
framework of columns and beams allows the maximum admission of light while
simultaneously transmitting wind, floor, and roof loads directly through the peripheral girders to the massive columns at the base of the building and hence to the
footings; the fixed size of the openings was regarded by Pei as preferable to the
irregular window sizes of many apartments; and the transformation of the wall into
a bearing structure reduces the number of columns and eliminates the "scatter"
columns often introduced to accommodate varying room sizes. As the elevations of

Fig. 17. Edith Farnsworth house, Plano, Illinois, 1950. Ludwig Mies van der Rohe, architect.

Fig. 18. Edith Farnsworth house. Plan.

17

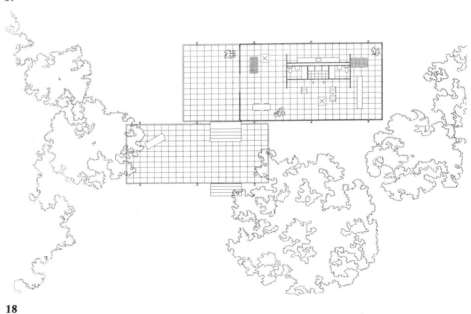

18

Fig. 19. Apartments, 900 North Lake Shore Drive, 1955–58. Ludwig Mies van der Rohe and Pace Associates, architects.

Fig. 20. Apartments, 2400 Lake View Avenue, 1961–62. Ludwig Mies van der Rohe and Greenberg and Finfer, architects.

19

20

61

Fig. 21. Apartments, 2400 Lake View Avenue. Site and ground-floor plan.

Fig. 22. *Left:* Apartments, 3410 North Lake Shore Drive, 1950–51. J. Marion Gutnayer and Louis R. Solomon, architects. *Right:* Apartments, 3440 North Lake Shore Drive, 1955–56. Louis R. Solomon, architect.

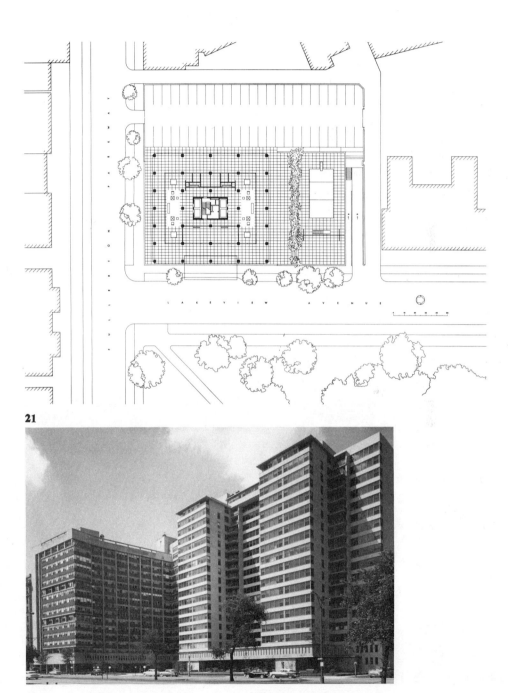

21

22

Fig. 23. Apartments, 5740 Sheridan Road, 1961–62. J. Marion Gutnayer, architect.

Fig. 24. 5740 Sheridan Road. Typical floor plan.

Fig. 25. University Garden Apartments, 1451 East 55th Street, 1959–61. I. M. Pei and Associates and Loewenberg and Loewenberg, architects.

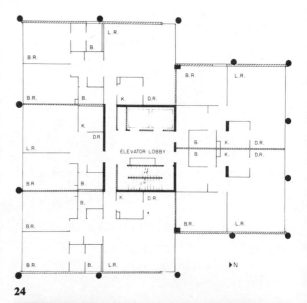

24

23

25

Fig. 26. Apartments, 227 East
Walton Street, 1954–55. Harry Weese
and Associates, architects.

26

the University Garden Apartments indicate, the screen wall combines lightness and openness with strength and mass. The two buildings face inward toward a handsomely landscaped interior plaza, but their location on an island in the middle of the widened street effectively walls them off from the surrounding area and has justifiably earned them the local name of Monoxide Island.

The load-bearing screen offers structural and economic advantages, but its unified appearance is often in fact a monotonous repetition of extremely simple, identical shapes, a characteristic that only serves to intensify the visually empty quality of most contemporary architecture. The Chicago architect who has most valiantly and successfully struggled to avoid this tedium is Harry Weese. In the apartment building constructed in 1954–55 at 227 East Walton Street he revived the vertical row of oriel windows or projecting bays that constituted the distinguishing feature of the hotels and apartments of the Chicago school (fig. 26). The Walton tower faces a narrow street on an even narrower lot, and its combination of discreetly projecting windows and brick panels gives the street elevations a welcome variety of color and shape while offering both privacy and openness on the restricted site. More imaginative in both plan and elevation is the group of apartments and town houses forming a single four-story enclosure at 235 West Eugenie Street (figs. 27, 28). Built in 1961–62, the block reveals an association of traditional and contemporary elements, respectively, in the bearing walls of brick that close the ends and form the interior partitions and in the broad areas of glass along the upper stories of the facade. The plan represents an ingenious use of the compact space: the first two floors are divided into eleven one-bedroom apartments and six garden-studio units; the third and fourth floors are devoted to a row of two-story town houses with living-dining areas on the lower level and bedrooms on the upper, the latter of which are set back along the street to provide a little terrace or deck for each dwelling. The whole design represents the modern style at its best; yet the warm tawny brick and the modest scale allow the building to harmonize nicely with the late Victorian architecture of its Old Town setting.

The most prominent of the Weese apartment commissions is the John M. Fewkes Tower, opened in 1967 at 824–38 North Dearborn Street (figs. 29, 30). The slender thirty-story shaft, supported by a flat-slab frame of reinforced concrete, was built under section 231 of the National Housing Act to provide subsidized middle-income housing for retired schoolteachers but was later opened to all tenants whose incomes fall below the specified limit. Covering only one-third the area of its site, the building contains 236 apartments, a penthouse solarium and roof garden, and a 200-seat meeting room, and the raised terrace around its base provides underground and surface parking for 113 cars.[8] The walls in all four elevations of the high square prism have oriel or projecting windows similar to those of the Walton Street apartments. The roots of the form lay in the Chicago tradition, as the designers of the Weese office were well aware and as the commentator for *Architectural Record* pointed out. "This tower . . . strongly recalls the 80-year old beginnings of modern skyscraper design in Chicago. The apartments within, filled with daylight and a heightened sense of space, demonstrate the continuing relevance of this tradition for the city in which it was begun."[9]

Another architect who in the late fifties was moving toward an even more radical break with the ruling mode is Bertrand Goldberg. The Astor Tower at 1300 North Astor Street, built in 1961–62, might be described as an orthodox version of the novel forms that were already taking shape in the Marina City group (fig. 31). The extremely attenuated twenty-eight-story tower, again a square prism in shape, is carried by a concrete structure composed of twelve peripheral columns, a solid-walled core that was poured by the slip-form technique, and the floor slabs that act as rigid diaphragms in transmitting horizontal forces to the shear walls of the core. Several unusual features appear in this elegant building of the inner Gold Coast: the glass curtain walls, occupying the entire space between the thin edges of the slabs, are protected from solar radiation by permanent jalousies fixed to a light interior framework; the base is open to a height of forty feet to lift the lowest apartments above the roofs of the surrounding houses and the pollution of the encompassing streets. This provision, however, has proved to be increasingly futile as the inner area of the Gold Coast has been progressively destroyed by indiscriminate high-rise building and the associated traffic now flooding horse-and-carriage streets.

No privately sponsored apartments have attracted more attention or have been more extensively involved in the urban ecology than the Marina City project, which was conceived initially by Bertrand Goldberg and planned in detail by the architects and engineers of his office.[10] The history of this extraordinary idea for a microcity in the urban core began when the Real Estate Research Corporation undertook a survey of inner-city housing needs and issued a report of the results in April 1959. The chief conclusion was that the demand for apartment space within walking distance of the Loop would swell to a total of 39,000 units by 1980. The first organization to act on this knowledge was the Building Service Employees International Union, whose president, William L. McFetridge, saw an opportunity to invest his health and welfare fund in a way that would simultaneously bring a good annual return and increase the available jobs for building service workers. The union purchased the 3½-acre site on the north bank of the river between State and Dearborn

Fig. 27. Apartments and town houses, 235 West Eugenie Street, 1961–62. Harry Weese and Associates, architects.

Fig. 28. 235 West Eugenie Street. *Left:* First-floor plan. *Right:* Floor plans of a typical three-floor town house.

27

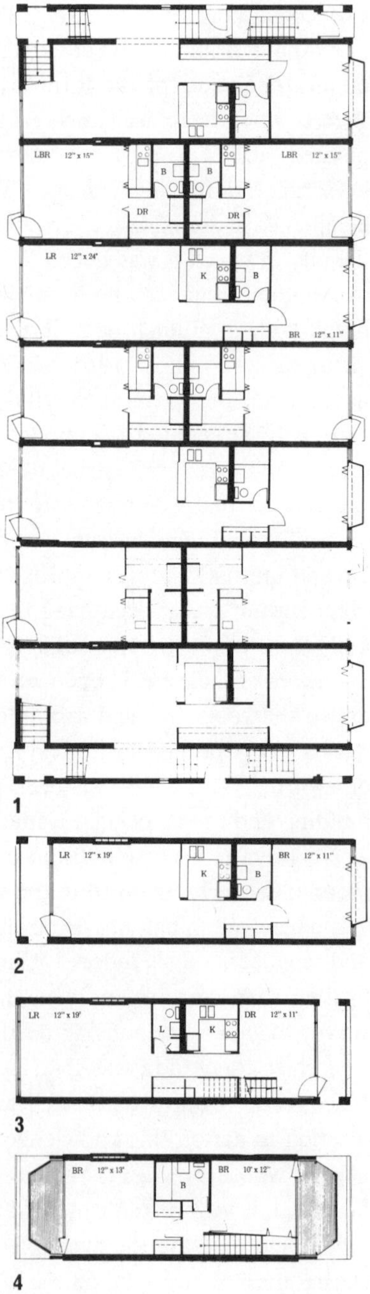

1

2

3

4

28

Fig. 29. John M. Fewkes Tower, 838 North Dearborn Street, 1965–67. Harry Weese and Associates, architects.

Fig. 30. John M. Fewkes Tower. Typical floor plan.

Fig. 31. Astor Tower, 1300 North Astor Place, 1961–62. Bertrand Goldberg Associates, architects.

29

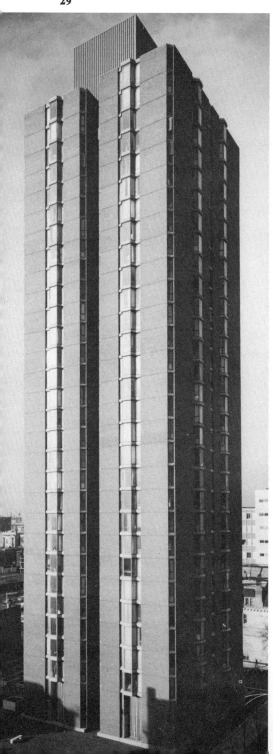

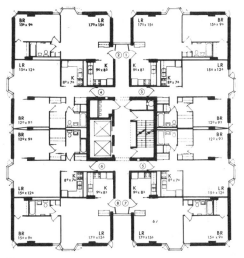

30

31

from the Chicago and North Western Railway for $3,000,000 and awarded the architectural commission to Bertrand Goldberg Associates, who submitted their first plan in September 1959. This scheme embraced two forty-story apartment towers of conventional rectangular form, a ten-story office building, a four-story area surmounted by a plaza with shops, restaurant, and parking space, a marina, an auditorium, a swimming pool, and a landscaped space with fountains, the whole complex to cost about $25,000,000. Financing for this unprecedented enterprise and the insurance of mortgage loans by the Federal Housing Authority proved to be a difficult problem because of objections to the intimate mixture of residential and commercial uses and to the absence of any provision in the project or in the neighborhood for families with children, so that the necessary funds were not fully available until September 1961, although the construction period had been originally planned as 1960–62.[11]

But Goldberg's original plan possessed one serious defect for the restricted site. The two forty-story towers, embracing a total of 1,120 apartments within their plane-walled surfaces, would have covered an excessive proportion of the site and would have stood too close together for comfortable and visually satisfactory apartment living. Before the end of 1959, accordingly, Goldberg submitted a radically different plan involving a wholly new spatial concept. To avoid overloading the site he proposed two sixty-story cylindrical towers, each to contain forty floors of apartments above a two-story mechanical level and a parking garage in the form of a continuous helical ramp rising through the equivalent of eighteen stories. This fantastic idea alone was enough to extinguish the enthusiasm of bankers and insurers, for the towers were to be the tallest cylindrical buildings ever erected, and the skyscraper helix had as a precedent only the much smaller and more conservative spiral ramp in Wright's Guggenheim Museum in New York. Elsewhere on the site the Goldberg staff squeezed a marina, plaza, shops, restaurant, bar, office building, bank, television studio, theater, skating rink, and sculpture garden, an assortment that required the engineers to exhaust every technique of concrete construction developed up to the time. The total number of apartments was reduced to 896, with associated garage space for 900 cars, and the rent schedule was fixed at a minimum of $115 per month for studio apartments and a maximum of $295 for the two-bedroom units (these rates were subsequently raised). With enough money in hand and structural design sufficiently advanced to get the project under way, ground was broken on 22 November 1960.[12]

The cylindrical-tower form offered a variety of structural and economic advantages that the designers thoroughly exploited, although geometric exigencies imposed some peculiar problems on the design of individual apartments that were only partly solved (figs. 32, 33). The circular plan allowed a minimum perimeter for a given floor area, with a consequent saving in structural materials and in heating and air-conditioning loads, and a minimum length of access corridor around the central service core. The sectorial shape of the individual apartment made possible the concentration of the smaller service spaces along the corridor, thus opening the broader areas toward the perimeter to living space. The structural efficiency arises from the minimizing of the wind load on the cylindrical surface and the high resistance of the solid-walled cylindrical core to horizontal bending and shearing forces, a resistance that is uniform regardless of the direction in which the force acts. The circular plan offers a minimum obstruction to the view from any apartment or from the plaza, an advantage that is enhanced by raising the first apartment floor to the twenty-first story, above the low buildings on the north side of the river and above the greatest concentration of atmospheric pollution.

The chief functional divisions of the towers are clearly manifested in their external appearance: the unmistakable helical parking ramp occupies the first eighteen stories; the utility spaces are marked by the break at the nineteenth and twentieth floors; the apartments extend upward from the twenty-first to the sixtieth floor, their individual floors cantilevered outward at every bay into a semicircular balcony (fig. 32). The repetition of these outward-curving flower-petal shapes gives the two buildings their chief visual interest, a quality that was hardly enhanced by the decision of the owners to add television transmission towers and of various tenants to paint soffits and rails in colors other than the original choices. The structural system is visible in all its major parts only at the garage levels. The chief bearing and wind-resisting element is the core that rises to a height well above the roof line, but this is supplemented by inner and peripheral rings of columns joined to the core by radial girders and to each other around the ring by circumferential beams (fig. 33). The core sustains about 70 percent of the bending and shearing forces and a little less than one-half the gravity loads. To obtain maximum strength and rigidity of the core wall it was necessary to stagger the openings at the ends of the elevator lobby floor by floor and to use a horseshoe shape, which minimizes the high stress concentrations that occur at sharp corners and at the line of contact between the floor slab and the cylindrical wall. The circumferential beams offer the liveliest play of purely structural shapes: since they are continuous members and sustain cantilevered areas as well as the radially supported slabs, they curve upward and outward from their haunched ends at the columns to the midpoint of the segment between any pair of adjacent columns. Haunches also appear at the connections of columns and radial

Fig. 32. Marina City, north bank of
the Chicago River between State and
Dearborn streets, 1960–64, 1965–67.
Bertrand Goldberg Associates,
architects

32

Fig. 33. Marina City. A construction photograph showing the cores and peripheral columns.

Fig. 34. Marina City. *Left:* Core plans. *Right:* Floor plans.

Fig. 35. Marina City. *Left:* Site plan. *Right:* Vertical section through the plaza levels and the buildings.

33

34

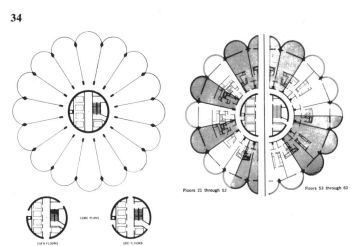

35

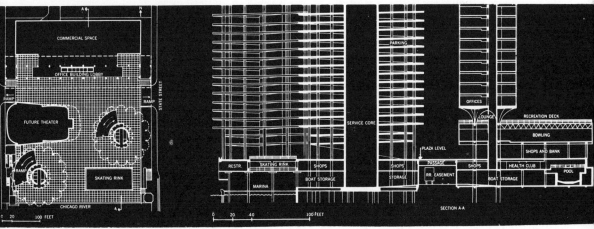

girders, both of which are exposed on the inside of apartments and on the soffits of the balconies to gain some sculptural effect through these heavy plastic forms. Unfortunately, however, the massive structural elements are out of scale with the details of the small apartments and bulk intrusively into these intimate surroundings.[13]

The apartment towers of the Marina City complex were completed in 1964, although tenants had begun to occupy finished apartments as early as June of the previous year. If the sectorial plan offered certain visual and functional advantages, it also imposed an awkward association of spaces through the need to adjust the necessary rectangularity of kitchens, bathrooms, and large pieces of furniture to a basic radial pattern (fig. 34). Kitchens, especially, emerged in a badly squeezed state, and the intrusion of massive structural elements into these already restricted spaces not only cramped them still further but led to extreme spatial contrasts between the narrow compass within the enclosure and the unbounded vista beyond the balcony. The mechanical services were organized according to a carefully analyzed plan comparable to that followed in a subdivision of single-family residences: the utilities serving the entire tower area are limited to cold water, waste disposal, sewerage, electricity, and vertical transportation, whereas hot water, heating, and air conditioning are provided by separate units in the individual apartments. The advantages of this system, which reinforced the microurbanistic character of the Marina group, accrue both to the owner and to the tenants, since the former is protected to some extent against the cost of obsolescence, and the latter enjoys a reduction in his own maintenance costs. The heating and air-conditioning elements, however, had to be located at the base of the window wall, which not only marred its appearance but caused a minor hazard in the form of an obstruction at the base of the doorway leading to the balcony.[14]

The multilevel plaza that covers the marina at water level and houses a restaurant, bar, shopping center, entrance lobby, and skating rink is divided at the original grade level by the North Western rail line, the two portions being linked by a tubular bridge (fig. 35). The tracks, serving the plants of three Chicago newspapers, several warehouses, and Navy Pier, are successors to the original Galena and Chicago Union line of 1848, and the site is part of block number one in the original town of Chicago. The various levels of the plaza are carried by a typical column-and-slab frame. The ten-story office building along the north strip of the site, erected in 1962–64, is carried high above the upper plaza level by a series of concrete groin vaults supported by slender, widely spaced columns. The floors above these vaults rest on transverse beams spanning between load-bearing screen walls composed of a dense array of extremely attenuated columns. Under the groins the architects slipped a low boxlike enclosure containing a bank, health club, swimming pool, and bowling alleys. In such space as remained in this tightly packed area the Marina complex was rounded out by the construction in 1965–67 of the television studio of the ultra-high-frequency station WFLD and the Marina Cinema theaters.

The structural character and visible form of this grotesque lead-sheathed enclosure, looking very much like an inflated whale carcass, was primarily the work of Hanskarl Bandel of the Severud engineering firm. Every surface of the building is curved and every corner rounded for acoustical purposes, and the entire exterior is covered with lead to deaden the sound of rain, hail, aircraft, and street traffic. The hyperbolic-paraboloidal roof is a concrete shell supported by a doubly curved space truss of steel springing from two massive concrete piers that rise like vertical wings from the plaza surface at the sides of the building. The form is as novel as that of the towers themselves, and it is unfortunate that it lies buried in their shadow. The structure represents a unique combination of major twentieth-century innovations in building technology. Since the top surfaces of the arched members in the space truss are buried in the concrete shell, the two had to be designed for composite action between the steel and the concrete. The truss ordinarily sustains the dead weight of the shell, but under the live loads induced by wind the two act as a unit in sustaining the shearing and bending forces. It is all hidden away but perfectly at home in the staggering exhibition of structural virtuosity embodied in Marina City. The question of the setting for this complex may be debated as long as it lasts, but if one were free to choose a site the world over, the vivid and compelling and even violent forms that stand regularly spaced along the sweep of Wacker Drive and the river might seem most perfectly appropriate.

One would suppose that anything following the Marina group would be an anticlimax, but amazing feats of the architectural imagination do not go long unchallenged in Chicago. At the time the Marina City apartments were opened two young and relatively unknown architects, George C. Schipporeit and John C. Heinrich, received the commission for Lake Point Tower, which in its size and form constitutes another original contribution to the building arts (figs. 36, 37). The immense building, designed in collaboration with the architectural firm of Graham, Anderson, Probst and White and the structural engineers William Schmidt and Associates and constructed in 1965–68, towers seventy stories or 645 feet above the street and contains 900 apartments distributed over 1,300,000 square feet of living space. Its isolated site on the man-made peninsula at the base of Navy Pier immediately east of

Fig. 36. Lake Point Tower, 505
North Lake Shore Drive, 1965–68.
Schipporeit-Heinrich Associates and
Graham, Anderson, Probst and
White, architects.

36

Fig. 37. Lake Point Tower. Typical
floor plan.

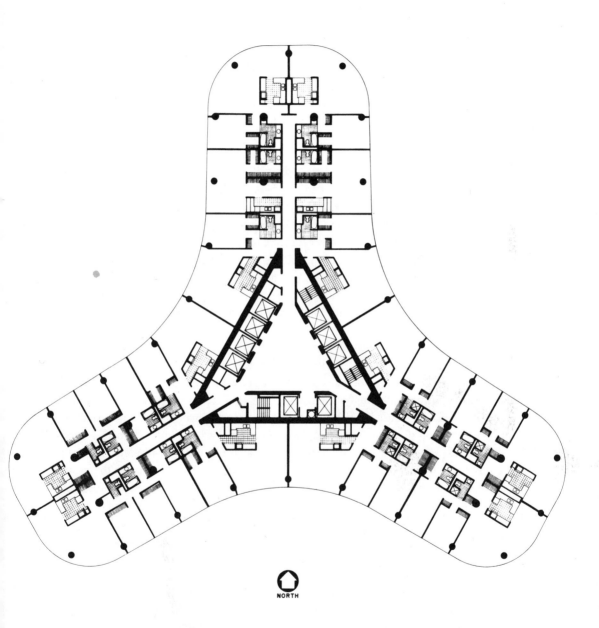

Lake Shore Drive gives it a commanding presence. At the time of its completion it was the highest apartment building in the world and the highest reinforced concrete structure.

More impressive than its size, however, is the curving or undulating form of its three-lobed envelope, whose ancestry makes it especially appropriate to Chicago. In a project presented for an exhibition of the Berlin Novembergruppe in 1919 Mies van der Rohe proposed an asymmetrical curving and angular glass-walled skyscraper with floor slabs spreading out from a shear-wall core of concrete, the odd shape adopted for a narrow triangular site on the Friedrichstrasse. In the following year he offered an even more radical concept in the form of a thirty-story glass-curtain skyscraper with floor slabs cantilevered from a central core and undulating walls disposed in a free-form curve. Both the Marina City and the Lake Point towers were derived from these celebrated projects, but it is the Lake Point design, with its continuous swelling and undulating walls of amber-tinted glass, that represents their fullest realization. As graduates of the architectural program at IIT and products of the Mies office, it is understandable that Heinrich and Schipporeit were deeply imbued with the Miesian spirit.

The tower rises from a two-story base structure that contains space for mechanical and electrical equipment, a parking garage for 700 cars, a lobby, restaurant, coffee shop, and community rooms, and is covered by a landscaped area embracing a swimming pool, ornamental lagoon, putting green, and children's play space. The intermediate level of the base is a concrete slab cast integrally with a two-way system of beams, and the top deck is a solid flat slab 15 inches thick designed to carry a load of 600 pounds per square foot imposed by the earth fill, water, and planting. Both slabs rest on a conventional system of columns. In the seventy-story tower the gravity loads are divided between peripheral columns and a service core in the form of a triangular prism whose walls taper from a thickness of 4 feet at the base to 12 inches at the fifty-ninth floor (fig. 37). Wind loads are sustained entirely by the core, the triangular section offering greater rigidity to bending and shear than the common rectangular variety. An unusual feature of the Lake Point structure is that the building functions as a continuing laboratory for the measurement of wind and seismic deflections and their associated stresses and thus constitutes a unique example of experimental science applied to building technology after as well as before the completion of the work in question. A variety of measuring instruments—strain meters, strain gauges, seismographs, anemometers, and brass-button reference points, some used only during the construction period, others permanently retained —are distributed throughout the caissons and the structural frame. This valuable program of research was established and continues to be maintained through a collaborative effort of various engineering and trade associations and the University of Wisconsin.[15]

The three-lobed plan of the tower is in some ways an aesthetic tour de force, and although it minimizes direct or frontal wind resistance it produces pressure changes arising from airfoil effects caused by wind blowing across the great concave surfaces between the lobes. From the standpoint of interior planning, however, the form offers several advantages. The corridor run in any one wing is short, with a maximum of six apartments in a wing and a minimum of four, the basic module being the two-bedroom apartment. The small number of apartments assures a high degree of privacy in the wing, and the three-wing system with axes at 120 degrees makes it impossible for one tenant to look into his neighbor's apartment (a problem the extent of which does not seem to have been precisely ascertained). The living units were designed so that the owner can expand or reduce the size of individual apartments at moderate cost and so increase or decrease the total number of units to fit changes in the market. The architects followed the conventional practice of locating individually controlled heating and air-conditioning elements in a housing below the sill line of the window walls, the location being marked by the air-intake grills on the exterior of the curtain. The three-lobed form and the necessity for peripheral columns, on the other hand, led to some unavoidably awkward planning of interior enclosures: certain rooms took on odd shapes—trapezoidal, pentagonal, and oval-ended rectangular—and the small cantilever along the edge of the floor slab caused the massive cylindrical columns to intrude into the room along the middle of the wall at the ends of the wings.[16]

But the one serious criticism of Lake Point Tower concerns the relation of the site to urban ecology. As I said in *Chicago 1910–29* (chaps. 1 and 5), the public development of the lakefront terminated in the downtown area at Randolph Street below the river and at Ohio Street above it, leaving a gap of about half a mile in which the riparian land has remained in the hands of private owners. The south portion is held by the Illinois Central Railroad and the north by the Chicago Dock and Canal Company, although it was the intention of the Plan Commission under the Burnham proposals to acquire this property for public recreational and harbor uses, as the construction of Navy Pier as a municipal enterprise indicates. The Park District recognized the value of maintaining the continuity of land along the lake, but it allowed the opportunity to pass without acting on it. Since the municipal government, in its desperate need to raise tax revenue regardless of the civic cost, has adopted a zoning program that places few practical restrictions on building density, this prime area for the construction of high-rise luxury apartments will eventually be drastically overbuilt and the lakefront at the river will be blocked from public access.

Achievements like Lake Point—however admirable in themselves and however seminal for the future development of the building art—or like the scores of upper-income apartment towers along the lakeshore to the north and south, few of them possessed of any architectural distinction, could not by their inherent character satisfy the overwhelming need for low- and middle-income housing. The condominium apartment met a special kind of need, one in which the purchaser wanted to own his own home under a full and clear title but preferred to be free of the cares of maintenance and repair, and as long as the purchase price of the apartments remained around $25,000, they lay within reach of middle-income families. The condominium was introduced into Chicago by the Dunbar Builders Corporation in a small building of fifty-four units erected in 1962–63 at Ridge Avenue (2200W) and Devon (6400N). With a maximum price of $20,500 and a maximum mortgage-payment period of thirty years, the apartments were readily available to families in the middle range. The Dunbar program proved successful and reached an uncommon quality of design in the two Thorndale Beach apartment blocks (1965–66), well sited between Sheridan Road and the lake at Thorndale Avenue (5900N). Again, the maximum price of $28,400 kept the group at the middle-income level. The more elegant glass tower along Lincoln Park at 339 West Barry, designed by Fridstein and Fitch and constructed in 1963–64, clearly fell in the upper-middle bracket, with a $53,850 maximum price, and within two years Gold Coast condominiums were to offer apartment units in the hundred-thousand-dollar range, with an architectural quality that in no way corresponds to the price.

Steeply and irresistibly rising construction costs eventually nullified the promise of every program of middle-income housing, and it finally became obvious that federal subsidies would be necessary if families with incomes below $12,000 per annum (1970 price level) were to survive in the residential market. Subsidized middle-income housing under private sponsorship was introduced into Chicago in 1962 under the terms of section 221(d)3 of the National Housing Act, and in the first five years of the program Chicago builders erected the largest number of subsidized apartment units in the nation, the total running to 9,298 in seventy-six projects. The individual figures varied, but ordinarily the program involved relatively low ceilings on family income, rents, and the rate of return to the investor. These ceilings were maintained through direct payments by the Federal Housing Authority to financial institutions in order to make up the difference between the current interest rate and the low rate of about 3 percent that the borrower was obliged to pay. This large body of construction, with its relatively stringent limitations on cost and hence on design flexibility, brought to the fore the architectural firm of Dubin, Dubin, Black and Moutoussamy, who steadily improved the quality of planning until it stood not far below the average of unsubsidized work such as Marina City.

Considered for its full urbanistic significance as much as for its design, the most important of the Dubin projects is the extensive South Side complex known as Theodore K. Lawless Gardens, constructed between 35th and 37th streets along Rhodes Avenue in 1967–69. The enterprise was sponsored by a consortium of black business and professional men known as the Service Development Association, who purchased the thirteen-acre site from the city's Department of Urban Renewal for $391,000. The entire group, planned as an association of high- and low-rise blocks, parking areas, drives, and landscaped plazas, embraces two twenty-four-story apartment buildings, fifty-four town houses, and a two-story office structure. The two high towers of reinforced concrete framing are characterized by strongly articulated walls of continuous columns, broad baywide window groups, and recessed and molded spandrel panels, all very much in the Chicago tradition.[17] The same architects used a somewhat similar design for the big thirty-story block constructed at Michigan Avenue and 20th Street in 1968–70, which was also financed under the terms of section 221(d)3. The great value of the Michigan project is that it marks the first step in the conversion of the area between Grant Park and Cermak Road (2200S) from its present conglomeration of marginal or derelict commercial properties into blocks of low- and middle-income housing. The building itself is marked chiefly by the presence on all four elevations of load-bearing screen walls with extremely attenuated, closely ranked columns. This feature became a hallmark of the Dubin work, but unfortunately, the very source of its economy and efficiency is what makes it the most monotonous in appearance of all structural systems.

In the design of individual houses Chicago never regained or even remotely approached the preeminence it had achieved at the beginning of the Burnham period. Many of those that revealed some architectural distinction were erected in the suburbs, where the work of Edward Dart had established itself in the front rank by the decade of the sixties. Modern domestic architecture returned to the city proper with the house erected in 1947 at 4912 South Woodlawn Avenue from the design of Ralph Rapson and John Vander Meulen, but only the latter elected to remain in Chicago. Over the years a few possessed enough architectural excellence to qualify for various awards, but a high proportion of these were confined to the Hyde Park area. Among the best of the single-family variety are the house at 5617 South Kenwood (1957–58) by Harry Weese and Associates, the atrium row houses at 1366–

1380 East Madison Park (1960–61) by Yan C. Wong, and the group of detached units designed by Edward Dart and erected at 58th Street and Dorchester Avenue in 1962–63 for the faculty of the Chicago Theological Seminary (fig. 38). The houses are arranged in a U-shaped site plan around a landscaped central court for maximum privacy, and their steeply pitched roofs—a high fashion by the mid-sixties —form a lively pictorial composition of sloping planes. Among straight-line row houses several groups of American Institute of Architects award winners were built as part of the conservation and renewal program in the Lincoln Park area, but they are pitifully few in the light of the neighborhood needs—sixteen units at 515 West Belden Avenue (2300N), designed by Anderson and Battles and erected in 1967–68; six at 2110 North Hudson (432W), built in the same years from the plans of Booth and Nagle; eight at 424 West Webster (2200N), by the same architects and opened in 1970.

But these little essays, scattered through neighborhoods that retained some measure of urbanity, only served to emphasize the mortal sickness of residential construction in Chicago. It was sick of every ailment—greed and cynicism and civic indifference, zoning provisions that allowed indiscriminate building to any height and density, minimal design and jerry-building, and inflation that year by year eroded away the minor gains in productivity. The cancer started at the top and ate downward through every economic stratum, from the few rich to the multitude of poor: urban disaster, like Death in his proud tower, looked down on all alike. The real estate and building interests demanded and received from the city council the freedom to build at whatever density they chose in order to develop the land at maximum profit to themselves. The most extreme intensity of land use occurred along the lakefront, especially along and east of Michigan Avenue below Oak Street, in the Gold Coast area, and on Sheridan Road above the north end of Lincoln Park. The vicious spiral of overbuilding and inflated land values was pointedly described by the architect Harry Weese, who retained a civic conscience that was lacking in many of his fellows.

I have given up on the lakeshore. It is becoming a Chicago version of Rio de Janeiro's Copacabana—a solid row of high-rises with Appalachia directly behind. High-rises attract high-rises. As soon as one goes in, the land tends to go up in value and price. The higher the land costs go, the higher the buildings must go in order to bring a maximum return on the investment. More and more are piled on until they cancel each other out.[18]

While the big-time operators created canyons of skyscraper vulgarity, the lesser exploiters, not to be outdone in rapacity, introduced little jerry-built apartments

Fig. 38. Chicago Theological
Seminary faculty houses, Dorchester
Avenue at 58th Street, 1962–63.
Loebl, Schlossman, Bennett and
Dart, architects.

known as four-plus-ones that began to mushroom like noxious weeds in the better inner-city residential areas, particularly Rogers Park and Lake View. By dropping the ground floor a little below grade the builder could hold a five-floor apartment building below fifty-five feet and thus, according to the code, use a framing system of wood rather than steel or concrete. Ugly, shoddy, dangerous, minimal in utilities and design, the four-plus-one simultaneously guaranteed the destruction of good housing and the creation of slums where none existed before.

This rage to build anywhere for a quick profit resulted at the very least in street congestion, lethal atmospheric pollution, and the burying of decent neighborhoods of single-family houses and walk-up apartments in the shadows of lumpish and disfigured giants. But that proved to be only a beginning, for the worst consequence was the literal destruction of neighborhoods and of the last vestiges of community life. The most extreme damage has been wrought in the inner Gold Coast, where the reckless building of high-rise apartments along the narrow tree-lined streets such as North State, North Dearborn, Astor, and the intersecting arteries has brought many parts of the neighborhood close to devastation. Great architectural landmarks, unprotected by a council desperate to increase the tax return at all costs, fell along with more conventional houses that retained a dignity and charm preserved for generations by the aristocracy of Chicago. Since the great majority of apartments in the new towers are the studio and efficiency variety, the unmarried tenants, coming in and moving away every few months, obviously have no interest in schools or neighborhood amenities. Nothing could be more bitterly ironic in the city of the Burnham Plan than this disappearance of civic standards, this collapse of urban taste that signifies the spiritual bankruptcy of middle-class America. As of 1970 there was no evidence that the trend would be arrested.

In the upper-income areas along the lake the symptoms of civic deterioration took the form of a frightening concentration of tin-can skyscrapers, but for the low- and middle-income areas—the overwhelming bulk of the city's residential land—the disease took precisely the opposite form. In these neighborhoods housing began literally to disappear. By 1970, according to a survey undertaken by the Metropolitan Housing and Planning Council of Chicago, the production of low- and middle-income housing, privately sponsored, subsidized, or public, had dropped nearly to the vanishing point: of the 1,300,000 dwelling units in the city 61.5 percent had been built before 1920 and 20 percent in the decade ending in 1929, while 21 percent of the total fell below the minimum standards of housing fixed by the federal Department of Housing and Urban Development. Proposals for the meaningful enforcement of the housing code were nullified by a politically attuned judiciary or by the indifference of the city council, but even if such plans had been adopted, economic inflation provided the final and insurmountable barrier. The high cost of construction, high interest rates, the evaporation of mortgage funds, the general decline of home building in favor of the more profitable military and industrial operations—these together brought housing to the final crisis. By 1970 the situation was such that a family with an income below $12,000 per annum could not afford to buy a newly built house or to rent an apartment in a newly constructed building, a massive economic fact that effectively barred 80 percent of the population of Chicago from moving out of their decaying blocks or the skyscraper prisons of the Chicago Housing Authority.

There was a small stream of well-intentioned plans, programs, and odds and ends of council ordinances, but results were nonexistent. The building code for dwellings was among the best in the country. There were housing courts to enforce it, independent aldermen who offered excellent proposals for upgrading substandard units, and a receivership program for rescuing derelict properties; but in the richest nation in the world there was no money to carry out such enterprises because there was no profit in them. The Planning and Housing Council precisely summarized the appalling truth.

[Chicago has] as many instruments as any city in the nation for housing and community betterment. . . . Yet all these programs combined do not add up to a meaningful strategy for managing and preserving the existing housing, or for coping with the disastrous housing deficiency. . . . We are mired in a bureaucratic system where court action adds up to a slap-on-the-wrist enforcement and is not a deterrent to violation of the city's codes. . . . Because of the lack of alternative housing, Housing Court judges hesitate to order the demolition of structurally sound buildings, even though many serious violations exist. . . . [The result is that] deterioration is spreading; building abandonment is on the rise; low-income housing is disintegrating faster than it is being built. Chicago is running out of housing.[19]

And as the housing ran out, the health services collapsed: in 1970 the city had two thousand fewer physicians than in 1930, and those who remained were distributed 97 percent among the white neighborhoods and 3 percent among the black, although the latter accounted for 33 percent of the total population. Half the low-income minority were forced to go to Cook County Hospital, which had deteriorated so badly that it could not fill half its quota of medical school graduates. As a human habitation, Chicago had come perilously close to total failure, as a decline of 183,000 in population between the censuses of 1960 and 1970 clearly indicated.

Office Buildings

It is necessary to establish this failure of the privately financed housing industry in order to make a proper urbanistic assessment of the extraordinary achievements of Chicago architects and engineers in the office building boom of the 1960s. Construction in the city's core was late in beginning, and for a decade after the end of the war real estate activity was not only moribund but showed no promise of freeing itself from that state. An ironic curiosity of postwar urban expansion is that the first buildings to be erected in the inner-city area are factories, both excellent works of industrial architecture in the glass-walled mode of the thirties. The earlier is the addition to the R. R. Donnelley and Sons Company's plant, erected in 1946 along the Illinois Central tracks below 23rd Street and designed by the Albert Kahn firm as a simplified version of the previous building by Howard Van Doren Shaw. The second is the Florsheim Shoe Company factory at the northwest corner of Canal and Adams streets (1948–49), a handsome work of ribbon-windowed flat-slab framing designed by Shaw, Metz and Dolio (fig. 105, left background). For three years after the completion of this building construction in the central business district lay dormant, but it was suddenly and finally shaken out of its slumbers by the erection of the Prudential Insurance Company's headquarters in 1952–55. The forty-one-story steel-framed tower, with a gross floor area of 1,763,000 square feet, was designed by Naess and Murphy and constructed on air rights over the Illinois Central Suburban Station on Randolph Drive; it was the first Chicago office building since the completion of the Field in 1934 and the first air-rights structure since the opening of the Merchandise Mart in 1930. Although it is an emasculated variation on the skyscraper verticalism of the late twenties, the Prudential served two valuable functions: it demonstrated the willingness of a major corporation to invest a large sum of money in its Chicago facilities, and it reminded the building and real estate interests that if any substantial demand for space appeared, there was nothing of prime quality available beyond five thousand square feet. Moreover, the construction of the Prudential came shortly after a drastic revision of the Chicago building code in 1950 which substituted performance standards for the traditional specification of materials. It was a model for the entire country, and it eventually proved to be a potent stimulus to new construction.[20]

The revival of building in the Loop followed quickly after the Prudential's completion. The initial work was the Inland Steel Building, designed by Skidmore, Owings and Merrill and erected at the northeast corner of Monroe and Dearborn streets in 1955–57 (fig. 39). It is modest enough in size, with its nineteen-story height, but

85

Fig. 39. Inland Steel Building, northeast corner of Monroe and Dearborn streets, 1955–57. Skidmore, Owings and Merrill, architects.

Fig. 40. International Minerals and Chemical Corporation administrative and research center, 5401 Old Orchard Road, Skokie, Illinois, 1957–58. The Perkins and Will Partnership, architects.

40

39

its structural and architectural design includes valuable innovations. The structure as a whole is divided into two radically distinct parts, one the main enclosure embracing the rentable floor area, the other a slender utility tower containing all service elements, the two being joined by a connecting wing that is simply an extension into the main volume of the successive elevator lobbies. The "served" areas, as the architect Louis Kahn later described them, are sheathed in blue-green glass, the "servant" space in stainless steel. To free the working floor space of structural as well as mechanical obstructions the architects reduced the number of columns to seven pairs situated entirely outside the long elevations of the building and connected by transverse floor girders extending across the 58-foot clear span. Overlying the tinted windows and the stainless-steel sheathing of the spandrel girders is the familiar Miesian tracery of continuous mullions, whose close spacing nicely establishes the human scale in this glistening integument. The entire work reveals the influence of Mies van der Rohe's 860–80 North Lake Shore Drive apartment towers, and the debt is one that the partners of Skidmore's Chicago office are happy to acknowledge. The Inland Steel Building represents technology celebrated according to the Miesian canon: its structural system and its functional divisions can be clearly read in its exterior forms, and this combination of simplicity, clarity, and elegance made it immensely influential in the coming construction boom.[21]

The neutral curtain wall of glass and enameled steel that was made popular by Lever House in New York (1950–52) remained the ruling fashion throughout the decade of the fifties. The most prominent example in Chicago is the Borg-Warner Building (1957–58), erected on the site of the old red-brick Pullman Building at Michigan Avenue and Adams Street. The design was a collaborative work of A. Epstein and Sons and the New York architect William Lescaze, who was the first to import the so-called International Style into the United States. A more elegant work in the Miesian spirit is the administrative and research center of the International Minerals and Chemical Corporation, designed by Perkins and Will and constructed during the same years at 5401 Old Orchard Road in Skokie (fig. 40). The presence of continuous mullions and a bolder use of color add a liveliness to the elevations that the more conventional essays like the Borg-Warner lack. The impressive feature of the Minerals and Chemical group, however, is the imaginative landscaping of the plaza, which is divided into discrete rectangular areas of flowers, shrubbery, and gravel organized by a grid of five-foot squares that extends into the horizontal plane the similar pattern formed by windows and spandrels in the building. Franz Lipp, the author of this little-known masterpiece, received a national landscaping award for his creation. The pure Miesian style done in stainless steel came with Skidmore,

Owings and Merrill's addition to the Harris Trust and Savings Bank Building (1958–60), at the southwest corner of Monroe and Clark streets. The handsomest part of the design is the recessed connecting wing that joins the main addition to the original building: here nothing interrupts the broad panes of glass except the narrow spandrels, and they rise in a clean glittering sweep within this shadowed bay.

As the building boom approached an explosive level around 1960, several great men of the past, architects who stood among the earliest creators of a modern style, reached the end point of their long lives. On 9 April 1959 Frank Lloyd Wright died at Phoenix, Arizona, two months short of what proved to be his ninety-second birthday. Through his enormously prolific life he had persistently understated his age by two years, apparently as one of the many little acts by which he built up the myth that was inseparable from the man. Six months later, on 17 October, Richard E. Schmidt died at the age of ninety-three, so old that his birth had occurred when his native Bavaria was still an independent kingdom. The following year, 6 October saw the death at the age of eighty-eight of Hugh Mackie Garden, an early associate of Richard Schmidt and one of the founders of the productive and influential partnership of Schmidt, Garden and Martin. More shocking was the death on 28 September 1962 of Louis H. Skidmore, whose sixty-five years seemed almost youthful beside the life spans of these aged pioneers. Much of the success of the Century of Progress Exposition could be attributed to his work, as we have seen (pp. 3–22), and when he founded the office of Skidmore and Owings in 1936 it might have been possible to predict something of its success and influence.

By the time Skidmore died it had become obvious that the Loop was entering into a building boom comparable to those of the 1880s and the 1920s, although it never reached the intensity of the latter, the best year of the sixties seeing only two-thirds the area of office space installed during the more boisterous stretches of the twenties.[22] The last of the curtain-wall mode that was fashionable during the fifties is the sixteen-story building of the Home Federal Savings and Loan Association, a smooth tower of dark-tinted glass and black spandrel panels from the office of Skidmore, Owings and Merrill. Erected in 1961–62 at the southeast corner of State and Adams, it is the only office building on State Street except for the celebrated though fading Reliance and is the largest structure to appear on the great shopping artery since the opening of the Palmer House in 1925. The construction of the Home Federal headquarters required the demolition of the Republic Building of Holabird and Roche, since the remodeling cost proved to be higher than that of putting up a new building. It was a tragic year for the cause of good architecture: a veritable orgy of destruction swept away the Republic, the Cable, the Majestic Hotel, and the Garrick Theater Building, the last being the victim of a barbarous act of vandalism carried out in the name of an expanding economy.[23]

The demolition of the Cable Building at the southeast corner of Jackson Boulevard and Wabash Avenue cleared the way for the Continental Center, which marked a decisive and apparently permanent break with the smooth curtain walls of the previous decade. The twenty-two-story steel-framed block, erected in 1961–62 from the plans of C. F. Murphy Associates, is a large rearward extension of the Continental Companies headquarters at 310 South Michigan Avenue (figs. 41, 42). The articulated walls of the Continental addition are so emphatically drawn from the central tradition of the Chicago school as to make it seem as though the long discontinuities between past and present had never existed. The U-shaped plan of the building made it possible to restrict the elevators and the central utility shafts to the open court embraced by the arms of the U and to free the office areas of columns by means of the unprecedented bay span of forty-two feet (fig. 42). Long spans, of course, mean deep girders, and the resulting sacrifice of overhead space in the Continental was minimized by passing ducts and conduits through rectangular openings cut in the webs of the girders, a technique which in effect turned them into Vierendeel trusses. The expense of fabricating such steelwork is partly offset by a reduction in the number of columns and hence of the costly caissons. The massive steel frame of the Continental Center is expressed in the street elevations with a relentless assertiveness, so that there is no mistaking what lies behind.

The old Chicago practice of increasing apparent height by means of continuous projecting columns, emphatically revived in the Inland Steel Building, is the distinguishing feature of the richly clad central office building of the United States Gypsum Company (fig. 43). Standing at the southeast corner of Wacker and Monroe Street, where it was constructed in 1961–63, the Gypsum building embodies so many extraordinary features that it suggests that the architects, Perkins and Will, were aiming to produce a lasting novelty.[24] The most obvious characteristic is that the slender nineteen-story tower, a square prism in its geometric form, is rotated at forty-five degrees on its site, so that the four elevations face diagonally to the ruling grid of the street system, leaving four little triangular plazas at the corners of the lot. With all sides of the structure thus exposed to view and with a generous foreground provided by the double-deck, dual-pavement boulevard, the owners decided to clothe their corporate seat with a measure of costly splendor. The continuous columns of the steel frame are sheathed in marble, the spandrel panels are rough-faced slate, and the windows that fill the narrow bays are a blue-gray tinted glass. The marble ceiling above the space between the columns and the entrance-elevator lobby

89

Fig. 41. Continental Center,
southeast corner of Wabash Avenue
and Jackson Boulevard, 1961–62.
C. F. Murphy Associates, architects.

Fig. 42. Continental Center. The
steel frame during construction.

42

41

is formed into a series of shallow dihedral angles, while at the very top the columns terminate in sharp-pointed marble-clad polyhedra. Their shape was derived from the crystalline form of calcium sulfate, or gypsum, but the source of this ornamental detail very likely eludes the average spectator. The wall paneling in the company's executive offices, on the other hand, is composed of wood so exotic that at least its high cost cannot escape the visitor.

The area lying on both sides of the river, from Wacker Drive to Canal Street in the vicinity of Union Station, was filled with spacious sites either opened up by the extension of the drive or long available in the form of air rights over the station's extensive track and platform system.[25] In the summer of 1961 a consortium of New York and London builders announced a grandiose scheme for burying the vast Union Station complex between Canal Street and the river under a linear series of skyscrapers, the total investment to run as high as $200,000,000. The figure was high enough to arouse the suspicion that the ambitious plans would never be realized, and before another year had passed the two promoters, Diesel Construction Company and City Center Properties, Limited, were actively scaling down their program. Yet the development of this prize site held great economic and social implications for the city. The Chicago Central Area Plan of 1958 (pp. 271–72) designated it a transportation center in which a tightly knit group of rail, air, helicopter, and bus terminals would constitute the focal point of a line of skyscrapers above the tracks. The coming construction of the University of Illinois campus eight blocks to the southwest, scheduled to begin in 1963, was to provide additional impetus to the redevelopment of the West Side (pp. 181–89). The Central Area Plan had much to recommend it, but it was also marked by a considerable measure of unreality. The Union Bus Terminal had been built in 1949–50 on Randolph Street between Dearborn and Clark, where it was in no immediate need of expansion. The airline ticket offices had long been established in the vicinity of Monroe Street and Wabash Avenue, on the opposite side of the Loop, and no one could discover any demand for public helicopter space. At the very moment that the air-rights proposals reached their grandest scope Erwin S. Wolfson, the president of the Diesel Construction Company, died, and the failure to raise more than a fraction of the capital brought the whole enterprise to collapse. But the enormous potential of the site remained, and events had proceeded far enough so that the Tishman Realty and Construction Company was able to rescue the operation and restore it to life by the end of 1962.

The several buildings that eventually rose over the station tracks are known collectively as Gateway Center and individually by various addresses on Riverside Plaza, a public-relations name felt to be more appropriate than the homely, histori-

Fig. 43. United States Gypsum
Building, 101 South Wacker Drive,
1961–63. The Perkins and Will
Partnership, architects.

Fig. 44. Gateway Center I and II,
between Canal Street and the South
Branch of the river, from Madison
Street to Adams Street, 1963–65,
1965–67. Skidmore, Owings, and
Merrill, architects.

44

43

Fig. 45. Montgomery Ward Store, Adams between State and Dearborn streets, 1890–91, 1964–65. The original Fair Store was designed by William Le Baron Jenney, the modernization by the Perkins and Will Partnership.

Fig. 46. Hartford Insurance Building, 100 South Wacker Drive, 1959–61. Skidmore, Owings and Merrill, architects.

45

46

cally meaningful Canal Street. Skidmore, Owings and Merrill had already been chosen as architects, and the first of four projected buildings to come from their office was constructed in 1963–65 over the track area bounded by Madison and Monroe streets (fig. 44). The twenty-one-story block is a conventional work of steel-framed Miesian architecture, but the delicately articulated walls were handled with the finish and assurance that mark many of the large commissions of the Skidmore firm. The finely drawn black vertical tracery and the sea-tinted glass are well set off by the long travertine-paved plaza along the river. The structural system is marked by unusually long, narrow bays, measuring 18 feet on the longitudinal line and 45 feet on the transverse. The larger dimension was dictated by the need to provide a clear span over two tracks and two half-platforms in the station below, and the shorter was adopted to reduce vibrations in the framing caused by passing trains. The second Gateway Center followed in 1965–67, an exact copy of the first, and the third was placed under construction in 1969 as an unusual combination of interior steel framing and external bearing walls of concrete framing that function as wind-bracing as well as supports for gravity loads. Since the builders were determined to use the Adams-Jackson block in their overall plan, this visually uninteresting work of commercial architecture required the demolition of the superbly vaulted concourse building of Union Station.[26]

A relatively minor enterprise in the boom of the sixties was one that brought the original and the renaissance phases of the Chicago school into immediate physical association. William Le Baron Jenney's Fair Store (1890–91), extending from State to Dearborn along the north side of Adams Street, was acquired by Montgomery Ward and Company in 1957 to provide a downtown retail outlet and to improve its competitive position with Sears, Roebuck, whose store at State and Van Buren streets had also been designed by Jenney. The old Fair, however, was in many ways a monstrosity in its external appearance, and no one could make a case for it as a landmark. The new owners accordingly commissioned Perkins and Will in 1964 to undertake the design of an extensive remodeling, and the result was opened in the following year as the largest department-store investment in the Loop in thirty-five years (fig. 45). The handsome renovation, very much in the Chicago spirit, preserves the power of the original articulated walls at the sacrifice of their tasteless ornament. In the new work the second and third stories are windowless, but above them rise the familiar baywide Chicago windows, the deep reveals, and the continuous piers with projecting moldings at the edges, all nicely set off by the smooth limestone veneer.

Most of the office and store buildings that sprang into being during the prolific sixties are steel-framed structures strongly marked by the native or the Miesian tradition, or by both in harmonious association.[27] The ascendency of concrete, however, coincided with the enormous expansion of building activity in the decade, and the innovations in concrete construction that characterized the new apartment towers began to appear in their office counterparts. The first of these and the most thoroughly imbued with the Chicago spirit is the Hartford Fire Insurance Company's building, designed by Skidmore, Owings and Merrill and erected in 1959–61 at the southwest corner of Monroe Street and Wacker Drive as the first step in the filling out of the sites along the new southward extension of the drive (fig. 46). The twenty-story structure is a prize example of simplicity and clarity: the thin-edged floor slabs, the slender columns, and the shallow haunches at the column tops are directly presented in all four elevations, with only a polished granite sheathing on the outer surfaces of the concrete as a formal addition. The curtain walls of glass are drawn back 4 feet 6 inches from the outer plane of the concrete frame for a variety of functional and aesthetic reasons—to provide a screen against solar radiation and a convenient platform for washing windows, and to add an exaggerated sharpness and incisiveness to the appearance of the frame. If the Inland Steel Building represents the celebration of technique, one might very well argue that the Hartford is technique uncelebrated. The second Hartford, at Adams Street on the south half of the block, was added in 1968–70. A reinforced concrete tower covered with polished black-granite veneer to frame its dark-tinted glass, it is an example of another fashion that became popular in the late sixties and that might be characterized as the empty, featureless, or literally monotonous elevation.

A more imaginative work that represents a powerfully stated realization of technical potentialities is the group of buildings constituting the executive offices and the training center of the United Air Lines (figs. 47, 48). Set in a fifty-one-acre site along Algonquin Road in Elk Grove Township, the administrative and original training centers were constructed in 1960–61, but a third building for the training of stewardesses and management personnel was added in 1966–67, all of them products of the Skidmore office. The two original buildings are extremely elongated in their main horizontal dimension, possibly to an unmatched degree: two stories in height, the administration building alone extending 700 feet in length and the individual bay stretched to 66 feet, the two structures are exercises in linearity as emphatic as the prairie horizon itself (fig. 47). It was only by using prestressed concrete that the architects could adopt the extreme bay span without an unmanageable depth of girder. The strong rectilinear articulation in the United Air Lines structures is again intensified by the device of drawing the glass walls well back from the outer

Fig. 47. United Air Lines administrative and training center, Algonquin and Linneman roads, Elk Grove Township, Illinois, 1960–61, 1966–67. Skidmore, Owings, and Merrill, architects.

Fig. 48. United Air Lines group. Interior court of the administration building.

47

48

Fig. 49. Brunswick Building, 69 West Washington Street, 1963–65. Skidmore, Owings and Merrill, architects.

Fig. 50. Brunswick Building. Typical floor plan.

49

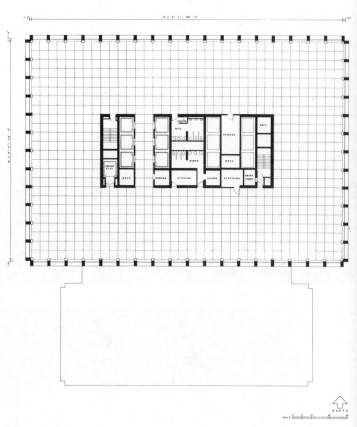

50

surfaces of the framing members, a feature which emerges most emphatically in the enclosed landscaped areas of the interior courts (fig. 48). The specific author of the airlines group among the Skidmore designers was Myron Goldsmith, a graduate of Mies's architectural program at Illinois Institute of Technology and of the institute's civil engineering department as well. He is perhaps the leading exponent of the Miesian dictum that "wherever technology reaches its real fulfillment, it transcends into architecture."[28]

The largest and most impressive work of concrete framing in the Loop is the Brunswick Building, at the southwest corner of Dearborn and Washington streets, where it was constructed in 1963–65 simultaneously with the Civic Center that faces it on the north side of Washington (figs. 49, 50). The Brunswick is another distinguished work to emerge in good measure from the talents of Myron Goldsmith, the Skidmore partner who acted as senior designer, but the tightly ranked members of its load-bearing screens lie at the other end of the spectrum from the extended horizontality of the United Air Lines group. The thirty-eight-story height of the Loop building made it the highest structure with a load-bearing wall erected up to the time of its completion, and the division of gravity and wind loads between the external framework and a shear-wall core made it the first of its kind to have a column-free interior. These are planning and structural distinctions of a high order, but they may take second place before the four-story base, where a combination of aesthetic, technical, and economic decisions led to a solution unique in multistory construction. The problem arose from the question whether the numerous columns of the screen wall should be carried to grade level, and if this was not done, what alternatives were available and how they were to be managed. The decision that was finally made posed a challenge that the architects met with characteristic boldness.[29]

It was obvious from the beginning that carrying the screen wall to bedrock through a multitude of small caissons was inadmissable because of the high cost and the difficulties of sinking the caisson wells. It then followed by logical necessity that a transfer girder would be required to distribute the loads of the many small columns to the relatively few caissons underpinning them, and the question then arose whether this massive girder should be located above grade or below. The architects decided on the former course in order to provide an open area around the lobby walls that would visually balance the extremely long spans and generous heights at the base of the Civic Center to the north (pp. 134–41). What followed offers a good example of the art of structural and architectural design: if the openings between columns of the Brunswick base were too great, they would require a transfer girder of unmanageable depth; if too small, they would appear shrunken and underscaled compared with those of the Civic Center. The ultimate solution was to transfer the loads of the four screen walls to ten columns around the full perimeter of the building, with the columns set 57 feet center-to-center on the long elevations. The members necessary to sustain the loads are undoubtedly the largest structural elements ever used in conventional building (as opposed, for example, to track-floor frames in railroad terminals): the individual column is a huge pier of square section, 7 feet on a side; the ring girder is staggering in its size, extending through the depth of one and a half floors, or 24 feet 5½ inches.[30] Instead of trying to disguise these elephantine members, the architects proclaimed them clearly enough so that everyone can see how this lofty cage is lifted and held securely above the ground.

In its architectonic character the Brunswick is obviously a distinguished work, superior to anything else of its kind, but the formal treatment of the elevations makes us realize that like a pennant-winning baseball team, even the best performers are capable of errors. Because the column depth of the screen wall was much less than the thickness of the ring girder, the designers were faced with the problem of providing a satisfactory transition from the huge scale of one element to the relative delicacy of the other. Their solution was to avoid the awkward step-back by introducing an inward-curving face at the foot of the column, much like the curve at the second-floor line of the Monadnock Building four blocks to the south. But the absence of a terminating feature in the Brunswick and the illusions of perspective cause the cagelike tower to diminish into weakness and irresolution at the top. The way of avoiding this phenomenon is also present in the Monadnock—the outward curve of the walls at the parapet—but while the partners of the Skidmore office are happy to admit their debt to Mies van der Rohe, they would never allow themselves to make such obvious use of a nineteenth-century solution. But there is a more serious defect than this, and it probably arose from concessions to corporate bad taste. The screen walls, the ring girder, and the base piers are all concrete, and however disparate their shapes and proportions, they function as a unified working system. This unity is denied by covering the girders and the piers with materials that are not only misleading but inharmonious: the piers are clothed in the ubiquitous travertine, and the great girder in a high-density paneled concrete that looks like limestone of inferior quality. It was all meant to convey a sumptuous character that bare concrete lacks, but it serves only to look like what it is, an irritating mistake.

The role of the Brunswick Building extends further than what is implied by the visible portions above grade level. Underneath it there spreads the beginning of an underground city that will hopefully come to rival the multilayered core of Montreal. Opened in 1966, this 45,000-square-foot area embraces a variety of small stores,

Fig. 51. First National Bank
Building, Madison Street between
Dearborn and Clark, 1965–69. C. F.
Murphy Associates and the Perkins
and Will Partnership, architects.

restaurants, bars, service facilities, a barber shop, and a branch of the Chicago-Tokyo Bank. In itself it is a modest start, but it is the center of a system of broad pedestrian passageways that extend north to the Civic Center, east to the Dearborn and State Street subways, and west through the Civic Center area to the old City Hall and County Building on Clark Street between Randolph and Washington. Eventually, following the completion of the First National Bank Building and the long-delayed Federal Center, passageways are to extend southward to these buildings and to others along the way. The system represents the first step in creating a below-grade equivalent of the elevated walkways and special entrances that connect the rapid transit Loop with various department stores and LaSalle Street Station, but it is still far removed from either Montreal or the ancestor of all such developments, the immense Grand Central Terminal complex in New York City.

All the postwar skyscrapers of the core, whether steel-framed or concrete, constitute a preparation for the two highest buildings of any description so far erected in Chicago. The first to reach completion is the First National Bank, which was constructed in 1965–69 at the exact geometric center of the Loop, on the block bounded by Madison and Monroe streets to the north and south and by Dearborn and Clark to the east and west (fig. 51). The demolition necessary to clear the space for this block-long, sixty-story, 850-foot behemoth was staggering: it included not only the bank's existing seventeen-story building but the two parts of the Morrison Hotel, the tower of which was forty-five stories in height, and a host of lesser office areas, shops, bookstores, restaurants, and bars. However valuable one may consider the addition of a great financial and office center to the city, it is obvious that construction on this scale can be accomplished only at the cost of permanent damage to the life of the urban core, especially to the life after hours, when the bank and the offices are closed. At the same time, the officers of the bank clearly recognized the value of the site, and the rapidity with which the office space was leased long before construction was completed confirmed their judgment. Midway between the department stores of State Street and the financial institutions of LaSalle, with a direct underground entrance to the adjacent Dearborn Street subway, equidistant from all the elevated stations and from the suburban rail lines to the east and west, the $106,-000,000 investment and its happy rental history provide a potent demonstration to urban ecologists of the importance of public transportation, even in a nation infatuated with the automobile.

The commission for the design of the huge building went to two of the largest architectural-engineering firms in the city, C. F. Murphy Associates and the Perkins and Will Partnership, whose collaborative achievement clearly fits into the classic

Chicago tradition of articulated walls and continuous projecting columns. The distinctive feature of the tower is the shape of the external envelope, an inward-curving form that reminds us, not entirely by coincidence, of the Eiffel Tower in Paris. Underlying this novel deviation from the conventional geometry is a floor-use and circulation problem peculiar to the large bank in Illinois. The First National claims to be the world's largest financial institution in which all business must be carried on at a single location because of a primitive Illinois law that prohibits branch banking. Thus the bank is compelled to provide under one roof all the facilities necessary for its financial operations, including a commercial savings department unparalleled in size and scope. Translated into architectural terms, these conditions required that the maximum floor area be at and near the ground level to accommodate the heavy public traffic, whereas the financial and administrative activities dictated a progressively diminishing floor area throughout the first forty-two stories occupied by the bank and tenants. In the remaining eighteen floors, given over to rental space and utilities, the stories retain the conventional uniform area to the top.

What Charles Brubaker of the Perkins and Will office called this "hierarchical arrangement of functions" dictated a tapering envelope, but the precise parabolic curve adopted for the long elevations was chosen in good measure on aesthetic grounds. The tower, occuping 46 percent of its site at the base, contracts in floor area from 59,000 square feet at grade to 29,000 square feet in the tenant stories. Of the total floor area available the bank occupies about 1,000,000 square feet. Extending outside the main enclosure on the short elevations are two blunt wings that house the elevators and the service facilities, their location thus leaving a maximum area of unobstructed space and maximum flexibility for the banking activities.[31] The entire building is a powerfully expressive revelation of its complex internal functions and its dominant structural system of column-and-girder framing. The inward curving envelope of the central enclosure, the lofty ground floor with its curtain of glass, the articulated walls in their granite sheathing, the baywide window openings, the precise separation of the servant areas from the served—all together express in a single unified form the essential parts and the internal activities of the whole work.

The structural framework of the First National Bank involves two deviations from straightforward rectilinearity, the obvious one, of course, being the inward curve of the external columns. This curve does not begin at grade level, although it appears to do so: the individual column follows an inclined tangent to the fifth floor, a parabolic segment from the fifth to the forty-second, and a vertical tangent through the remaining height. The curvature of the columns outside the long elevations results in an inclined thrust with a horizontal component that is sustained by posttensioned tie rods extending between opposite pairs of columns immediately below grade level. The vertical component is carried by the outermost rows of columns in the four subbasements. The outward spread of the columns, although fundamentally dictated by the changing floor areas, also increases the resistance of the building to wind, and in this respect the Chicago structure is similar to the Eiffel Tower, whose outward-curving base frames were exactly calculated to provide maximum rigidity against wind loads.[32]

The internal frame of the First National Bank includes the second deviation in the form of trusses that extend across the transverse dimension at the fifth, twenty-fifth, and forty-second floors. Those at the two lower levels carry columns that are offset to allow an optimum column distribution in the big public and office spaces, where obstructions had to be held to a minimum. The trusses at the forty-second floor, however, play a more complex role which requires the transfer of all interior column loads above the forty-second floor to the exterior columns. The primary purpose of this transfer is to take advantage of a provision in the Chicago building code that allows the designer to use 33 percent of the total compressive stress in a column for resistance to wind loads. Since the external columns are most susceptible to wind action, and since a heavily loaded member offers greater resistance to bending and shearing forces than one carrying a lesser load, it proved more economical to increase the dead load on the column than to increase the cross-sectional area of the long member exclusively to increase its resistance to wind. A lesser advantage is that the transfer of loads to the outer columns minimizes the differential elongation and contraction between interior and exterior columns that results from temperature changes. These structural niceties are for the most part hidden in the interior enclosures of the building, but they are among the factors that give visual prominence to the most striking feature of the First National building—namely, the powerful upward sweep and the massive rhythm of the huge outer columns.[33]

The second of the two buildings that ushered in another drastic jump in the urban scale is the John Hancock Center, constructed on a vacant lot at 875 North Michigan Avenue over a period of nearly six trouble-plagued years, from early 1965 through 1970 (fig. 52). Sponsored initially by Jerry Wolman, the owner of the Philadelphia Eagles football team, and continued by the John Hancock Life Insurance Company when construction difficulties exhausted Wolman's resources, the one-hundred-story skyscraper, rising 1,107 feet to the roof and 1,449 feet to the top of the television towers, is by long odds the most complex and the most original postwar structure to come from the prolific Chicago office of Skidmore, Owings and Merrill, or any other architectural firm.[34] As preliminary consultation and planning

Fig. 52. John Hancock Center, 875
North Michigan Avenue, 1965–70.
Skidmore, Owings and Merrill,
architects.

progressed among the architects and engineers, boldness and imagination came increasingly to the fore, until a rather orthodox initial idea had given way to a work wholly unique in its size, its internal planning, and its structural character. The first proposal was a conventional one consisting of two prismatic towers, one of forty-five stories for offices, the other of seventy stories for apartments, both about equal in measured overall height because of the greater ceiling height required for office occupancy. But the scheme revealed serious defects: the two buildings covered nearly all of the spacious site; the problem of siting the two with respect to each other and the surrounding area in order to insure privacy, quiet, and unobstructed views raised insurmountable difficulties. Rejecting all the alternatives because of inherent disadvantages, the architects finally hit on the novel scheme of placing the apartment tower on top of the office, and the office tower in turn on top of all the public spaces. The result is a megastructure on the grand scale, a microcity embracing activities of work, dwelling, shopping, recreation, and transportation in which another hierarchical distribution of functions by floor dictated the uniformly tapering envelope. By extending the height the architects reduced the occupancy of the site to somewhat less than half the area for the building proper, exclusive of the helical concrete ramp on the east side that provides access to the garage levels.[35]

The truncated pyramidal form required some adjustments in the ideal floor dimensions to conform to its geometric character, but it emerged very nearly as a logical outgrowth of the functional determinants. As with the First National, the public shopping and banking facilities demanded the largest floor areas, which would permit arrangements at maximum depth from the wall, and these had to be as close to the ground as possible. The garage and office spaces called for an intermediate range of dimensions, with the most extensive reserved for the garage, which would also be as near the ground as feasible. In the apartment volume the lower floors, embracing the larger areas, were reserved for the one-bedroom and efficiency units, since these could be disposed at the greatest depth from the outside walls and would generate the maximum elevator traffic, which would thus be concentrated on the lower apartment levels. The two-bedroom apartments were distributed through the intermediate floors and the large three- and four-bedroom units were restricted to the topmost stories for maximum privacy, view, and status. Further, this distribution of space uses permitted an optimum arrangement for the system of vertical transportation. By placing the apartment lobby at the forty-fourth floor, the elevator banks could be stacked one above the other, one lower bank serving the office floors, another providing express service to the lobby, the upper bank serving the apartment floors, and one through shaft carrying express cars direct to the observatory and restaurant.

The ingenuity that entered into the floor planning of the Hancock is more than matched by the innovative spirit behind its structural frame. The foundation system, on the other hand, is novel only in its magnitude, and its installation would have been a straightforward operation had it not been for a peculiar and potentially dangerous series of mishaps that resulted in long and costly delays in the construction process. The footings are carried on a total of 239 caissons, of which 57 extend into bedrock at a maximum depth of 191 feet below grade level, and 182 into hardpan at a maximum depth of 88 feet. The caissons are relatively small compared to those under the First National and the Brunswick, for example, the maximum diameter being 10 feet. The problem of fixing or "planting" the caisson involved difficult operations of drilling the well in the hard dolomite and keying the concrete into the rock mass to form a watertight seal. It was hazardous work, but the trouble came with the familiar process of pouring the concrete in the upper length of the caissons. The first sign that something had gone wrong was scarcely noticeable, but its implications were alarming in the extreme: in the summer of 1966, during the placing of a twelve-ton column section on the base plate at the top of one caisson, a workman saw the plate tip slightly from the true position, although its surface was everywhere in contact with the solid concrete. The foreman wisely ordered that the column segment be lifted off the plate, and the foundation contractor (Case Foundation Company) concluded that the caisson would have to be examined for internal defects. A core drilling revealed a large void in the concrete extending from 50 feet to 64 feet below grade, a defect that would have led to an appalling calamity if the member had survived the construction of many stories of the framework. All steel erection was suspended and all caissons were drilled for a total of 12,000 lineal feet of cores two inches in diameter. This costly exploration revealed a similar void in one caisson and the presence of earth, sand, and other foreign material in three others.

The defect had arisen from careless pouring of concrete, inadequate or missing caisson liners, and irresponsible supervision on the part of inspectors and construction superintendents. To make matters worse, identical trouble occurred at the same time during the erection of the office building at 500 North Michigan Avenue (1965–67), which was also designed by Skidmore, Owings and Merrill.[36] When the frame reached the twenty-third floor, cracks appeared in the first three floor slabs above grade, and core borings in the caissons revealed a clay-filled void in one member at a depth of forty-five feet below grade. The immediate cause was careless

pouring in an unlined well; the secondary cause was an obscuring of the view into
the well by vapor condensate that formed in cold weather over the warm concrete,
heated by the exothermic chemical reaction of setting; but in spite of this obviously
hazardous situation, the inspector failed to halt operations until he could see what
was going on. The costs of repair were high and the delays were long for both buildings—six months and more than $1,000,000 in the case of the Hancock—but these
were minor compared to what might have happened if the caissons had survived
until the two buildings were occupied. The difficulties posed a moral issue that demanded a full critical airing, and the editors of *Engineering News-Record* were
quick to assume their responsibilities in the matter.

Caisson troubles that have come to light in Chicago ought to give the entire construction industry a very severe case of the shudders. . . . The first suspect is, of
course, construction's perennial weakest link—inspection. Yet the whole design-
construction-inspection chain rates reconsideration. Is concreting a drilled hole, unprotected by a steel shell, a sound method of constructing a caisson column foundation? This was the method used on 500 North Michigan Avenue, and it didn't
work. . . . Cold weather formed a sight-obscuring fog that prevented anyone peering
in the hole from seeing the concrete. If this is so, why was such an obviously hazardous concreting technique tolerated by the architect-engineer, by the contractor, by
the A-E's inspector, and by the city's building department? . . . The cost of repair
and delay to the John Hancock Center will be ridiculous, compared to the cost of
having put down sound caissons in the first place. . . . Cost in dollars or in lives from
damage that might have befallen a completed 100-story John Hancock Center if
its faulty caissons had settled years hence is just too horrible to dwell upon.
Immeasurable also is the cost to the image of the entire construction industry
that has already resulted from faulty inspection and construction of the Chicago
caissons. It is not for anyone in this industry to say, "There but for the grace of God,
go I." The whole shocking experience will be for nought if the whole construction
chain, particularly inspection, isn't strengthened through the industry as a result.[37]

The steel structure of the Hancock can be fully understood only by placing it in
the context of skyscraper history since the time of the First World War. The emphasis in the structural system has gradually shifted from a primary concern with
resistance to gravity loads, arising chiefly from the dead weight of the building itself,
to a concern with total rigidity, or resistance to horizontal as well as vertical forces.
The reasons for this development may be found in changes of structural and formal
design which we have traced in earlier chapters. The skyscrapers of the twenties,
except where interior exigencies required long clear spans, were carried on frames

with modest bay spans, seldom more than twenty-five feet, whereas their counterparts of the fifties and sixties were built with bay spans of forty feet or more. Interior
subdivisions in the earlier period were usually made by partitions of hollow-tile construction, but these gave way in later years to light, movable, free-standing screens
of prefabricated material. Finally and most conspicuously, the prestige buildings of
the twenties were covered with a limestone veneer that sometimes accounted for a
major portion of the total wall area; but under the influence of Mies van der Rohe
the masonry was superseded by glass and light insulating panels. The primary structural consequence of this evolution has been a reduction in total weight and a concomitant decrease in the total rigidity of the building. From the economic standpoint
the results were an increase in the cost of constructing an adequate moment-resisting
frame and an increase in space sacrificed to bracing devices. The Hancock building
is the first on the order of magnitude of the RCA, the Chrysler, and the Empire
State in New York to be built with glass walls, and its enormous open volume
within these brittle shells threw the problems of structural design and cost into high
relief.

The new approach to the traditional framing design appeared in the early sixties
when various engineers and theorists recognized that if the exterior walls could be
treated as rigid diaphragms rigidly joined to each other, the result would be a hollow
boxlike or tubular vertical cantilever that would resist horizontal forces without the
customary internal bracing. In other words, under tubular construction the size,
cost, and weight of internal columns, girders, and joints could be drastically reduced,
and bracing elements could be largely eliminated. An office building, however, cannot be constructed with walls in the form of solid diaphragms, but the equivalent of
their action can be obtained by treating the wall as a rigid truss, either a Vierendeel,
as in the World Trade Center in New York, a lattice, as in the IBM Building in
Pittsburgh, or a multipanel triangulated form, as in the Alcoa Building in San Francisco. The specific form of wall chosen for the Hancock is a conventional truss with
double diagonals, but its simplicity could be achieved only through the use of enormous individual members, each diagonal except for the top panel crossing eighteen
floors. The resulting system may be called a trussed or braced vertical tubular cantilever or an "optimum column-diagonal truss tube" (the last by Fazlur Khan of
Skidmore, Owings and Merrill).[38] The rigid-tube action of the Hancock arises from
a precisely determined pattern of exterior columns and diagonals: the governing
principle was that the four half-diagonals forming a single panel must meet a column
and a spandrel girder at a single point, where an octagonal gusset plate could then
bind the eight members (columns above and below the floor, spandrels to right and

left, and four radiating diagonals) into a tight unit. The intricate calculations having to do with the investigation of alternatives, the slight variations in inclination of the diagonals, wind pressures, and sizes of members and joints were all accomplished by computer analysis. In spite of the wide spacing of the columns and contrary to the action of horizontal trusses, the wall frame behaves as a homogeneous cantilever in which a load on any two columns at or near the top is distributed uniformly through all of them at the bottom and the diagonals under almost all conditions are in compression.

The background to this important forward step in the building arts tells us much about the roles of tradition and innovation in the evolution of technology. The idea of diagonal bracing as a method of obtaining rigidity in a vertical frame is as old as the timber truss bridge and the timber trestle, the supports for both of which were frequently tapering bents with double diagonals in each panel. Derivative and very elegant forms in iron were developed by Gustave Eiffel for a number of French railway viaducts constructed in the 1860s and 1870s. A free-standing tapering tower one thousand feet high, circular in horizontal section, and braced with two diagonals in every panel, was proposed by Clarke and Reeves for the Centennial Exposition at Philadelphia in 1876. A twentieth-century counterpart is the braced tower of the vertical lift bridge—for example, that of the Pennsylvania Railroad over the Chicago River on the line of 20th Street. One might multiply other examples, but they appear to have had little influence on the structural frames of buildings until the post–World War II period, except for the traditional wind bracing composed of diagonal members set in the bays of the internal frame. In 1953 Mies van der Rohe proposed an exhibition hall for Chicago in the form of an unprecedented kind of structure: an immense square 720 feet on a side and 112 feet high was to be roofed by a continuous space frame 30 feet deep which was to be carried to base piers by four Warren trusses 60 feet deep set in the wall planes. There were to be no intermediate supports, and the entire enclosure was to act as a rigid trussed cage or box. It has been a continuing misfortune of the building arts that this masterpiece of constructive architecture has never been brought to realization.

The man who appears to have been most immediately influenced by Mies was Myron Goldsmith. As early as 1955 he proposed a circular covered stadium whose roof was to be supported on a circular Warren truss with a double-diagonal web system, or as it is sometimes designated, a bearing wall with a double system of inclined columns. Having joined the office of Skidmore, Owings and Merrill, Goldsmith was given the opportunity to see his project translated into physical reality when the city of Oakland, California, commissioned the architects in 1962 to design a sports and exhibition stadium. It was completed five years later exactly in the form of the original concept save for the omission of an unnecessary intermediate chord. Who was initially responsible for adapting the idea to the usual rectangular form of the office building is a matter of conjecture. Among the pioneers in the United States have been various members of the Seattle engineering firm of Worthington, Skilling, Helle and Jackson. But the decisive steps for the specific design of the Hancock building seem to have come from the Skidmore office, and the two leading structural engineers of the staff were the major contributors. Fazlur Khan introduced the tubular-cantilever system to Chicago with his design for the De Witt–Chestnut Apartments, erected in 1962–63 at the intersection from which the building takes its name. In this forty-four-story tower the rigid tubular prism consists of a reinforced concrete framework much like that of the Brunswick Building. The next step, indirectly involving Goldsmith's talents, lay closer to the structural character of the Hancock.

In 1964 Mikio Sasaki, a student in the Department of Architecture at Illinois Institute of Technology, submitted a building project as his thesis for the Master of Science in Architecture, and his faculty advisor in the preparation of this work was Myron Goldsmith (fig. 53). The proposal that Sasaki offered is a steel-framed office tower of fifty-four stories that was designed for Tokyo and hence specifically framed to resist earthquake forces as well as gravity and wind loads. There are several differences of design and action between the student's project and the Hancock Center, but the fundamental similarities are obvious. The exterior walls of both buildings are diagonally braced trusses, Sasaki's work having three parallel trusses extending up the height of each elevation, the Hancock having only one, but the panel unit in each case is eighteen stories, and the aim in both cases was to reduce the amount and hence the cost of steel required for the conventional internally braced, moment-resisting frame.

The decision to adopt the trussed tubular cantilever left one problem to be solved before final testing and construction could begin. Since the glass curtain wall would lie on the median plane of the structural frame, that is, midway between its inner and outer surfaces, the interior half would lie in a fixed-temperature environment, whereas the outer would be exposed to the vicissitudes of the weather, with its extreme variations of temperature and solar radiation. The thermal expansion and contraction arising from such changes would obviously result in unacceptable or even irreparable damage to interior partitions, floor slabs, and exterior glass curtain walls. The structural members thus required an insulating cover as well as fireproof cladding, and these had to be sheathed in a corrosion-resistant envelope. For the latter the architects considered various materials, finally selecting black-anodized aluminum because of its resistance to chemical action and the ease with which it can be fabricated, put in place, and maintained. An aluminum model of the building at a scale of $\frac{1}{300}$ was tested in a wind tunnel under wind velocities up to 130 miles per hour (equivalent to a pressure of sixty-one pounds per square foot) to determine the capacity of the frame to withstand direct dynamic loads, static pressure, differences in pressure between surfaces, and turbulence. Resistance to wind-driven rain was determined by testing a full-scale replica of part of the aluminum and glass curtain wall. Although construction of the foundation brought unexpected troubles, the far more forbidding frame went up with no more than the usual difficulties. The steelwork of the first six stories was erected from the ground by crawler cranes, and the remaining ninety-four by creeper cranes that were hauled by cable up the sides of the framework as the structural members were put in place.

The external form of the Hancock appears to have been dictated wholly by science and utility, but as we have seen, alternative forms of truss framing were available, and the one that was chosen was retained as much on visual as on structural grounds. Although the great size of the tower and its primary components seems overwhelming to many, the long diagonals play a major role in bringing the succession of expanding geometric patterns into a harmonious progression. The human scale is fixed by the individual window, and from there the eye moves successively through the individual bay, the long horizontal band of the single floor, the four triangles defined by the intersecting diagonals, the trapezoidal panel, to the whole tapering silhouette. As James Hornbeck concluded in his thorough analysis of the building,

The manner in which the parade of diminishing X's overlays, yet reinforces, the rectilinear pattern of spandrels and columns, sets up a geometry that lends appropriate scale and visual interest to the giant façades that might otherwise overwhelm nearby buildings. Happily, these diagonals—unlike those in other structural walls—will not act visually to deny the expression of recurring horizontal floors, but will actually strengthen it.[39]

If the Hancock in itself may be regarded with good reason as an architectural triumph, one is nevertheless compelled to raise serious questions about its location and its consequences for the urban ecology. The owners, quite understandably, wanted a site of maximum prestige, and North Michigan Avenue has no competitor in this respect; yet the choice is plainly an error when measured against the complex of urban functions that a hundred-story megastructure cannot help but disturb. The tower is grossly out of scale with the buildings around it and inharmonious in its

111 Fig. 53. Project for a Master of
Science thesis in architecture, Illinois
Institute of Technology, 1964. Mikio
Sasaki, designer.

53

form, dominating them by its physical presence and by its very shadow. The nearest rapid transit station is half a mile away, and the vehicular traffic generated by the building increases the total volume on Michigan Avenue by 10 percent, even though the street reached its rush-hour capacity long before the Hancock opened. If a building of such magnitude belongs anywhere, it is on the west side of the core area, along Wacker Drive, or on rescued rail property to the south, where it can form a backdrop to the city's homogeneous skyscraper masses and where suburban railroad and rapid transit lines are close at hand. More ominous than the physical presence of the Hancock is the generous zoning allowance by which it came into being, one of a long series of special amendments passed by the city council granting building privileges wherever the building interests saw the opportunity of expanding profits. The architects were quick to defend their handiwork: William Hartmann and Bruce Graham of the Skidmore, Owings and Merrill office claimed that no traffic congestion would result, and Nathaniel Owings argued that "our approach was to decide what was needed to solve urban and suburban problems, and the 100-story tower is part of the answer—denser housing to make way for open space."[40]

These assertions, however, are contradicted by the facts, and there were compelling voices to call attention to the other side of the coin. The most radical attack came from Wolf von Eckardt, the perceptive and literate architectural critic of the *Washington Post*. "Chicago," he wrote, "is building an ugly steel-braced colossus 1,100 feet tall, the John Hancock Center, which will at least contain apartments as well as offices, but which, nevertheless, promises to disrupt not only the appearance but the urban ecology of the downtown area."[41] The success of the Hancock combined with unprincipled zoning quickly led to plans for competitors even higher than the Michigan Avenue tower, so that by 1970 the inner meaning of Chicago commercial architecture was thrown into naked relief. M. W. Newman, von Eckardt's counterpart on the staff of the *Chicago Daily News*, most effectively exposed the fundamental truth.

Competition in big-time architecture now bizarrely revolves around the question of who can announce plans for the tallest skyscraper of the week. The "corporate image," signposts in the sky, are what these giant buildings basically are all about. They tell us more about our civilization than they do about architecture, a captive art which now appears to be a branch of outdoor decorating, a subsidiary of the public-relations industry. . . . Strongly shaped, black-coated and austere, [the Hancock] symbolized Chicago muscle and technical daring. Then along came the grotesque top-floor "crown of light" and "I am Curious (Orange and Yellow)" antennae to contradict the effect. . . . Hancock's tapering 100 stories serve primarily as

Fig. 54. Edens Theater, 303 Old
Skokie Highway, Northbrook, Illinois,
1961–63. The Perkins and Will
Partnership, architects.

54

support for these big-dollar TV masts. They have become its true abstract image, lacking only a huge S sign running through them to complete the $ symbol.[42]

Money and technology underlay these potent works of modern structural art, and there was enough of both to maintain an ever expanding tide of office construction, which approached the records of the twenties in 1970, when more than 2,000,000 square feet were opened to use.[43] The rage to demolish and build anew reached a kind of frenzy, and no one seemed to have the time in the summer of the previous year to mourn the passing of the man who more than anyone else had shaped the course of large-scale urban building after World War II. On 17 August 1969, at the age of eighty-three, Mies van der Rohe reached the end of the most extraordinary life in the history of architecture. Through his own thirty-one-year career in Chicago and through the work of his many students, he left a mark on the metropolitan area so profound that one could find a parallel only in imperial Rome, or Florence under the Medici, or Paris in the heyday of the monarchy. At the time of his death his office was more active than ever before, his students were flourishing everywhere, and his influence was apparent in the major cities of the world.[44]

Outside the city proper, among buildings in the inner ring of suburbs that compel attention for their architectural character, one is an office building that springs indirectly from the Miesian authority. The Fountain Square Plaza group, erected in 1967–69 at Orrington Avenue and Davis Street in Evanston, is a product of the office of Schipporeit-Heinrich Associates, whose founders were students of Mies at Illinois Institute of Technology, designers in his office, and the authors of Lake Point Tower after they had established an independent firm. The steel-framed buildings, all marked by the familiar vertical tracery here executed in bronze-anodized aluminum, include a twenty-one-story office tower, a one-story circular public banking area of the State National Bank, and a long two-story building for Walgreen Drug Store and a group of second-floor offices. The drugstore block is the only building to bear some relation to a long-forgotten project of Mies's for a summer house in Jackson's Hole, Wyoming. Very much at odds with the metallic elegance of the Evanston buildings is Edens Theater at Northbrook, Illinois, a product of the Perkins and Will office erected in 1961–63 (fig. 54). This attractive suburban theater is distinguished by a shell roof in the form of a hyperbolic paraboloid 221 feet long and 4 inches thick, but supported at only two points. It was the largest and most delicately poised concrete shell constructed up to its time, but the thick edge beams that are typical of American work obscure the aerial buoyancy of the form. More sober because of the educational and publishing functions of its owner is another sub-

Fig. 55. Scott, Foresman and Company administrative and editorial center, 1900 East Lake Avenue, Glenview, Illinois, 1965–67. The Perkins and Will Partnership, architects.

Fig. 56. Scott, Foresman and Company group. One of the interior courts.

55

56

urban triumph of Perkins and Will, the Scott, Foresman and Company group erected in 1965–67 at 1900 East Lake Avenue in Glenview (figs. 55, 56). Set in an extravagant site of forty-four acres and planned around handsomely landscaped interior courts, the three buildings form a series of rich and harmonious compositions of sand-blasted concrete, dark tawny brick, and tinted glass.

So the architecture commanded by mercantile oligarchy and municipal authority flourished as vigorously as it had in the halcyon days of the past. Chicago again led the way, for however much the business community despised the arts, it saw money and prestige in new architecture and was willing to pay for the best. Franz Schulze, an art critic for the *Daily News,* explained it very well in a brief but penetrating appraisal of the city's character.

Chicago's earliest greatness is its present and enduring greatness. It is a rough crossroads giant of the machine age which believes in what it sees, what it can figure out and what it can get done. It is pagan, materialistic, bourgeois and pragmatic, and it likes the stock report and the steam hammer a lot more than it cares for poetry—unless the poet is himself willing to celebrate such a hierarchy of values. Chicago has neither the spiritual wherewithal nor the historic depth to be patient with intellectual subtlety, abstractions, ironies or the ambiguities of artistic feeling that are tolerated and even encouraged by a number of still greater modern cities. Chicago could not create, or at any rate could not suffer very long, an Henri Matisse or an Andy Warhol. Perhaps it will never be much of a town for painters, or actors or the classical ballet. But it understands commerce and technology as it reveres them, and it happily raises temples to these contemporary deities, attaining its most admirable creative momentum in the process. Architecture is thus the one art Chicago's spirit can serve, at least—and probably only—as long as architecture returns the favor.[45]

NOTES TO CHAPTER 3

1. See table 3.
2. For the IIT buildings, see pp. 173–76.
3. Mies van der Rohe, quoted in "Mies van der Rohe," *Architectural Forum* 97(November 1952):99.
4. Ibid., p. 94.
5. Except for high temperatures generated by the absorption of solar radiation, necessitating the installation of individual air-conditioning units in the various apartments, and except for inadequate facilities for garbage disposal, the 860–80 apartments have been a utilitarian and economic success. Known as a mutual ownership coop-

erative under Illinois laws, the building group offers the tenant a substantial initial investment with a relatively low monthly payment, which in turn allows the sponsor a small mortgage, equivalent to 60 percent of the building cost, and the short amortization period of twenty years. The total cost of the two buildings was $4,404,000 in 1952 (about $9,688,000 at the 1972 price level), giving a unit cost of $10.38 per square foot of floor area, a comparatively modest figure in spite of the high cost of foundation work in the lakeshore fill, the special expense of providing outside drapes for a uniform color behind the nontinted glass, and the cost of an underground garage for 116 cars.

6. The collaborating architects on the 900 North Lake Shore project were Pace Associates and on the 2400 Lake View Greenberg and Finfer. The builder in both cases was Metropolitan Structures, Incorporated, founded by Herbert Greenwald and Samuel Katzin. Other apartment groups in Chicago for which Mies was the controlling architect are the following: the six buildings of the Algonquin Apartments, East End Avenue at 50th Street, 1950–52, designed in collaboration with Pace Associates and Holsman, Klekamp and Taylor, and the two buildings of Commonwealth Plaza, Surf Avenue (2900N) between Sheridan Road and Commonwealth Avenue, 1955–58, with Pace Associates again acting as collaborators.

7. Innovations in plan and construction respectively characterize two conspicuous buildings in the inner city. On the Gold Coast Hausner and Macsai adapted the exposed concrete frame of Mies's Promontory Apartments to the quarter-circular plan of the apartment building erected in 1956–58 at 1150 North Lake Shore Drive. This unusual form, possibly unique at the time, was dictated by the need to provide a lake view for a large number of apartments squeezed into a site formerly occupied by a single Gold Coast mansion.

   The hotel known as Executive House, constructed in the same years at 71 East Wacker Drive, is a work of relentless ribbon-windowed horizontality designed by the architect Milton Schwartz and the staff of the Miller Engineering Company. The process of construction and the structural system embody several features of major importance to the development of the building arts. The installation of foundations was radically speeded up through the use of the Benoto caisson drill in sinking caisson wells. A French invention which found one of its early American uses in the construction of Executive House, the drill reduced by more than two-thirds the time formerly required for this tedious operation. The wind bracing in the high, narrow hotel is unique and represents a step in the direction of the solid-walled core such as that used in the 5740 Sheridan building: two rigid slabs in the end walls extending from the first to the sixth floor, a massive connecting slab extending the length of the sixth floor, and four shear walls paired in tandem across the width of the building provide resistance to the shearing and bending forces of the wind.

8. The total cost of the building when it opened was $2,607,800, or $12 per square foot. Rents were typical for the middle-income range in Chicago: the minimum was $135 per month for the studio apartments, and the maximum $185 for the two-bedroom units.

9. "In the Spirit of the 'Chicago School' . . . ," *Architectural Record* 144(July 1968): 109.

10. A structural work of the magnitude of Marina City is usually designed only after extensive consultation with outside engineers. Associated with the Goldberg office in structural design and analysis and in foundation work were the following engi-

neering firms: Severud, Perrone, Fischer, Sturm, Conlin and Bandel; Mueser, Rut-
ledge, Wentworth and Johnson; and Ralph Peck (foundations only).

11. Under the terms of the final arrangements financing for Marina City was divided
among three organizations as follows: Building Service Employees International
Union, $13,180,900; Institutional Securities Corporation (an ad hoc consortium
formed by nineteen eastern banks), $17,819,100; Continental Illinois National Bank
and Trust Company, $5,000,000; total $36,000,000. The difficulties of completing
these arrangements indicated that the officers of banks, insurance companies, and
the FHA were not only unfamiliar with the idea of a microcity, that is, a diversified
body of urban functions in a single unified development on a compact area, but
were unable to comprehend its validity. This myopia is one of the products of the
radical separation between suburban living and inner-city working.

A major factor in the financial stability of the Marina project is that the substantial revenues from the garage, restaurant, bar, office building, and marina have made
it possible to hold rents below the average for inner-city apartments, with the result
that the vacancy rate has been negligible. The helical garages, for example, were
leased in 1961 to the Marina City Garage and Parking Corporation for twenty-five
years, in which period the operators of the parking facilities guarantee a minimum
of $5,000,000 to the owners of the whole complex.

The argument of the FHA that Marina City had no provision for children was
irrelevant. It was obvious from the start that the location of the apartments close to
the Loop and remote from schools, parks, and residential areas indicated a special
kind of tenant who would ordinarily be relatively young, unmarried, or if married,
childless, and employed in the Loop area. The pertinent argument is that the overwhelming need in Chicago is for low- and middle-income housing, not luxury high-
rise apartments, but this is another matter that we will consider later (pp. 150–66).

12. Details of the preliminary structural planning of Marina City reveal the special
problems associated with this novel form. Once the final scheme had been approved,
Goldberg proposed that the towers be built as true core-and-cantilever construction
in which the hollow cylindrical core would sustain all gravity and wind loads. The
form would offer maximum efficiency in the distribution of material and in structural action because the circular floor provides a maximum area for a given length
of perimeter (or minimum perimeter for a given area), and the cylindrical core
offers maximum and uniform resistance to horizontal forces acting in any direction.
Goldberg believed, on good theoretical ground, that the monolithic cantilever system would provide greater rigidity than a steel frame. The idea had been given only
one practical demonstration, namely, in Wright's research tower for the S. C. Johnson Company at Racine, Wisconsin (1947–50), but at less than one-quarter the
height of the Marina buildings. Fred Severud argued, however, that the cantilever
scheme involved serious and possibly insurmountable difficulties: first, the effects of
wind loads on a high cylinder carrying a multitude of cantilevered disks were unknown; second, the necessary radial girders would have had to be so deep as to make
the increased floor-to-floor height and hence the total height prohibitive in cost and
to make room planning unmanageably difficult; and finally, caisson construction
under the core would have presented peculiar difficulties in form and size of the
caissons and in the clear possibility of nonuniform loading on the foundation system.
Because of these problems Severud proposed the more conservative idea of supplementing the core action with a double ring of columns (see text, below).

The 896 apartments in the two towers are distributed by size as follows: 256 efficiency units; 576 one-bedroom; 64 two-bedroom. The two-bedroom maximum indicates that the designers believed the apartments would seldom be occupied by families with children.

13. The core of the individual Marina tower was constructed by pouring concrete from one-ton buckets hoisted by climbing hammerhead cranes. As each lift set, the ring form, cylindrical on its interior surface and prismatic on its exterior, was dismantled and reassembled at the next level. In spite of the unprecedented height of the cylindrical tower, no more than routine difficulties arose. This is more than can be said, however, for the familiar but still hazardous process of sinking caisson wells. The 154 caissons underpinning the Marina complex were sunk 118 feet below grade under conditions made extremely troublesome by the presence of groundwater that appeared in layers, first in the mixture of water and sand near the river surface, second in the abandoned narrow-gauge freight tunnels at −60 feet, and last in the watery silt overlying the bedrock of impervious Niagara dolomite at −118 feet. The use of double linings, the outer to hold back water and finely divided soil and the inner to contain the concrete, solved this complex of problems, but they were compounded by other difficulties. The simultaneous construction of Dearborn Street bridge (1959–63) at the west edge of the Marina City site required the sinking of caisson wells for the north abutment close to the line of some of the Marina wells. The resulting soil movements into the excavated space around the caisson liners for the bridge abutment induced movements of water and saturated sand that increased the instability of the already fluid mass, with consequent delays that reached many months in the case of the bridge (p. 234).

14. The Marina City apartments, as we have seen, are not above criticism, but the defects have not discouraged tenants from keeping them fully occupied. The characteristics of the first group to move in give some idea of the continuing occupants: the project was racially integrated from the beginning as a matter of official policy, and four apartments among the first group to be leased were occupied by black tenants; the average annual income of the whole group was $16,108, ranging from a minimum of $4,000 to a maximum of $90,000; the majority fell below $10,000, which suggests a high proportion of single people and a consequent rapidly changing tenancy.

15. The distribution of instruments in Lake Point Tower is as follows: twelve strain meters, one in each of twelve caissons, to measure changes in compressive stress during strong winds; ten strain meters in a single caisson, set at seven-foot intervals along the caisson depth, to determine stress variation throughout the length of the members under wind deflection and the effects of skin friction resulting from the transmission of building loads through the caisson to bedrock; reference points in the form of brass buttons placed in three identical columns at every story from top to bottom to measure elastic deformation of columns under wind loads; a special strain gauge twenty inches long to make readings at every story as the load increased during construction in order to measure creep in concrete members (creep is the slow deformation of a member under prolonged load and is a problem of particular concern in concrete structures); various gauges for the continuing measurement of creep in columns and slabs to determine the magnitude of the phenomenon and to calculate the resulting changes in the modulus of elasticity of concrete; seismographs and anemometers for the measurement of direct seismic and wind forces.

The $250,000 cost of the instruments was borne by Hartnett-Shaw and Associates of Chicago, the developers of the property, and Fluor Properties, Incorporated, of Los Angeles, the owners.

The participating organizations are the Reinforced Concrete Research Council of the American Society of Civil Engineers, the Portland Cement Association, the National Association of Architectural Metal Manufacturers, Wiss, Janney, Elstner and Associates, and the Civil Engineering Department of the University of Wisconsin.

16. The following schedule of minimum rents was adopted at the time Lake Point Tower was opened to tenants: convertible bedroom (studio) apartment, $169 per month; one-bedroom center, $247; one-bedroom corner, $263; two-bedroom center, $371; two-bedroom corner, $382; three-bedroom, $518.

17. The following rent schedule was initially adopted for the Lawless Gardens apartments: one-bedroom, $115 per month; two-bedroom, $135; three-bedroom, $155. The total project cost in 1969 was $7,800,000, of which a $7,000,000 loan was insured by the FHA under section 221(d)3, which provides for a forty-year mortgage at 3 percent interest but limits the sponsor's return to 6 percent per annum on his investment. Income limits were fixed at the time at $7,250 per annum for a family of two, $8,550 for a family of three or four, and $9,850 for a family of five or six.

18. Quoted in M. W. Newman, "Our Super City in the Sky," *Chicago Daily News,* 9 August 1966, p. 38.

19. Quoted in Thomas M. Gray, "Building Code Enforcement by City Is Weak," *Chicago Sun-Times,* 27 April 1970, p. 22. For the role of the Chicago Housing Authority in the creation of this crisis, see pp. 163–66.

20. Various details of the genesis and construction of the Prudential Building were important for the revival of large-scale building in Chicago. As a city with more downtown rail property than any other in the world, it offered unparalleled opportunities in both extent and urban value for air-rights developments, and the Illinois Central Railroad's immense holdings east of Michigan Avenue and north of Grant Park offered the greatest possibilities for exploitation. The Prudential Insurance Company was not the first to propose building over these tracks. In 1929 the Crane Company and the railroad jointly planned a seventy-five-story Crane Tower over the new suburban station, but although the proposed building would have been superior to the Prudential in its formal design, it was killed by the depression, never to be revived.

The problem of air-rights construction above the Illinois Central tracks at the site in question was a peculiarly difficult one, and the city is indebted to the Prudential company for cracking this obstinate nut. The rights were sold outright rather than leased, but the negotiations for the sale required eighteen months to consummate. The difficulties arose from the need to define exactly the separate parcels of property at ground level for caissons and column footings and the space volumes below the basic air-rights plane needed to contain the lowermost columns, girders, and bracing elements, the parcels and volumes together totaling 550 units. In addition to these complexities the railroad reserved for its own use small areas of land over the footings and volumes of air around the lower halves of the girders to provide an adequate clearance envelope around the catenary structure of the electrified suburban terminal. These expensive negotiations, added to the cost of digging 110-foot caisson wells by hand, greatly increased the final cost of the building, but they produced an excellent guide for similar construction in the future.

The extreme liberality of the Chicago zoning ordinances is demonstrated not only by the absence of setbacks in the Prudential Building. The code allows any shape so long as the building floor area at this site does not exceed 144 times the lot area; but given the generous size of the Prudential lot, extending a full block from Randolph to Lake Street, this formula would have left the company free to construct 20,520,864 square feet of floor space.

21. The planning innovations of the Inland Steel required certain structural novelites. The 58-foot length of the main girders was at the time the longest ever used repetitively in a multistory frame, and the necessary depth of 36 inches required that openings be cut in the webs for the passage of ducts, pipes, and electrical conduits. The ruling module was fixed by the spacing of the mullions at 5 feet 2 inches center to center. The columns are spaced at a conventional 25 feet 10 inches on centers, but their section is unique, being an expanded H with flanges at the ends of one vertical bar.

The chief problem in the design of the frame arose from the decision to place the columns outside the wall plane of the long elevations, with the consequence that no direct connection could be made between the column and the longitudinal spandrel girder. The solution required that the two members be joined by an extension of the massive transverse girder and that the resulting double joint be rigid enough to provide resistance to the high torsional forces accompanying the bending and twisting induced in both the column and the girder by wind action.

22. See table 2.

23. The Republic (1905, 1909) and the Cable (1898–99) were the work of Holabird and Roche, the Majestic (1892–93) came from the office of D. H. Burnham and Company, and the Garrick (1891–92) was a unique masterpiece by Adler and Sullivan.

24. For the extension of Wacker Drive south of Lake Street, see pp. 232–33.

25. The double track layout of the station, from throat to throat, covers about six blocks, three on either side of the former concourse building. The third to the north (Washington–Madison) was covered by the Daily News Building in 1929, and the second one to the south (Van Buren–Harrison) was covered by the Central Post Office in 1932. By 1960 three blocks of exposed train sheds still remained.

26. Various quantitative details of the Gateway Center project reveal elements of the contemporary urban economy. The rent level of the center was well below that of new buildings in the Loop or east and north thereof, the basic figure being $5.00 per square foot at the time of leasing, with a minimum as low as $4.50 on lower floors if the tenant took an entire floor. Two factors underlay this low schedule: the positive was the favorable terms of the air-rights lease, which carried a rental of $440,200 per annum for the three-block area, and the negative was the unfavorable character of the West Side site, remote from shops and restaurants and close to Skid Row with its inconvenient drunks. Offsetting these disadvantages was the proximity

of first-class public transportation provided by the North Western Railway at Canal and Madison, the Burlington and the Milwaukee in Union Station, and the Chicago Transit Authority on Wells Street, a little more than two blocks to the east. Surveys conducted during the planning of the third Gateway Center revealed that 50 percent of the employees of one insurance company intending to lease space in the building traveled by rapid transit and bus, 43.5 percent by train, and only 6.5 percent by car. Facts such as these ought to be extremely instructive to the makers and unmakers of cities, but for most of them they have generally gone unheeded. The chief result of these discoveries was that rents rose from $5.00 per square foot in Gateway I to $8.50 in Gateway III.

The presence of nonelectrified railroad lines introduced a problem that was solved by techniques first developed for the Daily News Building in 1928. Fumes from diesel-electric locomotives are drawn into isolated vertical ducts by means of a collecting chamber and discharged through stacks in the roof.

The stake of the rail companies in terminal air rights and hence their willingness to sacrifice great station buildings may be readily judged from the situation of the ailing Pennsylvania Railroad, 50 percent owner of Union Station, for which the therapy of air-rights rentals held in a little life during the bankruptcy that followed its awkward marriage with the slightly less sick New York Central (the declaration of bankruptcy came in 1970).

27. For other steel-framed skyscrapers erected during the sixties in the Loop area, see under Public Buildings, pp. 126–41.

28. The principle has been repeated many times, in this case in connection with a critical interpretation of Goldsmith's work by Allen Temko in "Goldsmith: Chicago's New Structural Poet," *Architectural Forum* 116(May 1962):135.

29. The dimensions of the structural unit in the load-bearing wall are close to the average for high buildings of this form: the columns are spaced 9 feet 4 inches on centers, and the cross-sectional area of the individual column is 13×19 inches at the foot, but this is diminished floor by floor as the direct load and the bending moment decrease with increasing height.

Associated with Goldsmith on the Brunswick project was Bruce Graham, the partner in charge of the design.

30. The transfer girder extends from a plane 4 feet 8½ inches below the third floor level to the plane of the fourth floor; it has a maximum thickness of 7 feet 6 inches, a unit weight of 28,000 pounds per lineal foot, and a minimum compressive strength of 5,000 pounds per square inch. Since the girder is continuous over the base piers, it is subject to both positive and negative bending and thus requires longitudinal reinforcing near both the top and the bottom planes, these bars being supplemented by hoops at variable spacing in the vertical plane and by shear bars bent into a trapezoidal pattern over the intermediate piers. The continuity of the girder at the corners is maintained by joining the two ends through steel plates welded to the reinforcing bars, which are themselves butt-welded. A special problem in the use of concrete members of such great size and under such high loads is that of transmitting the load from the ring to the piers. The solution adopted for the Brunswick is a four-ply bearing assembly consisting of a steel plate on top of the pier, a copper sheet, an intermediate or transfer plate, and a top plate, the four plates fixed in position to withstand horizontal forces by an 8-inch shear pin. A grid of reinforcing bars welded to the top plate and imbedded in the girder forms a rigid connection between

the two concrete members. The elimination of columns between the core and screen walls reduced the number of caissons to ten, the largest being 14 feet 9 inches in diameter and carrying a load of 9,500 tons, all caissons extending to an average depth of 110 feet below grade. The floor slabs over the clear span of 39 feet around the core are sustained by a coffered slab or two-way system of beams. Since the structural members of the screen wall are exposed to outdoor temperature changes and hence subject to thermal expansion and contraction, the floor slabs are joined to the inner faces of the members by hinged connections to prevent cracking arising from differential expansion between walls and flooring.

31. The overall dimensions in plan at the base of the First National are 200 × 300 feet and at the top 95 × 300 feet. The columns of the main block and the framework of the utility wings necessitated an underpinning by eighty-five bedrock and ten hardpan caissons.

    The distribution of floor assignments is as follows: bank, 1–22, 57 (executive dining room); tenants, 23–59; utilities, 6, 7, 26, 27, 43, 44, 60.

32. The columns of the First National are built-up hollow-box members with sectional dimensions that vary from a maximum of 34 × 96 inches at grade to a minimum of 34 × 33 inches from the forty-second floor to the top.

    The particular curve of the four base frames of the Eiffel Tower was calculated with a scientific exactitude that one ordinarily finds only in bridge construction: the axis of the individual frame conforms as closely as the rigid geometry of the iron structure will allow to the bending-movement curve of the wind load.

33. The analysis of the role of the trusses in the framing of the bank building is based in good part on a personal letter, dated 21 January 1966, to the author from Carter H. Manny, Jr., a partner in the C. F. Murphy organization.

34. Because of the magnitude of the Hancock project and the range of its innovations, it is useful to assign specific credit for the various aspects of the design. The following individuals and offices played major roles in the preparation of plans: William E. Hartman, partner-in-charge, Skidmore, Owings and Merrill; Bruce J. Graham, partner-in-charge of design; Albert Lockett, partner-administrator; Richard E. Lenke, project manager; Fazlur Khan, project structural engineer, Skidmore, Owings and Merrill; E. Alfred Picardi, chief structural engineer, Skidmore, Owings and Merrill; Paul Weidlinger, Ammann and Whitney, John Goldberg, consulting structural engineers; Richard Warfel, project mechanical and electrical engineer, Skidmore, Owings and Merrill; Edison Price, lighting consultant; Bolt, Beranek and Newman, acoustical consultants.

35. The Hancock contains the following distribution of functions and activities by floor:

    Concourse level (below grade): skating rink, restaurant, small shops, bank, stockbroker.

    Floors 1–5: large clothing store (Bonwit Teller), small shops, bank.

    Floors 6–12: parking for 1,200 cars.

    Floors 13–41: office space (net area 812,160 square feet).

    Floors 42–43: mechanical and electrical equipment.

    Floors 44–45: upper plaza and apartment lobby, specialty and service shops, swimming pool.

    Floors 46–93: apartment space (700 apartments, rents at the time of completion ranging from $175 a month for an efficiency to $750 for a four-bedroom unit).

    Floor 94: observatory.

Floors 95–96: two-level restaurant and bar.

Floors 97–100: mechanical equipment, television and radio stations.

Roof: two television transmission towers 344 feet in height and one FM radio transmitter 100 feet in height.

The area of the individual floor diminishes from 41,000 square feet at the base (approximately 165 × 265 feet) to 16,200 square feet at the 100th floor (ca. 100 × 165 feet). The reduction in floor width is thus a little under 8 inches per story and in length 1 foot per story. The total floor area of 2,800,000 square feet makes it the largest multipurpose building in the world. The final cost of $95,000,000 was somewhat less than that of the First National Bank Building's $106,000,000.

36. The 500 North Michigan building is supported by a concrete frame with external load-bearing walls. It is a relatively small structure twenty-five stories in height.

37. "Dirt in the Caissons," *Engineering News-Record* 177 (13 October 1966): 238.

38. The reduction in the weight of steel following the adoption of the tubular cantilever principle is spectacular: unit weight in the case of the Hancock is 29.7 pounds per square foot of floor area as opposed to 45–50 pounds for skyscrapers with conventional moment-resisting frames. The quotation is from Khan, "The John Hancock Center," *Civil Engineering* 37 (October 1967): 38.

39. James S. Hornbeck, "Chicago's Multi-Use Giant," *Architectural Record* 141 (January 1967): 141.

40. Quoted in "Skidmore, Owings and Merrill: An Architectural Community," *Engineering News-Record* 176 (26 May 1966): 188.

41. Wolf von Eckardt, "New York's Trade Center: World's Tallest Fiasco," *Harper's Magazine* 232 (May 1966): 96.

42. M. W. Newman, "Chicago: City of the Big Tombstones," *Chicago Daily News Panorama,* 24 January 1970, p. 4. The "competition" that Newman refers to is the 80-story Standard Oil Company building, on Illinois Central Railroad property east of the Prudential, and the 110-story Sears, Roebuck and Company headquarters, on Wacker Drive at Jackson Boulevard, both placed under construction in 1970. The expression "I Am Curious (Orange and Yellow)" is an allusion to the title of a popular Swedish movie showing in several Chicago theaters at the time the article was prepared.

It was obvious to anyone not blind to the urban milieu that the building industry of Chicago served organized power exclusively, but it was equally obvious that it continued to command an unlimited reservoir of talent, as many of the buildings of the sixties demonstrated. Chief among those not discussed above are the following:

United Parcel Service Distribution Center, 1400 South Jefferson Street, 1964–65; Edward D. Dart, architect.

Blue Cross–Blue Shield, southwest corner of Wacker Drive and Dearborn Street, 1965–68; C. F. Murphy Associates, architects and engineers (the first core structure in the mass-concrete mode fashionable at the time).

Arvey Corporation office building, 3450 North Kimball Avenue, 1966–67; Fridstein and Fitch, architects.

Central Switching and Exchange Building, Illinois Bell Telephone Company, southwest corner of Canal and Madison streets, 1966–70; Holabird and Root, architects (the heavy switching equipment required a massive superrigid welded steel frame).

Time-Life Building, Fairbanks Court between Ohio Street and Grand Avenue,

1968–70; Harry Weese and Associates, architects (gold-reflecting tinted glass and Cor-ten self-weathering steel on a concrete frame impart a welcome richness of color and texture to the four elevations of this imaginatively planned building).

111 East Wacker Drive, 1968–70; Office of Mies van der Rohe, architects (constructed on Illinois Central Railroad property east of Michigan Avenue and hence the first step in a vast and potentially calamitous project planned to cover the rest of this superb site).

IBM Building, north side of the river between State Street and Wabash Avenue, 1969–71; Office of Mies van der Rohe and C. F. Murphy Associates, architects (at fifty-two stories, the largest building in the United States to employ the strict Miesian classicism).

43. See table 2.
44. Up to the time of his death Mies's office had been responsible for the design of the following works in the Chicago area: twenty-two classroom, laboratory, heating, and commons buildings at Illinois Institute of Technology; fourteen apartment towers, two corporate office buildings, the federal court building (pp. 129–34), the federal office building and post office (still incomplete as of 1971), and one private residence. There were many more in New York, Baltimore, Washington, Detroit, Houston, Des Moines, Montreal, Toronto, Mexico City, and Berlin.
45. Franz Schulze, "The New Chicago Architecture," *Art in America* 56 (May–June 1968) : 70.

4. Public Building

Public Institutions

The postwar renewal and expansion of Chicago's public institutions coincided very closely with the revival of commercial building in general, although most of the works that have attracted the greatest attention for their architectural character did not begin to appear until the mid-sixties. Considered from a strictly chronological standpoint, the Art Institute again led the way, as it did in the immense upsurge of civic construction in the period following the adoption of the Burnham Plan. On the basis of old endowment funds and recent gifts the trustees authorized two large additions to the main building facing Michigan Avenue, one at either end, both pulled far back from the street along the Illinois Central tracks to minimize formal interference with the handsome Renaissance design of the 1893 structure and any disturbance to the flanking areas of Grant Park. The Benjamin Ferguson wing to the north was erected in 1957–59 to provide additional work space for the examination and care of paintings, and the Sterling Morton wing was built to the south in 1961–62 chiefly for additional gallery space. Designed by Shaw, Metz and Associates, both are simple limestone-clad volumes that extend the Art Institute complex over the entire two blocks between Monroe Street and Jackson Boulevard and thus constitute backdrops for the newly landscaped spaces flanking the main building.[1]

Public building gathered momentum at the end of the mid-century decade, but the quality of the architecture hardly suggested an exciting new era of civic design. Presbyterian–Saint Luke's Hospital began a $21,000,000 expansion of its medical and housing facilities at the West Side Medical Center with the construction in 1959–60 of the big surgical and laboratory center known as the John F. Jelke Memorial Building, but the design prepared by Skidmore, Owings and Merrill did nothing to improve the monotonous if soberly functional character of most hospital work. In the training academy of the Chicago Fire Department, erected in 1960–61 at 558 West De Koven Street, the architects Loebl, Schlossman and Bennett added some much-needed color to the area west of Canal Street. The academy is sheathed in bright red glazed brick and located on the site of the O'Leary home, where the Chicago fire started on 8 October 1871, both features making it a memorial to Chicago's incendiary history. Other works came around the same time, ranging from a little child-care center on University Avenue at 55th Street by George Fred and William Keck (1962–63) to the first of the city's giant rubbish-disposal plants, the Southwest Incinerator at 1400 West Pershing Road (1961–63), but there was little to suggest the great days of the Burnham period.

Something of the scale if not the quality of that spacious age returned with the construction of the Metropolitan Fair and Exposition Building, but its location represented a barbarous denial of everything that Burnham stood for as a planner. The history of this monstrous structure was loaded with ironies of a Swiftian character. In 1952 the South Side Planning Board, an agency of the South Side Redevelopment Program, asked Mies van der Rohe to prepare a preliminary design for an exposition hall of a size appropriate to metropolitan needs which was to be erected on blighted residential and commercial property on the near South Side.[2] The hall, whose structural characteristics we considered in connection with the background of the Hancock building, was to have the form of an immense square 720 feet on a side and 510,000 square feet in free internal area, with a seating capacity for 50,000 and a contiguous parking space for 10,000 cars. It was to include theaters, restaurants, truck drives, and railroad spurs as well as space for exhibitions and athletic events. The whole concept was very much in the spirit of the Chicago Plan, although Burnham had devoted more attention to sports and gymnastics than to exhibition facilities. But the South Side Planning Board's great project was never realized, first, because the appropriate offices of the state and municipal governments had other and grossly inferior plans and, second, because the Chicago government usually rejects proposals that do not originate in city hall. The result of this rejection was serious damage to the urban fabric eventually compounded by disaster.

In 1957 the state established the Metropolitan Fair and Exposition Authority and granted it the power to issue revenue bonds to the amount of $34,000,000, the expected cost of the new exhibition building. Instead of taking advantage of the opportunity to clear underused blighted land, as proposed in the South Side program, the city offered the state a prize recreational site in Burnham Park at the east end of the 23rd Street viaduct. This gesture absolutely contradicted Burnham's plan of reserving the entire lakefront for recreational purposes and very possibly stood contrary to the legislation establishing the public parks in Chicago, although this had not yet been tested in the courts. There was immediate opposition to this decision from civic and professional organizations and private citizens, who pointed out the numerous errors in choosing to locate an exhibition building on lakefront land: first and most obvious was the destruction of the scenic and recreational potential of the shore area; second, the necessarily huge parking areas would turn the beauty of the landscaped spaces into acres of concrete ugliness; third, the site is far from the hotels, restaurants, theaters, and entertainment centers of the Loop; fourth, it stands at a high-speed traffic interchange between South Lake Shore Drive and 23rd Street, where traffic would move with great difficulty and even danger; and finally, the whole venture placed public land and public revenues ultimately derived from the taxpayers at the service of private business enterprise. But the city and the state were not to be deterred from realizing their program, however questionable it was in the light of sound urban planning, and the project was quickly brought to realization.[3]

Officially designated McCormick Place because the *Chicago Tribune* under the ownership of Robert R. McCormick was the most vigorous journalistic proponent of the hall and its lakefront site, the Metropolitan Fair and Exposition Building was constructed at the foot of 23rd Street in 1958–60, on the basis of plans prepared by the architectural office of Shaw, Metz and Dolio in collaboration with Holabird and Root and Burgee and Edward D. Stone, and by the engineering firm of the Ralph H. Burke Company. The immense structure, measuring 340 × 1,050 feet to the edges of the flat-slab roof, consisted of three main parts, the open exhibition space of the main floor, a five-thousand-seat theater at the south end of the enclosure, and a variety of special areas—meeting rooms, art galleries, cafeteria, entrance and exit drives—on the lower level. Parking accommodations were provided chiefly in the simplest and most destructive way, by paving over several acres of once-landscaped grounds to the north and south of the building. This huge volume posed a challenge to the architects, who met it with a minimum of imagination: the precast concrete wall sheathing, its smooth planes interrupted only by narrow, widely spaced panels of relief sculpture executed by Constantine Nivola, looked like a giant sarcophagus, as lifeless in appearance as the corpses one tended to associate with it. Yet the internal structural system possessed great visual possibilities, and it was unfortunate that the architects made no attempt to exploit them. The roof rested on steel-truss purlins carried in turn by eighteen rigid-frame bents of trusswork spaced 60 feet on centers and spanning 210 feet clear between the legs, but this lively play of steel framing members was entirely hidden under various coverings of conventional character and rather cheap appearance.

The controversy over the location of the exposition building broke out with renewed fury in the spring of 1966, when the authority announced its intention of expanding the existing facility by 204,000 square feet, or more than 60 percent of the original main-floor area. Opposition to this further violation of the lakefront recreational areas quickly arose under the leadership chiefly of the Chicago Chapter of the American Institute of Architects, the Welfare Council of Metropolitan Chicago, and the Chicago Heritage Committee, all of whom offered a variety of useful alternative proposals. The Plan Commission and various business organizations, on the other hand, applauded the exposition authority's decision and urged its immediate implementation. The attitude of those who controlled the industrial and political machinery of the city was most succinctly and unambiguously stated by Thomas H. Coulter, the chief executive officer of the Chicago Association of Commerce and Industry. "Our lakefront," he told an interviewing reporter, "is not much more than a wasteland. Oh, it has some trees, but the only time I've been on the lakefront in the past 30 years has been to McCormick Place."[4] The opposition, however, had reached the level where it was politically expedient to listen to its voice, and accordingly Mayor Richard Daley proposed the compromise of building the addition westward on air rights over South Lake Shore Drive and the Illinois Central tracks, a suggestion that was accepted by the authority on 5 January 1967. But the people of Chicago were to be spared a further expansion of the original work: on 16 January a fire spreading among combustible contents in a cavernous building drastically short of sprinklers raised the internal temperatures to the point where the unprotected steel frames buckled and brought about a swift collapse of roof and walls. All parts of the structure except the foundations and the supporting framework of the main theater were a total ruin. There was nothing to do but begin over again after the insurance settlement, but the rebuilding was at least placed in more competent architectural hands.

Before the second McCormick Place reached the final design stage the character of large-scale public building in Chicago was drastically improved, chiefly through the direct activity and the indirect influence of Mies van der Rohe. His first opportunity to play such a role came with the commission for the extensive Federal Center, a complex of office, court, and postal buildings that was to cover the entire block bounded by Adams, Dearborn, Jackson, and Clark streets and nearly half the block east of Dearborn between Adams and Jackson Boulevard. Associated with Mies in this $100,000,000 project were three among the largest firms of architects in the city—A. Epstein and Sons, C. F. Murphy Associates, and Schmidt, Garden and Erickson. The background to such portions of this scheme as were eventually completed was marked by the errors and insufficiencies that ordinarily characterize the absence of genuine urban planning. The original plan, advanced in the spring of 1959 by the General Services Administration of the federal government, called for a single court and office building on the east side of Dearborn Street to extend the length of the block and rise to no more than forty-two stories, but further reflection during the ensuing year revealed that the height would very likely have to be seventy-five stories. The Plan Commission and the local chapter of the American Institute of Architects objected on the ground that a building of this formidable size and heavy public traffic would seriously obstruct pedestrian and vehicular circulation in the Loop. They proposed as an alternative the division of the single block into two buildings, one on Congress Parkway, a block south of the Loop, and one on South Wacker Drive, two blocks to the west. The General Services Administration accepted the idea of two buildings originally sixteen and twenty six stories in height but insisted that they be built on both sides of Dearborn Street on the Adams-Jackson block, thus revealing that its officers had not comprehended the point of the initial criticism.

Moreover, the Dearborn scheme as modified by the General Services Administration in 1960 embraced so many defects of site planning that the city's Plan Commission protested that it was unacceptable. The chief shortcomings had to do with circulation: there was no separation of pedestrian and vehicular traffic over the heavily traveled thoroughfare that split the site into two unequal parts; there was no link with the underground pedestrian system serving the two subways and the municipal complex in the area of Dearborn and Washington streets; and insufficient space was provided east (to the rear) of the east building for service vehicles, although the rear area offered the only space where such vehicles could be parked. Beyond these failures were two relating to open space: the public plaza on the main block west of Dearborn, which was now to contain a post office, was much too small for the crowds involved, and since there was to be no pedestrian subway, there was no provision for a sunken plaza area that might be used for other commercial and public purposes. In what was alleged to be a satisfactory compromise reached in October 1960 the General Services Administration rejected all the city's proposals except for an agreement to add a little tree-lined mall and an oval cul-de-sac for service vehicles behind the east building.

The plan that was finally adopted and on which construction was initiated in 1961 embraced a thirty-story court building on the east side of Dearborn Street and a forty-five-story office building and lofty one-story post office on the Dearborn-Clark block (fig. 57). The courthouse and its associated utility building were completed in 1964 at a total cost of $41,700,000, but aside from the subgrade framing system of the office building, post office, and plaza, no further progress on the Federal Center had been accomplished by 1971 (figs. 58, 59). The completed structure is a high, narrow prism of column-and-girder framing in welded steel of which the four elevations are covered with the familiar vertical tracery formed by continuous steel mullions. The close spacing of these members and the depth of the spandrel panels

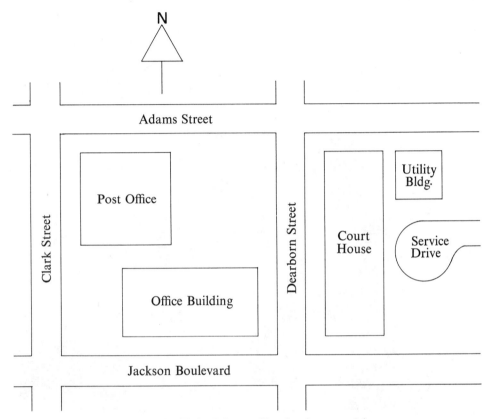

Chicago Federal Center: Site plan (not to scale)

yield a system of proportions that makes the elevations the most impressive of all Mies's steel-and-glass curtain walls: they possess to the utmost degree the paradoxical combination of tension and weight with delicacy and transparency.[5] The sense of openness is intensified not only by the usual glass walls of the setback lobby, but more by its great area of 35 × 116 feet and by the reduction of its contents to two monumental benches and a central information kiosk. The sheathing of the elevator bays, the inner end walls of the lobby, the lobby floor, the benches, and the paving of the surrounding arcaded area are everywhere a uniform gray granite. The materials of all the visible surfaces are dark-tinted glass, black-painted steel, and polished granite: in few other buildings did Mies achieve a more thoroughly unified monumentalism, possibly carried to the point of an almost inhuman exactitude.

Fig. 57. Federal Center, Dearborn, Adams, and Clark streets and Jackson Boulevard, 1961–64, 1966, 1971–. Architects: Ludwig Mies van der Rohe; C. F. Murphy Associates; Schmidt, Garden and Erickson; and A. Epstein and Sons.

Fig. 58. Federal Center. Federal Court House, facing Dearborn Street between Adams and Jackson, 1960–64.

57

58

Fig. 59. Federal Center. Federal
Court House. Floor plan and
longitudinal section.

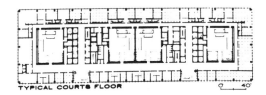

TYPICAL COURTS FLOOR

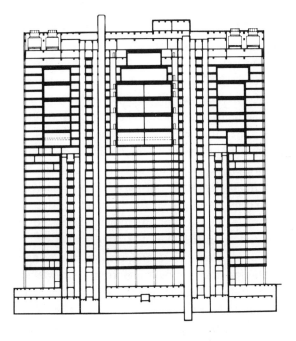

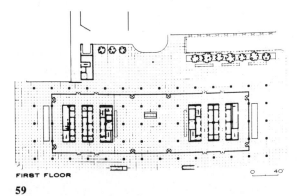

FIRST FLOOR

59

The interior of the Federal Court House is more complex than what is suggested by the elegant simplicity of the exterior. The planning of the building and part of the framing system were designed to accommodate a number of interior courtrooms that are themselves monumentally simple in character (fig. 59). There are fifteen such rooms, each two stories in height and two column-free bays in both horizontal dimensions, distributed throughout floors seventeen to twenty-eight, and the architects made provision for five more courtrooms which can be added without structural or mechanical changes. The materials of the interior are reduced to brown wool carpeting, walnut furniture and wall panels, black leather chair covering, and aluminum ceiling grills. These darkly sumptuous enclosures are wholly isolated from the exterior walls and from the surrounding elements of the building: they are served by their own elevators and lavatory facilities; they are cooled or warmed by their own air-conditioning and heating systems; and they are acoustically insulated from the surrounding noises. One view holds that these walled-off cells symbolize the repressive injustices of the police state, another that they represent a reflective justice uncontaminated by the prejudices and passions of the marketplace. The one obvious truth of the whole design, however, was summarized in a single sentence by Donald Canty: "The new Federal building by Mies van der Rohe [is] surely the most refined architecture ever to make its way through the General Services Administration."[6] It was perhaps the precipitating factor in bringing Mies the gold medal of the Chicago Chapter of the American Institute of Architects in 1966.

The next stage in the development of a new civic architecture in Chicago is almost as deeply imbued with the Miesian spirit as buildings from his own hand. The city and Cook County needed new court and office space as much as the federal government, and planning for what was to be known as the Chicago Civic Center began in June 1959, when the city's Public Building Commission voted to issue the necessary bonds. The architects were chosen in the following year—C. F. Murphy Associates, with Jacques Brownson of the Murphy staff in charge of the design, were the controlling office, and the collaborating firms were Skidmore, Owings and Merrill and Loebl, Schlossman and Bennett. The generous site that they were given for their handiwork is another full block, in this case the one lying immediately east of the original City Hall–County Building and bounded by Dearborn, Washington, Clark, and Randolph streets, in clockwise order.[7] The original plan prepared by the Murphy office and retained with minor variations through nearly two years of financing problems called for two separate buildings placed to one side of a double-level landscaped plaza, the lower level of which was to be ringed with shops, restaurants, and exhibition space. This last provision was an essential part of the plan if the full potentialities of the urban core were to be realized. When an entire block of highly diversified inner-city buildings is demolished it is inevitable that some part of the city's day-and-night life is destroyed along with the material fabric, and this was particularly true with the Civic Center, since two of the buildings that were sacrificed housed the Erlanger Theater and Henrici's Restaurant, the latter a Chicago institution established in 1868. The difficulty of raising the necessary capital, eventually acquired only through a supplemental federal grant and additional borrowing power that had to be authorized by the Illinois legislature, led to the inevitable scaling down of the original plans, and the valuable idea of diversified plaza use was the first to be sacrificed.[8]

The program that was finally adopted in the spring of 1962 embraced a single-level illuminated plaza with landscaping accents and a fountain at one corner, a single thirty-one-story tower rising to a height of 648 feet, two basements extending under the entire block, and pedestrian subways connecting the subgrade lobby with the City Hall to the west, the Brunswick Building on the south, and the Dearborn and State Street rapid transit subways to the east. The building was to occupy about 35 percent of its site at the north side of the block, along Randolph Street, the remaining area to be disposed in a spacious plaza on the south side and a thirty-foot-wide strip around the other three sides. The decision to build a single tower rested mainly on common-sense economics and to a lesser degree on the visual relations of the necessarily huge structure to the open plaza and the surrounding buildings. The merger of the two buildings into one freed a considerable area of the site from any encumbrance, allowed improved floor planning through more usable space per floor, and secured economic advantages through a reduction in physical maintenance, in number of separate service facilities, and in maintenance personnel.

The most striking feature of the Civic Center as it was constructed is the giant scale—the great height for a modest thirty-one floors, the immense bays, and the extremely generous openings of the base (figs. 60–62). These characteristics constituted a bold assertion of utilitarian necessities. The center was designed to house 120 courtrooms and hearing rooms, conference rooms, judicial and other offices, the library of the Chicago Law Institute, provision for future court space, and large public lobbies. To provide an adequate ceiling height and to minimize interior obstructions the architects raised the floor-to-floor height to 18 feet and reduced the number of primary columns to sixteen, which required the unprecedented and even unimagined bay span of 47 feet 8 inches on the transverse dimension and 87

Fig. 60. Civic Center, facing
Washington Street between Dearborn
and Clark, 1963–65. Architects:
C. F. Murphy Associates; Skidmore,
Owings and Merrill; Loebl,
Schlossman and Bennett.

60

Fig. 61. Civic Center. *Left:*
Longitudinal section. *Right:*
Transverse section.

Fig. 62. Civic Center. The steel
frame during construction, showing
the trusses of the floor framing
system and the spandrel panels.

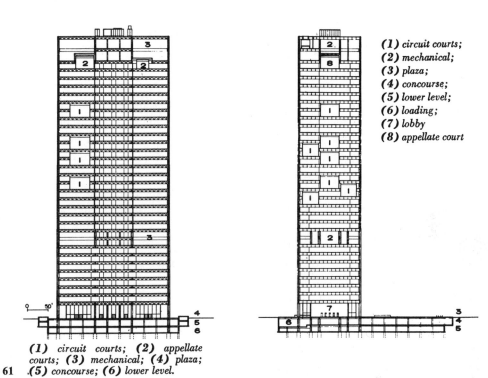

(1) circuit courts;
(2) mechanical;
(3) plaza;
(4) concourse;
(5) lower level;
(6) loading;
(7) lobby
(8) appellate court

(1) circuit courts; *(2)* appellate
courts; *(3)* mechanical; *(4)* plaza;
(5) concourse; *(6)* lower level.

61

62

feet on the long.[9] Construction on the basis of this program was initiated in the spring of 1963 and completed late in 1965, but the installation of all interior furnishings was delayed until the following year.

The structural system of this mammoth building exhibits the kind of geometric simplicity that one finds in first-class bridge design. The sixteen primary columns are cruciform in section, their equal axes 6 feet in length at the base, and their cross-sectional area is reduced at intervals up the height of the building, as the vertical loads and wind moments diminish. The floor framing system is composed of Warren trusses 5 feet 4 inches deep, a depth that was adopted for the long span of 87 feet but held constant throughout the frame to simplify fabrication and erection and to provide openings betwen the diagonal web members for ducts, pipes, and conduits. The depth of the floor trusses and the additional space occupied by the fireproof cladding and acoustical tile left a floor-to-ceiling height of 12 feet, sufficient for all spaces except the largest courtrooms, which had to extend through two stories to gain a ceiling height of 26 feet (fig. 61).

The rigidity of the primary framing system is provided by the conventional form of portal bracing in which the girder is rigidly fixed throughout its depth to the column. Supplementing the primary frame are the secondary columns that constitute the framework of the elevator shafts, continuous openings that are vulnerable to wind action and hence require additional bracing that in this case has the form of K-trusses set between adjacent columns. All connections of the Civic Center frame are welded, making it the largest all-welded skeleton erected up to its time. Between the primary trusses that join the columns are trusses of identical depth spanning the short dimension of the bay and spaced at 9 feet 8 inches to carry the metal decking which in turn supports the concrete floor slab (fig. 62 illustrates many of these structural details). The big spans demanded costly steelwork and made the erecting process difficult and expensive, but these were offset to some extent by the reduction in the number of caissons to fifty, with a maximum diameter of 13 feet 10 inches and an average depth of 120 feet below street grade.

The exterior of this magnificent steel framework was treated by the architects with the quiet assurance that marks the work of those who need no sensational novelties to attract attention. The columns are exposed as continuous members outside the planes of the steel and glass walls; between them stretch the horizontal bands of the six-foot-deep spandrel panels and the 12-foot-high windows. The rhythmic play of voids and solids is so subdued as to possess a kind of reticence; yet it speaks directly of an almost overpowering technology. The exterior covering of the structural members is a self-weathering steel known as Cor-ten which reacts with the oxygen of the air to form an impervious iron oxide coating.[10] The amber tint of the glass and the color and texture of the oxide patina provide the appropriate finish for these giant elevations: the deep red-brown tone with a bluish overtone and its suggestion of translucency convey simultaneously the rude enduring strength of steel construction and the unassuming dignity of its formal expression. The honors that came to the Civic Center were richly deserved: the Award of Architectural Excellence of the American Institute of Steel Construction in 1966, and the Honor Award of the American Institute of Architects in 1968.

The building so obviously and with such conviction expresses the Chicago as well as the Miesian spirit that one would place it immediately in its milieu and might suspect that its chief begetter, Jacques Brownson, was not only a student of the old master but spent many months talking to him about the design of the building. The meaning of the Civic Center is thus historical as much as structural and architectonic. The *Forum* commentator saw the beginning of what the center implies.

This is as "pure" a structure as has been built in or out of Chicago in a long time; and it is as "universal" a space-container as has been devised anywhere in recent years to cope with an unpredictable future. . . . Chicago's new Civic Center speaks for itself—clearly, nobly and monumentally. It also speaks for its godfather (who happens not to have been involved in its actual design at all): Mies van der Rohe. For this 648-foot-high monolith is, quite possibly, Mies's greatest tower to date. The outstanding team of Chicago architects who did, in fact, design this big monolith would probably be the first to insist that his name should head the list of credits. What makes the Civic Center a Mies building is the clarity and precision of its detail and its form; and second, the universality and flexibility of its spaces.[11]

It was the English critic Reyner Banham, however, who saw the full historical implication of the center.

[The] last building in the [Museum of Modern Art] exhibition is [the Chicago school's] most striking monument to date, the civic centre building. The civic centre seems to me to be a unique, and uniquely Chicagoan, achievement. . . . Technically this somber prism of civic pride is remarkable enough, but what is really remarkable is this simple fact: this is the first public building in the world which is both modern and conceived in the local building tradition. Chicago has no tradition but modern; almost as long as it has been a city, its natural style has been the most severe metal skeleton construction. No wonder the spirit of Modern Architecture U.S.A. presides over it as one of those tutelary goddesses in a mural crown who watch over the good fortune of cities in late Classical manuscripts.[12]

But the final chapter in the creation of the finished Civic Center involved still another development of twentieth-century art, one leading to ironies that the sobriety of architecture can seldom afford. To the astonishment of the art dealers' and collectors' establishment, a deputation led by the Skidmore partner William Hartmann persuaded Picasso in the summer of 1966 to donate the forty-two-inch maquette for a monumental statue of a woman's head, which could probably have fetched a price on the market of better than $100,000.[13] The very idea of such a work on a prominent site in the middle of the Loop aroused immediate controversy marked by the usual attacks on modern art by the lumpenbourgeoisie. And the presence of the physical object itself, the achievement of an artist holding vaguely communist convictions, in the front yard of Chicago's political machine could only be regarded as a complex ironic joke. But the city's acceptance was conveyed in the proper spirit, the $300,000 cost of the completed work was borne by various charitable foundations, and the fifty-foot statue was fabricated from Cor-ten steel by the American Bridge Division of the United States Steel Corporation in 1966–67.[14] The formal unveiling in the summer of 1967 rounded out the irony with a full measure of official pageantry: before 15,000 spectators in the Civic Center plaza congratulatory telegrams from Picasso and President Lyndon Johnson were read, the Chicago Symphony Orchestra played appropriate music, Archbishop John Cody invoked the benediction, Gwendolyn Brooks read the poem she had written for the occasion— all prelude to the climax that came with the removal of the billowing plastic wrappings. Yet when the arguments finally died away the big oxide-covered head of steel seemed perfectly at home before the same material spread out in the building's austere geometry. The best of the many last words on the whole subject of center, plaza, and statue came from the editorial writer of an out-of-city newspaper, the *Saint Louis Post-Dispatch*.

We confidently predict that . . . the day will not be far off when an army of Chicagoans will spring to the defense at the very thought of doing away with it.

Picasso's political views, the tired old argument over abstract art, the debate over what the sculpture "represents," are all . . . irrelevant. The impressive thing is the perfect way Picasso's welded steel design fits in the monumental open space before the city-county-state office building, and enriches that handsome contemporary building itself.

Whatever the views on Picasso's art, we hope Chicagoans appreciate what they possess in this Civic Center on the north edge of the Loop. They have something as exciting as St. Mark's Square in Venice, an open space in the midst of cliff-high office buildings, surrounded by Nineteenth and Twentieth Century architecture amicably intermixed, which virtually commands pedestrian traffic across it. It is the people, in a way, that make the center so striking. People walk, and gawk, and chat and stand: and if the Picasso gives them something to stare at and talk about, so much the better. What is really significant is that the Civic Center-cum-Picasso acts as a powerful magnet, bringing people together in the heart of the city, giving them a common bond of light, air and satisfying design, creating an island of pedestrianism in a sea of skyscrapers and wheels.

Cities too often, especially downtown, offer their people little but means of getting from here to there. An open space which insists on being used in common gives a rare lift to community spirit.[15]

The completion of the Civic Center in all its details put the crown piece into the transformation of Dearborn Street from a drab and fading artery into an architectural showplace of worldwide importance. The immense program of building that began in 1955 constituted the foremost example in the United States of the spontaneous reconstruction of the urban core; indeed, possibly the only other city in the world that has experienced a similar remaking is Montreal. The sheer volume of construction is remarkable enough, but what renders it unique is that a unified system of structures, spaces, and pedestrian passageways was put together by very nearly every organization, institution, and economic interest that is involved in the sponsorship of buildings. Commerce, finance, housing, municipal, state, and federal governments, each constructing to satisfy its own need, produced an excellent example of urban planning that for once showed a proper respect for the street.[16] Dearborn thus emerged by 1970 to play a dual role in the economy of the core: not only had it become a thoroughfare of major importance in its own right, but it had come to form a connecting link between the shopping centers of State Street and the financial institutions of LaSalle. With the construction of the projected Loop subway (p. 249), this process of what we might call integrated diversification would gain momentum as it spread into other parts of the core area.

The third of the great public buildings to grow out of the Miesian renaissance is the reconstructed McCormick Place. Its final design proved to be another triumph of intelligence and imagination, but the series of decisions that led to its rebuilding formed a comedy of ineptitude that was finally ended only by the intervention of the state and municipal governments. The officers of the Metropolitan Fair and Exposition Authority made a single wise move in awarding the commission for the design of the new building to C. F. Murphy Associates early in 1967, but this seems to have exhausted their capacity to deal forthrightly with the problems involved. Much of the ensuing year was occupied with the tedious business of insurance settlements, which included the decision to use the original foundations, footings, caissons, and basement slabs, undamaged by the fire, and hence to keep the building on its bitterly contested lakefront site. Architects, planners, architectural educators, civic groups of various kinds urged the city and the authority to adopt Mies van der Rohe's project of 1953 both in design and location, advancing potent arguments for its value to the whole city, but since the municipal government does not act on public proposals arising spontaneously from private citizens' groups, the scheme died as the result of official indifference. The directors of the authority insisted on their own plan, to be implemented through the use of public land, and they moved with a haste and privacy that still further aroused popular suspicion.

The first plan designed to the new and enlarged prescription was submitted by the Murphy office in the summer of 1967: its chief characteristics were the division of the building into two parts, an exhibition space and a theater, five levels for exhibits, curtain walls of marble or granite sheathing, and a roof frame of Pratt trusses on steel columns. The plan was rejected by exhibitors on the ground of inadequate area, the separation of the main parts, and the high cost. The architects accordingly prepared a second plan, submitted in October 1967, that expanded the total floor area and placed all the facilities within a single enclosure. Its remarkable feature was the presence of suspended construction on the grand scale: the vast roof was to be carried by cable hangers suspended from four parallel main cables supported by four pairs of steel towers set beyond the end walls. The primary structural system and the necessity for anchor cables brought the project closer to pure suspension-bridge construction than any building erected or proposed in the previous forty-five years. Having secretly ordered this plan to circumvent the demands of public bodies opposed to further encroachment upon the lakefront, the authority unanimously adopted it without discussion in another secret meeting. The directors appeared to be moving in panic, and it was finally realized by the enlightened newspapers and responsible public bodies that the battle would have to be joined. In November the Metropolitan Housing and Planning Council strongly denounced the exposition authority's usurpation of lakefront land for commercial purposes, then announced a set of principles that were to be followed in the reconstruction of the hall. These were concerned mainly with public hearings on all decisions having to do with expansion and rebuilding, the relation of the structure to the city's lakefront plan, the elimination of all outdoor parking, the use of adjoining railway air rights for future expansion, and a unified plan for the development of an exposition complex.

The authority accepted the principles, called for a third plan presumably drawn up to meet all objections, and held a public hearing on the design in mid-December. The architect in charge of the project was Gene Summers, who had recently joined the Murphy associates after several years in Mies's office. Construction was finally initiated in May 1968, but before another six months had passed the authority discovered that it lacked $10,000,000 to complete Summers's admirable plan. The causes of this latest episode in the comedy were, first, a $6,000,000 miscalculation in estimating the cost of the underground garage and, second, the expectation that the Park District would pay the $4,000,000 cost of an eleven-acre fill east of the building, although no such agreement existed between the two agencies. The consequence was that the plans went back to the architects for a fourth revision, while all concerned discussed the alternatives that remained to the authority. Jack Reilly, the mayor's representative on the Metropolitan Fair and Exposition Authority board, expressed the opinion that these repeated errors made the officers look silly in the eyes of the public, a sentiment with which there was widespread agreement. Much of the difficulty arose from the inexperience of the authority's general manager, Edward J. Lee, who was familiar with the management of fairs and exhibitions but not with the administration of big building projects. He attempted to blame the architects for the errors, bad judgments, and erratic orders of the authority's officers, but his charges were carefully answered in a letter written by Charles F. Murphy in response to this attack. The upshot of these recriminations was that the board asked the architects to revise the plans to keep the cost within the earlier budget of $72,000,000.

Fortunately for the whole enterprise, however, the state, the Public Building Commission of Chicago, and leasing arrangements with a private garage operator brought in additional funds sufficient to include the underground parking area and the landscaped lakefill to the east of the hall. The design that ultimately emerged under Gene Summers's direction is another superb example of Mies's generalized space defined by glass set in a steel and concrete frame (fig. 63). The huge complex is made up of two different enclosures separated on the main level by a 180-foot wide mall on the line of 23rd Street, but the three elements lie under a single roof measuring 610 × 1,360 feet overall, or nineteen acres in area. The northern and larger of the two enclosures is the exhibition space, with an area of 576,000 square feet divided about equally between a main and a lower level; the southern is a reconstruction of the original theater reduced in capacity from 5,000 to a little less than 4,500 seats. Extending south of the exposition hall is an underground garage with space for 2,100 cars and direct pedestrian connections to the hall, where the vertical transportation between the various levels is provided by elevators and escalators.

The only fixed limitation imposed on the spatial and structural design of McCormick Place was the requirement that the architects use the foundations and main

Fig. 63. McCormick Place, Metropolitan Fair and Exposition Building, lakefront at 23rd Street, 1968–71. C. F. Murphy Associates, architects.

floor of the original building, so that these structural elements constituted the basis of the lower exhibition level of the new work. The optimum system of primary supports, allowing for the maximum extent of unencumbered interior space with a reasonable depth of the roof framing system, was one consisting of four rows of nine columns per row, all columns uniformly spaced at 150 feet in both directions. These cruciform columns are reinforced concrete covered with steel plate and stand 50 feet high to the center of the hinged bearings at their upper ends, where they carry a roof frame of steel Warren trusses arranged in a two-way grid having a uniform depth of 15 feet throughout the roof area. These trusses are cantilevered 75 feet beyond the outermost columns to provide generous sheltered spaces beyond the glass walls on all four sides of the building. The only deviation from strict rectangularity in the roof frame occurs at the columns, where the ends of the trusses rest on four cantilevered arms which are themselves trusses set on the diagonal lines and extending 30 feet from the bearing at a depth of 15 feet 6 inches. This head assembly is made up of welded pieces, but all other connections in the main trusses are bolted. The roof trusses are everywhere visible outside the enclosure on the four elevations, so that the formal excellence of the hall is derived in good measure from the easy poise with which this vast framework rests on the high, slender, widely spaced columns.[17] The new hall was opened early in 1971, its final cost of $97,000,000 far exceeding the budget that the hapless exposition authority had fallen back on two years earlier.

While Chicago was adding to its corpus of civic buildings by means of new constructions in the $100,000,000 range, private bodies were struggling to find housing for cultural institutions of a public or quasi-public character. Since in most cases they established themselves in prize buildings of the past, their existence came to be inseparably bound up with the city's program of landmark preservation. A belated recognition of Chicago's architectural heritage came in 1960 with the establishment of the Commission on Architectural Landmarks, which came into existence under a municipal ordinance that granted it neither money nor power. Since it was impotent, its initial designation of thirty-eight buildings as official great works aroused little controversy, and five were soon demolished.[18] Recognizing the inadequacy of this program, the general assembly in the summer of 1963 passed an act empowering the city to create a new ordinance that gave it not only the authority to designate landmarks but the tools to protect them. For more than four years the city did nothing, but under increasing pressure from private individuals as well as professional and civic bodies the council at last acted by passing in January 1968 a model law that established an advisory committee and a permanent commission with the means to protect a given building under private ownership or, as a last resort, to lease it for preservation or to acquire it under the right of eminent domain. The one weakness of the ordinance is that no structure can be designated a landmark without the approval of the council, which meant that under the extreme intensity of land use in the inner city political and financial considerations would take precedence over civic excellence. The consequence of this vulnerable point was that although the advisory committee quickly recommended sixteen buildings as landmarks, only three had been officially designated by the end of 1970—the Clarke house, built in 1836 and the oldest structure in the city, the Glessner house, and the Carson Pirie Scott Store. The establishment of a category of National Historic Landmarks under the federal National Park Service indirectly helped to preserve two more, but the program was equally limited by lack of funds and genuine authority.

Two buildings in this pathetic group survive because they were transformed into the homes of quasi-public institutions. Wright's celebrated Robie house, at 58th Street and Woodlawn Avenue, was threatened with destruction by the Chicago Theological Seminary, which was willing to make the sacrifice when it was faced with the necessity of enlarging its facilities.[19] The house was temporarily rescued by the Webb and Knapp Company, the main contractor for the Hyde Park–Kenwood renewal program (pp. 208–14), who used it as a field office until 1962, when it was donated to the University of Chicago. An ad hoc committee raised enough money by 1965 to begin a badly needed restoration, the university being either unwilling or unable to turn it into a functioning element of the campus, and the designation of the house as a National Historic Landmark brought honor but little in the way of funds. Rescue and hopefully permanent protection came two years later, when the newly founded Adlai Stevenson Institute of International Affairs acquired the house as its headquarters and undertook a sensitive renovation and refurnishing carried out under the direction of Walter Netsch of Skidmore, Owings and Merrill.

The Glessner house, at Prairie Avenue and 18th Street, was the only structure whose owners actively sought landmark status. The house for a number of years had been owned and actively used as an office by the Graphic Arts Technical Foundation, but this organization abandoned its quarters when it moved to Pittsburgh in 1966. The Chicago School of Architecture Foundation, hastily created the same year with an awkward name, brave plans, and little money, raised a sufficient endowment to buy the house in the spring of the year. So little money was left, however, that restoration had to be limited to the basic utilities and none was available to turn the house into an active element of the city's cultural life, although plans had been proposed to use it as the office headquarters of various organizations and as a center for lectures, seminars, and exhibitions in the building and civic arts. A later and successful money-raising campaign led to the realization of most of these plans by 1971.

Outside the circle of active institutions housed in rescued landmarks, there are two that qualify partially for this status. In another act of violence visited upon the civic body, the city in 1962 swept away the entire working Hull House group, ten buildings designed by Irving and Allen Pond and erected between 1890 and 1908, as part of the clearance necessary for the construction of the University of Illinois Chicago Circle Campus (pp. 181–89). The demolition left only the useless Charles Hull family house, built in 1856 at 800 South Halsted Street as a not very interesting example of the Italian style. But the house was designated a National Historic Landmark as a memorial to Jane Addams, faithfully restored in 1966–67, and then left to stand little used in its academic sea. There is small value in restoring and preserving a once functioning building if the result is an empty shell, the artificial newness of its physical fabric intensifying the sense of pointlessness. The rescue of Richard Schmidt's Albert Madlener house, on the other hand, provides an excellent contrasting example. Built in 1903 at State Street and Burton Place (1500N), the house was acquired by the Graham Foundation for Advanced Study in the Fine Arts and expertly renovated for office use in 1963–64, with the architectural firm of Danforth, Brenner and Rockwell in charge of the project.[20] The Madlener house was designated a landmark under the original program, and if it has not recovered that status under the new law, it is at least a functioning part of the living, working city, actively maintaining the continuity of past and present.

D. H. Burnham's Orchestra Hall (1904), on Michigan Avenue between Adams Street and Jackson Boulevard, was never designated a landmark, although there is every reason why it should have been. By 1960 it had deteriorated to the point where extensive renovation had become a matter of urgency. The Orchestra Association hoped for a bequest, but when the only one that was offered came under terms it could not accept, it boldly and perhaps recklessly dipped into its endowment fund to pay the $2,000,000 cost of a brilliant interior remodeling completed in the summer of 1966 from the design of Harry Weese and Associates. This program involved the addition of lounges, locker and dressing-room space, a conductor's suite, a recording room, a library, rehearsal and warm-up rooms, a marked acoustical improvement, and central air conditioning, as well as the usual carpeting, upholstering, painting, and plastering. The whole enterprise was a model of how such things ought to be done, and a matter of simple propriety for one of the great symphony orchestras of the world; but the price was so high that the recovery and expansion of endowment became a matter of desperate necessity.

The musical arts have always fared better than the visual in Chicago, and given the latter's stepchild role, one might argue that the establishment of the little Museum of Contemporary Art in 1967 was comparable in its field to the remodeling of Orchestra Hall. Situated at 237 East Ontario Street, the renovation of the existing building again the work of Danforth, Brenner and Rockwell, the museum filled a need for many contemporary artists that the Art Institute was increasingly unable to satisfy.

But these various achievements, each valuable in its way to the artistic and intellectual life of the city, were overshadowed by the greatest work of restoration and revival ever undertaken in the city, if not in the nation as a whole. The Auditorium Building had been rescued from final oblivion when it became the property of Roosevelt University in 1946, but the immense theater within it lay dark, begrimed, and apparently unwanted. Once the home of the Chicago Symphony Orchestra and the Chicago Opera Company, it declared itself bankrupt in 1941 and was shortly padlocked for the failure to pay more than $1,000,000 in accumulated taxes. No cause looked more hopeless than the restoration of Adler and Sullivan's masterpiece, and the abortive attempts of 1956–58 to bring it back to life only underscored the obvious fact. But the vision of the Auditorium freshly restored to its golden splendors would not die, and because there were individuals who insisted on transforming the vision into reality, Roosevelt University in 1960 established an Auditorium Theater Council to make one more effort to raise the necessary funds. It made little progress until its chairmanship passed to Beatrice Spachner, a Highland Park woman endowed with the kind of energy that spurs an individual to greater efforts the more formidable the challenges grow. The estimate of the cost of restoration had grown to about $4,350,000 by 1962 because of the supposed water damage to plaster as well as the need to replace all seating, carpeting, and electrical installations and to clean and repaint all surfaces.

At this point, however, the architect Harry Weese was invited to take charge of the restoration, and with the thoroughness and sensitivity that characterize his architectural work, he conducted an investigation that revealed far less damage than had previously been supposed to exist. The building had suffered unequal settlement between the massive bearing walls and the less heavily loaded iron columns, but although this resulted in the crowning of floors and distortion of door frames, it had caused no damage to the structure, to its superb acoustical properties, or to the utilities. Weese, with the enthusiastic cooperation of the contractor, the Sumner Sollitt Construction Company, was able to demonstrate that the minimum restoration for immediate use could be accomplished for $2,750,000, although the improvement of antiquated backstage facilities would require additional funds. By the summer of

1967 Mrs. Spachner's council had raised all but $500,000 of this total. With more pledged and with the promise of an expert yet highly economical job of renovation to be carried out by the Sumner Sollitt staff, she was emboldened to restore the theater to regular usage. The official opening came in October 1967 with a performance of the New York City Ballet Company, although there had been a previous testing of the new facilities when the theater had been used for a memorial service for Adlai Stevenson in October 1965. By 1968 the Auditorium had become an active theater in the Chicago system, having a season of its own devoted largely to musical and ballet performances sponsored by a variety of independent organizations. The ultimate challenge was more than a matter of restoring a four-thousand-seat theater to working order, because an essential part of the agreement between Roosevelt University and the theater council was that the Auditorium enterprise could never go into debt. The revival of this grandeur of another age was thus compelled to be a continuing success.

Public Housing

After fifteen years of stagnation on the part of the construction industry the need for low- and middle-income housing in Chicago at the end of World War II was a matter of desperate urgency. Much of what survived from earlier periods was literally worn out or was at various stages approaching that condition, and the scattered wartime enclaves of public housing met only a small fraction of the long-frustrated demand. For nearly a decade after the war the Chicago Housing Authority, with limited resources, not only tried to make strictly quantitative progress in meeting the need, but followed a policy of designing projects to make them assets to the community and to keep them racially integrated. The period of civic enlightenment for the CHA culminated in the three years of 1948–51 under the chairmanship of Elizabeth Wood. She adopted and valiantly struggled to maintain a policy based on two principles—the selection of sites without regard to race wherever housing was needed and wherever suitable land existed, and the maintenance of a balanced racial composition in individual projects by the technique of holding a proportion of apartments open during tenant application for whatever racial population was needed to preserve the balance. Except for three aldermen out of a total of fifty, Miss Wood's program clashed with the views of the city council, whose members preferred to retain the status quo. As a consequence, she resigned in 1951 and was replaced by administrators who followed a policy of racial segregation until they were exposed by the courts nearly twenty years later.

In the first postwar decade public housing was supported by state and municipal funds made available mainly from the proceeds of two state bond issues floated in 1945 and 1948. Since the period of greatest activity coincided with Miss Wood's tenure, the projects opened in these years reveal the highest architectural, functional, and social standards of all the CHA groups. Racine Courts (1949–50), designed by Perkins and Will and situated in the immediate vicinity of 107th Street and Racine Avenue (1200W), consists of 122 units arranged as an informal series of small two-story apartment blocks on curving interior streets with relatively generous landscaping of trees and shrubs. In 1968 the CHA sold the Racine apartments to tenants through a tenant-owned cooperative known as the Foundation for Cooperative Housing. It marked the first time that urban public housing in the United States was sold to its occupants, and the plan under which this was carried out made it possible for families with an income range of $5,700 to $7,500 per annum to become householders.[21] The typical apartment groups erected in the first few years after the war are clearly inferior to the Racine Courts. Wentworth Gardens (1945–47), for example, retains something of the human scale in its two- and three-story buildings, but the separate structures are laid out in an unrelieved grid-iron pattern that follows the monotonous geometry of streets and alleys. The Wentworth units were constructed in the area of 37th Street and Princeton Avenue (300W) from the plans of Loebl, Schlossman and Bennett. A much larger project by the same architects, and one that gives an ominous hint of future deterioration in standards, is Dearborn Homes (1948–50), a group of cruciform apartment blocks in the dreary institutional style centered at 25th and State Street.[22]

Two comparable projects from the Elizabeth Wood legacy are Le Clair Courts (1949–51), far out on the periphery of the city at 44th Street and Cicero Avenue (4800W), and Ogden Courts (1949–50), on the diagonal Ogden Avenue at 14th Street. The former was designed by Friedman, Alschuler and Sincere and Ernest A. Grunsfeld, Jr., as a group of relatively attractive two-story blocks constructed of brick and wood siding over timber framing and disposed in parallel series with their narrow brick ends facing the streets. The 315 family units are distributed among 55 buildings, the simple and repetitive structure of which held the unit construction cost to $9,800. In the Ogden group, designed by Skidmore, Owings and Merrill, the authority turned to the intermediate-size apartment block: the 136 units are divided between two seven-story buildings set well back from the busy artery (fig. 64). The two buildings are T-shaped in plan and are saved from the customary institutional aspect through the use of an exposed concrete frame, baywide window ribbons, warm red brick, and outdoor galleries along one side of the rear wings, with panels of blue and white glazed tile arranged in a checkerboard pattern to form a kind of protective partition along the outer edges of the galleries. The superior quality of the Ogden design was a consequence of the moderate flexibility in the public housing budget that was allowed under the state bond issue, as opposed to the rigid ceiling in construction costs fixed by the Public Housing Authority in Washington. Elizabeth Wood could thus raise the unit cost to a little more than $11,210 per apartment, which would have risen to nearly $27,600 by 1972, and she felt free to authorize the architects—in a sentence that reflects a happier and healthier time—to "give us the best you have."

The CHA managed to maintain a reasonably human scale for individual buildings, a modest size for the whole development, and relatively high architectural standards for the next two years, while limiting the cost of construction to around $12,500 per unit, but rising costs and the pressure of housing needs rendered extreme by ruthless destruction for the city's renewal and expressway programs quickly swept away these principles. The last of the projects to be built under city-state financing and the tenure of Elizabeth Wood is the Prairie Avenue Courts, constructed in 1951–52 from the plans of George Fred and William Keck and extending southward from 26th Street along Prairie Avenue (figs. 65, 66). Because of its location in the densely built South Side ghetto, the CHA found it necessary to increase the number of dwelling units to 326 and to turn to high-rise construction for one of the thirteen separate buildings. The exposed concrete frame, tawny brick, and outdoor galleries appear again in the Prairie Avenue group, enhanced by strong visual accents in the form of brightly colored doors, but the chief excellence of the design lies in the well-planned association of low-, intermediate-, and high-rise blocks, ranging from two, through seven, to fourteen stories. The authority once more held the unit construction cost close to the average for the past three years, the precise figure being $12,237.[23]

The departure of Elizabeth Wood saw the beginning of steady deterioration in site planning and exterior design and a concomitant increase in the size of both the project and the individual buildings. The deliberate practice of racial segregation, maintained by the device of building only in the ghetto, where the demand for housing exceeded by many times the available space, meant that public housing was to become a prime factor in perpetuating the urban diseases it was once hopefully designed to cure. The first backward step coincided with the return to federal sponsorship: Harold L. Ickes Homes (1952–55), the work of Skidmore, Owings and Merrill, extend for three blocks along State Street below Cermak Road (2200S) and embrace 799 units in a mixture of nine seven- and nine-story buildings (fig. 67). The exposed frame adds the only visual interest to these long blocks that are mo-

Fig. 64. Chicago Housing Authority. Ogden Courts, Ogden Avenue at 14th Street, 1949–50. Skidmore, Owings and Merrill, architects.

Fig. 65. Chicago Housing Authority. Prairie Avenue Courts, Prairie Avenue at 26th Street, 1951–52, 1958. George Fred Keck and William Keck, architects.

64

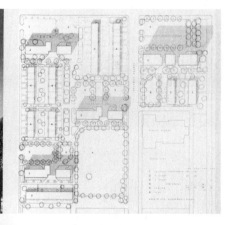

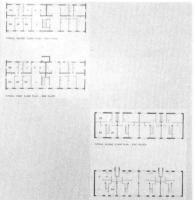

65

154

Fig. 66. Prairie Avenue Courts. Views of low- and high-rise buildings and floor plans.

Fig. 67. Chicago Housing Authority. Harold L. Ickes Homes, State Street from Cermak to 25th, 1952–55. Skidmore, Owings and Merrill, architects.

66

67

155

Fig. 68. Chicago Housing Authority. Stateway Gardens, State Street from 35th to Pershing Road, 1955–58. Holabird and Root and Burgee, architects.

Fig. 69. Chicago Housing Authority. Washington Park Homes, scattered sites in the Washington Park area, 1960–62. Lichtman and Kalischer, architects of row houses.

68

69

Fig. 70. Chicago Housing Authority.
Robert R. Taylor Homes, State
Street from Pershing Road to 54th
Street, 1959–63. Shaw, Metz and
Associates, architects.

157

Fig. 71. Chicago Housing Authority. Raymond M. Hilliard Center, Cermak Road at State Street, 1964–66. Bertrand Goldberg Associates, architects.

Fig. 73. Raymond M. Hilliard Center. Typical floor plan of one of the segmental (twenty-two-story) buildings.

Fig. 72. Raymond M. Hilliard Center. Typical floor plan of one of the cylindrical (sixteen-story) buildings.

71

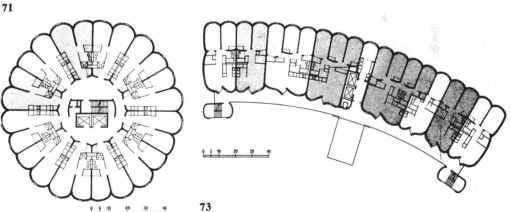

72

73

notonously industrial in appearance. The unit cost of slightly over $13,500 indicates that the authority was questionably holding the line in the face of continuously rising prices. What followed was much worse: the 1,900-unit extension of the Cabrini Homes along West Division Street (1955–58), distributed through buildings of seven, ten, and nineteen stories, proved a fertile ground for breeding every ill of poverty and discrimination, and the resulting violence of daily life eventually reached a fury that focused the attention of the entire world on the horrors of the American city.

A certain measure of structural imagination was brought to bear on Holabird and Root and Burgee's design of Stateway Gardens, erected along State Street below 35th in 1955–58, but it could have been put to better social and architectural uses (fig. 68). The underlying structure of these ironically named Gardens is a box frame of reinforced concrete, and thus marks a considerable departure from the monotonous repetition of conventional short-span column-and-girder frames that characterize the other CHA projects. In a box frame the working structure is a rigid series of contiguous rectangular cells bounded by vertical as well as horizontal concrete slabs. The chief advantages are the economy arising from the simplified formwork and the rigidity under wind loads of the solid-walled boxes, but these are somewhat off-set by the fixed interior partitions of concrete. But the exterior design of Stateway Gardens reveals nothing of this novel structural system—possibly the largest example of it in the world—and the concentration of 1,644 apartments in eight buildings of ten-story and seventeen-story height carried a step further the iniquitous practices inaugurated in the Ickes project.

Worse was to come with the decade of the sixties, but it must be pointed out in justice to the CHA that not all the blame attaches to the local authority. In the three years of 1958 through 1960 the directors submitted repeated plans to the Public Housing Authority office in Washington for more imaginative projects—groups of eight-story buildings with four-bedroom apartments to be constructed along State Street, mixtures of two-story row houses and high-rise apartment blocks on scattered sites, small neighborhood buildings with single-bedroom units for the elderly, and high-rise towers to be erected on air rights over expressways. In every case, however, the projected cost exceeded the ceiling of $17,000 per dwelling unit arbitrarily established by the bureaucracy of the Public Housing Authority: for the straight-forward medium-height buildings on State Street, for example, the unit cost in the low bid came to $19,000. The Chicago office accordingly conducted an investigation into the matter in 1959, and the conclusions strongly suggested that compared with the world of public housing the novels of Franz Kafka and the movies of the

Marx Brothers are examples of stark realism. The CHA discovered a world of contradictions and paradoxes: if the directors chose big projects instead of the more costly small ones, only the very largest contractors could undertake the job, thus nullifying the economic advantages of competitive bidding; the inflexibility of bureaucratic methods led the public housing authorities to cling to administrative practices when nothing compelled them to do so and everything indicated the benefits to be derived from abandoning them; instead of building on vacant sites or on derelict property left by rail lines, open-air businesses, and the like, the authority always built in densely occupied slum areas where the high costs of clearance and excavation offset any economies of construction; the adoption of new techniques of construction was viewed with abhorrence, even when they had been tested and found to yield economies. The Public Housing Authority office in Washington conducted its own investigation but could find no causes for the high Chicago costs and therefore insisted blindly on their reduction.

The contractors and the architects, who could point to lower costs in comparable private construction, revealed still other problems. Housing distributed in small groups on scattered sites made it prohibitively expensive to build large and efficient centralized heating plants and impossible to install plumbing and electrical conduits in central utility shafts serving a great number of apartments. Particular deficiencies of certain sites, such as voids within older foundations or local peculiarities of drainage around rail embankments, sometimes required caissons even for low buildings on the scale of row houses or walk-up apartments. Routine practices of the housing authority suggested to contractors a kind of carefully plotted madness: decisions reached by the local office were often changed or nullified by the Washington office after plans were completed, with inevitable conflicts that went on for months while work was suspended; the final payment to the contractor was frequently delayed for three or four years after completion, compelling the general contractor to carry the operation at a deficit in order to pay his subcontractors; payments of certain bills were sometimes renegotiated years after the allegedly final settlement.

In the wake of these disclosures the CHA submitted a body of recommendations to the mayor's office that left the authority complete control in preparing a program of requirements while granting similar control to architects and engineers in the preparation of plans. This report presumably reached the mayor, but if it achieved any results, they were scarcely visible in the subsequent activities of the authority. Of the 7,801 units of housing constructed between 1959 and 1963 somewhat more than 7,400 were in the dreary high-rise blocks with their rows of uniform windows punched out of clifflike walls of brick, and all the sites were distributed through the ghetto areas of the South, Near West, and Near North sides.[24] The single deviation from this fixed pattern of high-rise construction is Washington Park Homes, an immense project of 1,445 units built in 1960–62 on twenty-eight scattered sites in the Washington Park area on the South Side (fig. 69). The major portion of the apartments are in seven sixteen-story blocks, but the remainder are divided among sixty two-story buildings that constitute a welcome change from the inhumanity of the skyscraper fortresses. The architects of the two-story structures were Lichtman and Kalischer, and those of the high-rise units Shaw, Metz and Associates.

But the Washington Park apartments stood by themselves, an oasis in the arid mountains of concrete and brick, and in the year following their completion the CHA opened what is undoubtedly the worst example of low-income housing ever conceived in the history of the program. The Robert R. Taylor Homes, designed by Shaw, Metz and Associates and constructed over the four years from 1959 to 1963, embrace 4,328 units disposed in a battery of sixteen-story slabs extending southward between State Street and the New York Central–Rock Island tracks from Pershing Road (3900S) to 54th Street, a distance of nearly two miles (fig. 70). A few amenities—3,500 three- and four-bedroom apartments, a community center in part leased to the Chicago Park District for recreational and educational purposes, the settlement center known as Firman House, the Beethoven School of Perkins and Will (p. 169), fifty-six apartments designed to be used as kindergarten and elementary-school classrooms—are overwhelmed by what can only be described as a vast urban disaster. Housing 28,000 residents in its brick and concrete warrens, it represents a full complement of all the ghetto ills: poverty, economic and social discrimination of the most blatant variety, the shabbiest forms of victimization underlying the other marks of urban pathology, broken families, hopelessness and apathy, endemic and daily crime, drug addiction, random violence, delinquency, dirt, and anarchy. "Taylor Homes," in the precise summary of Joseph Black, "[is] one of the worst tragedies that architects have created, and surely among the world's ugliest buildings."[25] There was no reason for anyone to be ignorant of life in this most prominent aspect of the American city: it was exhaustively presented in a series of articles by M. W. Newman published in the *Chicago Daily News* in April 1965, a series that constitutes an impressive and moving example of American journalism at its best. It was Newman who coined the expression "the $70,000,000 ghetto" to designate this costly encapsulation of urban inhumanity.[26]

The construction of Taylor Homes gave the CHA the momentum of an irresistible tide that apparently allowed little time to reflect on the consequences of its activity. In 1963, however, the authority introduced a drastic change in the direction of its program, if not in its methods and their results: instead of concentrating exclusively on the construction of family housing, the CHA began the practice of building small dwelling units for elderly people living by themselves or as couples without children, and for the remainder of the decade its new projects consisted almost entirely of this type of housing.[27] Because they were designed for occupancy by people suffering from the usual infirmities of old age, they contained a number of novel features that at last brought the CHA a measure of favorable attention. Kitchen utilities include cabinets everywhere easily reachable from the floor, a built-in oven at eye level, a walk-in closet with broom and shelf space easily accessible to the hand. Showers are equipped with a wide range of sprays for therapeutic uses, and stout metal grips are strategically placed on bathroom walls. Stairs are minimized and doorways built to special widths to accommodate wheelchairs. Outside the individual apartments are community rooms with kitchen facilities, equipment for handicrafts, and sheltered outdoor decks.

The need to make daily living as easy as possible brought out the best in architects. One of the early projects, the Judge Harry M. Fisher Apartments, designed by Loewenberg and Loewenberg and built at Broadway and Ardmore Avenue (5800N) on the Far North Side, is a slender twenty-story tower distinguished by a broad V-shaped plan and ribbon windows enclosed between narrow brick spandrels. On a number of sites equally far to the south in the Hyde Park–Kenwood renewal area the CHA broke completely with its own tradition by constructing a total of thirty-four atrium houses, row houses, and low apartment units in 1966–67 from the plans of Y. C. Wong and Hannaford Associates. These are concentrated along Woodlawn, Blackstone, Dorchester, and Kimbark avenues between 51st and 56th streets. In the following year the authority returned to the North Side to erect the twenty-six-story apartment building at Sheridan Road and Devon Avenue (6400N), a high, narrow slab designed by Dubin, Dubin, Black and Moutoussamy, who used the densely patterned load-bearing screen wall of concrete that became the hallmark of their work. The Devon tower, completed in 1970, is the first of the CHA projects to be built under a "turnkey" program: the structure was erected by the development firm of McHugh-Levin Associates and sold to the CHA complete except for turning the key in the main entrance door. The entire project, with its adjoining community building, marks a hopeful forward step in the rescue of the Loyola University area at the south edge of Rogers Park, where neglect and decay had been taking a visible toll in the years following the Second World War, in spite of the presence of a large area of open land, the Sheridan Road elevated station, two bus lines, two movie theaters, and a university.

The program of low-income housing for the elderly proved enough of a stimulus to the architectural imagination to lead to one work of genuine distinction in site planning, design, and structural character. The Raymond M. Hilliard Center, built in 1964–66 along Cermak Road west of State Street, is another of Bertrand Goldberg's essays in cylindrical geometry (figs. 71–73).[28] The project is unique not only to public housing but at the time of completion to the building art in general, and with respect to the physical fabric itself, it at least suggests a long-hoped-for promise of better things to come. The entire group is composed of two sixteen-story cylindrical towers, two twenty-two-story structures having the form of shallow cylindrical segments, an outdoor amphitheater, and a one-story community center, all of reinforced concrete. The lower residential buildings are restricted to elderly tenants without children and the higher to families. The structural system is composed of curving scalloped exterior walls and radial interior partitions, the whole complex forming a rigid monolithic system of relatively light concrete slabs and curving segments (the floor plans, figs. 72 and 73, show the distribution of bearing walls). The windows throughout are oval, to smooth out the flow of tensile and compressive stresses around the openings while providing a form that would take the conventional sliding sash in the central area. The architects developed the internal plan by starting with the living spaces and their customary arrangements of furniture, then organizing the bearing-wall envelope around them. The small apartments of the elderly were best fitted into the compact cylindrical towers, but the more spacious multiroom family units required a greater outside wall area and hence were more appropriate to the narrower segmental form (figs. 72, 73). The scalloped construction of the exterior walls was adopted to increase rigidity and to indicate the internal divisions of the floors on the outer surfaces of the walls. The repetitive pattern of swelling curves, the external galleries and stairways of the higher buildings, and the brightly colored doors add a lively visual interest to these unusual structures.[29]

The numerous amenities and the high level of design brought a demand for apartments from elderly white people as well as from the black people whose ghetto area stretched for miles to the south and west, and there was some hope that a genuinely integrated settlement would emerge. The housing authority's attempt to attract eligible white families, however, resulted in failure because of the poor quality of ghetto schools and the fear of racial conflict. But the policies of the CHA were likely to guarantee that the Hilliard Center could be no more than an unstable island in a sea of troubles. The choice of its site simply added to the enormous concentration of high-rise public housing along the State Street spine of the ghetto and thus extended a little further all the ills attendant upon this concentration. The choice had been made in spite of the fact that the land had been repeatedly proposed as a site for a new high school to relieve the overcrowded and deteriorated schools of the area. The planning decision to separate the family units from the elderly intensified another kind of segregation from which all of American society suffers. These decisions, it turned out, were made on the basis of building costs and the existing distribution of underground utilities, not on the basis of social need and urban health.

Paralleling the increasingly fruitless efforts of the CHA were the attempts of the younger Chicago Dwelling Association to add to the supply of low- and middle-income housing, but the latter accomplished so little that it was questionable whether it had any effect at all on the housing crisis. The association was established in 1948 as a nonprofit corporation to employ funds provided by the state and the city as equity, on the basis of which it was to raise conventional mortgage money guaranteed by the Federal Housing Authority for the construction and rehabilitation of middle-income housing. By 1965 the Chicago Dwelling Association had constructed 112 single-family houses and 728 apartment units, an achievement so modest in its magnitude that both the federal Department of Housing and Urban Development and the municipal Department of Urban Renewal decided that it was necessary to add resources for an expanded program. The upsurge of activity that followed these efforts led to the addition of 210 single-family detached houses on various sites in the South and West sides and the rehabilitation of about 500 apartments acquired through receivership and financed by local banks. The total was hardly spectacular, and the cost of the rehabilitation program so far exceeded the association's resources that it had to be abandoned. By 1969 the Chicago Dwelling Association was for all practical and useful purposes out of business. Another step that ended as ignominiously was the CHA plan of 1968 to build low-cost houses of prefabricated components with funds provided by the Illinois Housing Development Authority. Attended by great advance publicity designed to impress the delegates to the National Convention of the Democratic Party, the plan was launched with the aim of producing a minimum of two thousand houses. After one hundred demonstration units were completed the program collapsed because the CHA failed to satisfy the requirements of the FHA for insuring mortgage funds.

These examples could be multiplied at length through any inquiry into the administrative techniques of the Chicago Housing Authority and its associated bodies, but they are less serious than the civic damage wrought by the authority's policy of building inhuman skyscraper ghettos within the existing ghetto—machines for non-living, they might be called, totaling 36,056 dwelling units as of the early part of 1970.[30] A policy so massive, so thoroughgoing, so persistently adhered-to down through the years in the face of riots and violence was not the result of errors of management or of good intentions gone awry. It was eventually discovered to be the consequence of a deliberate political decision. Since the CHA owns properties with an aggregate value of around half a billion dollars, the attitude underlying its policy can be understood only as an outgrowth or expression of the climate of opinion that came to exist at the top level of the city's municipal, financial, and industrial establishment. When the values that are embodied in the political and economic institutions of Chicago and hence that govern much of its public life are applied to public housing, they almost necessarily lead to the creation of a physical and moral wasteland.

The mental and emotional state that underlies the ruling public attitudes appears to be a fear of many things that are at odds with conventional middle-class views—of persons of predominantly non-European origin, chiefly Negroes, Indians, Mexicans, and Puerto Ricans, of the more obvious forms of dissent, novel ideas and art forms, obviously different modes of personal behavior, all impulsive acts, and all conspicuous forms of sensuous and emotional indulgence. These fears manifest themselves in a host of ways—in the absurdities of police censorship visited upon owners of bookstores and movie theaters, in the infamous local laws that allow arrest for loitering, disorderly conduct, and the charge of resisting arrest that often follows a beating at the hands of the police, in the thousand devices by which darker-skinned peoples are kept in their place, in hidden trusts, contract sales, and panic buying, struck down from time to time by the courts but, like the Hydra, growing two new heads as soon as one is cut off. But the underlying prejudice and ignorance might be offset on a higher level were it not that many of the same views are shared by those who make the important decisions. They appear among some elements of the business community as well as among the ruder types at city hall, as some of the more obvious examples demonstrate. In February 1968 twelve hundred members of the Executives Club applauded George Wallace, and in the following month they snubbed Senator Charles Percy when he made a devastating criticism of Wallace's arguments.

With opinions and views such as these at the upper levels, it is not surprising to find more outrageous variations among the politicians, or to find them translated into brutality on the part of the police. The Chicago force inherited a long history of repression and harassment, but in the decade of the sixties these practices came to be increasingly directed against black people and dissenters of any description. The climax came in 1968, when the police on three occasions mounted attacks against unarmed citizens—first in the West Side ghetto, after the assassination of

Martin Luther King, when Mayor Daley ordered the police to shoot suspected arsonists and looters on the streets; second, in the same month, when they attacked peaceful men and women demonstrating at the Civic Center against the Vietnamese war; and finally and most infamously, during the Democratic National Convention in August, when an army of police and national guardsmen struck down youthful dissenters who had come to protest the same war—the attack in this case so unbridled and widespread as to lead the attorney and former president of the Chicago Crime Commission, Daniel Walker, to call it a police riot. Exceeding the violence of these acts was the killing in December 1969 of two black men, Fred Hampton and Mark Clark, by a squad of city police acting under the orders of the state's attorney. The same indifference to the poor, the nonwhite, and the morally courageous who cry out against injustice has characterized the municipal services down through the years. Paul Cornely, the president of the American Public Health Association, described Chicago slums as "the most depressing I have seen," and regarded the city's attempts to alleviate the sufferings of the slum dwellers as deliberately calculated to degrade them still further. "While Chicago is known for its police brutality," he said, "there is another kind of brutality here. That is the brutality of the city's agencies, its health department and its hospital system."[31]

Behind these Swiftian ironies stands the elected first citizen, who does much to set the city's ethical tone, and at the time of the Chicago Housing Authority's degradation he was Richard J. Daley, a man of inexhaustible political sagacity and of great ambitions for the city, but at the same time possessed of a very limited idea of civic excellence. The newspaper columnist Mike Royko characterized him in these words:

Daley likes to build big things. He likes high-rises, expressways, parking garages, municipal buildings and anything else that requires a ribbon-cutting ceremony and can be financed through federal funds.

He isn't that enthusiastic about small things, such as people. Daley does not like civil rights demonstrators, rebellious community organizations, critics of the mediocre school system, critics of any kind, or people who argue with him. . . . He has simple tastes. Nobody catches him chatting about literature, music or French cooking. He likes White Sox games, fishing and parades. He has led more parades than anyone since Rome fell apart. . . . He is old-fashioned. Other city machines took up civil service and other bad habits. They fell apart. The old-fashioned Daley organization controls about 60,000 patronage jobs. It has thousands of others in unions, private industry, utilities, at race tracks. . . . Everyone can join if they do what they are told. It is truly democratic in a dictatorial sort of way.[32]

Behind the municipal politicians are those of the state, and Illinois has long been one of the most backward. The Chicago newspaper editor Milburn Akers most accurately described the essence of the Springfield milieu.

Overall, politics in Illinois are venal. The politicians play group against group, section against section, and . . . a legislature is noted for its auction-block character. These characteristics are not confined to either party. Springfield is and long has been especially amenable to pressure groups. If there is a lack of scientific brains in the state, as the secretary of defense indicated, there is also a lack of public and political morality.[33]

In such a moral climate it is understandable that the directors of the Chicago Housing Authority were emboldened and indeed encouraged to exhibit a disregard for the purposes both of civil rights legislation and of public housing. The first to attack the practice of ghettoizing the ghetto was Theophilus M. Mann, a member of the CHA board, who made the original charge in August 1961. No response came until four years had passed and a neighborhood community group known as the West Side Federation complained to the secretary of housing and urban development that the CHA was guilty of practicing racial discrimination by building in the ghetto and by not admitting Negroes to white projects. The possibility of effective action emerged in August 1966 when the American Civil Liberties Union filed a suit on behalf of six public housing tenants to compel the authority to follow an integrated housing program. The CHA first sought dismissal and was refused, then denied the allegations only to have the denial exposed as false through documents uncovered by ACLU attorneys. The consequence was that Judge Richard B. Austin of the United States District Court in February 1969 ruled that the authority was guilty of racial discrimination in selecting building sites and assigning tenants, and in submitting sites to selected aldermen who reflected their constituents' racist sentiments, and required it to cooperate with the union in developing a plan of remedial action. Such a plan was drawn up and rendered mandatory through a court order issued by Austin in July of the same year, the chief provisions of the program being the construction of small buildings on scattered sites with a racially balanced tenancy.[34] Charles Swibel, the director of the CHA, accepted the order without appeal, did nothing for a year, then suddenly reversed his earlier decision and directed his legal staff to file an appeal, having previously argued through attorneys "that 'political considerations' made it unwise to act more promptly."[35] Meanwhile, the CHA built no housing of any description.

Schools and Universities

School buildings of every type and in every district constituted the city's most crucial need after low- and middle-income housing. The more prosperous suburbs resumed the construction of schools shortly after the end of the war, and the leadership in design quickly fell to the office of Perkins and Will, who worked from principles developed for and tested at Crow Island School (pp. 30–32). Although Chicago had only twenty new schools to show for the entire wartime decade, the board of education did not mount an attack on the formidable backlog until the first of a series of $50,000,000 bond issues for school construction was approved by the voters in 1951. Five such issues eventually provided a capital of $225,000,000 for the decades of the fifties and sixties, but under the combined forces of economic inflation, rapidly rising school population, and physical deterioration, the sum proved far from generous. The quantitative dimensions of the problem alone were enough to discourage the most ambitious administrator: the school population increased by 10,000–12,000 children a year throughout the fifties; a deficit of more than 5,000 seats at the beginning of the decade forced 11,000 children into double sessions (two sessions scheduled in succession during a single day), but the number was to grow to 24,800 at the worst; a high proportion of the school buildings (174 all told) had been erected before the acceptance of the Burnham Plan in 1910. The board of education adopted various measures to cope with the problem in addition to going to the voters at regular intervals for money. Of these the most important were the appointment of Benjamin C. Willis as superintendent of schools and the termination of the traditional practice of using staff architects to design school buildings. Willis was brought to the city from Buffalo, New York, precisely for the purpose of administering a huge construction program with little disturbance to the existing set of racial and class relations, two tasks in which he was eminently successful. The decision to commission "outside" architects led to some improvement in the quality and a marked reduction in the cost of the educational plant. By the end of the decade these measures appeared to be yielding the desired results, and there were 82 new schools to show for the effort, but as the sixties progressed this proved increasingly to be a tragic illusion.[36]

The new order in architectural design and site planning began to manifest itself in the mid-fifties. Among the larger elementary and secondary schools Stephen Ting Mather High School attracted attention not only because of the general excellence of its design but because its cost fell $200,000 below the budgeted figure and the school grounds were incorporated in Mather Park, which was opened shortly after the school was completed. Constructed in 1957–59 from the plans of Loebl, Schlossman and Bennett, the school lies at the south end of the park bounded by California Avenue (2800W) and Richmond Street (2932W) on the east and west and by Thorndale (5900N) and Peterson Avenue (6000N) on the south and north. The disposition of interior elements—classrooms in the main block and special facilities in the wings—represents a variation on planning principles that go back to the time of Dwight Perkins, but the irregular asymmetry, the simple volumes, and the elongated wings reflect the contemporary idiom.

The most prominent and the most impressive of all the public facilities built under the jurisdiction of the board of education is Chicago Teachers College North, designed by Perkins and Will and erected in 1959–61 on a spacious campus extending westward along Bryn Mawr (5600N) from Saint Louis Avenue (3500W).[37] Except for the six-story tower housing faculty and administrative offices, the college is a continuous single-story building with its wings disposed in the form of a double open rectangle marked by an extreme horizontal extension of the narrow enclosures (figs. 74, 75). The separate facilities are distributed according to a long-established plan: the gymnasium and pool are at the west end, library, auditorium, and cafeteria in the central area, faculty offices to the east, and classrooms, laboratories, and study carrels are scattered throughout the long wings. The dominant rectangularity of the college is interrupted by the hexagonal plan of the office tower and its awkward honeycomb sunscreen, but the window walls, the colored tile pattern in the covering of the spandrel strips, and the grass-covered courts gave the college a bright and sunny quality that made it particularly inviting among scholastic institutions. Unfortunately, this open plan did not long survive: built for 2,100 students, the college saw its enrollment rise to 6,200 by 1968, with the inevitable consequence that the spacious courts and campus had to be filled in by new expansions. Under a law passed by the general assembly in 1964 Chicago Teachers College North and all other collegiate facilities built and operated by the Chicago Board of Education passed to the jurisdiction of the state board. It was a necessary step for the overburdened city system, but it ended local control of the municipal colleges.[38]

Among the numerous elementary schools several erected around 1960 most emphatically reveal the changes that had been made by breaking out of the old architectural mold. The Richard E. Byrd School (1958–60), designed by Perkins and Will and constructed at 363 West Hill Street as part of the Chicago Housing Authority's Cabrini Homes extension, is a concrete-framed, glass-walled structure divided into three separate but connected pavilions set in a landscaped court, the first Chicago school to be planned in this way. The James R. Doolittle, Jr., School (1960–61), erected at 37th Street and Cottage Grove Avenue from the plans of Skidmore, Owings and Merrill as part of a renewal project, is a long two-story block of finely detailed concrete framing built around a generous central court. Another Perkins and Will essay, close in its community role and its design to the Byrd facility, is the Ludwig van Beethoven School, constructed in 1960–62 at 25 West 47th Street (figs. 76, 77). Built as part of the Robert R. Taylor project of the CHA, the school is also divided into three separate pavilions, but they lie on a straight line rather than forming a triangle like the Byrd towers. Distinct from the ruling mode of Perkins and Will designs is the Jens Jensen School (1961–63), built at 3030 West Harrison Street after the plans of Harry Weese Associates (fig. 78). The various enclosures take their form from the hexagonal classroom unit that constitutes a geometric motif extending throughout the informal plan. The careful preservation of a scale suitable to the physical range of children and young adolescents, the warm brickwork, and the unity of form in a diversity of spaces give the Jensen school a humanity sorely needed in the inner-city milieu.

The flow of money from successive bond issues allowed the board to maintain through the sixties the pace of construction that had been established in the previous decade, but by 1967 space as well as money began to run short. Very nearly the last of the major buildings to be carried out under the program initiated by Benjamin Willis and maintained by his successor, James F. Redmond, is Jones Commercial High School of Perkins and Will, an unusual work of scholastic design and an institution involved in the history of Chicago schools from the beginning of their present organization. Established in 1873 to provide secretarial and office training for girls and named after William C. Jones, the president of the board of education, the school was housed for ninety-four years in an antiquated brick building at State and Harrison streets. The replacement of this building was considered by the board as early as 1909, and in the following year Dwight Perkins proposed a plan for a skyscraper school that would have been not only unique at the time but another indication of its author's farsightedness. The new Jones high school, however, was not constructed until 1965–68, but in one respect, at least, it embodied the ideas of the elder Perkins. The school is divided into three main buildings, of which the most prominent is a six-story classroom tower that is framed in reinforced concrete for an additional sixteen floors; flanking it on two sides are the auditorium and the gymnasium buildings, both two stories and both connected to the academic tower by covered passageways.

Jones and the long delayed extension of South Shore High School, designed by

Fig. 74. Chicago Teachers College
North (now Northeastern Illinois
University), Bryn Mawr Avenue
at Saint Louis, 1959–61. The Perkins
and Will Partnership, architects.

Fig. 75. Chicago Teachers College
North. Perspective drawing of the
campus plan.

74

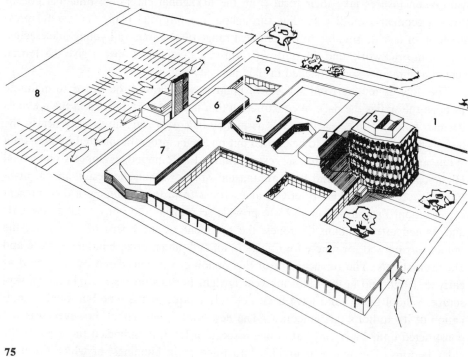

75

171

Fig. 76. Ludwig van Beethoven Elementary School, 25 West 47th Street, 1960–62. The Perkins and Will Partnership, architects.

Fig. 77. Ludwig van Beethoven Elementary School. First-floor plan.

Fig. 78. Jens Jensen Elementary School, 3030 West Harrison Street, 1961–63. Harry Weese and Associates, architects.

76

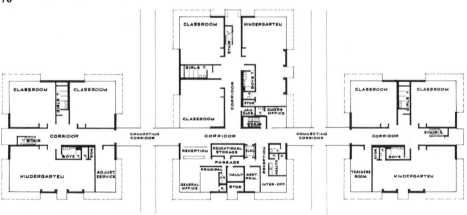

77

78

Fridstein and Fitch and opened in 1969, brought the major phase of postwar school construction to a close, but the need for additional facilities, for teachers, and for nothing short of a revolution in the schools serving low-income neighborhoods had grown to such proportions that nearly twenty years of building seemed only to have resulted in retrogression. The promise of satisfying some part of the physical need came in 1969, when the Chicago Public Building Commission was authorized by the city council to issue bonds up to a total of $160,000,000 to finance the construction of schools and to bring them into close association with proposed branch libraries, health centers, and recreational facilities. These hopeful beginnings, however, were in good part nullified by the appalling decision of the board to locate new schools in parks, specifically such masterpieces of their genre as Douglas, Humboldt, and Washington, in spite of the fact that the city had only 2.1 acres of parkland for every 1,000 inhabitants, about half of the proportion recommended by the new Comprehensive Plan (pp. 270–82). A taxpayers' suit to prevent this alienation of public land was denied by the state supreme court, so that the way was cleared for the damage to parks to continue and to be made permanent. "To place schools in them," the *Daily News* editorialized, "would set disastrous precedents for the plundering of priceless assets that cannot be replaced."[39] Washington Park was the first to suffer when the Vincennes School was placed under construction in 1970, and although the Park District was opposed to alienating any more than the twenty-six acres the board originally requested, the precedent, like that of McCormick Place, implied that no public land was safe from bad planning or the narrow parochialism of public and private institutions.

But the expansion of the physical plant alone could do no more than temporarily relieve one symptom of the sickness that afflicted the public school system. The root of much of the trouble was the racial segregation of the school population, which had increased until by 1969–70 Chicago shared with Gary, Indiana, the distinction of having the most thoroughly segregated schools outside the South. Black students constituted 52.9 percent of the total enrollment; of these 75.9 percent attended schools where 99 percent of the students were black, whereas only 3.2 percent attended schools where white students formed a majority. The failure of ghetto schools to offer a meaningful educational experience—to do little more, as a matter of fact, than maintain a simulacrum of external order while merely passing the hours of the day—was reflected in a dropout rate of 56 percent in 1969, the worst in the previous twenty years of the city's history. In 1968 Illinois ranked forty-ninth among the various states in the proportion of personal income devoted to public schools, and although the total sum was substantially increased under the administration of Governor Richard Ogilvie, Chicago remained below such comparable cities as New York and Washington in school expenditures per student. The reading skills of students declined steadily as they advanced through the elementary grades, so that they fell progressively below the given grade level in ability the more they were exposed to the educational system. The vocational training program, for which the city had once been famous, deteriorated steadily in the postwar period, and the refusal of the craft unions to accept members of minority races as apprentices reached the point where blacks disappeared from the construction and mechanical trades. In 1966 the educational theorist Robert J. Havighurst of the University of Chicago drew up a report containing twenty recommendations for the city's schools, only to see fourteen of the most important, ranging from teacher training through special programs for dropouts to an increase in mechanical aids, left to die on the shelf from inaction or unconcern. It was a dismal picture, and as the one hundredth anniversary of the organized school system approached, there were few reasons to celebrate the event.

At the other end of the educational spectrum, ironically enough, the universities of the Chicago area entered into another great period of physical expansion and intellectual development at the end of the war, a progress that included the creation de novo of two entire campuses. In the vanguard by virtue of its early start and the fame of its physical achievement was Illinois Institute of Technology under the presidency of Henry T. Heald and the architectural chairmanship of Mies van der Rohe. IIT came into existence in 1940 with the merger of Lewis and Armour institutes, but the event that was ultimately to bring it world attention was the Hitler government's closing of the Bauhaus at Dessau, Germany, in 1936. Three of its most celebrated faculty members fled to the United States in the next two years, Walter Gropius to Harvard University, Laszlo Moholy-Nagy to Chicago to found the Institute of Design, and Mies to the school of engineering and arts that was taking shape under Heald's guidance.[40] From the time of his arrival in 1938 Mies began the work not only of organizing an enlarged department of architecture and urban planning in collaboration with his compatriot Ludwig Hilberseimer, but of designing a new campus for the university. The final scheme for the campus plan that Mies and Hilberseimer proposed in 1940 included twenty buildings disposed in a balanced pattern on either side of 33rd Street as the cross-axis, between State Street on the east and the New York Central–Rock Island line on the west. The rhythmic spacing of the buildings and the forms of the structures themselves were based on a twenty-four-foot module, which is the bay span of the steel or concrete frames and the adoption of which facilitated future expansion without sacrificing the unity of the overall plan. The institute adhered to this plan with unusual fidelity, but the rapid growth of new construction necessitated in part by the institute's useful and remunerative industrial research program compelled it by 1950 to expand east of State Street and to locate faculty and student housing as far east as Michigan Avenue.

The first work from Mies's hand is the Minerals and Metals Research Building, constructed at the west edge of the campus beside the railroad embankment in 1941–42. Before his retirement in 1958, when he was also dropped as institute architect in an incredible act of administrative blindness, he designed twenty-one others, a total that includes industrial research laboratories, faculty apartments, a heating plant, a commons building, and a chapel as well as typical academic buildings of classrooms and offices. All of them are characterized by welded steel frames and walls predominantly of glass except for the five structures of the IIT Research Institute, the two of the Institute of Gas Technology, and two faculty apartments, which are brick-paneled enclosures with strip windows carried on column-and-girder frames of reinforced concrete. The Miesian approach in the design of these now celebrated works is one of a perfection of detail so pure and rigorous that it would do credit to the most Platonic of mathematicians. The result of this Germanic thoroughness is an exactitude and a delicacy of form that has been duplicated only by the master's ablest students. The comment by an anonymous curator of the Museum of Modern Art in New York, made in reference to the Metals Research Building, applies equally well to all of them. "The function and form of each element has been so carefully studied and the relationship between materials so delicately adjusted, that the resulting structure is superbly well integrated, technically and aesthetically, perhaps to the critical point of over-refinement."[41]

With the end of the war IIT entered a twenty-year period of expansion that is unparalleled among privately endowed universities. Buildings appeared at an average rate of one a year, all of them together exhibiting a considerable variety of form dictated by functional requirements, in spite of the rigid mathematical order imposed by the architect. Alumni Memorial Hall (1945–46) was the first postwar work and the first in which Mies used glass in panes broad enough to fill the width of an entire bay. The Chemistry Building (1946–48), marked by relatively small sash set four to a bay, became the standard for all subsequent classroom structures and for the administration and laboratory buildings of the Association of American Railroads (respectively 1949–50 and 1952–53). The heating plant (1949–50) falls into a separate class by virtue of its special function, a high, narrow brick shell without interior divisions in which a marked vertical accent arises from the continuous steel-plate covering of the columns. The little chapel (1952) is another unbroken volume clothed in brick except for the largely glass facade. The Commons Building (1953–54) is unique because of the absence of intermediate mullions, the broad sweep of glass filling the entire twenty-four-foot bay above shallow panels of brick. Most of the IIT buildings were designed in collaboration with architects whose larger staffs handled the structural and mechanical details—the production as opposed to the design, as the architects put it. The associated firms were those of Holabird and Root for Alumni Memorial Hall and the classroom buildings and Friedman, Alschuler and Sincere for the remainder (the chapel was too small to warrant a collaborator, and the heating plant was largely a matter of power-plant engineering).

The culminating work in this outpouring of architectural virtuosity is Crown Hall, designed in collaboration with Pace Associates and constructed in 1955–56 to house the institute's departments of architecture, planning, and design (fig. 79). This elegant, rhythmically articulated prism of glass is on its main level a single enclosure measuring 120 × 220 feet in plan and 18 feet in clear interior height above the main floor. The structural system is reduced to its ultimate essentials: four rigid frames of welded steel carry roof purlins by means of little hangers suspended from the soffit of the girders that stand at their full height above the roof plane.[42] The exterior walls are divided between and beyond the frames by free-standing mullions set at 10-foot intervals, and this module is further subdivided by an upper fixed sash of clear glass and two lower movable sash of sandblasted glass. The service facilities and small classrooms of Crown Hall are confined to the lower floor, which is constructed according to a conventional system of concrete columns supporting the main floor slab and concrete-block partitions enclosing the various spaces. The *Architectural Forum's* correspondent asserted that "the structural clarity of IIT's newest building is unlikely ever to be surpassed in steel," echoing with minor variation Mies's own comment, "I think this is the clearest structure we have done, the best to express our philosophy."[43]

With one exception all the buildings erected on the IIT campus after Mies's retirement were designed by Skidmore, Owings and Merrill. The first of these is the student union, Grover M. Hermann Hall, which was constructed in 1960–61 as an inferior version of Crown Hall (fig. 80). The primary structural system consists of a series of simple girders that stand clear above the roof but are supported by columns set in from the ends of the girders, so that the vertical members can be seen only on the inside of the building. The consequence is that the walls of dark-tinted glass are pure curtains divided only by the thin mullions. The architects followed the same design and the same structural system for the John Crerar Library

(1961–62) but adopted a questionable plan for the interior in which the main entrance lies a full level below grade while the chief public facilities such as the catalog and the circulation desk are on the level above.[44] The twenty-story IIT Research Tower (1963–65), designed by Schmidt, Garden and Erickson, and the Arthur Keating Gymnasium (1965–67), from the Skidmore office, represent independent essays of which the latter is unusual by virtue of its four tinted-glass elevations in factory sash. In the two final buildings of the decade, however, the architects turned to strictly Miesian forms established more than twenty years earlier: the centers for Life Sciences (1966–67) and for Mechanical and Aerospace Engineering (1967–68) are exact copies of Alumni Memorial Hall except that the presence of air conditioning in the newer structures made the older movable sash unnecessary.

The postwar growth of the University of Chicago was perhaps quantitatively equal to that of IIT, but the already extensive area of the older institution made it less noticeable. The first wave of new construction was devoted almost exclusively to the expansion of the medical school: between 1950 and 1966 ten new buildings and wings were added to the existing plant, including the Argonne Cancer Research Hospital (1952), which is operated by the university for the United States Atomic Energy Commission. The expansion of the main academic campus to the east along the Midway began with two building groups that brought Eero Saarinen to the Chicago architectural scene for the first time. His initial work is the dormitory known as Woodward Court and constructed in 1957–58 on Woodlawn Avenue at 58th Street, across the street from the Robie house. The second is the far more impressive law-school complex erected in 1958–60 on the south side of 60th Street adjacent to the existing law group done in Henry Ives Cobb's Tudor style. Saarinen respected the formal continuity that had been maintained over the years on the campus, and he took great pains to adapt the rhythms and proportions of his own work to those of the older buildings without in any way imitating the past (fig. 81). The law-school group includes a concrete-framed library sheathed in folded (or more accurately, pleated) glass walls, a circular auditorium with exterior walls in the form of an eight-point star, and a low rectangular classroom wing. The three main units form an L in plan, the two arms embracing a pool and fountain in the open area facing the Midway.

The Saarinen work ushered in a period of great architectural diversity on the visually stable and conservative campus. In Stanley R. Pierce Hall, a dormitory constructed in 1959–61, Harry Weese and Associates used the oriel windows and the warm brickwork that they had already employed effectively in inner-city apartments (fig. 82). The trustees moved to the other end of the architectural spectrum when

Fig. 79. Illinois Institute of
Technology. Crown Hall, State Street
at 34th, 1955–56. Ludwig Mies van
der Rohe and Pace Associates,
architects.

Fig. 80. Illinois Institute of
Technology. Grover M. Hermann
Hall, 33rd Street near State, 1960–61.
Skidmore, Owings and Merrill,
architects.

178

Fig. 81. University of Chicago. Law School group, 60th Street between University and Ellis Avenue, 1958–60. Eero Saarinen and Associates, architects.

Fig. 82. University of Chicago. Stanley R. Pierce Hall, 5514 South University Avenue, 1959–61. Harry Weese and Associates, architects.

81

82

Fig. 83. University of Chicago. School of Social Service Administration, 60th Street at Ellis Avenue, 1963–64. Ludwig Mies van der Rohe and J. Lee Jones, architects.

Fig. 84. School of Social Service Administration. Main-floor plan.

Fig. 85. School of Social Service Administration. Main lobby and general meeting space.

83

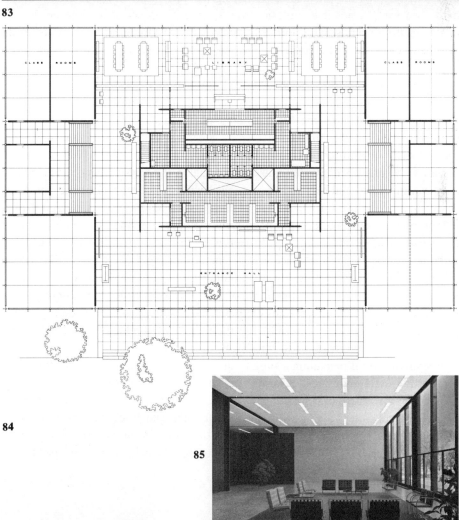

84

85

they chose Mies van der Rohe to design the new building for the School of Social Service Administration, erected in 1963–64 as the third step in the university's expansion into the residential area south of 60th Street. But before construction began the decision plunged the institution deeply into the urban ecology of which it had long appeared to be ignorant. With available land in the area north of the Midway running out, the administration adopted a plan in 1960 to extend the campus into the densely built Woodlawn ghetto, which suffered from all the ills that afflicted such areas elsewhere in the city. The resulting friction was intensified when the city council passed an ordinance in 1961 designating two pieces of university property south of 60th Street as renewal areas, and was brought close to the danger point when the university adopted the practice of protecting its "turf" with steel-link fences topped by barbed wire. A possible explosion was averted by an act of wisdom on the part of the ghetto residents, who founded The Woodlawn Organization in order to demand and to be granted a voice in all subsequent plans affecting both the university and its neighbors. The result was that the renewal of the border area was carried out in a reasonably peaceful manner under neighborhood control.

Mies's building remains so far the prize work of the 60th Street row (figs. 83–85). The welded steel frame, the black-painted mullions and fascia panels, the broad panes of glass—all the familiar elements—are here modified from the archetypal form in such ways as to give the building a paradoxical combination of weight and density with great openness that makes it unusual in the Miesian canon. The interior plan is symmetrical and carried out in a split-level two-floor arrangement: the public spaces occupy the central area, from which stairways lead at both ends upward half a floor to classrooms and downward to faculty offices (fig. 84). The main feature is the two-story lobby that measures 40 feet in depth by 120 feet in length and serves as both a public circulation space and a general meeting area (fig. 85). The extensive open volume in this relatively small building, the glass wall that allows the inner space to merge with the broad expanse of the Midway outside, the austere geometric harmonies set forth in partitions of cream-colored brick, space dividers of walnut paneling, and black steel handrails—all these features combine to make the lobby the handsomest interior space in Mies's Chicago work.

The architectural pendulum swung to the other extreme in the Henry Hinds Laboratory for the Geophysical Sciences, constructed in 1967–69 from the plans of I. W. Colburn Associates, working with J. Lee Jones as a collaborating architect. Reinforced concrete framing with waffle floor slabs and brick bearing walls under limestone sheathing form the structural basis of a work in the new fashion of plastic or sculptural masonry. Colburn's love of what might be called a modern picturesque style is here expressed in his own highly personal idiom of slender, nervous towers, pierced free-standing slabs, and heavy projecting masses. Few can handle this neo-medievalism well, but he is one of the masters. Competition for architectural attention at the University of Chicago, however, appears to have been permanently ended by the monstrous Joseph Regenstein Library, designed in the Skidmore office under the direction of Walter Netsch and built on the former site of Stagg Field in 1967–70.[45] It cost more than $20,000,000 to complete this repository for 3,000,000 volumes; yet for all its size and intricacy, it is expertly designed to provide the scholar with a full measure of comfort and to place him as close as is physically possible to the books of his particular discipline—the latter a problem of peculiar difficulty because of the multidisciplinary character of much contemporary research. The exterior appearance of the huge building makes it formidable in its overwhelming mass, but the narrow slotlike windows and the vertical bands of limestone were again dictated by the desire to establish some formal unity with the Tudor Quadrangles.

Lying outside the campus but close to it physically and associated with it in its curriculum is the Lutheran School of Theology, built at 55th Street and Greenwood Avenue in 1966–67 as Perkins and Will's contribution to the university's architectural ménage (figs. 86, 87). The three connected buildings that form a U in plan are elongated prisms carried on reinforced concrete Vierendeel trusses that are lifted a full story above grade by a structural system unique to the Chicago area. The chief compression members in this system are four squat piers cruciform in section and pyramidal in silhouette above a flaring base. Hinged or rocker bearings at the tops of these piers carry the massive bottom chords of the trusses, which extend longitudinally in pairs, one for each of the three main enclosures. The clear span is 110 feet center-to-center of the bearings, but the truss is cantilevered 32 feet beyond the bearing at each end.[46] This structural tour de force, derived directly from the forms of Vierendeel-truss bridges with parallel chords, is partly hidden by the dense vertical tracery of the upper elevations, but the piers and the lower chords are prominent enough to suggest something of its full character.

Nothing in the scholastic history of the city demonstrated the magnitude of the postwar education boom more forcefully than the creation of the Chicago campus of the University of Illinois. And it might be added that nothing better demonstrated the ruthlessness of the educational empire builders and their political allies. It was ridiculous that the metropolitan branch of a leading institution of higher learning like the University of Illinois should have been confined for twenty years to a junior college thrust into the lake on Navy Pier, and the trustees' decision in 1957 to establish a proper city campus was long overdue. But the desperate need for land in an age of endless inflation and of organized rapacity in the consumption of urban space quickly brought out the worst in those responsible for implementing the decision. The campus, which was expected to serve at least twenty thousand students, required a minimum of one hundred acres, and so the trustees turned their attention to finding open land lying in or near the city that was properly located for access and for neighboring residential development. With astonishing unconcern for the recreational needs of the metropolitan inhabitants, the trustees in 1959 selected as their first choice the extensive field known as Miller Meadow in the Forest Preserve area of suburban Maywood. The commissioners of the Forest Preserve District had through the years steadfastly refused to give up any forest land, and they had no intention of losing their wisdom and foresight in this instance. The university trustees next considered Meigs Field, the small airport laid out for private planes on Northerly Island, the peninsula extending south of the Adler Planetarium.[47] This choice bordered on idiocy: it would have been nearly inaccessible and useless for residential construction, and the inevitable development of commercial services would have completed the ruin of the lakefront in the vicinity. The third choice, Garfield Park on the West Side, would have wrought equal damage to the urban fabric, but a suit to prevent the alienation of parkland was decided by the state Supreme Court in favor of the university early in 1961. The bitter opposition of civic organizations and local residents, however, forced the trustees to abandon their plan the following month.

Meanwhile, the municipal government in the person of the mayor made the one intelligent and enlightened proposal in the whole sorry business. As early as 1958 he had suggested that the railroads using Dearborn, LaSalle, and Grand Central stations (the three south-of-the-Loop properties) move their trains into Union Station, so that the university could build its campus on the large area of vacated land, and the trustees had tentatively accepted the idea even before the Miller Meadow fiasco. It was similar to the proposal for station rearrangements made long ago by Burnham and Bennett, and there was every reason to adopt it: Union Station and its associated coach yards included plenty of reserve capacity; the affected rail lines crossed the Pennsylvania Railroad access tracks at either Englewood or at the big Archer Avenue–21st Street ganglion and the Burlington tracks at Western Avenue; the clearance of the trackage and its replacement by a great university with its surrounding development would have conferred immeasurable benefit on the entire city. Like all enlightened civic plans in the postwar age, however, it died because of the inertia of the railroads and the failure of the city to compel them to relinquish their property. Instead, the power of the municipality was used to do maximum

183

Fig. 86. Lutheran School of
Theology, 55th Street at Greenwood
Avenue, 1966–67. The Perkins and
Will Partnership, architects.

Fig. 87. Lutheran School of
Theology. Plaza floor plan.

86

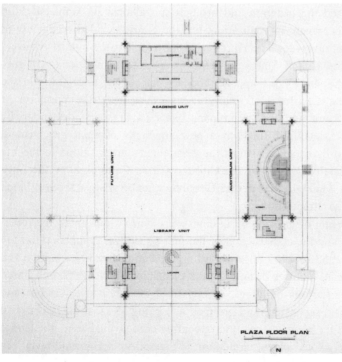

87

damage when it could have been used to obtain maximum advantage for the city.

The final choice, proposed by Mayor Richard Daley in September 1960 and officially recommended by the site-selection committee in February of the following year, was the West Side neighborhood surrounding Hull House and bounded by Harrison, Halsted, Taylor, and Morgan streets and Blue Island Avenue. A densely built area of homes, apartments, restaurants, bars, and shops, it was a multiethnic enclave predominantly of Greek, Mexican, and Italian character with perhaps the liveliest community life of any neighborhood in the city. It offered many advantages for a university, to be sure—accessibility to public transportation, proximity of part-time employment for students, the Loop a mile to the east and the West Side Medical Center a half-mile west, and an area of substandard dwellings that was already in process of renewal—but these were far outweighed by the destruction of a neighborhood and the uprooting of people, businesses, and traditions. Compounding the injury was the arbitrary way the Chicago Land Clearance Commission declared the entire neighborhood a renewal area and recommended demolition of 98 percent of the structures standing within it. A community organization known as the Harrison-Halsted Group under the leadership of Florence Scala vigorously opposed the program and brought suit against the university and various city agencies to prevent its realization, but the courts decided repeatedly in favor of the institutions involved. The Harrison group reached the end of the road in May 1963, when the United States Supreme Court refused a hearing on successive dismissals of the suit by the appeals and district courts. Everything in the area except the useless Charles Hull mansion was destroyed, the purchase of land having already begun and the preliminary plans having been drawn up by Skidmore, Owings and Merrill. In this way a new university campus was created, and its benefits were to be weighed against the permanent damage done to the life of the city. It was officially designated the Chicago Circle Campus after the huge circular interchange of Kennedy, Ryan, and Eisenhower expressways about a block to the east of its Halsted Street boundary.

The plan and the design of individual buildings were carried out under the direction of Walter Netsch, and the construction of the first phase was completed in little more than two years, 1963 to 1965 (figs. 88–91). The campus exhibits unique and permanently controversial features because of the principles on which Netsch based this grand scheme: the various buildings, except for those devoted to science and engineering, are planned, separated, and grouped according to function rather than discipline; the big lecture rooms constitute a central core available to the entire campus and roofed by a focal plaza; circulation is divided into a ground-level system of local access ways and an elevated walkway that extends like an expressway from the rapid transit station on the north, through the campus on a straight line with one displacement at the plaza, to the parking areas far to the south. The functional concept underlying these principles was that of emphasizing social communication as much as classroom and library work, but unfortunately Chicago weather through much of the academic year inhibits even such primitive forms of communication as girl-watching. The various buildings extend in irregular, roughly parallel lines on either side of the central walkway, which acts as a unifying spine centering on the broad and rather forbidding area of concrete that roofs the lecture center. Construction is everywhere reinforced concrete and brick except for the costly granite slabs that form the elevated walkway, not merely as surfacing but as the material of the deck itself.

The design of individual buildings was carried out under principles adopted to impose visual unity on this diversity of functions, so that if there is little at the Circle of architectural distinction, the balanced grouping of the different masses yields impressive, highly urbanistic vistas. All structural systems represent variations on reinforced concrete framing characterized by a material of uniform strength and minimal reinforcing. The differences in load and hence size among individual members are expressed by the coarseness of the aggregate, which is exposed by sandblasting the surfaces: the lighter elements have the finer aggregate, the heavier the coarser. The emphasis everywhere is on durability, and all the hard abrasion-resistant surfaces are exposed, the concrete frames, precast concrete sash, brick infilling, and granite walkway and posts along the edge. This hardness of surface is harsh and unrelieved, so that the campus is in no way visually pleasing except when it is filled with people on a comfortable, softly lighted spring or autumn day. Each building type has its own scale, again graded like the aggregate and the structural members, and the utilities common to all of them are left exposed underneath the concrete floor structure. A fundamental system of proportions derived from the rectangle of the Golden Section was used throughout the campus as a purely formal device, although one might raise the question whether the concept has not long ago lost its mystical and symbolic meaning. A final measure of unity arises from the presence of amber-tinted glass in all windows, which was thought to render shades unnecessary but which actually underscores the necessity of leaving the control of natural illumination in the hands of the building's occupants. The concrete frames of the various buildings are all strictly rectangular except in the lecture center, where the sectorial shape of the enclosures dictated a radial system of girders.

Among individual buildings the science laboratory center, the office tower, and

Fig. 88. University of Illinois, Chicago Circle Campus, Halsted Street from Harrison to Taylor. Phase I, 1963–65. Skidmore, Owings and Merrill and C. F. Murphy Associates, architects.

Fig. 89. University of Illinois, Chicago Circle Campus. University Hall, 1963–65. Skidmore, Owings and Merrill, architects.

88

89

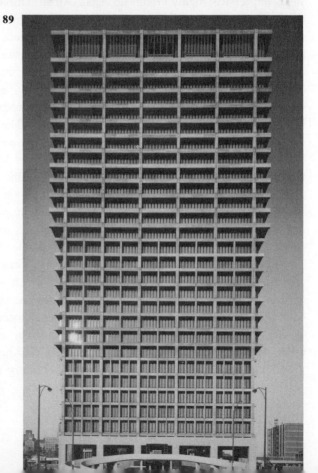

Fig. 90. University of Illinois, Chicago Circle Campus. Library, 1963–65. Skidmore, Owings and Merrill, architects.

Fig. 91. University of Illinois, Chicago Circle Campus. Classroom group, 1963–65. Skidmore, Owings and Merrill, architects.

90

91

the library are most prominent for their size and their architectonic character. The building housing the science and engineering laboratories is unique in the campus group because of its giant scale and its steel roof frame (fig. 88, left background). In order to free the interior of columns the architects adopted a two-way system of steel girders to support the roof over a clear transverse span of 75 feet and a longitudinal span of 112 feet between columns. This framework is carried by two rows of tapering concrete columns standing outside the long elevations, the individual columns being 60 feet high and 5 feet square in section at the base. The walls themselves are windowless bearing elements of oversize brick uniform in color with all other brickwork on the campus. University Hall is a twenty-eight story tower housing faculty and administrative offices in which the concrete frame constitutes the entire means of formal expression (fig. 89). Instead of following the usual practice of diminishing the sectional area of the column as loads and bending moments diminish from bottom to top, Netsch elected to decrease the number of columns. The bay span in the wall is 7 feet 6 inches for floors three to eight, doubled for the next eight stories, then doubled again for the remaining thirteen. At the third floor the whole system of wall frames is supported on a massive rigid bent in which a huge ring girder transfers the wall loads to six pierlike columns. The proportions of the various heights marked off by particular column spacings, taken in successive pairs, are close to the Golden Section ratio: five floors to eight yields a ratio of 1/1.6, and eight to thirteen a ratio of 1/1.625.[48]

The library at the Circle Campus is distinguished by an emphatic horizontality of structure and thus stands in strong contrast to the office skyscraper but in harmonious association with the adjacent plaza (fig. 90). The most prominent elements of the exposed frame are the deep longitudinal girders that are supported in pairs at the ends of blunt brackets cast integrally with the columns. The paired arrangement made it possible to reduce the depth of the girder necessary for the long spans and thus to avoid the concomitant sacrifice of vertical space. The transverse girders are Vierendeel members adopted so that the openings could be used for the passage of ducts, conduits, and other utilities. The modest classroom buildings are constructed of ordinary column-and-beam frames that are distinguished only by the window-wall panels of precast concrete frames and tinted glass (fig. 91). They represent the human scale on the campus, and their little clusters set off by grassy areas and a few trees offer an intimacy and warmth missing among the larger buildings. The passage between groups of these buildings at ground level, however, is often rendered forbidding by the merciless wind-tunnel effects produced by the overhead walkway.

Circle Campus, indeed, can in no way be regarded as an unqualified success: the building of it rested on damage to the neighborhood that has not been undone by any subsequent programs of community activities; its second phase, placed under construction in 1967, extended the campus still farther into the surrounding area and pushed the parking lots deeper into residential and commercial land on the periphery. The new additions include three fantastic spatial agglomerations in the Arts and Architecture, the Science and Engineering South, and the Behavioral Sciences buildings, which were planned on the basis of an eight-point star, although it is difficult to discover the symbolic or functional basis of this odd form. The campus is full of bold and novel elements, some of undeniable power, and it has led to a comparatively enlightened form of urban rehabilitation in the area lying between it and the Medical Center, but in its day-to-day working life it satisfies neither its students nor its faculty. They are separated from each other, from the harsh objects that they must use in the educational enterprise, and from the community they ultimately exist to serve.[49]

Northwestern University produced nothing as grand as the Circle Campus, but the total volume of building that came with the great expansion initiated in 1955 was comparable in quantity and it was eventually marked by two distinguished works of architecture as well as the creation of the very soil on which they stand. Numerous additions to the professional schools and hospitals on the Chicago campus provided much needed space, but they did so by replacing the attractive landscaped strip along Superior Street with a collection of ill-assorted and unattractive buildings. The Evanston campus, whose original bounds were substantially filled out with the completion of the Technological Institute in 1941, fared far better until an unwise decision of 1969 led to irreparable damage to the original campus plan. Blocked from further acquisition of land in Evanston because the city could not afford to drop any more property from the tax rolls, the trustees decided in 1961 to follow the Chicago practice of filling in the lake along the existing shoreline. In this way sixty five acres of land enclosing a lake-connected lagoon were added in 1962–64 to provide space for the ambitious building program that had already been adopted.[50] The first five buildings to occupy the new site were designed by Skidmore, Owings and Merrill under the direction of Walter Netsch, who deliberately sought the maximum diversity in his choice of forms, except for the low glass-fronted computer center and heating plant, which are identical in external appearance though by obvious necessity radically different in their internal arrangements.

The second structure to be erected in the lakefill group is the Lindheimer Astronomical Research Center, constructed in 1965–66 on the northeast corner of the fill to place it as far as possible from the haze and smog of the surrounding metropolitan area (fig. 92). The center consists of three parts radically distinct in function, structural character, and appearance. One is the building proper, which is composed of two hemispherical domes housing a sixteen-inch and a forty-inch telescope and the curtain wall enclosing the stairways and elevators providing access to the elevated instrument floors. These domes and other enclosing walls are folded or ribbed sheet metal carried on a light internal framework of steel. Second, entirely hidden by the metal coverings and separated from their structural frames, are the concrete mountings of the telescopes that are carried by piers resting on independent footings and caissons. Third and most conspicuous of all is the external space frame or three-dimensional truss that supports and braces these seventy-foot-high, lightly clad hollow spaces against the storms of the exposed site. This white-painted framework, strongly etched against the sky or the shore, introduces a dynamic quality into the static observatory shapes that unites space and structure into a single form.

The largest and most impressive of the lakefill buildings to arise under the authorship of Walter Netsch is the Core and Research Library, erected immediately behind Deering Library in 1966–69. This model work of library planning for which faculty committees worked with the architects through two years of preliminary study is divided above its associated plaza into three connected pavilions devoted respectively to an undergraduate core collection and to research collections in the humanities and the social sciences. Below the plaza level are the public, administrative, and service spaces—catalog, circulation desk, offices, and the like—and the reference and periodical departments. Several fundamental characteristics of structural and functional planning place the Northwestern library in the front rank of university facilities. The defining spatial principle in each tower is a circular-radial stack system with central reading areas and a geometrically appropriate arrangement of concrete framing elements, all placed in a square-prismatic envelope. The radial scheme appears in the elevations of the towers through the device of setting the rectangular embayments enclosing the study carrels along radial lines, as though someone had sliced across four mutually perpendicular chords and through the sectorial elements of an immense cylindrical volume. The result is that the pavilions exhibit a strong vertical pattern on the exterior that is formed by the narrow windows and the projecting ribbons of limestone. The interior planning of the library is a masterly example of providing a great diversity of reader spaces while bringing those spaces into the closest proximity to the book stacks. Lounges, studies, reading rooms, audio-visual centers, and lecture areas were designed to allow for the simultaneous presence of 3,200 persons pursuing all the possible activities that the library

191

Fig. 92. Northwestern University,
J. Roscoe Miller Campus, Evanston,
Illinois. Lindheimer Astronomical
Research Center, 1965–66. Skidmore,
Owings and Merrill, architects.

92

generates. This lavish space combined with sumptuous furnishings suggests that the Northwestern facility is a model of extravagance, but precisely the opposite is true: its unit cost of $30 per square foot of net interior area is below that of comparable university libraries erected in the postwar years.[51]

The excellence of the new lakefill buildings, however, was offset by an extraordinary blunder with respect to the existing campus along Sheridan Road. As I noted in *Chicago, 1910–29,* the campus plan in its prominent aspect along the thoroughfare is a shallow arc containing a mixture of buildings and informal areas of small groves and bordering shrubs balanced on either side of the broad Deering Meadow. In 1969 the trustees decided to locate the new buildings for the schools of education and business administration in such a way that their intrusive bulk cuts directly across the arc at right angles to its chord and extends outward to the edge of the sidewalk along the street. The plan as spatial form and sequence has been permanently damaged and the broad sweep of meadow and woodland has been destroyed by this thoughtless intrusion. It recalls the far worse decision to drop Mies van der Rohe as the architect of the IIT campus and makes us realize that the educational establishment, like the military and the industrial, has an inherent need to destroy the human qualities of the environment, for it is only in this way that money and practical demands can be fully served.

In the scholastic community of Chicago De Paul University and George Williams College had long been stepchildren; yet when the building program of the sixties reached boom proportions, they were destined to share richly in the bequests and grants that made it possible and to emerge suddenly into the architectural front rank. De Paul cast its faded little campus into the shadow at one stroke when it erected the Arthur J. Schmitt Academic Center in 1965-67 on a lofty terrace well above Seminary Avenue (1100W) in the block between Belden (2300N) and Fullerton (2400N). C. F. Murphy Associates here produced a stately example of the new plastic-sculptural style done in mass concrete, its "New Brutalist" surface carefully roughened by refined mechanical devices. The gravity loads and horizontal forces of the Schmitt center are divided between shear-wall cores and twenty massive hollow piers disposed around the periphery, eight on each of the long elevations and two on each of the short. George Williams College, founded in 1890 by the YMCA to train leaders of social and humanitarian organizations, moved its Chicago campus to Downers Grove in 1965 and focused its new buildings around the Leisure and Creative Arts Center, designed by Mittelbusher and Tourtelot and opened in 1967 (fig. 93). The center is one of the few works of concrete shell construction in the Chicago area: the swimming pool is roofed by five parallel shell vaults set with their long axes on the transverse line, and the gymnasium by a groin vault supported only at its corners by pier-buttresses sloping in the line of thrust. The shells are four inches thick and are supported by posttensioned concrete ribs that provide unobstructed floor areas for both enclosures of 112 × 112 feet.

The plastic forms of concrete and brick appeared in a growing number of schools and ecclesiastical buildings scattered through the metropolitan area in the decade of the sixties. Among schools none could compare in size, prestige, architectural quality, and the wealth of its district with the West Branch of New Trier Township High School, erected near the Forest Preserve area of Northfield in 1964–66 from plans jointly prepared by the Perkins and Will Partnership, the Architects Collaborative of Cambridge, Massachusetts, and the landscape designer Lawrence Zuelke (fig. 94). The campus embraces six buildings joined by covered walkways and disposed around a sunken central court. The academic and library buildings are constructed of reinforced concrete frames with brick panels, and the gymnasium, swimming pool, and music and drama buildings are covered by roofs on steel frames supported by brick bearing walls—all of them reflecting the new spirit of richness and mass but here disciplined by the geometry of structure. Pure brick masses in smooth planes characterize two schools from the Harry Weese office: one the almost romantically picturesque Institute for the Visually Handicapped, a training and therapeutic center in the West Side medical enclave constructed in 1964–65 (fig. 95); and the other the Chicago Latin School, more imposing and rectilinear in character, opened in 1969 on Clark Street at North Avenue.

A number of suburban churches erected in the decade of the sixties carried the romantic revival into ecclesiastical design. The temple of North Shore Congregation Israel in Glencoe (1961–63) brought Minoru Yamasaki to the Chicago area for the first time, and he characteristically transformed the tense and dynamic structural forms enclosing the tabernacle space into wedding-cake architecture by means of creamy white paint and amber-tinted glass. No such pretty covering hides the fairy-castle brickwork in the pierced screens, the nervously attenuated columns, and decorative groin vaults of Saint Anastasia Church in Waukegan (1964–65), the most fanciful work of self-expression from the hand of I. W. Colburn (fig. 96). More sober in its prismatic forms and unbroken planes but equally rich in the brickwork of its smooth bearing walls is the Holy Apostles Church, erected at the same time in Westchester from the plans of Loebl, Schlossman, Bennett and Dart (fig. 97). By the time the church was placed under construction Edward Dart had become the leading ecclesiastical architect of Chicago, and it was under his direction that the building was designed. For the most part its structural system is as orthodox and

Fig. 93. George Williams College. Leisure and Creative Arts Center, 555 Thirty-first Street, Downers Grove, Illinois, 1965–67. Mittelbusher and Tourtelot, architects.

Fig. 94. New Trier Township High School West, Happ Road, Northfield, Illinois, 1964–66. The Perkins and Will Partnership and the Architects Collaborative, architects.

Fig. 95. Illinois Institute for the Visually Handicapped, Illinois Medical Center, 1115 South Wood Street, 1964–65. Harry Weese and Associates, architects.

93

94

95

Fig. 96. Saint Anastasia Church, 624 Douglas Avenue, Waukegan, Illinois 1964–65. I. W. Colburn, architect.

Fig. 97. Holy Apostles Church, 2501 South Wolf Road, Westchester, Illinois, 1964–65. Loebl, Schlossman, Bennett and Dart, architects.

96

97

traditional as its liturgy, but the twentieth century intrudes in the nave, where the concrete roof slab is supported at its corners by concrete columns with flaring octagonal capitals. Dart employed common forms of brick and timber construction in the irregular and highly expressive geometry of the Emmanuel Presbyterian Church at 1850 South Racine Avenue in the city, the third work of its kind to be completed in 1965. His masterpiece, however, is the Benedictine Abbey of Saint Procopius in Lisle (1968–70), a multibuilding complex superbly shaped to fit the contours of the moraine on which it stands. The largest and most costly of the new churches brought ecclesiastical building to the immediate periphery of the Loop: the Seventeenth Church of Christ, Scientist, designed by the Harry Weese office and erected in 1966–68 on the little triangle bounded by Wacker Drive, South Water Street, and the narrow flank of Executive House, is a semicircular structure under a conical roof supported by radiating concrete girders. It is a handsome and imaginatively planned work for its awkward site, but one might raise the questions whether it belongs formally to this world of skyscrapers and whether the city can afford to remove from the downtown tax rolls a thin pie-slice of property valued at $466,000.

NOTES TO CHAPTER 4

1. The construction of the Ferguson wing was preceded by a short-lived legal controversy that arose because the trust fund established by Benjamin F. Ferguson in 1905 was to be used, according to the terms of his will, for statues and monuments to be erected in the city's parks. Little of it was devoted to this end, and so a half-century later it had grown to a sizable sum of money. Since modern sculpture has little memorial or emblematic character and since there is as a consequence a limited popular interest in it, the trustees of the institute understandably felt that the money could be put to better uses. Various parties led by the Chicago Heritage Committee argued that to expand the museum facilities constituted an illegal use of the fund, but the controversy soon died.
2. For the history of the South Side Redevelopment Program, see under Renewal and Reconstruction, chap. 5. The precise area to be covered by the Mies project was a square roughly half a mile on a side bounded by Cermak Road (2200S) on the north and South Parkway (now Martin Luther King, Jr., Drive, 400E) on the east. A good part of this space is now occupied by Stevenson Expressway (p. 243), the new Mercy Hospital buildings, and a few marginal industrial and commercial properties along Cermak Road.
3. A minor but pointless extenuation raised by various spokesmen for the Chicago Park District and the Plan Commission had to do with the condition of the lakefront in the area of 23rd Street. In 1948 a number of railroad companies organized the Railroad Fair, a traditional combination of exhibits and pageantry which was

held on the 23rd Street site during the warm-weather seasons of 1948 and 1949. When the temporary tracks and structures were cleared the park area was left in a disreputable condition, and since the Park District had no funds to restore the landscaping, it was happy to be relieved of the consequences of its irresponsibility by the new exposition authority.

4. Quoted in Mike Royko, "Lakefront Isn't a Wasteland—But It Will Be," *Chicago Daily News,* 16 December 1966, p. 3.

5. The narrow slablike form of the Federal Court House is revealed in its major dimensions: it measures 112 × 364 feet overall in plan and 382 feet in height; the bays are uniform at 28 feet square, except where interior courtrooms required that they be doubled to 56 feet; the thin mullions are actually 8-inch wide-flange members of I-section; the total gross floor area is 1,389,000 square feet.

6. Donald Canty, "Chicago's Dearborn Street . . . ," *Architectural Forum* 122(April 1965):40.

7. For the earlier City–County Building of Holabird and Roche, see Carl Condit, *Chicago, 1910–29* (Chicago: University of Chicago Press, 1973), pp. 178–79.

8. The difficulty in financing the Civic Center arose because the investment houses would not buy the bonds of the Public Building Commission until the commission owned the land, cleared the site, and was prepared to start construction, the last of which it could not undertake unless architectural and engineering plans were on the way to completion. The federal grant was necessary to complete the plans, and the state authorization to purchase land and demolish the existing buildings. The Chicago Public Building Commission was established in 1956 with its own bonding power, and under the capable administration of Robert W. Christensen, appointed director by Mayor Daley in 1961, the organization proved to be the solution to the problem of moving many public projects from the planning to the execution stage.

9. The distribution of functions by floor in the Civic Center is as follows:

   Lower basement: Chicago Board of Health Laboratories
   Upper basement: board of health offices and public spaces
   Floors 1–2: lobby, exhibit, and utility spaces
   Floors 3–5: various offices
   Floors 6–8: offices of clerks of courts and other judicial officials
   Floor 9: mechanical and electrical equipment
   Floors 10–12: offices of clerks of courts and other judicial officials
   Floors 13–28: Municipal Court of Chicago and Cook County courts
   Floor 29: Library of the Chicago Law Institute
   Floor 30: Supreme Court and appellate courts of Illinois
   Floor 31: mechanical and electrical equipment

   The gross floor area of the building is 1,465,723 square feet, of which 1,050,000 square feet represent net usable space. The cost of construction when the building was opened in 1965 was $49,725,000 (a unit cost of a little under $34 per square foot of gross area), and the total cost, including land, demolition, and furnishing, was $87,000,000.

10. Cor-ten steel was developed by the United States Steel Corporation in 1933 for railway hopper cars, but it does not appear to have been used in building before the Chicago Civic Center and the John Deere Company administration building at Moline, Illinois, designed by Eero Saarinen and erected in 1963–64. The word Corten is a trade name telescoped from the phrase corrosion-resistant high-tensile.

11. "Big Steel: Chicago's Civic Center Complete," *Architectural Forum* 125(October 1966):32.

12. Reyner Banham, "The Missing Motel," *Listener* 74(5 August 1965):192. The exhibition to which Banham refers was mounted by the Museum of Modern Art in New York in the summer of 1965 under the title "Modern Architecture USA."

13. The other members of this party were the Chicago architects Charles F. Murphy, Jr., and Norman Schlossman, and Picasso's biographer Sir Roland Penrose, but Hartmann's repeated visits and his friendly personal relations with the artist were the chief factors in the success of the enterprise.

14. Although the statue weighs 272,000 pounds, the relative thinness of the plate of steel in contrast to its extensive flat area posed a problem in wind resistance and uniform stress distribution the solution of which required modifications in the form of the base and the body. The engineers of the steel company sent an aluminum model embodying the necessary changes to the artist and proceeded with the work only after securing his approval. It was a lesser modern-day parallel to Gustave Eiffel's designing the steel frame for the Statue of Liberty (1883–86).

15. "The Picasso Square," editorial, *Saint Louis Post-Dispatch;* reprinted in *Chicago Sun-Times,* 30 September 1967, p. 27.

16. The architectural distinction of Dearborn Street becomes obvious if we set down in order the entire group of important buildings that lined the street in 1971 from the north bank of the river to Congress Parkway, a distance of less than a mile. In order from north to south, with location by block and dates of completion, they are the following:

    Marina City group, north bank of river (1964, 1967)
    Blue Cross–Blue Shield, Wacker Drive (1968)
    Civic Center, Randolph–Washington streets (1966)
    Unity, Randolph–Washington streets (1892)
    Brunswick, Washington Street (1965)
    First National Bank, Madison–Monroe streets (1969)
    Inland Steel, Monroe Street (1957)
    Montgomery Ward Store, Adams Street (1891, 1964)
    Marquette, Adams Street (1894)
    Federal Court House, Adams Street–Jackson Boulevard (1964)
    Monadnock, original, Jackson Boulevard (1891)
    Monadnock, addition, Van Buren Street (1893)
    Fisher, Van Buren Street (1896)
    Old Colony, Van Buren Street (1894)
    Manhattan, Congress Parkway (1891)

    The dates reveal the concentrated character of the building periods and the long hiatus that separated the earlier from the later, a time in which all the buildings except the Marquette and the Monadnock suffered varying degrees of deterioration.

17. The roof frame of McCormick Place was designed for the relatively high live load of 80 pounds per square foot. The supporting system of this 829,600-square-foot slab required 1,050 separate trusses ranging in length from 30 to 120 feet. These lengths were fabricated on the ground and lifted into place, with very few exceptions, by long-boom cranes located on the ground because the existing 4½ inch floor slab would not support the weight of heavy erecting machinery.

    This floor slab was increased to a depth of 13½ inches in the new building, suffi-

cient for a floor load of 400 pounds per square foot. The structural system supporting the slab is a straightforward work of concrete construction: cylindrical columns
spaced on 30-foot centers and terminating in large mushroom capitals carry the
common two-way or waffle grid cast integrally with the slab.

A serious defect in the original McCormick Place and a major factor in its destruction by fire was a sprinkling system of only one thousand heads. This number
was increased to twenty thousand in the new hall.

The area that was to be occupied by Mies's exposition project of 1953 was in
large part given over to the east end of Stevenson Expressway and to the new building for Mercy Hospital, which was founded in 1849 and which constructed the first
of its own quarters in 1863 at 26th Street and Calumet Avenue. This increasingly
antiquated red-brick structure survived until 1967, when it was replaced by the
handsome concrete-framed building that C. F. Murphy Associates designed.

18. The first Chicago landmarks, listed in chronological order, were the following (* =
demolished by 1971):

*First Leiter Building, William Le Baron Jenney (1879)
Rookery, Burnham and Root (1885–86)
Glessner house, H. H. Richardson (1886–87)
Wirt Dexter Building, Adler and Sullivan (1887)
Auditorium Building, Adler and Sullivan (1887–89)
Monadnock Building, Burnham and Root (1889–91)
Carrie Elizabeth Getty Tomb, Adler and Sullivan (1890)
*Garrick Theater Building, Adler and Sullivan (1890–92)
Charnley house, Adler and Sullivan (1892)
*A. W. Sullivan house, Adler and Sullivan (1892)
*Meyer Building, Adler and Sullivan (1893)
*Stock Exchange Building, Adler and Sullivan (1893–94)
Reliance Building, D. H. Burnham and Company (1894–95)
Francis Apartments, Frank Lloyd Wright (1895)
Fisher Building, D. H. Burnham and Company (1895–96)
Heller house, Frank Lloyd Wright (1897)
Gage buildings, Holabird and Roche (1898)
*Cable Building, Holabird and Roche (1898–99)
McClurg Building, Holabird and Roche (1899–1900)
Carson Pirie Scott Store, Louis Sullivan (1899–1906)
Schoenhofen Brewing Company powerhouse, Richard E. Schmidt (1902)
Chapin and Gore Building, Richard E. Schmidt (1904)
E-Z Polish Company factory, Frank Lloyd Wright (1905)
Magerstadt house, George W. Maher (1906)
First Congregational Church of Austin, Guenzel and Drummond (1908)
Hunter Building, Christian A. Eckstrom (1908)
Robie house, Frank Lloyd Wright (1908–9)
Carl Schurz High School, Dwight H. Perkins (1908–10)
Grover Cleveland Elementary School, Dwight H. Perkins (1909–10)
Dwight Building, Schmidt, Garden and Martin (1911)
*Edison Shop, Purcell, Feick and Elmslie (1912)
Reid, Murdoch and Company Building, George C. Nimmons (1912–13)
Krause Music Store, Louis Sullivan (1922)

Third Unitarian Church, Schweikher and Elting (1937)
5551 University Avenue Apartments, George Fred and William Keck (1937)
IIT Campus, Mies van der Rohe (1941–56)
860–80 North Lake Shore Drive Apartments, Mies van der Rohe (1949–52)
Inland Steel Building, Skidmore, Owings and Merrill (1955–57)

19. This amazing contempt for educated world opinion, paralleled only by the destruction of the Larkin Building in Buffalo, is alleged to have inspired one of Wright's most devastating comments: "It proves that you cannot trust theologians with spiritual matters" (possibly apocryphal; source unknown).

20. The foundation was established under the will of Ernest R. Graham, cofounder of Graham, Burnham and Company and Graham, Anderson, Probst and White and the leading example of an architect who had grown wealthy by investing in the successful buildings that these enormously prolific architects designed.

21. The sale of publicly built housing to private owners had two precedents that were established when the federal government sold the planned communities built by the Farm Security Administration (the so-called Greenbelt towns) and by the Tennessee Valley Authority to privately financed organizations. The Racine houses were sold to their tenants under the following terms: initial down payment of $200, followed by another of $250 payable over twenty-five months without interest; monthly payments not to exceed rents, at the time $87 to $149 per month; interest rates ranging from 0 to 6 percent, scaled to income so as to keep payments at a level of 21.8 percent of income; acceptance by the CHA of a 100 percent forty-year mortgage of $1,715,000, the cost of the project in 1950. Those unable to purchase homes were offered apartments in other CHA projects.

22. Wentworth Gardens contains 422 units in 37 walk-up apartment blocks. Dearborn Homes, built under federal sponsorship, marks the CHA's first step in the direction of high-rise blocks: the 800 units are divided among 16 seven- and nine-story buildings. The total development cost was $9,491,700 in 1950.

23. Two earlier projects reveal the architectural quality of the Ogden group, but their location in areas of extreme atmospheric pollution has brought about marked deterioration in their external appearance. Loomis Courts (1950–51), at Loomis Street (1400W) and 14th Place, was designed by Loewenberg and Loewenberg, Harry Weese, and John Vander Meulen; its 126 units, divided between two seven-story buildings, were built at a cost of $12,104 per unit. Archer Courts (1951–52), in a trapezoidal area bounded by Princeton Street and the Pennsylvania Railroad east and west and by Archer Avenue and 23rd Street north and south, was the work of Everett Quinn and Alfred Mell; two seven-story buildings with outside galleries contain 147 units constructed at an average cost of $12,673.

24. The one exception to construction in brick walls, though it remains typical in all other respects, is the William Green Homes, designed by Pace Associates and constructed in 1960–62 on Division Street (1200N) east of Ogden Avenue. The 1,096 units are distributed through five fifteen-story and three sixteen-story buildings in which the spandrels between the exposed columns are precast concrete panels. The baywide window groups and the subdued articulation of the walls give the Green project a little more visual interest than exists in comparable high-rise groups.

25. W. Joseph Black, "The Renewed Negro and Urban Renewal," *Architectural Forum* 128(June 1968):63.

26. For Newman's articles, see the Bibliography. The total development cost of the Taylor project was $70,091,800, of which the construction cost was $62,791,800. The unit construction cost was thus $14,508 and the unit development cost $16,195.

27. The last project composed only of family units is Lake Michigan Homes, erected in 1962–64 at 41st Street and Lake Park Avenue from the plans of Shaw, Metz and Associates.

28. The site of the Hilliard Center was long a barren slum of scrap-metal yards, weed-filled lots, and decayed row houses, but it was once rich in a vanished tradition that is particularly expressive of Chicago's more sumptuous days. The neighborhood long ago was a notorious center of prostitution known as the Levee. For ten years after the turn of the century its most celebrated institution was the Everleigh Club, established and presided over with regal splendor by the Everleigh sisters, who had made it possibly the most elegant house of prostitution in the country. Patrons met their partners of the night or weekend in a library or music room or a gallery of painting and sculpture, the choice depending on the artistic tastes of the habituées. The club was closed by Mayor Carter Harrison in 1911, and the sisters left the city, reputedly with a million dollars derived from the unspeakable pleasures they offered in their silken chambers.

29. The Hilliard Center was planned as a showpiece of public housing, but its imaginative structural system and the use of the slip-form technique in constructing the outer walls held the unit cost well below the average at the time. The twenty-two-story buildings were designed for 173 apartments each, and the sixteen-story for 182 units each, for a total of 710 units. The site area is 12.5 acres, yielding a density of 56.8 units or somewhat under 200 persons per acre. The construction cost was $7,926,134, or $11,164 per unit, and the total development cost was $11,650,000, or $16,408 per unit. The minimum age for tenancy in the apartments reserved for the elderly was sixty-two years, and the average age at the time of completion was sixty-seven years. These units include various special features necessary for the safety and comfort of the elderly: waist-high ovens, easily reached cabinets, sliding windows, sit-down showers (no tubs), and safety handles.

30. The properties and population of the CHA in 1969 were as follows: 35,587 dwelling units; 150,666 residents, divided between 51,980 adults (34 percent) and 98,686 children (66 percent). The foregoing quantitative data on public housing have been provided largely by the Office of Public Information, Chicago Housing Authority.

31. Quoted in Betty Washington, "Slums Here Called Worst in Nation," *Chicago Daily News,* 10 July 1969, p. 6.

32. Mike Royko, "The Anatomy of Dick Daley," *Chicago Daily News,* 20 August 1968, p. 3.

33. Milburn P. Akers, "Illinois: An Age of Decadence," *Chicago Sun-Times,* 10 September 1962, p. 24.

34. The ACLU–CHA plan, if implemented, would constitute a model program of public housing. Its chief provisions are the following: (1) three housing units must be constructed or leased in white census areas for one in black areas and in buffer zones one mile deep surrounding them; (2) new buildings containing family units must be limited to three-story height and 120 persons, except under "unusual circumstances" which might allow a maximum of 240; (3) the CHA must attract low-income white families to public housing, since qualified whites outnumber blacks two

to one; (4) in new projects 50 percent of the units must be reserved for people in the immediate neighborhood; (5) public housing units now mostly white must be desegregated.

35. Quoted in Barbara Polikoff, "How Can We Lose When We're So Sincere?" *The Brief,* September 1970, p. 2. Judge Austin's original decision was upheld on all appeals.

36. See table 5.

37. Both the college building and the curriculum represent the culmination of an educational program that was inaugurated shortly after the Civil War. In response to a need generated by a rapidly growing population, especially in the Chicago area, the Illinois General Assembly in 1869 authorized the establishment of normal schools in the counties of the state, following the precedent of Cook County, which had been operating such a school at Blue Island since the end of the war. The County Board of Supervisors opened a new school in 1869 in the town of Englewood, but the control of this institution passed to the city of Chicago when it annexed the smaller community in the same year, with the consequence that the training of teachers became the obligation of the Chicago Board of Education. The curriculum, originally covering only six months, was extended to two years in 1899 and to four for undergraduates in 1938, when the state authorized the granting of bachelor's and graduate degrees. By the end of the Second World War the Englewood campus had become grossly inadequate, and so various branches were established throughout the city in 1949. These proved to be temporary expedients, and in 1957 preliminary plans were drawn up to establish a new campus on the North Side and to enlarge the existing campus at Englewood. At the same time the board of education in consultation with the Ford Foundation broadened the educational program at both facilities to emphasize a general liberal education as well as teacher training.

38. In addition to the two teachers colleges (that on the South Side is now designated Illinois State College) the municipal system embraced the following junior colleges, collectively designated the Chicago City College, in 1969–70:

    Amundsen-Mayfair Campus
        Amundsen Unit, 5110 North Damen Avenue
        Mayfair Unit, 4626 North Knox Avenue
    Bogan Campus, 3939 West 79th Street
    Fenger-Southeast Campus
        Fenger Unit, 11220 South Wallace Street
        Southeast Unit, 8600 South Anthony Avenue
    Kennedy-King (formerly Wilson) College, 7047 South Stewart Avenue
    Loop College, 64 East Lake Street
    Malcolm X College, 840 West 14th Street
    TV College, 5400 North Saint Louis Avenue (incorporated with Chicago Educational Television Center)
    Urban Skills Academy, 153 North Michigan Avenue
    Wright Campus, 3400 North Austin Avenue

A new West Side campus designed by C. F. Murphy Associates to take the place of the old Malcolm X building and the first to be built specifically as a junior college was under construction in 1970.

39. "Parks versus Schools," *Chicago Daily News,* 3 June 1970, p. 18.

40. The Institute of Design was originally established in the old Marshall Field residence on Prairie Avenue in 1937, but it closed within a year and was reestablished by its intrepid founder in 1939 in a bakery at 247 East Ontario Street. It lived a precarious existence during the war, and when Moholy-Nagy died in 1946 the school was compelled to accept absorption into Illinois Institute of Technology as the price of survival.

41. *Built in USA, 1932–1944* (New York: Museum of Modern Art, 1944), p. 96.

42. These frames are spaced 60 feet on centers and span the full width of 120 feet between columns. The girder or horizontal portion of the frame is 6 feet deep. The purlins are cantilevered 20 feet at each end beyond the end frames. This primary structure constitutes a clear example of Mies's willingness to sacrifice organic form to the ruling geometry. Since the girder is welded throughout its depth to the columns, it is a fixed-end beam that transforms the three members into a rigid frame. The pattern of bending in the frame is such that an organic form would have a maximum depth at the knee, where there is a complex pattern of high stresses, a somewhat smaller depth at the midpoint, with its lesser stress concentration, and a minimum depth at the base of the leg, where the bending moment is theoretically zero. The structural engineer of Crown Hall was Frank J. Kornacker.

43. "Mies' Enormous Room," *Architectural Forum* 105(August 1956):105. The structural clarity and purity of Crown Hall were at least equaled in Mies's Galerie des zwanzigsten Jahrhunderts in Berlin (1968–69).

44. The Crerar is a research library of science, technology, and medicine established in 1894 by the industrialist John Crerar. It was housed in the Marshall Field Store until 1920, when it was moved to its own quarters in an office building constructed in that year at 86 East Randolph Street. Rising costs and fixed endowment compelled its merger with the IIT library in 1962.

45. The site of the Regenstein Library was once the university's sports stadium, Amos A. Stagg Field, but it is now a National Historic Landmark commemorating the first self-sustaining nuclear reaction, achieved under the direction of Enrico Fermi on 2 December 1942. The strip of lawn west of the library contains Henry Moore's sculptural celebration of this dubious accomplishment, a mushroom cloud in bronze entitled quite obviously *Atomic Energy*. The name Stagg Field—and it is no more than that—came from the name of a former football coach and represents the surviving memento of the days when the University of Chicago not only had a football team but competed effectively with its Western Conference rivals.

46. The individual Vierendeel truss at the Lutheran School is 175 feet long, 36 feet deep, and two feet thick, and is cast integrally with the floor and roof slabs. The individual bearing was designed for a maximum load of 2,800,000 pounds.

47. For Meigs Field and other depredations of the lakeshore in this area, see pp. 141–46, 243, 258.

48. The proportions of the sides in the Golden Section rectangle are $1/\{1 + \frac{1}{2}[-1 + \sqrt{5}]\}$, or $1/1.618$ to three decimal places. The irrational number arises from the quadratic equation that must be written to determine the ratio of the sides in the Pythagorean figure.

49. The eight-point star as a basis for building form has been ably defended by Walter Netsch in an elaborate set of concepts that he calls *field theory,* although the doctrine bears no discernible relation to the meaning of that expression in physical science

and mathematics. Its ultimate validity appears to rest on the assertion that it would provide students with an environment which would "expand their conception of space." (Quoted in John Morris Dixon, "Campus City Continued," *Architectural Forum* 129[December 1968]:33.)

50. The Northwestern University fill measures approximately 1,200 × 2,600 feet exclusive of the new swimming beach at its north end and was emplaced by methods long followed by the city of Chicago. A permanent seawall of rubble topped and flanked on the outer face by huge rectangular blocks of limestone formed a cofferdam enclosure within which sand from the Indiana dunes was deposited by clamshell buckets that lifted it from the top of decked barges.

51. The Core and Research Library was designed for the simultaneous use of 2,200 undergraduates, 800 graduate students, and 200 faculty members. In addition to bookstacks, special and general areas for reading, talking, and lounging, and communications facilities, there are 18 seminar rooms, 136 faculty and graduate studies, and 2,000 carrels. The total construction cost, including furnishing and architects' fees, was $9,897,939. The unit cost of $30 per square foot may be compared to $30.50 for Indiana University, $32.50 for the University of Chicago, and $40.50 for the University of Michigan.

5. Renewal and Reconstruction

Like public housing, the renewal program of Chicago, on final balance, resulted in damage to urban life and to the urban fabric that considerably outweighed the benefits it conferred. The need for this complex program of municipal, state, and federal activities arose from the failure of the private sector of the economy to provide not only low-cost housing for the poor but also housing, services, and neighborhood amenities for middle-income groups who wanted to live in the inner and intermediate areas of the city. The decline of this aspect of the urban economy was obvious throughout the nation, but in Chicago there were ominous indications that its continuing and increasing deterioration was irreversible. The sociologist Pierre de Vise discovered that the proportion of the national population and employment in the metropolitan area began a steady decline in 1960, contrary to the rapid expansion that occurred up to 1920 and the average stability that persisted through the succeeding forty years by virtue of a gradual change from continuing rise to leveling off and descent. The recognition that the federal government would have to provide at least part of the funds for housing and urban services for all economic levels up to upper income came shortly after the end of World War II and was embodied in the renewal provisions of the National Housing Act of 1949, under which the government was to pay two-thirds of the cost of land, demolition, and construction in renewal projects (the proportion was to rise in later years). This act was modeled to a certain extent on the Blighted Areas Redevelopment Act passed by the Illinois General Assembly in 1947. Surprisingly enough, however, in view of the subsequent failure of official planning in Chicago, various private and public bodies working cooperatively anticipated the state's concern by two years.

In 1945 Michael Reese Hospital, centered at 29th Street and Ellis Avenue (540E) on the South Side and the largest privately endowed hospital in the United States, established the South Side Redevelopment Agency and provided it with a planning staff under the direction of Reginald R. Isaacs. The hospital, like its neighbor Illinois Institute of Technology, was faced with a familiar problem: situated at the edge of one of the worst slums in the nation, unwilling to abandon a $10,000,000 investment, and under the necessity of drastically expanding its facilities, its directors realized that its survival depended on the creation of a decent human habitation in its South Side neighborhood. IIT, which was involved in similar concerns because of the campus expansion it had initiated in 1940, was the first institution to join the hospital in the redevelopment program. Other public agencies and organizations and two business establishments with local investments soon followed—the Chicago

Housing Authority, the Metropolitan Housing and Planning Council, the Roman Catholic Archdiocese of Chicago, the AFL–CIO, the printing firm of R. R. Donnelley and Sons, and the Illinois Central Railroad. The program drawn up by Isaacs and his staff took on a grandiose character, looking eventually to the rebuilding of the immense area extending from Roosevelt Road (1200S) to 47th Street, and from Burnham Park along the lake to the Pennsylvania Railroad's main tracks (450W), an area of about 5.5 square miles, but the plan that finally emerged was marked by a well-balanced association of high-density housing, open spaces, schools, and shopping centers, with industry segregated near the rail lines on the east and west sides. The execution of this scheme began in 1947 with the assembly of land for the expansion of the hospital's campus, and by 1970 a piecemeal and defective realization of other parts included the Reese building program, the IIT campus, three renewal projects, Mercy Hospital, a high-rise middle-income apartment, and a great battery of public housing groups, most of which we considered in the preceding chapter.

The first residential project in the South Side renewal program was Lake Meadows, built by the New York Life Insurance Company under the federal plan of cost sharing but retained by the sponsor as a profitable investment (fig. 98). Constructed in 1952–60 along South Parkway (later Martin Luther King, Jr., Drive) from 31st Street to 35th Street and designed by Skidmore, Owings and Merrill, the extensive group includes ten high-rise apartment buildings, an office building, a shopping center, recreational facilities, and a community club. The benefits that came from the construction of Lake Meadows are obvious: the seventy-acre site is almost excessively generous; the apartments and the subsidiary facilities are racially integrated; the individual buildings are well-designed works of glass-and-steel curtain-wall construction, the best being the Miesian block at 600 East 32nd Street; the landscaping is pleasant though conventional; the community center is a handsome piece of window-walled timber framing under a low pyramidal roof. One has to inquire more closely to see the real and disturbing failures, but the first is prominent in the very appearance of the project. Planned like Le Corbusier's skyscrapers in a park, it shows no respect for streets or children: most of the thoroughfares were taken up to preserve the continuity of the park setting, the recreational facilities were clearly designed for adults, and the empty, lifeless lawns are just as clearly prohibited to children. Such community life as there is is confined to decorous bourgeois activities in the community club. The 2,033 apartments of the project took the place of 3,416 units originally occupying the site, the new built to rent at three times the previous levels, and since Chicago has never developed a relocation program, nearly all the families dispossessed from the area added to the already dangerous overcrowding of the neighboring ghetto.[1]

The New York Life Insurance Company, benefited by liberal tax concessions, earned a comfortable return on its investment and in 1969 sold the project to the Draper and Kramer Company of Chicago for $28,500,000. In these simple economic facts one may discover why urban renewal came to be called Negro removal in the black communities. The city's Land Clearance Commission assembled the land at the going price and sold it at a reduction in cost to the sponsor, who was then granted tax concessions in addition to this bargain. In its failure to retain title to the land it had cleared and in its acceptance of the principle that the sponsor is to earn a profit from his investments, the city guaranteed that the supply of low-income housing was to shrink still further while space was made available for a few of the respectable middle classes. Beyond these features there was the underlying practice of declaring a neighborhood a renewal area, then demolishing everything in it down to the ground. The damage wrought by this bulldozer approach was compounded in the Chicago program by delays averaging nearly eight years between clearance and reconstruction. The process was to be repeated again and again until the opposition to these iniquities finally reached a level that compelled a somewhat more civilized means of dealing with the problem.

Although Michael Reese Hospital had initiated the planning and redevelopment program for the South Side, its own contribution to the new housing supply was delayed until the late fifties. The hospital's renewal program outside its own campus is the group of apartment buildings known as Prairie Shores, constructed in 1959–62 along South Parkway between 28th and 31st streets from designs prepared by the architectural firm of Loebl, Schlossman and Bennett, the structural engineer Eugene A. Dubin, and the landscape architects Stephanie S. Kramer and Sasaki and Walker (fig. 99). The 1,677 apartments are divided among five nineteen-story buildings that are set at an angle to the line of the boulevard with their narrow elevations toward the artery. The consequence of this simple device is that the high, narrow volumes form a series of partially overlapping screens that provide strong vertical accents in the form of lofty planes standing free among the long horizontal lines of the South Park area. This screenlike quality is enhanced by the skillful treatment of the curtain walls composed of ribbon windows above narrow spandrels painted in a different color for each of the buildings. If the Prairie Shores project suffers from the same defects as Lake Meadows, it at least provides an excellent example of how the brittle curtain walls fashionable in the fifties served more effectively as pure space delineators than any other architectural mode.

As IIT, the Chicago Housing Authority, various private developers, and the board of education filled in block after block in the South Side plan, one large area bounded by Michigan and Prairie Avenue and running from 26th Street to 31st

Street lay cleared and fallow for so many years that it came to be known simply as "the Gap," as though it were some kind of topographic feature. It was finally developed as a middle-income housing enclave by the building and real estate firm of McHugh-Levin Associates working in collaboration with the Community Renewal Foundation. Known as South Commons and placed under construction in 1966, it was designed by Ezra Gordon and Jack M. Levin and L. R. Solomon–J. D. Cordwell Associates as a model example of a renewal project that it was hoped would answer some of the objections to the usual variety. The group of 1,406 apartments and houses with their associated shopping center, malls, school, and recreational facilities was consciously planned as a bridge between the low-income public housing along State Street and Prairie Avenue and the upper-middle-income apartments on South Parkway—in other words, as an economically as well as a racially integrated community. The site plan and the design of individual structures were carried out in consultation with the city's Department of Urban Renewal and a panel of architects under Edward Dart and Charles Goodman, who selected the McHugh-Levin scheme as the best of a number of alternative plans. The result is a diversified association of twenty-one- and twenty-two-story towers, walk-up apartments, row houses, and small scattered parking lots, arranged in groups around pools, playgrounds, malls, and commons. With costs partially subsidized under section 221(d)3 of the National Housing Act, rents were held below market levels for the various accommodations offered, the range at South Commons extending from $95 to $350 per month, and the prices of town houses covered a wide spectrum of $27,000 to $60,000. Construction continued through 1970, by which time the aims appeared to be realized: a stable community was forming, with 95 percent of the leases renewed; the racial composition was somewhat unbalanced at 70 percent white and 30 percent black, but the income spread of tenants and owners was extraordinary, ranging from $6,400 to $60,000 per annum.

Close to the South Side Redevelopment area physically, chronologically, and in its dependence on the success of all rebuilding enterprises is the Hyde Park–Kenwood Renewal Program, the largest, most thoroughly organized, and most effectively controlled on the local level among similar programs in the United States. Yet its success hangs in the balance, for the fundamental reason that unless the whole city can be redone under similar circumstances, no local program can ever bring a single community to the point of continuing stability. The once spacious town of Hyde Park, extending twelve miles from 39th Street to the forests and marshlands along the Calumet River at 138th, was annexed by the city of Chicago following a popular vote on 29 June 1889, but the present neighborhoods of Hyde Park and

Fig. 98. Lake Meadows, South Parkway (now Martin Luther King, Jr., Drive) from 31st Street to 35th Street, 1952–60. Skidmore, Owings, and Merrill, architects.

Fig. 99. Prairie Shores, South Parkway from 28th Street to 31st Street, 1959–62. Loebl, Schlossman and Bennett, architects. Michael Reese Hospital in the background, along the Illinois Central Railroad line.

98

99

Kenwood cover only a small north-central part of this area. The founding of the University of Chicago in 1891, the extension of the Chicago and South Side rapid transit line in the following year, the Columbian Exposition of 1893, the Illinois Central's excellent suburban service, the proximity of Jackson Park and the lakeshore—these together guaranteed, it would seem, an attractive, flourishing, and stable community. For nearly forty years this proved true, but depression, war, crime, spreading urban blight, and the pressures of the expanding ghetto to the north and south took the inevitable toll, so that by 1950, although Hyde Park remained in many ways the most urbane and handsomest residential area in the city, the community and the university were seriously threatened. The latter, indeed, began to lose students and faculty at a rate that made a solution to the forbidding problem a matter of desperate urgency. The attack began in 1949, when the first steps were taken by private citizens through churches, synagogues, and citizens' groups to create the most democratically organized and racially balanced redevelopment program in the nation. The planning agency that undertook to translate the preliminary plans into practical action was the South East Chicago Commission, established in 1952 under the sponsorship and with the potent backing of the university.

Such local participation in urban renewal was authorized and encouraged by the Urban Community Conservation Act passed by the Illinois General Assembly in 1953, while the university's planning role was much enlarged through a grant of $100,000 from the Marshall Field Foundation in the following year. The organization, work, and initial successes of the commission and its associated planning conferences were summarized by the political scientists Rossi and Dentler in their exhaustive study of the whole Hyde Park program.

Location of the planning unit in the neighborhood and its sponsorship by a local institution probably made the Planners more sensitive to local interests and more attentive to local needs. . . . The leadership and staff functions provided by citizen organizations in the Hyde Park–Kenwood community might be best summarized under three categories:

Stabilization: The reduction of population turnover and the enforcement of local housing and zoning regulations.

Renewal Planning: The drawing up of specific proposals for the renewal of the community.

Obtaining approval: The obtaining of the support of the local community for the plan and making representations of such support to public officials empowered to make final decisions. . . . These functions were performed with some success under an informal division of labor, in which the University of Chicago acting through its

Planning Unit and the South East Chicago Commission drew up the plan and handled relations with municipal agencies while the Hyde Park–Kenwood Community
Conference took on the role of building popular acceptance of the concept of planning and publicizing the specific plans developed by the Planning Unit. . . . It is hard
to see how [metropolitan agencies] can effectively take over the functions provided
by the Conference.[2]

The physical implementation of the Hyde Park–Kenwood program began in
1954, although the plan was not officially approved and the city's share in the project authorized until 1958. The first step was an immense though carefully defined
clearance operation necessary to remove blighted areas in which housing and other
buildings had deteriorated beyond repair. This demolition was concentrated along
55th Street west of the Illinois Central Railroad embankment and along Lake Park
Avenue, adjacent to the embankment on its west side. Progressive construction in
the cleared areas was initiated in 1958 and under the stimulus of renewal work began to expand into available sites eastward toward the lake, northward to 47th
Street, and southward toward the university's property along 58th Street in 1961.
By 1970 it was obvious even to the casual visitor that an enormous amount of new
building had been completed, a volume totaling at least $300,000,000 from private
investment and another $100,000,000 from the University of Chicago and various
public agencies. This work, most conspicuous along 55th Street, includes row
houses, large elevator apartments, town houses, shopping centers, a unique center
for artists and craftsmen known as Harper Court, and small groups of public housing, which was not originally planned but was rightly demanded by the Cardinal's
Conservation Committee of the Catholic Church.

Since the redevelopment was carried on initially by the Webb and Knapp Company, the row houses and large apartments in the immediate area of 55th Street were
designed by the company's staff architect, I. M. Pei, in collaboration with the Chicago firm of Loewenberg and Loewenberg. The first of the row-house units was
completed in March 1959 at 1408 East 54th Street, an extremely simple, almost
cubical structure in buff brick closed largely at the second floor toward the street
and opened to window walls facing the small patio at the rear, a discreetly appropriate form that was repeated in all subsequent construction of the same type.[3] The
only large apartment buildings to come under the Webb and Knapp sponsorship are
the University Garden Apartments, at 1451 East 55th, designed by the same association of architects and erected in 1959–61 as one of the two pioneer works of
load-bearing screen-wall construction (pp. 58–64).[4] Outside the ruling mode of
row houses and apartments on 55th Street there are several groups of town houses

arranged as planned enclaves around central landscaped courts or plazas. The ante-
cedent for all these essays is a closed group of town houses surrounding a block-long
park together known as Madison Park Place and built at the turn of the century
between Dorchester and Woodlawn avenues approximately on the line of 51st
Street. The Pei and Loewenberg offices designed a similar group of two rows of
town houses facing an oval landscaped divider separating the two halves of Harper
Avenue between 56th and 57th streets. The prize work of this type, however, is the
Common, constructed in 1965–66 at 52nd Street and Kimbark Avenue from the
plans of Ezra Gordon–Jack M. Levin Associates (fig. 100). The combination of
simplicity, richness of texture and color, and privacy in this little group of town
houses surrounding a series of landscaped brick-paved courts continues the great
tradition of Hyde Park urbanity established long ago by the university's Quadrangles.

Among commercial structures a unique work by virtue of its social function is
Harper Court, designed by Dubin, Dubin, Black and Moutoussamy and erected in
1964–65 on Harper Avenue between 52nd and 53rd streets on land deliberately set
aside for the purpose by the Department of Urban Renewal. The university neighborhood had attracted artists, craftsmen, and teachers of music and dance from the
time the institution was founded, but the various quarters they once occupied had
to be sacrificed in the demolition of substandard structures. The court, erected by a
nonprofit ad hoc foundation with funds provided by a local bond issue and a loan
from the Small Business Administration, was consciously planned and designed to
offer artists and craftsmen a center for work and for the exhibition and sale of their
creations. The building forms an open rectangle under a traditional gable roof and
houses a variety of studios, galleries, and shops in which the rent is limited to $100
per month. It has led an uneasy existence even on these modest terms, yet it fulfills
a need that exists in many communities though it is seldom satisfied.

The Hyde Park–Kenwood Renewal Program is in many ways a model of its kind:
in spite of its great size and complexity and the great sums of money invested in it,
it has been carried out with a degree of local participation unmatched in extent and
sophistication. The level of education among the citizens of the area and their strong
institutional, professional, and intellectual commitments implied that if the job could
be done properly at all, it ought to achieve success in this community. Yet there are
signs that the essential problems remain unsolved. The chief obstacle to rounding
out the plan is 47th Street immediately west of Lake Park Avenue. A major commercial artery and the boundary between the ghetto to the north and the university
enclave to the south, its role in the redevelopment scheme was never exactly determined, and the various plans proposed for its reconstruction emerged as either so

Fig. 100. The Common, 52nd Street and Kimbark Avenue, 1965–66. Ezra Gordon, Jack M. Levin and Associates, architects. Part of the row-house group and associated plazas.

100

controversial or so insecurely founded that the necessary financing has proved elusive. As a consequence large areas of land lie fallow, strewn with the rubble of a once flourishing neighborhood, precisely in the border zone where tensions are most easily exacerbated and a genuine integration is most crucial. And for all the democratic participation, the citizens' stake in the community, and the volume of high-quality building, Hyde Park was being deserted at an alarming rate by those who could escape. Between 1960 and 1970 the community lost 27.9 percent of its population, an attrition exceeded by only four of the city's seventy-six census "neighborhoods," three in the South Side and one in the West, ghetto or border areas that had been mercilessly cut to pieces by the construction of expressways and the University of Illinois campus.[5]

Woodlawn, immediately to the south of the Midway, was one of the neighborhoods to suffer a greater population loss than Hyde Park, but its problems were among the most serious of any urban area, and the city for a long time showed a characteristic failure of responsibility and imagination in dealing with them. Planning for renewal of the community was initiated by the Department of City Planning (later Urban Renewal) in 1961, but these preliminary plans quickly led to controversy. The South East Chicago Commission, representing the University of Chicago, wanted the entire row of blocks extending the length of the Midway between 60th and 61st streets cleared for academic use and proposed that the additional strip extending to 63rd Street be declared an official redevelopment area. The Woodlawn Organization, under the leadership of Arthur M. Brazier, demanded a voice in any deliberations affecting the neighborhood and was supported in the issue by the Industrial Areas Foundation, an organization established chiefly by Saul Alinsky to develop community power under local leadership, ideally to the point where it could control its own destiny in its relations with city hall. The consequence of these conflicts was that the 60th Street plan was repeatedly revised and eventually resubmitted in the summer of 1966 with official federal approval. The new proposal granted the university very nearly everything that it had requested, in return for which the Department of Urban Renewal sold a large block of land lying between 61st and 63rd streets along Cottage Grove Avenue, at the west end of the renewal area, to an association of the Woodlawn Organization and the Kate Maremont Foundation. Their intention was to build a middle-income housing group of small walk-up apartments rather than the high-rise variety that the Department of Urban Renewal wanted.

This occasion proved to be one of the few times the department listened to the voice of the low-income majority, its role ordinarily being that of representing the interests of the municipal government in the city's residential neighborhoods. With the land acquired and funds available under section 221(d)3 of the National Housing Act, TWO began building a model housing project in 1969 on the basis of plans prepared by Stanley Tigerman. The final scheme, developed after the study of one hundred preliminary plans, called for a total of 504 apartment units distributed among 27 different buildings. The architect based the plan of the individual block and the arrangement of all of them in the group on a module of six apartments occupying two floors, this working unit susceptible to a variety of arrangements which were ultimately established in such a way that each module would be associated with its own enclosed outdoor space. These modular-spatial units were then arranged in a linear series on both sides of Cottage Grove as the central artery, which was paralleled by subsidiary walkways extending through the interior areas. This simple but perfectly functional plan is matched by the economical construction of the buildings: the loads are divided between timber frames and concrete-block partitions; floors are built up of a thin layer of concrete poured over plywood panels carried on timber joists; walls are brick sheathing. The rectangular blocks of brick are reduced to the point of monastic severity, but the generous windows provide some relief. The whole project, drawing for its construction on the maximum participation of small black contractors, is in many respects an admirable example of its kind, designed and erected without any cooperation from the Department of Urban Renewal, but it suffers from two defects: its 504 units are less than half the number displaced by the expansion of the university, and its income limits are too high for the neighborhood.[6]

The largest of all the Chicago renewal projects to be concentrated on a single site expressly cleared for the purpose is Carl Sandburg Village, covering the four full blocks running from Division Street (1200N) to North Avenue (1600N) between Clark Street and LaSalle and a half-block strip along the east side of Clark between the street and an interior alley (figs. 101, 102). The Chicago Land Clearance Commission (later merged into the Urban Renewal office) cleared the site in 1960–61 and offered it for sale under the stipulation that the developer was to build a total of 1,200 units together with adequate shopping facilities. Before the project was rounded out nearly ten years later the number of dwelling units had risen to more than double the requirement, but the shopping center largely remained in the planning stage. The developer who offered the highest bid for this plum of prime urban land was a syndicate composed of various real estate firms, building contractors, and architects, among whom Arthur Rubloff and Company was the largest and most potent. The city council once expressed some concern over the replacement of low-rent apartments by high-rent skyscrapers and high-priced town houses,

216

Fig. 101. Carl Sandburg Village, original area, between Clark and LaSalle streets, from Goethe Street to Burton Place, 1962–66. Louis R. Solomon, John D. Cordwell and Associates, architects.

Fig. 102. Carl Sandburg Village. General view of high-rise apartments, town houses, and plaza areas.

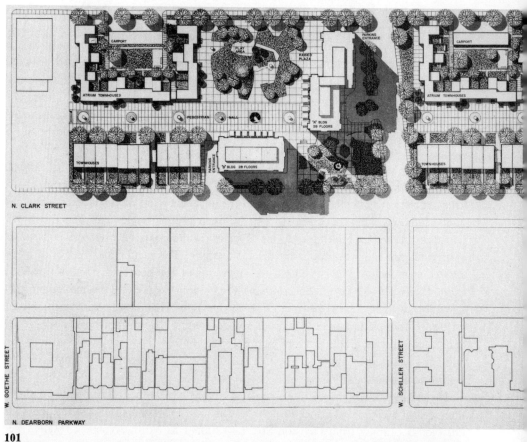

101

102

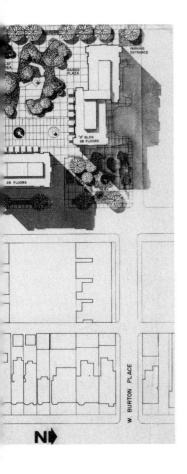

and John J. Egan, director of the Catholic Archdiocesan Conservation Council, urged that the project be balanced between high-rise luxury apartments and middle-income units, but these prejudices were quickly brushed aside in the face of the profitable possibilities arising from the demand for inner-city apartments.[7] The only proposal that survived among those offered by the archdiocesan council was the requirement of racial integration, which the city council established by an amendment to the original acceptance act.

Construction of the huge project began in the spring of 1962 on an eight-acre area between Goethe Street (1300N) and Burton Place (1500N), from plans prepared by Louis R. Solomon–John D. Cordwell Associates, a relatively young firm of Chicago architects who quickly rose to the front rank in the number of commissions for large apartment towers. The original plan was altered in various details during the successive expansions of Sandburg Village, but the essential balance and arrangement of building types remained. The first group, containing a total of 1,902 dwelling units, consisted of twenty-eight-story rental towers arranged in two linear series, ten-story blocks of cooperative apartments, atrium houses disposed in three U-shaped groups, trilevel town houses, and associated elevated and contoured plazas, walled playgrounds, studios, malls, a central exhibition area, and kiosks. The rent schedules adopted in 1962 called for a maximum figure of $270 per month for apartments and $360 for town houses, and the sale price of the atrium houses was fixed at $38,000 per unit, all of which have subsequently been raised.[8] Additional plans for a primary-grade school and a center for the performing arts have so far gone unrealized. The first phase of the Sandburg project was completed in 1966, and the second, which added another high-rise tower, a group of fourteen town houses, and four artist's studios, was built in 1968–69. This expansion required the demolition of the Red Star Inn, a celebrated German restaurant constructed in 1899 as another of those eating institutions intimately bound up with the higher hedonistic aspects of Chicago's history. The final phase added still another skyscraper and a variety of lower structures on the east side of Clark Street to bring the final total of dwelling units to 3,166.[9]

Neither the structural engineering nor the architectural design of Carl Sandburg Village is in any way distinguished. All the buildings are supported by conventional column-and-girder frames of reinforced concrete, and all of them, whatever their size, are characterized on the exterior by the common association of exposed concrete columns and brick panels alternating with baywide window groups, a formal quality which when repeated in block after block of structures conveys nothing so much as the tediousness of most modern architecture. The site planning, especially in the areas of plazas, malls, and low-rise groups, is much better, possessing an urbanity that is always missing in the skyscrapers-in-a-park schemes. But there are serious charges that can be brought against Sandburg from the standpoint of essential urban values: once again an entire neighborhood, ranging in character from marginal shops and apartments to the baronial Red Star Inn, was destroyed, and in its place rose a high-income housing enclave heavily weighted on the side of efficiency and one-bedroom apartments designed for the single tenants who guarantee community instability. The vast project was frankly designed to act as a stimulus to the redevelopment of the blighted areas to the west in the hope that the more respectable classes would continue to be attracted to the Near North Side, but the ironic result was that the blighted areas remained intact while high-rise developers ruthlessly destroyed the elegant and irreplaceable homes of the rich Gold Coast to the east.

Like proposals for rail terminal unification in the Burnham period, renewal and redevelopment plans fell like autumn leaves before the wind from the Department of Urban Renewal, but after the Sandburg completion only one more was to reach the stage of fulfillment by 1970. The little Noble Square project, limited to 482 units on a triangular site bounded by the diagonal Milwaukee Avenue, Kennedy Expressway, and Division Street, is a middle-income group sponsored and developed by the Foundation for Cooperative Housing and McHugh–Levin Associates, its severely simple design and site planning the work of the Perkins and Will office. Out of a total of fifty-four plans variously designated as redevelopment projects, conservation areas, and study areas, only eighteen could be regarded as having been fully completed by 1970 or presumably on the road to this state, like Hyde Park. An extensive rehabilitation project on the Near West Side adjacent to the Circle Campus of the University of Illinois was initiated in 1967 as a good example of spot clearance combined with the renovation of existing structures and was well advanced by 1970.

In spite of all the studies, the paper programs, and the expensive booklets with colored plates, there was little to show for the effort beyond these eighteen—high-rise luxury apartments along Lincoln Park and the South Shore, a depressing middle-income slab of concrete in Uptown, blocks of rubble and weeds where demolition had cleared the way for new construction that has never appeared, and closed streets for malls still to be built; yet the real disaster areas like the West Side ghetto of Lawndale and its Appalachian equivalent of Uptown sank further into poverty and blight, accompanied by the steady demolition of dwelling units. Agencies, councils, federations, conferences, foundations, ecclesiastical institutions, university departments, manufacturing and financial establishments vied with each other in producing inquiries and proposals for the improvement of Lawndale, but there was nothing to show for this tiresome repetition of the academically and politically fashionable "urban studies" beyond a few row-housing groups, some rehabilitation here and there, skyscraper islands of public housing, and a handful of schools.

Considered from a narrowly financial standpoint, there was no question that the urban renewal programs brought gains to the city and to certain segments of its economy. The total tax income of the first renewal projects more than doubled over the return from the same areas before rebuilding.[10] A great quantity of substandard property, with its attendant high cost of fire and police protection, was of course eliminated and replaced by sound construction, but only through the bulldozer technique that brought maximum and continuing hardships to the previous residents. In the case of businesses displaced by clearance, the city suffered a serious net loss because a high proportion of owners left the city or abandoned their businesses, the total of such loss running to 26.5 percent of all displaced properties as of 1966. Clear gains secured without damage to the urban fabric and society came from the construction on vacant land of hospitals, schools, recreational facilities, and industrial structures, and similar advantages with relatively small losses arose from the construction of new buildings on the periphery of renewal areas. But these gains were offset by disadvantages and losses beyond the fundamental one of uprooting populations. Foremost, perhaps, was the intolerable time lag between the designation of a renewal area and the execution of the project, which has run to an average of 7.75 years in Chicago. This was a consequence of a more fundamental failure, namely, a belief on the part of planners and redevelopers that whole communities, neighborhoods, or cities can be replanned and rebuilt as though they are inanimate machines or structures. This pernicious notion, reinforced by the idolatry of computers and systems theory, results at best in the failure to analyze a renewal scheme into workable and manageable units, with the consequent loss of time in execution, and at worst in sheer human suffering and degradation. Associated with this is the misunderstanding of the purpose of renewal arising from old New Deal misconceptions. The aim of renewal, indeed the ideal aim of all urban building, is not simply slum clearance but the rearrangement of urban technology to serve everyone equally well and at maximum benefit. But this cannot be accomplished if the city relinquishes its title to renewal land and its control of general land use and building construction to the developer who employs both only for his personal advantage.

The renewal program of the city was concerned primarily with residential, commercial, and industrial land that had to be rescued from blight in order to be restored to a useful and remunerative role in the urban economy. An essential part of such a program, however, is the improvement and extension of public and civic spaces, especially those devoted to recreational and cultural activities, and it is here that the city failed even more conspicuously than in middle-income housing. By contrast, the reconstruction of the city's core through the office-building boom of the sixties was accompanied by a considerable body of civic art that arose from the impetus to corporate prestige. The sponsors of the more elegant and expensive buildings began to vie with each other in laying out landscaped plazas to serve as foreground to the office towers, and in a few instances these little openings in the dense urban fabric revealed some civic distinction. The first of these spaces to grow from corporate munificence is the plaza of the old Daily News Building, completed in 1929, but the Field Enterprises, owner of the *Chicago Sun-Times* and later the *Daily News,* initiated the postwar development when they added a plaza in 1958 at the east end of their most undistinguished newspaper plant extending along the north bank of the river between Wabash and Rush streets (fig. 103). This richly planted microplaza is actually part of a pedestrian bridge that joins the Sun-Times Building to the space between the Wrigley tower and its annex, and thus serves as a green observation point for the stunning vista of river, boulevards, and skyscrapers that surrounds it. The space at the east end of the bridge, flanked by the two parts of the Wrigley group, is itself a plaza added by the Wrigley company in 1960–61 (fig. 104). Lying behind the ornamental screen of glass and enameled terra-cotta that joins the two buildings and including a central fountain and pool, the plaza is a deeply and pleasantly shadowed retreat on a hot day, although it is too isolated from the movement of people and vehicles that forms the lively drama of Michigan Avenue.

The rapid building up of the corridors lying along both banks of the South Branch of the river and flanked by the Wacker Drive extension on the east and Canal Street on the west introduced another group of plazas on the opposite side of the central business district. The first came in 1961 with the completion of the Hartford Building at Wacker Drive and Monroe Street (fig. 105). A slotlike space with a fountain at the river end, the Hartford court provides an opening to the river and the long travertine-paved strips that extend for three blocks over the Union Station tracks between the waterway and the three buildings of the Gateway Center, built over the years since 1963 (pp. 90–93). It was Michigan Avenue, however, that continued to bring out the best in the designers of civic space. The Apollo Savings and Loan Association, which later suffered financial collapse, was once so confident of the future that two years after its building at 430 North Michigan Avenue was completed in 1963 it added a Plaza of the Americas to provide proper foreground to the indifferent architecture of its headquarters (fig. 106). The distinguishing feature of the space is a double row of flags representing the nations of the American hemisphere, a hackneyed but colorful kind of display. The most spacious of all the plazas other than the great sweep before the Civic Center is the Pioneer Court of the Equitable Building, opened immediately south of the Tribune Tower in 1965 after the completion of the office structure (fig. 107). Only a major insurance company could afford this gesture—100,000 square feet of brick-paved space with fountain, trees, and glass-walled kiosk surrounding an escalator portal. Along the river a curving stairway descends to the original grade level, where shops, a restaurant, and the building's parking area underlie the court. The plaza contains little planting because it was meant to provide an open area defined by and providing a foreground to the river and the vivid skyscrapers of the Michigan–Wacker group. Bruce Graham, the Skidmore partner in charge of the Equitable commission, said that "in designing this court, we felt we ought to make a statement about how the river might be treated as a natural element that penetrates the metropolis. The design . . . makes you aware there is a river."[11]

The public lands under the jurisdiction of the Chicago Park District suffered steady deterioration compounded by official vandalism in the years following the Second World War, the nearly unbroken record of destruction wrought by time and municipal policy punctuated at long intervals by small additions and improvements, some so badly conceived that it would have been better if nothing had been done at all. Although most of the new constructions ranged from indifferent to atrocious, a few were prize works of architecture. The best is the little chess pavilion in Lincoln Park at the foot of North Avenue, a delicately poised cantilevered slab of concrete designed by Morris Webster. A much larger work and one of the few imaginative structures to be added to the city's zoos is the Seven Seas Panorama, an elevated tanklike enclosure built in the Chicago Zoological Park at Brookfield. Constructed in 1960–61 from the plans of Olsen and Urbain, the so-called Panorama is an aquarium for performing dolphins in the form of a steel-framed tank surrounded by an oval stadium for spectators and roofed by a glass vault.

The Lincoln Park Zoo and neighboring park areas were to receive the greatest attention, but some of it was sadly misguided. North Avenue Beach was widened to two hundred feet over the existing length of the beach from North Avenue (1600N) to Menomonee (1800N), and both the beach and the promenade were extended at the full width to Fullerton (2400N) in 1961–62, an operation that nearly quadrupled the area of this magnificent urban shoreline. The entire width of Lincoln Park was extended north from its old boundary at Foster Avenue (5200N)

Fig. 103. Sun-Times Plaza, Rush Street at the river, 1958. Atkinson and Fitzgerald, landscape architects.

Fig. 104. Wrigley Building Plaza, 400 North Michigan Avenue, 1960–61. Louis R. Solomon, John D. Cordwell and Associates, architects.

103

104

Fig. 105. Hartford Plaza, Wacker Drive between Monroe and Adams streets, 1961. Skidmore, Owings and Merrill, architects. Florsheim Shoe Company factory in left background.

Fig. 106. Plaza of the Americas, 430 North Michigan Avenue, 1965. Fred H. Prather, architect.

105

106

Fig. 107. Pioneer Court, 401 North Michigan Avenue, 1965. Skidmore, Owings and Merrill, architects.

to Hollywood (5700N) in a series of fills and landscaping steps that extended over much of the decade of 1950–60. The old and faded Zoological Garden was given a much needed addition of light and color when the little pavilion of the Children's Zoo was opened in 1959, but the garish, overscaled, and insensitive Farm-in-the-Zoo, a collection of imitation agricultural buildings completed in 1963, provided a foretaste of the brutalities that were to come. More than offsetting these additions, however, was the closing of the Zoo Rookery, a WPA project of 1936 that was the most impressive work of landscape architecture to come from the Park District staff since the days of Jens Jensen. The district's plan of 1968 for the extensive redevelopment of the Zoo would have been a total disaster had it not been for a public outcry accompanied by an imaginative proposal for rebuilding submitted by Harry Weese, a much compromised version of which was placed under construction in 1970.

The destructive forces of the Park District gathered momentum as its plans approached the grandiose scale. In 1961 the commissioners proposed the addition of a twenty-thousand-seat amphitheater for musical programs to the area of Grant Park east of Columbus Drive and below the Goodman Theater, even though the structure would have ruined this finest example of classical park design and would have far exceeded in size anything that the summer symphony program required. The proposal was bitterly fought by professional and civic organizations led by the small but vociferous Chicago Heritage Committee under the chairmanship of Thomas B. Stauffer. Lack of money and the possibility of lawsuits under the Montgomery Ward decisions (see *Chicago, 1910–29*) fortunately prevented the Park District from taking even a first step in realizing the plan. As it turned out, the Grant Park fiasco formed a prelude to the most appalling scheme in the history of lakefront degradation. In 1964 the Department of Public Works and the Park District announced a plan to widen and straighten South Lake Shore Drive from 47th Street to 67th Street, which would have required the cutting down of two thousand trees and the destruction of associated areas of lawn, shrubbery, and lagoon. After the contractor hired by the Department of Public Works had cut down five hundred trees and the Park District board had given the central lawn of Promontory Point to the military for radio microwave towers, a host of civic groups once again organized themselves for battle with the government, on this occasion under the leadership of the Daniel Burnham Committee.[12]

Opposition of such breadth and magnitude forced the city to make a show of bending before popular demand. The Department of Public Works curtailed its depredations in Jackson Park, which temporarily put an end to the provocative acts of cutting trees and uprooting lawns, and the Park District in 1966 engaged the landscape architects Johnson, Johnson and Roy to make a preliminary study as the basis for a comprehensive plan of the lakefront and to follow this with a body of recommendations for municipal action. The architects submitted a specific plan for Jackson Park in 1966 and a more comprehensive proposal two years later, but although certain of the aspects that were made public were laudable enough, they contained little that had not been proposed long ago in the Burnham Plan. The chief innovation was the nightmarish idea of an airport to be built on a polder in Lake Michigan, a monstrous scheme with a destructive potential matching its scope. Meanwhile, the Chicago architects Bruce Graham of the Skidmore office and Harry Weese offered a model plan for Jackson Park that would have restored much of its lost beauty, expanded its area, and placed the through boulevard entirely outside the park boundaries. The consequence of all this activity was that the city commissioned the planning firm of Barton–Aschman Associates in 1968 to offer an alternative plan that would have kept the "improved" traffic artery in the park, merely adapting it to the alterations proposed by Johnson, Johnson and Roy. At the same time the lakefront park system had been expanded slightly by the opening in 1965 of the little park at the west (shore) end of the fill placed for the new Central District Filtration Plant (p. 253); but this was offset by another proposal to destroy parkland for traffic, in this case to widen North Lake Shore Drive above North Avenue. This program was completed in 1969 at the usual cost of landscaped areas.

The entire series of these dismal events provided valuable lessons for those who sought to understand municipal government, especially in its public-works manifestation, as it had been developing after the Second World War. The city showed no intention of carrying out any of the valid schemes for Jackson Park, whatever their origin or their quality; instead, it offered a further revelation of what some reporters have called city-hall paranoia—the distrust and dislike of neighborhood organizations, the belief that people do not know what is good for them and do not even know what they want, the surrender to the big-money industrial and financial establishment. The behavior of officials in the Jackson Park case provided an ominous forewarning of what the citizen might expect in the future, as Paul Gapp of the *Daily News* most pointedly stated.

An imaginative plan to save trees and get the highway out of the park was conceived by two nationally prominent Chicago architects [Graham and Weese], praised by city officials, then squelched without warning or explanation.

Traffic volume estimates used by the city to document the need for the highway project were arrived at largely by guesswork.

The location of the present Jackson Park express route is in direct conflict with the city's master plan, which calls for keeping traffic out of the park. . . .

Chicago's lack of either a lakefront plan or a genuinely definitive city-wide master plan threatens to choke off all hope of rebuilding the city in an orderly aesthetic fashion. . . .

What kind of a city does Chicago want to be?

The question has not yet been answered. But the Jackson Park express route is a strong indication of what kind of city Chicago may turn out to be.[13]

Jay McMullen, in an earlier issue of the same newspaper, had correctly assessed the official mind in such matters, and although he was chiefly concerned with the long succession of Daley administrations, his characterization applies to the municipal establishment from the days of Mayor Edward Kelley, when sudden outpourings of New Deal largesse began to take the place of an ordered and humane development under a comprehensive plan.

The decision of the mayor to go ahead with the chopping down of 800 trees in Jackson Park—10 per cent of the park's total—to permit widening of S. Lake Shore Dr., portrays the curious "public works" character of Richard J. Daley's 10-year administration [grown to 16 by 1971]. . . .

While Daley has piled concrete on top of concrete, his administration has lacked a central motif, a human philosophy, a raison d'etre. Daley has been primarily a builder not given too much to fretting over human values. . . .

The traffic experts have won again. The nature lovers and conservationists have lost.

It points up the lack of any intellectual theme in the Daley administration's public works frenzy.

It is the same lack that permits the mayor to be more concerned about traffic congestion at 57th Street than he apparently is about deterioration in the city's library.

It is the same lack that permits the mayor to worry more about straightening out a kink in a highway than he does about the huge electric billboards sprouting up along those highways throughout the city.

It isn't that the mayor is anti-intellectual. It's just that his administration is dominated by un-intellectuals, the kind who would rip up 800 trees to widen a highway.[14]

As for the parks as a whole, their unhealthy state grew steadily worse: the Open Lands Project Committee of the Welfare Council of Metropolitan Chicago reported that the city's immense metropolitan area had become one of the most backward regions in the United States with respect to the preservation of open space and the establishment of adequate recreation areas. At the end of 1967 the city proper embraced 1.9 acres of parkland for every 1,000 inhabitants, behind New York, Los Angeles, Philadelphia, Boston, Detroit, and twenty-seven other cities of comparable size, in contrast with the recommendation of the National Recreation Association of

10 acres for every 1,000 persons. Moreover, as we have seen, parkland was steadily eroded away for expressways, schools, exposition facilities, and an airport, and the city had neither plans nor means for land acquisition to make up the deficit. The only redeeming aspect to this melancholy picture was the 55,000 acres of the Forest Preserve District, later to grow to 60,000 acres, but much of this land lay many miles from the inner city. The truth about the municipality itself was proclaimed in a single sentence by Jeffrey R. Short, Jr., the chairman of the Open Lands Project Committee. "The Chicago Park District, once world famous for its pioneer development of open space in the inner city, now lags far behind park systems in many other major cities."[15]

NOTES TO CHAPTER 5

1. The original rent schedule at Lake Meadows ranged from $83–$108 for efficiency apartments to $161–$189 for the three-bedroom units. The rents were subsequently raised.
2. Peter H. Rossi and Robert A. Dentler, *The Politics of Urban Renewal* (New York: Free Press of Glencoe, 1961), p. 291.
3. The row houses were designed for families and fall into two types, a larger unit of three bedrooms and 1,440-square-foot floor area exclusive of the basement (sale price at the time of construction $23,650), and a smaller one of two bedrooms and 1,152 square feet (price $19,865).
4. These apartments were designed for single persons and small families. The rent range in 1962 was as follows: efficiency, $115–$130; one-bedroom, $140–$165; two-bedroom, $175–$225. Similar in construction to the Chicago apartments and erected at the same time are the Kips Bay Plaza Apartments in New York.
5. The average loss of population and hence the loss for the city as a whole between the two censuses was 5.2 percent of the 1960 population (see table 1).
6. Woodlawn Gardens at the time of its construction was the largest low-rise project authorized under section 221(d)3. Its unit cost of $11.50 per square foot was modest enough at 1970 prices; its density of 55 persons per acre was less than half that of earlier renewal projects (115 at Lake Meadows and 140 at Prairie Shores), perhaps too low for the neighborhood; and its rent range of $95 to $160 was probably too high. Income maximums were fixed at $6,400 for a single person and $10,500 for a family of six.

   Stanley Tigerman was the leading figure among Chicago architects in his active concern with good renewal work and low-income housing. As chairman of the American Institute of Architects Chicago Chapter's Planning Committee in 1963, he persuaded the Department of Urban Renewal to establish an architectural review board to act as referee on renewal designs and to suggest improvements. The proposal bore fruit, as the South Commons project was the first to indicate.
7. On the extent of this demand, see under Marina City, p. 65.

8. The precise numbers of units in the first phase of construction at the Sandburg project were as follows: four high-rise apartments, two cooperative apartments, fifty-six atrium houses, and thirty-six trilevel town houses. The full rent schedule in 1962 was the following: studio apartment, $130–$150; one-bedroom, $152–$190; two-bedroom, $235–$270; town house, $310–$360. By 1970 minimum rents in new buildings had been raised to $180.

9. The original FHA-guaranteed loan from the Continental Illinois National Bank to the Sandburg developers was $19,878,000, but the total construction and land costs rose well beyond this figure.

10. The most spectacular increases in the tax returns of renewal projects occurred where blighted areas characterized by residential slums or marginal and derelict business properties were totally cleared and rebuilt in high-rent apartments or modern industrial facilities. In the case of Lake Meadows, for example, evaluation increased from $3,381,000 to $8,595,000, and the tax yield from $122,000 to $625,000. Sandburg Village, with Phase I still under construction, showed still better results: evaluation increased from $2,895,000 to $15,295,000, and the tax return from $151,000 to $1,146,000. The industrial renewal program of the West Side–Roosevelt–Clinton project showed the second greatest percentage increase in tax return because much of this area had been totally unproductive: evaluation rose from $1,073,000 to $3,799,000, and the tax yield from $53,000 to $286,000. Hyde Park, by contrast, showed relatively small increases because of the extensive areas of high-value property that remained untouched: valuation rose from $11,300,000 to $14,500,000 and the tax yield from $848,000 to $1,088,000. (Figures, based on 1962 tax rates and rounded out to the nearest thousand, provided by D. E. Mackelman, director, Community Renewal Program, and quoted in Ruth Moore, "The Cost of Urban Renewal . . . ," *Chicago Sun-Times,* 14 May 1964, p. 42.)

11. Bruce Graham, quoted in M. W. Newman, "A New Giant on the River Offers Lessons for the Future," *Chicago Daily News Panorama,* 17 July 1965, p. 1. The name "Pioneer Court" was chosen to memorialize the fact that the area was the site of the house built in 1816 by John Kinzie, an early trader in the Chicago area and sutler to Fort Dearborn.

12. An indication of the city's indifference to community interests was the universality of the opposition to the Jackson Park rape. Joining the Daniel Burnham Committee were the Chicago chapters of the American Institute of Architects and the American Institute of Planners, the Hyde Park–Kenwood Community Conference, South East Chicago Commission, Chicago City Club, Metropolitan Housing and Planning Council, Chicago Heritage Committee, South Shore Commission, the Woodlawn Organization, Greater Woodlawn's Pastors Organization, *Chicago Daily News, Chicago Sun-Times,* and Leon Despres, the alderman of the ward containing the park. The revised plans that the city offered were no better than the first and were quickly rejected. It was then (summer 1965) that the Plan Commission and the Department of Public Works began the usurpation of parkland for the execution of the traffic plan.

13. Paul Gapp, "The Untold Story of Jackson Park Battle," *Chicago Daily News,* 25 September 1965, p. 3. The city in the following year adopted a new comprehensive plan (see chap. 7), but it proved to be an innocuous volume since there were neither the resources nor the intention to implement it.

14. Jay McMullen, "Daley Shifts Gears—Good-by Trees," *Chicago Daily News,* 9 September 1965, p. 3.

15. Jeffrey R. Short, Jr., quoted in Robert Dishon, "City Park Crisis Feared," *Chicago Daily News,* 9 December 1967, p. 10. The Open Lands Project Committee followed this indictment with proposals for extensive improvements to and expansions of the park system of Chicago and Illinois. Reports of this kind coming from outside city hall invariably brought out the worst in the city's political and financial establishment: in 1968 Mayor Daley and the Chicago Association of Commerce and Industry released their first proposal for a sports stadium on the lakefront, in spite of the fact that on any list of urban priorities such a stadium, even if built on an acceptable site, would be at the bottom.

In 1969 the Chicago Park District included the following areas and facilities: 458 parks; 6,800 acres of total area (1.9 acres per 1,000 persons); 223 field houses; 103 swimming pools; 30 bathing beaches; 380 baseball diamonds suitable for hardball playing; 428 softball diamonds; 191 football and soccer fields; 884 basketball backboards; 408 volleyball courts; 626 tennis courts; 158 gymnasiums; 144 day camps; 64 craft shops; 823 club rooms. In addition the district maintains and operates Adler Planetarium, Lincoln Park Zoo, Lincoln Park Conservatory, Garfield Park Conservatory, Grant Park Band Shell, and Soldier Field, and provides land and some revenue for the Art Institute, Field Museum, Shedd Aquarium, and the Museum of Science and Industry (Source: Chicago Park District).

6. The New Transportation Pattern

Streets, Boulevards, and Expressways

The postwar transportation policy of the city and of the various privately owned carriers revealed a somewhat greater proportion of civic enlightenment than one could find in the renewal and recreational programs, although many of the earlier advances were undone by later errors. The basic street and boulevard system of Chicago and the immense number of fixed and movable bridges required by the widely ramifying pattern of railroads and waterways had been completed before the advent of the depression in 1930, and such additions to the street grid as were made after the Second World War were largely peripheral extensions in new real estate developments. The laying down of new thoroughfares and the widening of existing ones required by the Burnham Plan as well as by the automotive age were accompanied by a continuous program of grade-crossing separations and the ever expanding installation of traffic-control devices such as intersection and lane-control signals, directional signs, and pavement markings. The techniques of traffic control kept reasonable pace with the growing volume of vehicular traffic from the time the program was inaugurated at the end of the First World War, and the results in the form of greatly reduced numbers of serious accidents in proportion to motor-vehicle density gave Chicago an enviable safety record. In 1915, when there were only 97,830 registered vehicles in the city, the number of fatalities was 254, for a rate of 26 deaths per 10,000 vehicles. By 1962, when registration had passed well beyond a million, the number of fatalities was almost exactly the same (247), but the rate had declined to 2.4 per 10,000 vehicles, a reduction of 91 percent that earned for Chicago the National Safety Council's 1963 award for the best traffic safety record among cities over 1,000,000 in population.

In addition to installing a comprehensive system of traffic signals, adopting one-way streets in the Loop area, and maintaining aggressive patrolling in the core, in 1953 the Bureau of Streets and the Department of Public Works made a valiant effort to open congested streets and to reduce the number of standing vehicles by undertaking the construction of municipally owned parking garages in the downtown area. This program was completed in 1966, by which date the department had opened ten multilevel garages built above grade and two below grade, both of the latter situated under Grant Park to the north and south of the Art Institute.[1] A further reduction of cross-Loop traffic came with the extension of the double-level Wacker Drive southward along the line of old Market Street from its former western terminus at Lake to an interchange with Congress Parkway. Since each block of the new drive had to be completed before the next block of Market was torn up, to avoid obstructing more than one Loop artery at a time, and since the project involved the rearrangement of existing building footings as well as extensive demolition, the complex operation dragged on for nearly ten years, from 1949 to 1958. The completion of the Wacker extension, coinciding with the widening of Congress Street into Congress Parkway, closed an inner-ring boulevard system of which Michigan Avenue forms the east side and thus at last brought to reality the proposal that Burnham had made a half-century earlier in his Chicago Plan.[2]

Coincident with the initiation of work on the Wacker Drive extension came the construction of the new Greyhound Bus Terminal, erected in 1949–50 at the northeast corner of Clark and Randolph streets, on the site of Burnham and Root's Ashland Block (1890–92), which had to be demolished to make way for the new facility. Skidmore, Owings and Merrill acted as architects and engineers in the design of the commonplace structure that could only be regarded as a depressing anticlimax beside Root's masterpiece. The location, however, made it possible for buses to enter and leave the station via Garvey Court, which thus provides direct access from the subgrade bus concourse to the lower level of Wacker Drive and frees the surrounding Loop streets of the cumbersome bus traffic. The Greyhound terminal was planned as a union station and framed for the addition of an overhead twelve-story office building, but neither plan was realized: the Trailways Bus Station on Randolph Street between State and Wabash was retained, and the idea of a twelve-story office block became an anachronism in an age of one-hundred-story towers.

The most obvious and expensive aspects of street improvement are the bridges and viaducts built either to replace obsolete facilities or to separate streams of conflicting and disparate traffic. The creation of the city's expressway system required great numbers of such structures, but the sheer multiplicity of rail lines and waterways demanded a year-by-year program of repair and replacement within the bounds of the traditional street pattern. During the depression of the thirties this work was sponsored by the Public Works Administration, but the city's own Department of Public Works was well prepared with plans to resume activity at the point where the PWA had dropped it. The first postwar project was the replacement of the existing State Street bridge over the main river with a structure of the same double-leaf bascule type. Constructed in 1947–49 and officially designated the Bataan-Corregidor Memorial Bridge, the span won an honorable mention from the American Institute of Steel Construction in 1949 for bridges of the movable class, thus helping to maintain a Chicago tradition of prize designs that goes back nearly to the beginning of the institute's program of annual awards and continues to the present time.[3]

The longest of the street bridges built in the postwar period is the viaduct carrying Damen Avenue (2000W) over the yards and spur tracks of the Chicago Junction Railway from 37th to 47th Street, a $9,500,000 work of conventional steel-girder design that was opened in 1962. The most frustrating project, on the other hand, and the one offering the most impressive demonstration that the problem of sinking foundations in a water-bearing soil is never finally solved, is the new Dearborn Street bridge over the main river. Construction of what was expected to be a straightforward operation that had been repeated hundreds of times dragged on for nearly five years, from February 1959 to the fall of 1963. The strike of the United Steel Workers in 1960 delayed work for two months shortly after it had started, but the first of the difficulties arising from the construction process itself came in the fall of the same year, when the Wacker Drive foundations adjacent to the caissons for the south abutment began to sink as the result of the movement of sand into the caisson wells followed by a weakening in the bearing capacity of the overburden. More serious troubles with the north abutment came in 1961 because the simultaneous sinking of caissons for both Marina City and the bridge caused unsupported earth pressure to force the fluid sand-clay mixture into the space between the perimeter of the caisson well and the steel liner, with the consequence that the cofferdam for the north abutment sank downward and tipped outward into the water. Additional settlement of the upper deck of Wacker Drive, the difficulties encountered in underpinning the footings of the building extending along the north bank of the river to the west of Marina, and the pouring of saturated sand and clay into wells following the removal of the caisson liners caused further delays. The employment of high-speed caisson drills and soil-stabilizing chemicals eventually solved the various problems, and the bridge was finally opened two years behind schedule and $500,000 over the original estimate of its cost. The city's bridge engineers, under the direction of Stephen J. Michuda, did their design work well, as another American Institute of Steel Construction award testified.

The foremost grade-separation project other than those associated with the construction of expressways and viaducts above rail lines began as another act of lakefront vandalism, but ended as a tolerable compromise between good civic design and its antithesis. The need to smooth out the traffic flow at the Lake Shore Drive–Michigan Avenue–Oak Street interchange had become a matter of urgency by 1950, and the plan that the city finally drew up in 1961 represented the worst way to deal with the problem. The Department of Public Works, supported by such equally vigorous destroyers of cities as the Cook County Department of Highways and the federal Bureau of Public Roads, proposed a set of elevated connectors extending from Goethe Street (1300N) to Delaware (900N), at one stroke blocking the view of Oak Street Beach and the lake, walling off the west side of the Drake Hotel, and ruining the appearance of the north end of Michigan Avenue. The opposition of various citizens' and professional societies, united behind an ad hoc organization known as the Near Northsiders Save Our Shores Committee, compelled the city to withdraw its original proposal and to substitute a more costly but less destructive plan for underground connectors, which the Northsiders had first suggested. Although the final interchange system, constructed in 1963–65, involved the replacement of landscaped parkway strips along the drive with arid fields of concrete, the city provided some compensation by expanding the area of Oak Street Beach and extending the existing shore promenade from Oak Street to North Avenue Beach.[4]

All public works aimed at improving the circulation of vehicular traffic proved insignificant beside Chicago's immense expressway system, put together in eighteen years at a cost of about $1,100,000,000, only to reach a state in which rush-hour traffic moved at a lower average speed than it ever did on conventional boulevards (fig. 108). The pattern of high-speed limited-access traffic arteries actually had its origin in the system of diagonal metropolitan streets that Burnham and Bennett proposed in the Chicago Plan, although the concept that later came to be known as the superhighway or freeway lay in the future. Detailed planning for a radial system of expressways converging on the core area was initiated by the Cook County Department of Highways and the Chicago Department of Public Works during the war, so that both the city and the county were prepared to begin construction on certain routes shortly after the end of the conflict in 1945. The first segment of the system to reach completion was Edens Expressway, constructed in 1947–52 from a junction with the future Kennedy Expressway at Montrose Avenue (4400N) near Cicero (4800W) northward to the Cook–Lake county line. Since only 2½ miles of its 14-mile length lie within the city, the artery was very nearly a county project, although most of the cost of all freeways is borne by the federal government. At the time of its construction the length of Edens Expressway beyond the city limit lay in open country, so that the process of grading and paving was the least difficult of all the Chicago arteries, and its cost of $22,000,000 made it the least expensive on a per-mile basis. Little demolition was necessary, overpasses are relatively few, and there is only one marked change of grade, at the point where the roadway is carried

from its normal level at grade up to an elevation sufficient to clear the former catenary structure of the electrified North Shore Railroad at a crossing near the north
limit of Skokie.[5]

Almost simultaneously with Edens, its counterpart was being laid out on the south
side of the metropolitan area. Calumet Expressway was originally constructed in
1950–53 from 130th Street in Chicago southward to a junction with the Tri-State
Toll Road on the line of 172nd Street in Lansing, which meant that only the single
mile north of 138th Street lay within the city. The expressway, however, was subsequently extended northward to a junction with the future Ryan at 103rd Street in
Chicago, mostly along the line of Doty Avenue, skirting the west shore of Lake
Calumet, and southward to the Cook–Will county line. The original length was thus
little more than five miles and its cost of about $8,000,000 was a minor fraction of
the total expressway investment.

But these outlying segments proved to be preliminary exercises in engineering
complexity, traffic control, expense, and damage to the urban fabric. Before the two
north and south arteries were completed the city embarked on the Congress Expressway project, which required eleven years, 1949 to 1960, and the expenditure
of $183,542,000 to bring its 15.5-mile length to completion (fig. 109). The inner
end, extending from Halsted Street east through the length of Congress Parkway to
Grant Park, coincides exactly with the grand axis of Burnham's plan, but the continuous flood of trucks and automobiles, of course, is far different from the cere-
monial pageantry the planner envisioned. The west end is a junction with the main
segment of the Tri-State Toll Road. The building of Congress proved a much more
formidable task than any previous work that might be regarded as comparable to it.
First was the extensive demolition in the densely built West Side and the excavation
necessary to provide space for an artery of six to ten traffic lanes, a broad median,
and the necessary entrance and exit ramps. Both design and construction were com-
plicated by the number of intersections with multitrack north–south railroad lines
and by a unique series of engineering features at the east end of the expressway—in
tight succession from east to west, the passage under the track and platform area of
LaSalle Street Station, the interchange with the double-level Wacker Drive, the twin
bascule bridges over the South Branch of the river, and the passage through the
Central Post Office.

The great virtue of the Congress plan, however, is that it provides the first and
longest example of Burnham's far-sighted idea for traffic corridors in which the different forms of transportation would lie in contiguous rights of way screened from
the surrounding areas. The median strip of the Congress was reserved for the west-

ward extension of the Dearborn Street subway line, which occupies the median from the tunnel entrance approximately at Halsted Street (800W) to a point near the terminal at Des Plaines Avenue (7600W) in Forest Park. In addition, the walled cut containing the expressway was widened from Central Avenue (5600W) to Des Plaines to provide space for the tracks of the Baltimore and Ohio Chicago Terminal Railroad as well as the roadway and the rapid transit line. This brilliant concept makes it possible to minimize the damage done by building transportation arteries in the area, the conflicts that inevitably arise from destruction of the urban fabric, and the disputes over how the money is to be allocated among the different forms of transportation.[6]

Another engineering masterpiece among the Chicago expressways is also the system's leading fiasco of traffic planning. Chicago Skyway (originally and briefly known as Calumet) was constructed under the greatest pressure in two years, 1956–58, and at a cost of $101,000,000 to join the future Ryan Expressway at 63rd Street with the west end of the Indiana Toll Road at 106th Street, an alignment forming a near-perfect tangent of 7½ miles on the northwest–southeast diagonal. The skyway was built as a toll road from the proceeds of a municipal bond issue, and since it crosses the Calumet River on a high-level bridge, it is legally regarded as a toll bridge with a total of seven miles of east and west approaches. The planners of the artery proved to be wildly optimistic in their prediction of traffic volume: in 1970 this amounted to slightly more than 9,000,000 vehicles for the year, fewer than a third of the total expected years before, so that the toll revenues have never been sufficient to cover both the interest and the principal sum of the bond issue. The quality of engineering design is far superior to that of the traffic estimates. Chicago Skyway provides the clearest example of the Burnham principle of traffic corridors, since its elevated right-of-way is an expansion of the embankment that carries the lines of the New York Central and Pennsylvania railroads, each of which formerly operated four main tracks, although these were later reduced to two in the case of the Central. The Calumet River crossing is a fixed cantilever bridge of Warren trusses that provides the standard 135-foot clearance over this extremely busy waterway, its height, span length, and viaduct approaches making it by far the largest single-span bridge in Chicago.

The cost of the depressed or elevated freeway increased markedly for Northwest Expressway, which was constructed in 1955–60 and renamed after President John F. Kennedy in 1964 (fig. 110). Steadily rising prices, extensive demolition, the relocation of yard and main tracks of the Chicago and North Western Railway, and engineering complexities all contributed to the $238,000,000 cost of the artery, which

Fig. 108. The expressway system of
Chicago in 1969.

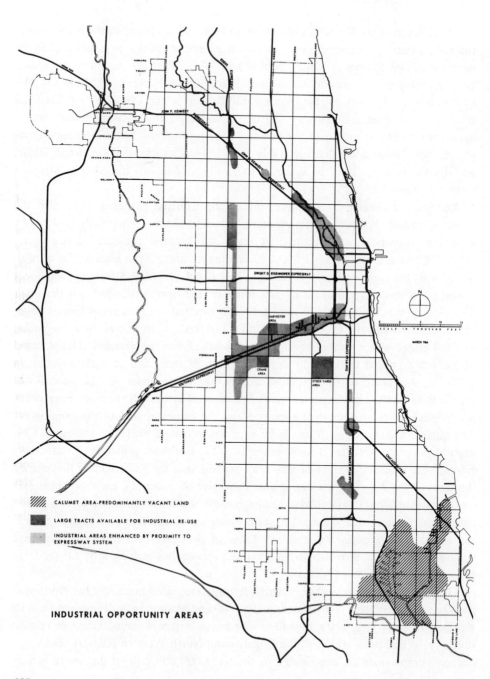

CALUMET AREA-PREDOMINANTLY VACANT LAND

LARGE TRACTS AVAILABLE FOR INDUSTRIAL RE-USE

INDUSTRIAL AREAS ENHANCED BY PROXIMITY TO
EXPRESSWAY SYSTEM

INDUSTRIAL OPPORTUNITY AREAS

Fig. 109. Congress (now Eisenhower)
Expressway, 1949–60. Chicago
Department of Public Works,
Bureau of Engineering, engineers.
The east end of the expressway near
the Central Post Office, with Chicago
Transit Authority line in the median.

Fig. 110. Northwest (now Kennedy)
Expressway, 1955–60. Chicago
Department of Public Works,
Bureau of Engineering, engineers.
Milwaukee Avenue overpass in
foreground and relocated tracks of
the Chicago and North Western
Wisconsin Division to right of artery.

109

110

Fig. 111. Abraham Lincoln Oasis,
Tri-State Toll Road, South Holland,
Illinois, 1967–68. David Haid,
architect.

111

Fig. 112. Ryan Expressway, with the Chicago Transit Authority rapid transit line in the median strip, 1967–69. Chicago Department of Public Works, Chicago Transit Authority, and De Leuw, Cather and Company, engineers.

Fig. 113. Kennedy Expressway, with the Chicago Transit Authority rapid transit line in the median strip, 1967–70. Chicago Department of Public Works, Chicago Transit Authority, and De Leuw, Cather and Company, engineers.

112

113

extends very nearly 17 miles from the interchange with Congress Expressway to the city's main airport at O'Hare Field (pp. 258–62). Most of the Kennedy is straight-forward expressway engineering, the chief exceptions being the overpasses of Mil-waukee Avenue and the Ontario Street connector. The first is a continuous-girder bridge of steel carried on rigid-frame bents, the long span and the unusual supports dictated by the sharply skewed alignment of the overhead street. The Ontario bridge may be unique: the deck of the overpass constitutes the upper flange of a continuous hollow-box girder of concrete that turns through a little more than 180 degrees and is carried by slab piers set on radial lines. Elsewhere the simple-span plate-girder bridge of conventional design is the rule. Kennedy Expressway forms another corri-dor throughout much of its length, since it lies adjacent to the line of the North Western Railway's Wisconsin Division.

South Expressway, later renamed Dan Ryan after a former president of the Cook County Board of Commissioners, formed the next and costliest step in the freeway pattern. The main stem, running from the circular interchange with Kennedy and Eisenhower (formerly Congress) to 99th Street, was constructed in 1957–62 at a cost of $282,700,000, but this route was later extended in two branches, southwest-ward to the Tri-State Toll Road of the Illinois state system and southeastward to a connection with Calumet Expressway (old Doty Avenue) at 103rd Street. The en-tire system was open to traffic by 1969. The high cost of the Ryan complex arose chiefly from its extreme width of fourteen lanes for a distance of about 3 miles below 28th Street and from the presence of a 2-mile-long eight-lane viaduct over the South Branch of the river and the numerous rail lines in its immediate vicinity. The river crossing is a fixed bridge that provides a 60-foot clearance, a height that represents a three-way compromise involving the city, the Bureau of Public Roads, and the Department of Defense. The city wanted a bascule bridge to allow uninhibited navi-gation on the river by masted vessels of any size; the military, on the other hand, demanded a fixed bridge, fearing a tie-up of vehicles in one of their imaginary wars; they were willing to settle for the customary 135-foot clearance, but the Bureau of Public Roads refused to bear the additional expense and demanded that the clear-ance be reduced to 60 feet. Thus the economy of the city paid the price of bureau-cratic inflexibility. From the line of 28th Street to near 63rd the depressed Ryan Expressway lies immediately contiguous to the embankment of the New York Cen-tral–Rock Island line that constitutes the approach to LaSalle Street Station, and the extreme width of the roadway added to the wide shoulders of the four-track rail embankment took a block-wide swath out of the South Side, where housing has always been in shortest supply. The division of Ryan into interconnecting through and local lanes is a particularly confusing example of super-clever engineering, which soon required a drastic reduction in the normal speed limit to cut the resulting accident rate.

Extensive open areas left from the draining of the old Illinois–Michigan Canal and simpler engineering problems kept the cost of Southwest Expressway to $115,-000,000. Constructed in 1959–64 and renamed Adlai Stevenson in 1966, the elevated freeway constitutes one element of a huge belt of contiguous land and water arteries. For most of its length west of Ashland Avenue (1600W) it lies between the lines of the Santa Fe and the Gulf, Mobile and Ohio railroads, the three together lying immediately south of the Sanitary and Ship Canal, and east of Ashland, to the junction with Ryan Expressway, the Stevenson lies adjacent to the Santa Fe, Gulf, Mobile and Ohio, and Illinois Central lines. An east–west link extending the Stevenson to a connection with South Lake Shore Drive roughly on the line of 24th Street was constructed in 1964–66 to provide two clear lessons demonstrating how expressways ought and ought not to be built. The west end of this connector is an immense elevated interchange all elements of which are segments of the Ryan-Stevenson viaduct system that stands high above a dense mass of rail lines, commercial streets, canal, and slips. The east end is a standard above-grade interchange with Lake Shore Drive that brought permanent ruin to fourteen acres of Burnham Park. Between these two junctions the Stevenson is depressed below all north–south streets and rail lines, but it was raised above grade precisely at the point where it would do maximum damage to public lands. Had the lesson of the Michigan Avenue connectors so soon been forgotten?

The city's expressways are supplemented by an extensive regional system of state-constructed toll roads, of which the circumferential Tri-State Toll Road extending from the Wisconsin to the Indiana state line is the most important for the movement of metropolitan traffic. Over much of its route this expressway lies close to the intermediate ring highway that Burnham and Bennett proposed for the outer metropolitan area. Engineering of the Illinois toll roads is straightforward work—steel-girder construction for long viaducts, precast and prestressed concrete girders for the numerous overpasses—but architectural elements of the Tri-State artery include a novel kind of restaurant in the form of glass-walled enclosures carried like bridges over the roadway. One of these so-called oases is a prize work of architectural design and steel-framed construction: the Abraham Lincoln Oasis, erected in 1967–68 in South Holland, was accorded an honor award of the American Institute of Steel Construction for the year of its completion (fig. 111). Designed by the architect David Haid and the structural engineering firm of Wiesinger-Holland, the installation includes a service station, parking space, landscaped areas, and access ramps as well as the restaurant. This window-walled enclosure, 90 × 225 feet in area of plan, is carried in a 135-foot clear span over the roadway by means of six-foot-deep plate girders at the edges of the roof and floor, the girders supported in turn by two pairs of columns set at the shoulders of the roadway. The concrete roof and floor slabs rest on a series of steel trusses that span transversely between the big peripheral girders. All exposed steelwork is the self-weathering variety, its natural oxide color harmonizing nicely with the amber-tinted glass. This lightly but securely poised prism of dark glass clearly indicates that its author was a product of the Miesian regimen at IIT.

The Chicago freeway system was to be rounded out with the construction of the costly, controversial, and in many ways problematical Crosstown Expressway, which was planned to extend down the west side of the city along the line of Cicero Avenue (4800W) from Edens to the south leg of the Ryan complex. Because of popular opposition to the destruction wrought by the building of expressways, the city and the federal Department of Transportation placed the design of the artery in the hands of a team of two architectural offices (Skidmore, Owings and Merrill and C. F. Murphy Associates) and two engineering firms (Westenhoff and Novick, and Howard, Needles, Tammen and Bergendoff) working under the direction of Joseph R. Passoneau, the former dean of the School of Architecture at Washington University in Saint Louis. Conceived as a means for enhancing neighborhood development rather than uprooting people, the Crosstown nevertheless required intolerable damage to the urban fabric, especially through demolition of housing, and the increase in the original cost estimate from $200,000,000 to nearly $1,000,000,-000 by 1971 made the possibility of realization according to the terms of the original plan seem remote.

In spite of the widespread destruction visited upon the urban fabric by the building of expressways and the increasing noise and atmospheric pollution attendant upon the mounting traffic, evils so obvious and so widespread that even rural legislators have become aware of them, there were numerous interests and organizations ready to demand an ever expanding program. Their chief spokesman is the Chicago Area Transportation Study, ostensibly an independent agency but actually supported by state and federal funds. In its report of 1962 the agency recommended the construction of a 232-mile system of expressways at a cost of $2,015,000,000 but suggested only a modest $185,000,000 for the Chicago Transit Authority. Since the expressway program would involve doubling both the investment and the mileage of the existing system, it was so widely attacked that the official spokesmen for the municipal establishment joined the opposition. The supporters of big expressway systems, whose lobbyists have been uniformly successful in opposing adequate transit support for Chicago, have been chiefly the Chicago Motor Club, Chicago Real Estate Board, Illinois Oil Council, Taxpayers' Federation of Illinois, Illinois Association of Real Estate Boards, and the pressure groups provided by the automotive and petroleum industries. The Chicago Area Transportation Study eventually became an agency of the Illinois state government.

Rapid Transit and Railroads

The event in transit history that aroused the greatest hope and eventually brought an equal measure of disappointment was the creation of a single public agency to own and operate the surface, elevated, and subway lines of the city. The Chicago Transit Authority was established as a public corporation operating within the city and in those suburbs where there were existing extensions of rapid transit, bus, and streetcar lines by an act of the general assembly passed in April 1945 and by a popular referendum held in the same month, and the new authority began the local transportation of passengers in 1947. The corporation was initially empowered to acquire all properties of the Chicago Rapid Transit Company and the Chicago Surface Lines, but within a few years it was expanded to include the Chicago Motor Coach System as well. The advantages expected from the coming of this long awaited new day, however, were in good part nullified by the irrational requirement that the authority earn all its operating expenses, interest charges on its debt, and its reserve fund for the replacement of equipment from fare revenues, although anyone possessed of a minimal acquaintance with the American economy should have known that transporting passengers without financial loss ceased to be possible in 1930.[7] The inevitable consequence of this folly was a constant increase in fares, totaling 600 percent in twenty-one years, each increment accompanied by a loss of riders and an intensification of street congestion until eventually the whole transit system was placed in jeopardy. This vicious circle could be broken only by a direct annual subsidy from the state and the city, as it was in such comparable transit systems as those of Boston, New York, and Philadelphia.[8] The CTA was helpless under the enabling legislation, since it granted bondholders the right to sue the authority either for a fare increase or for the replacement of management if at any time it fails to earn all operating expenses and fixed charges from revenues. In this way the people of the metropolitan area were forced to tolerate exorbitant transit fares so that holders of bonds, whose incomes are generally more than comfortable, could continue to enjoy a substantial return on their investment.

The creation of the CTA encouraged a revival in the making of transit plans, the authority itself proposing the seventh of the long series in 1958 and the Chicago Area Transportation Study the eighth in 1962, but the time had now arrived when some positive action in the improvement and extension of services was at last possible.

Coincident with the establishment of the authority, though planned under the old rapid transit system, was the construction of the Milwaukee Avenue–Dearborn Street subway in 1946–51 from Logan Square on the Northwest Side to a temporary terminal under Congress Street between Canal and Clinton, a distance of about six miles. This line was extended westward to Forest Park during the construction of Congress Expressway and was opened in 1958 as the first rapid transit line to be situated in the median strip of such an artery. It was not a net addition to the rapid transit mileage, however, since it replaced the existing Garfield Park line. The Milwaukee–Dearborn subway was the first segment of the Chicago system to be completely equipped with automatic block signals and automatic stop, the installation having been placed in operation in 1961.[9] A minor but useful line improvement came in 1960–62, when the tracks lying at grade level between Laramie Avenue (5200W) in Chicago and Harlem Avenue (7200W) in Oak Park were elevated to the existing right-of-way of the North Western Railway's Galena Division by the CTA's taking over one of the railroad company's four tracks and building a new track adjacent to it. The whole operation provided another example of transportation partnership of the kind that Burnham had proposed in his traffic corridors. Meanwhile, with funds secured from its initial bond issue the CTA began to replace the remaining wooden-body cars with all-metal varieties in 1950, a program dictated by the requirements of enlarged subway operations as well as by the sheer antiquity of the former rolling stock. The first group of new cars was rebuilt from high-speed lightweight streetcars, and they were the first in which the CTA introduced electric braking, which became standard for all subsequent additions to the authority's rolling stock.[10]

The first net addition to the CTA's rapid transit mileage followed the abandonment of all operations on the Chicago, North Shore and Milwaukee Railroad in January 1963.[11] The Chicago Rapid Transit Company had always owned the right-of-way and track of the North Shore's Skokie Valley line to the transit company's shops just west of McCormick Boulevard in Skokie and had operated local service to Dempster Street in the same suburb. When the interurban line abandoned service the CTA acquired the track as far as Dempster and revived shuttle service to the Howard Street terminal in April 1964. Unlike the old local run of the Rapid Transit Company, however, the new shuttle provides a high-speed nonstop service that the CTA claimed to be the fastest transit run in the world, the average scheduled rate for cars equipped with one-hundred-horsepower motors being forty-six miles per hour. The new extension provided an overwhelming demonstration of the demand for good rapid transit service in the suburbs: in the first year of its operation the Skokie branch carried nearly five times the anticipated number of passengers.

At the same time that it planned the new service the CTA began to replace the remaining rolling stock inherited from its predecessors. In the fall of 1961 the United States Congress authorized the Housing and Home Finance Agency to make loans to transit systems for the purchase of new equipment. It proved to be the little first step in the long-delayed entry of the federal government into the subsidization of metropolitan transit systems. The CTA applied for a loan of $7,500,000 in 1962, which allowed it to purchase 180 elevated-subway cars that were placed in service on the Lake Street and Douglas Park lines in 1964. The new cars were manufactured by the Pullman–Standard Division of the Pullman Company, a century-old Chicago institution, and embodied the new technology of transit rolling stock: air-conditioned, equipped with electric braking and one-hundred-horsepower motors that gave them a potential maximum speed of seventy-eight miles per hour, steel construction except for couplers and end plates of fiber glass and epoxy-resin, wide-windowed, quiet, and brightly lighted, they provided immediate visual and kinesthetic evidence of the benefits conferred by good urban rail service.

The greatest expansion of rapid transit mileage in Chicago since the basic system was laid down at the turn of the century followed the passage in 1966 of a general public-works bond issue amounting to $195,000,000. The sum included nearly $23,000,000 for the city's share in the cost of constructing a new elevated terminal at 63rd Street and Ashland Avenue in Englewood and new rapid transit lines in the median strips of Ryan and Kennedy expressways, the final cost of which rose to $113,000,000 before their completion.[12] The Ryan line was the first to be opened to service and was constructed in 1967–69 from a junction with the existing South Side elevated structure near 18th Street to a terminal in the expressway median at 95th. The connection with the original line allowed continuous runs over the Lake Street route and the Loop to the far South Side for a total distance of 21 miles, of which about 9.5 miles were new line (fig. 112). The track structure, though a conventional steel-rail system, reflected recent engineering developments in the use of welded rail supported by divided concrete ties whose separate halves are joined by steel bars. It is the signaling system, however, that constitutes the most striking technological innovation. Trains are operated without the use of wayside signals, which were replaced by continuously illuminated cab signals working in conjunction with the automatic train control. The interior equivalent of the block signal is the conventional three-color variety, but the novel feature is a circle of yellow light on the circumference of the speedometer dial that indicates the allowable speed limit at any part of the line, the minimum, of course, being zero in the case of a near approach to a standing train. If the motorman exceeds the limit shown by the yellow band, a whistle sounds in the cab; if he fails to heed the whistle by applying the brakes within 2½ seconds, the automatic control will bring the train to a stop.

The stations of the new line were designed by Skidmore, Owings and Merrill under the direction of Myron Goldsmith, who developed an impeccably functional form characterized by the clarity and delicacy of all his work. The large stations at street-grade level serve the feeder bus lines as well as the rail line, and the remainder are depressed below street grade at the track-expressway level. All wind breaks, dividers, and ticket booths are stainless steel; the supports of the transparent platform canopies and the structures of the station enclosures are white-painted steel frames, and the enclosures themselves are glass. The formal and functional criteria are everywhere perfectly satisfied: open, uncluttered, brightly lighted interior spaces; durability, safety, maximum efficiency of movement; lightness and purity of structure. The stations form an architectural equivalent to the 150 stainless-steel cars that constitute the new rolling stock designed for the Ryan and Kennedy lines.

The location of the Ryan–Lake Street run is such that it unites the South Side of the city with the West Side and the western suburb of Oak Park and thus serves two useful ends in the urban economy: it makes it possible for residents in the lower-income areas of the city to reach jobs in the suburbs, where many manufacturing and administrative centers have located during the postwar dispersal of industry, and it provides a similar service for suburban residents going beyond the center of the city, in both cases without a transfer from one transit medium to another. As a consequence of the advantages conferred by the location as well as the quality of service on the Ryan line, the average number of weekday passengers on the route rose to 99,000 per day by the end of 1970, 10 percent over the expected total, but the line possesses a far greater capacity to remove traffic from the adjacent expressway lanes.

The Kennedy–Dearborn–Eisenhower line (fig. 113), opened early in 1970, is similar to the Ryan in its technological and architectural characteristics, except for the subway extension from Logan Square to the expressway median near Kimball

Avenue (3400W). A questionable decision in the location of the terminal, however, held the traffic to little more than half that of the Ryan extension and well below the anticipated volume—59,000 passengers per weekday at the end of 1970 against an expectation of 70,000. The Kennedy line terminates at Central Avenue (5600W) in Jefferson Park, two miles short of the Harlem Avenue commercial concentration and nearly seven miles short of O'Hare Field. The design of stations and rolling stock offers every inducement to use the service, and its vast superiority to the older facilities is most potently demonstrated by Goldsmith's spacious, unobstructed, and brilliantly lighted subway stations at Logan Square and the Kimball-Belmont intersection.

At the same time, the Ryan and Kennedy lines share two handicaps that prevent them from being used to their full capacity. The narrow right-of-way restricted to two tracks made it impossible to operate both local and express service, and since all trains make all stops, the average speed on the nearly level Ryan route is held to twenty-eight miles per hour and on the Kennedy to little more than the system average of twenty-three miles per hour because of numerous curves and changes of grade between elevated structure and subway tunnel. Nor could the lines as built generate their full traffic potential, because the city lacked the money to build parking lots at the outlying stations. They proved, however, to be the beginning of a great rapid transit expansion: in 1968 the city announced plans for a new inner-city subway to replace the elevated Loop, secured the assent of the affected property owners to a special tax assessment to bear the local share of the cost, and in 1970 drew up a timetable of construction. The estimated cost, meanwhile, had risen from $539,000,000 to $750,000,000. The expansion of rapid transit, however, was partially offset for the general metropolitan area by the loss of two of Chicago's three interurban lines. The North Shore abandoned its Shore Line in 1955 and its prize-winning Skokie Valley Line in 1963, and the construction of Congress Expressway placed such serious handicaps on the operation of the Chicago, Aurora and Elgin that the company gave up entirely in 1957.

The railroad system of the Chicago metropolitan area had been substantially completed by 1910 and was brought to modern high-capacity standards in the thirty years between that date and the war. The vast complex of terminals and yards was desperately in need of renovation after the heavy wartime usage, but the disastrous decline of through passenger traffic after 1945 meant that little attention was paid to passenger facilities beyond the modernization of the interior of Dearborn Station in 1946. The virtual extinction of long-distance sleeping car trains was most perfectly and unhappily symbolized by the New York Central Railroad's abandonment of the Twentieth Century Limited in December 1967, after 65½ years of service. The train had become a national institution, a gathering place for celebrities and the epitome of the sumptuous life in travel, but in spite of the expensive new rolling stock with which it was twice reequipped (1938 and 1948), the truth was that the high point of its patronage had come nearly forty years before its demise.[13] The loss of through passengers and the continuing climb of suburban traffic accompanying the increasingly rapid expansion of both the area and the population of the outer suburbs meant that the time had come when the unification of rail terminals might at last be accomplished.

There was, as usual, no lack of plans: the South Side Planning Board submitted the first of the postwar series in 1949; the Illinois General Assembly passed an act in 1957 enabling the city to establish a railroad terminal authority, which was actually created the following year, when Mayor Daley proposed the use of cleared rail property for the University of Illinois; and various organizations offered three more merger plans in the two years of 1959–60. All these proposals involved removing one or more of the four terminals south of the Loop (Central, Dearborn, LaSalle, and Grand Central, from east to west), the most drastic being the perfectly feasible retirement of all of them, but once more inertia, indifference, and the failure of the municipal government to use the authority it possessed led to the customary absence of results. But dwindling traffic and the obvious reduction in expenses that would accompany the abandonment of redundant facilities eventually compelled some railroads to act on their own. In October 1968 the New York Central, after its merger with the Pennsylvania, shifted all its trains operated to Detroit, Cleveland, and the East from LaSalle Street to Union Station, leaving two trains of the old Big Four District to continue their eighty-year tenancy of Central Station. In the following year the merged Baltimore and Ohio–Chesapeake and Ohio system ended the active life of Grand Central Station by shifting the company's six remaining trains to North Western Station, raising the total traffic at the busy Canal Street terminal to 208 trains per day in 1970. The Baltimore and Ohio showed commendable reluctance to demolish the handsome Grand Central headhouse and balloon train shed, and various private groups initiated action to preserve it as a landmark, but without success.

The most remarkable as well as desirable feature of railroad developments in the postwar years was the resurgence of commutation traffic that coincided, as both cause and effect, with radical improvements in service. The renaissance began in 1950, when the Burlington took the first step by replacing its antique open-platform suburban cars with stainless-steel, air-conditioned coaches of novel design. The new rolling stock is distinguished by a double-level plan in which traditional double seats line either side of the main-floor aisle and two narrow rows of single seats occupy the upper or gallery levels, leading to the designation gallery car. The capacity of the individual car is 148 seats, and two rows of windows on each side provide each seating unit, upper and lower, with its own window opening. The Burlington eventually replaced nearly its entire fleet of suburban cars with the new equipment and simultaneously retired all its steam locomotives in favor of the diesel-electric variety. This drastic upgrading of service was unfortunately followed in 1969 by the demolition of the superb concourse building of Union Station to make way for the third Gateway Center tower.

The improvements on the North Western Railway were even more conspicuous: by the mid-fifties the company was approaching physical breakdown as well as bankruptcy, and the rescue operation performed by a new chairman of the board, Ben W. Heineman, required radical surgery to put the staggering road on its feet. Within a year of his election in 1956 Heineman replaced all steam locomotives with the existing diesel motive power, and three years later he began the installation of a fleet of gallery cars, certain units of which were equipped with the novel feature of locomotive cab controls that allowed the railroad to operate loaded trains on scheduled runs with the locomotive pulling at the front or pushing at the rear. Known as push-pull trains, they made possible the movement of outbound trains with the locomotive in pulling position and inbound with the power at the rear, in pushing position, which resulted in a reduction of expenses through more efficient use of motive power and freedom from the necessity of turning engines at terminals. A steady rise in traffic to a total of 90,000 inbound and outbound passengers per weekday, three-track lines on each of three divisions, automatic block signaling arranged for high-density train schedules, reduced maintenance costs for new equipment, 155- and 161-seat capacity per car—these factors placed the North Western in the unique position of not only offering the best suburban service in the United States but earning a profit on its operations. Its success in this enterprise led the Milwaukee and the Rock Island railroads to adopt a similar type of rolling stock during the decade of the sixties, leaving only the Illinois Central's electrified system, once the pride of Chicago commutation service, with worn-out equipment surviving from predepression days (the company began to follow its more enlightened predecessors in 1971).[14] The next two steps should have been obvious, but in a country lacking a national transportation policy and in a city without a unified mass transit–rail system it was questionable whether they would ever be taken: the first is the genuine integration of all transportation facilities on a metropolitan basis; the second is the introduction of high-speed rail passenger service at least at the level of 1950 schedules on all runs up to five hundred miles. The alternatives are airport and highway paralysis, continued environmental destruction, lethal atmospheric pollution, and an intolerable waste of material resources.

Water, Waterways, and Airports

The water resources of Chicago once seemed inexhaustible in quantity as well as in carrying and cleansing capacity, but by the mid-century decade they appeared terribly vulnerable to all the destructive agencies of a reckless industrial economy. The lake served simultaneously as the source of the city's domestic water, as the reservoir for the various canals and canalized rivers, which served both a sanitary and a freight-carrying function, and as its chief avenue of waterborne commerce. In this last respect the lake was suddenly to take on a new importance with the opening of the Saint Lawrence Seaway in April 1959, an event that made Chicago an ocean port comparable in its potential capacity to major East and West coast ports other than New York. Preparation for this addition of a substantial ocean cargo to the city's already huge volume of river and lake tonnage began in 1954, when the general assembly at Springfield passed an act establishing the Chicago Regional Port District, a public agency authorized to issue bonds in the amount of $100,000,000 for the construction of harbor facilities at 130th Street in Lake Calumet, chiefly for the handling of bulk cargo.[15] By 1959 Calumet Harbor was half completed, but sufficient dock, warehouse, rail, and trucking facilities were in place to handle the seaway shipments for the next several years. By 1965 the port district, various shippers, and shipping companies had built a liquid bulk-storage terminal in addition to expanding the existing dock and freight-transfer facilities to the point where they could handle the tonnage that was predicted for the mid-sixties, which proved to be much higher than the volume that actually materialized.

Other expansions and improvements of the Chicago harbor complex, though less spectacular in character, were equally important to the loading and unloading of cargo. The city's Department of the Port in 1960–61 reconstructed and expanded Navy Pier to provide docking and warehousing space for ocean vessels carrying general cargo and thus in part restored the pier to its original function, even to the extent of introducing a pedestrian promenade on the roof of the low freight shed that lies adjacent to the dock area. The Army Corps of Engineers finally turned its attention to the problems of the Calumet River, the access way from Lake Michigan to the new harbor in Lake Calumet, and in 1962 began a long-delayed program of improvements that was completed in 1966. The Engineers increased the depth to a uniform 27 feet, allowing its use by the largest lake freighters as well as ocean vessels, straightened the tightest curves, and replaced two dangerous center-pivoted swing spans with the vertical-lift type. At the same time the movement of river cargo into Lake Calumet from the west was greatly expedited by two projects of the Engineers: the widening of the Calumet–Sag Channel from 60 to 225 feet, an operation that began in 1958 and was still in process in 1970, and the replacement of the obsolete Blue Island Lock in 1965 by the Thomas J. O'Brien Lock and Dam at 134th Street in the Calumet River. The capacity of the whole harbor complex by the end of the sixties was probably double the actual tonnage that moved through it.[16]

The vast water-supply system of Chicago was without a near competitor anywhere in the world and was one of the most impressive achievements in the whole domain of urban technology, yet it was destined to undergo still another of its great expansive phases after the Second World War. The pumping system had been very nearly completed before the war and required the addition of only one more station in the postwar period. The mileage of supply and distribution tunnels was increased by 22 percent, but the filtration capacity was drastically expanded with the opening of the Central District Filtration Plant in 1964. Situated immediately north of Navy Pier on a long man-made peninsula extending into the lake, the plant was under construction for twelve years and emerged at a final cost of $115,000,000 (fig. 114). The architects and structural engineers of its finely detailed Miesian forms were C. F. Murphy Associates, who worked in collaboration with the engineering staff of the city's Bureau of Water, a division of the Department of Water and Sewers. The plant operates in essentially the same way as its counterpart of the South District (pp. 26–30) in providing filtered and purified water for 3,000,000 residents in that part of Chicago and in thirty-three suburbs lying north of Pershing Road (3900S). The main discharge tunnel connects the filtration plant with the Lake View Pumping Station on Wilson Avenue and normally carries 960,000,000 gallons of water per day, but in emergencies it must be able to supply most of the demand of the entire North and Central districts, or 1,700,000,000 gallons per day. By the mid-sixties the Chicago system was capable of delivering nearly 3,000,000,-000 gallons of water per day through seventy-five miles of tunnels and more than four thousand miles of pipes.[17]

The lake offered what was in effect an unlimited supply of water for domestic and industrial consumption, and theoretically it should have provided an equally generous quantity for sewage treatment and disposal, but an arbitrary limit on diversion through the Sanitary and Ship Canal and an overloaded system left the Metropolitan Sanitary District increasingly unable to meet the demands placed on its facilities. In 1954 the district adopted what appeared to be the easy solution in asking for federal legislation to increase the diversion of water from the lake beyond the 1,500 cubic feet per second fixed by a decision of the United States Supreme Court in 1930, but the bills submitted to Congress either failed to pass or were vetoed by President Eisenhower because of Canadian objections. A potential disaster for the city emerged in 1958 when six Great Lakes states brought suit against the district seeking to compel it to return all treated waste water to the lake, a demand which if granted would have required the expenditure of an incalculable sum of money to treat sewage to the point where the recycled water would equal the level of purity it possessed on the original diversion. Fortunately for the city, Judge Albert B. Maris of Philadelphia, acting as a Special Master in Chancery appointed by the Supreme Court, ruled in favor of Chicago in 1966 and granted the district the right to divert 3,200 cubic feet per second, 1,500 cubic feet directly into the waterways to carry effluent from the sewage treatment plants, and 1,700 for domestic and industrial consumption. Although the ruling saved the day, the district was left in the same position it occupied in 1930.[18]

Throughout the renewed controversy the Sanitary District continued under the pressure of necessity to expand its system of sewers, but except for the questionable and costly construction of sludge-drying incinerators, little was done to expand the treatment facilities themselves. The result was the discharge of half-treated and contaminated effluent along with massive quantities of industrial wastes into the Chicago rivers and canals and thence into the Illinois Waterway, which the United States Public Health Service designated in 1963 as one of the worst polluted streams in the nation. The pollution of the water, in close parallel to both the theme and the symbolism of Ibsen's *Enemy of the People,* was matched by widespread corruption among the district staff. Popularly elected trustees beholden to the political parties, particularly the impregnable Democratic machine of Cook County, free to dispense patronage, presiding over a sanitation empire with a capital investment of more than $600,000,000 and annual budgets above $70,000,000, were very likely to be tempted to place their personal ambitions above the public interest.[19] By the early sixties the newspapers had uncovered all the corrupt practices known to municipal politics—chiefly job selling, bribery, altering civil service examination scores, overpayments to favored contractors, kickbacks, and leasing deals—and the ensuing scandal forced Mayor Daley in 1963 to appoint a general superintendent pledged to genuine reform. His choice was Vinton W. Bacon, a sanitary engineer with an impressive career in state engineering agencies despite his youth.

Fig. 114. Central District Filtration
Plant, Chicago Water System, 1000
East Ohio Street, 1952–64. C. F.
Murphy Associates, architects.

Bacon cleaned out this Augean stable so thoroughly and improved the quality of operations so markedly that he soon won the profoundest kind of testimony to his ability. Within a year he earned the unquenchable hatred of the trustees, and in 1966 he was the object of an attempted murder by means of a dynamite bomb after he had uncovered evidence of the rigging of scores on civil service examinations. His farsighted plans and his improvements in the efficiency of the district's operations, revealed by an $11,000,000 reduction in the annual budget between 1963 and 1966, brought him more attractive honors from the side of civic decency: the mayor increased his salary, and the editors of *Engineering News-Record* chose him as Construction's Man of the Year for 1966. Enraged beyond endurance, frustrated in their repeated attempts to fire him by the usual public process, the trustees finally succeeded in removing him from office at a secret closed-door meeting held on 21 January 1970. It was the victory, again, of indifference to public trust over the knowledge, judgment, and honesty of a first-rate sanitary engineer and public administrator. The full background of the iniquity along with the vindication of Bacon came with the report issued in September 1970 by the Municipal Corporations Committee of the Illinois State Senate.

The trustees violated the law in discharging Bacon at an illegally convened meeting [and] did not have good cause for the discharge. . . . [The district demonstrated] inability to discharge its duties in a satisfactory manner. The board has ignored the Civil Service laws . . . squandered the taxpayers' funds . . . functioned flagrantly as an arm of the Democratic Party of Cook County . . . and failed to take positive action on Bacon's imaginative and well-engineered pollution abatement plans. . . . There is serious question as to the board's intention to carry out its commitment made to the general assembly and to the people when the board sought $380,000,000 non-referendum bonding power in 1969. . . .

After the district showed the general assembly item by item where the money would go, the general assembly granted this authority to make the 10-year clean-up program feasible. [The assembly] relied upon the testimony, assurances, and integrity of Bacon and the trustees in granting the authority to issue $380,000,000 in bonds.

Almost as soon as they obtained this ability to take the money from the residents of the district, the trustees discharged Bacon. Some of them openly disavowed the legislature and the idea of being bound by the commitment. . . .

The sanitary district is no longer viable as an independent government unit . . . its structure should be revised in the light of the fact that it is obsolete and frequently ineffective. The committee recommends that the general assembly set a high priority on the adoption of legislation correcting the faults of the district or providing a new structure.[20]

No action was taken on this report by the legislature that sponsored it, and only a small first step was made in executing Bacon's plan for cleansing the Chicago waterway system. Submitted in 1967 and estimated to cost about a billion dollars over a ten-year period, this program consisted of three major parts: the complete chlorination of effluent to kill all microorganisms; a filtration system adequate to remove solids and suspended matter from the effluent; a system of tunnels lying 600 to 900 feet below grade where storm water could be stored until it could be pumped to the surface for treatment, in place of the present method of discharging combined raw sewage and storm runoff into the waterways during periods of heavy rainfall. The execution of that part of the plan recommending tertiary treatment made some progress: a pilot plant was constructed in Hanover Park in 1967–68, followed by a much larger installation with a capacity of 15,000,000 gallons per day placed in service at the North Side treatment works in Skokie in 1969–70. In this system the effluent from the treatment plant is passed through a cylindrical microstrainer of stainless steel, which removes 75 percent of the remaining suspended solids, thence into a chlorination basin where it is disinfected by contact with potassium hypochlorite, and finally through a postaeration chamber on its way to the canal. During the process the strained microsolids are returned to the primary treatment plant. The advanced chemical technology of treatment was matched by progress in the mechanical technique of drilling deep tunnels. The major interceptor sewer for storm runoff installed in the suburb of Alsip in 1969–70, for example, was bored by a tunnel-drilling machine through solid dolomite at an average rate of six feet per hour and at a maximum rate of sixty feet for one eight-hour shift.[21] But the entire resources of the state were necessary to end the pollution of the Chicago waterways, and only many states acting in concert could prevent the destruction of Lake Michigan as a life-supporting and life-enhancing body of water.

The city's Department of Public Works was equally progressive in developing techniques for the disposal of solid refuse beyond the traditional incinerator using conventional methods of combustion. On the basis of an experimental crushing and baling plant completed at 103rd Street and Calumet Expressway (Doty Avenue) in 1968, and of a refuse-shredding plant built on Goose Island in the North Branch in 1968–69, the department constructed a combined incinerating, separating, and shredding installation known as Northwest Incinerator at Chicago Avenue near Kenton (4600W) in 1968–71. Designed by the consulting engineers Metcalf and Eddy following European prototypes, the plant has a capacity of 1,600 tons per day, making it the largest so far constructed in the United States. The combustion structure is built up of welded tubular steel walls that are water-filled and hence act as both a cooling jacket and a steam boiler. Domestic refuse is mixed with bulk refuse that is shredded after ferrous metals are removed by a magnetic separator, and the resulting mix is burned with coal as a fuel. The water-jacketed furnace operates at much lower discharge temperatures than conventional furnaces lined with refractory brick, but it also generates large quantities of steam, amounting under normal operations to 375,000 pounds per hour. About 20 percent of this steam is used to drive plant machinery, and it is hoped that the remaining volume can be sold for commercial purposes. The plant is very nearly free of atmospheric pollution: highly efficient combustion reduces solid matter to a negligible level, and electronic precipitators remove 97 percent of the fly ash.

If the air had become a dumping ground for much of the city's waste product, it had also come to be a major avenue of transportation, which contributed still further to its polluted state. Moreover, the first postwar step in the expansion of the Chicago airport facilities was also the first step in the usurpation of lakefront land on the South Side originally reserved for scenic and recreational purposes. The ninety-four-acre peninsula known as Northerly Island that extends south of Adler Planetarium, the one part of the lakefront to show a nearly exact realization of Burnham's plan for the entire shore and half the site of the Century of Progress Exposition, was converted in 1947 into an airport for privately owned planes, although together they constitute the smallest and least important segment of the nation's multidimensional transportation system. Officially designated Meigs Field, its traffic expanded one hundred times in the first ten years of its operation, and the officers of the municipal government, delighted with the kind of prestige that comes from such enterprises, added a new terminal building in 1960–61 to show their gratitude. Opposition to this devotion of public land to minor business uses arose somewhat belatedly in 1965, when the development of the commercial airline terminals had reached the stage where abandoning Meigs was a practical possibility. The opponents were the bodies that had assumed the responsibility of defending the civic patrimony—Chicago Heritage Committee, Daniel Burnham Committee, Welfare Council of Metropolitan Chicago, joined by three aldermen in this case, but their arguments were offset by the voice of the Association of Commerce and Industry, which explained the value of the field as a status symbol for corporate decision-makers who travel in their own or in company planes.

There was plenty of unused space at Midway Airport for the Meigs traffic after the city opened its new and vastly expanded second air terminal in 1962. The history of events leading to this achievement was marked by a shortsightedness on the part of the airlines that suggested they had learned nothing from the 125-year experience of the railroads in constructing metropolitan stations. Chicago acquired the military installation known as Edward H. O'Hare Field, west of the city between the suburbs of Bensenville and Des Plaines, in 1946, constructed a makeshift terminal building of transite sheathing, and began trying to persuade the airlines to shift their flights from the conveniently located but already overburdened Midway to the new terminal. The airlines refused to do so unless they were guaranteed that the change would add nothing to their landing and takeoff expenses, although this was obviously impossible. Having been left with inadequate resources after fifteen years of depression and war, the city turned to the state, but Governor Dwight H. Green cut the recommendation for state aid to airports to a little more than a third of the original figure. Since the federal government was not yet in the business of constructing airfields, the city turned to the airlines, whose spokesman declined to make any contribution and suggested the rather quaint proposal that concessionaires underwrite the costs of construction. In 1948 the city engineer and airport consultant, Ralph H. Burke, predicted that by 1960 Chicago would need a field capable of accommodating ninety planes on the ground at one time and 12,000,000 passengers per year, but responsible parties both at city hall and the airlines' executive offices refused to listen to him.[22] In 1949 Mayor Martin H. Kennelly announced that the city had no funds to build an airport for jet planes and ordered a halt to construction until the airlines agreed to pay for the facilities already installed. A tentative agreement came early in the same year to finance current operations, while those at Midway approached paralysis. In 1955 the airlines, still peculiarly blind to the expansion of jet traffic just ahead of them, finally agreed to a schedule of landing fees sufficient to allow the city to retire the bond issue necessary to underwrite the costs of building an adequate terminal.

The bonds were eventually sold; the commission for the design of the immense airport was awarded to the architectural and engineering form of Naess and Murphy in 1958, and construction began at last in June of the following year. Every airport poses special problems for the architectural designers, as the big metropolitan rail terminal did, and that they have not yet been solved is indicated by the variety of solutions that continue to be offered. The most vexing problem common to all airports arises from the great area of level space required for the movement of aircraft and from their awkward shape, which in turn make it peculiarly difficult to bring passengers and passenger facilities into reasonable proximity with the planes. These and other related problems were all intensified at O'Hare because of its extreme size of 6,600 acres, its status as the primary transfer point in the United States, the initial need for parking space for about 6,000 cars, and the high rate of traffic increase, amounting to 22 percent per annum when construction of the new field began. The unobstructed area of the original military field provided sufficient space for the 11,000-foot runways required by jet aircraft and made the spreading finger plan that the architects adopted the logical choice for bringing passengers and planes to-gether. The construction of the domestic terminal with its associated mail, cargo, baggage-handling, and fuel-storage facilities, repair hangars, telephone exchange, control tower, and generating plant was completed in 2½ years and opened for public use on 16 January 1962 (fig. 115). The international terminal was rebuilt from the original temporary structure and was opened in the following year (upper left, fig. 115). The total cost to the city of the entire domestic and international com-plex as it existed in 1963 was $155,000,000.

The architects' original plan of 1959 was modified somewhat before construction began, chiefly to expand the number of gates for aircraft parking. The final design as embodied in the completed structures is characterized by a polygonal site plan in which the two domestic terminal buildings, the main restaurant, the international terminal, and the connecting concourses extend along three sides of the hexagonal area of the parking lot. Springing from the transverse center line of each of the three terminal enclosures is a Y-shaped plane concourse with a stem 960 feet long and two branches of 1,160 feet each. Between the Y-shaped fingers are two straight con-course runs for the handling of miscellaneous cargo and mail. The main terminal buildings of the domestic complex are concrete-framed structures each 770 feet long, divided between a lower or grade level with baggage facilities for incoming passen-gers and a high-ceilinged glass-sheathed second level for departing passengers which includes the usual service elements such as ticket counters, newsstands, snack bars, lounges, telephones, and toilets. The dark glare-resistant glass in ½-inch thick sheets is divided into relatively narrow panels by the projecting mullions of the Miesian style. The overall design is simple, generally offering easy circulation from doorway to ticket office to plane gate, luminous by virtue of its light colors and lofty glass curtains, but suggesting an architectural formula of the fifties applied expertly if somewhat monotonously to these long interior spaces. The smaller international ter-minal, measuring 130 × 150 feet overall in plan, is in its formal character essentially a duplicate of the larger buildings.

The most interesting structural and planning features of the O'Hare complex lie outside the terminal buildings themselves. Each airline company has its own en-trance and exit doors facing the parking area and opening on a double-level ring drive whose upper deck is supported on V-shaped framed bents such as one finds in the bridges of the Italian engineer Riccardo Morandi. The ring drive is the end loop of the O'Hare extension of Kennedy Expressway connecting the field with the Loop

Fig. 115. O'Hare International
Airport, 11000 West O'Hare
Expressway, 1959–62. Naess and
Murphy, architects.

115

seventeen miles to the southeast.[23] Between the two domestic buildings stands a circular glass-enclosed restaurant and bar that is the only example in Chicago of suspended construction. The roof is composed of precast concrete slabs supported by a radial system of steel cables stretched between a tension ring of steel at the center and a peripheral compression ring of reinforced concrete carried on concrete columns. The roof cables were subjected to pretension by means of a 900-ton load of pig iron to bring them temporarily to their full elongation before the roof was sealed. The net area of 28,000 square feet in plan is sufficient to embrace a large dining room, a pancake grill, a coffee shop, and a cocktail lounge. Separated from all public enclosures at O'Hare Field is the heating and generating plant, a pure work of glass-sheathed diagonally braced steel framing that is the handsomest building in the whole vast complex, its nearest competitor being a cargo-handling terminal designed by Hammond and Roesch.[24]

Traffic at O'Hare Terminal grew at an unparalleled rate, indicating that if its construction had been delayed another year, the airport facilities of Chicago might have suffered total breakdown. In the first full year following its opening the number of passengers arriving and departing was 16,163,414, and this volume was nearly to double by 1968, when the total reached 30,124,543. The rate of increase slowed almost to a leveling off in the succeeding two years because of the economic recession, but this could only prove temporary.[25] This meteoric expansion of traffic, a high proportion of which arose from travel for business purposes, made a powerful impact on the urban economy. The areas of the city, suburbs, and unincorporated townships lying within a two-mile radius of the terminal buildings experienced a concentrated boom in the construction of office buildings, hotels, restaurants, manufacturing facilities, warehouses, and associated service enterprises. The chief arteries of the area—Kennedy and O'Hare expressways, Tri-State and Northwest toll roads, Mannheim Road, and River Road—were quickly lined with one of the greatest collections of garish motel and restaurant architecture in the nation, a concentration relieved only by the belt of forest preserve land lying along the Des Plaines River. This highly compressed reenactment of inner-city history on the metropolitan fringe was intensified by a number of other socioeconomic forces—the general expansion of the population, the shift of population and industry to the suburbs, the creation of the freeway network, and the land-development program of the North Western Railway in the broad corridor extending north from the company's Proviso Yard between its Des Plaines Cutoff freight line and the Tri-State Toll Road.

The chaos of new building along all the approaches to O'Hare was constructed without planning, in total disregard of the means for rational channeling of automotive traffic, and with blatant unconcern for the human needs of the residential population. At the same time the growing traffic at the airport produced an extent and concentration of noise, surface dirt, vehicular movement, and atmospheric pollution that had by 1970 reached intolerable levels of physical hardship and psychological damage to all persons living in the ring of suburbs surrounding the field. The Northeastern Illinois Planning Commission made a study of the region in the spring of 1970 in which it stated categorically that by 1975 the entire area within a 5-mile radius of the airport, an area of about 130 square miles outside the confines of the field itself, would be unfit for residential uses and daily work. The airport itself, considered from the strictly mechanical standpoint of accommodating passengers and planes, was at the same time approaching the saturation level. To relieve congestion the city expanded and rebuilt Midway Airport in 1966–68 from the plans of C. F. Murphy Associates, replacing the World's Fair Modern of its architectural decor with a long sweep of glass walls set in a black painted steel frame, but the airlines made only a negligible effort to shift their traffic to the revived terminal.

The city, however, had grander ambitions: a third airport was felt to be essential, and the only place to locate it so that the municipal establishment could benefit from the resulting commercial activity was in the lake off the South Shore. A single comparison between events at the beginning and the end of this history serves to reveal what had been accomplished: in 1910 the North Western Railway was about to open a terminal capable of accommodating 250,000 passengers per day on some forty acres of buildings and tracks, or 6,250 passengers per acre, while Burnham and Bennett had just proposed a lakefront plan designed to make 3,000 acres of scenic and recreational land available to the people at no sacrifice to the commercial value or to the purity of the lake; in 1970 the city proposed to offer an acre of space to every ten travelers and to ruin in the process the scenic and recreational potential of one of the greatest water resources in the world.

NOTES TO CHAPTER 6

1. The project also included the construction of an additional sixty-eight parking garages in intermediate areas of the city, chiefly where there were high concentrations of commercial buildings and major transfer points on the rapid transit system. The garage at 11 West Wacker Drive, built in 1955 from the plans of Shaw, Metz and Dolio, attracted particular attention because in place of the conventional walls and parapets the designers used stainless-steel cables strung in a dense vertical pattern between the floors of the flat-slab concrete frame. The resulting cagelike appearance

of the structure led to its popular designation of "Birdcage Garage." The replacement of landscaping above the Grant Park underground garages required the covering of the upper slab with large sheets of butyl-rubber membrane to prevent damage to the concrete and the cars from the seepage of rain and meltwater.

2. The extension of Wacker Drive followed the structural system of the earlier work in all essential details (flat slab, mushroom capitals, drop panels), but since it is set well back from the river's edge, it is fortunately free of the obstructions formed by the abutment enclosures of the bascule bridges along the main stem of the river. For an artery with ten traffic lanes exclusive of the entrance and exit ramps between levels, the extension is remarkably unobtrusive, the only serious damage wrought by its construction being the demolition of Adler and Sullivan's Walker Warehouse (1888–89). The opening of the drive, as we have seen, proved a potent stimulus to the building of new office towers, including the 110-story Sears, Roebuck giant (construction initiated 1970).

3. Chicago bridges selected by the American Institute of Steel Construction for awards in their respective classes are the following:

   Wabash Avenue bridge over main river, 1928–30; Department of Public Works, engineers; bascule Pratt truss; first-place award, 1930.

   Pedestrian bridge, 47th Street and South Lake Shore Drive, 1937–38; Chicago Park District, engineers; arched plate girder; honorable mention, 1938.

   Bataan–Corregidor Memorial Bridge, State Street over main river, 1947–49; Department of Public Works, engineers; bascule Pratt truss; honorable mention, 1949.

   South Pond Bridge, Lincoln Park, 1960–61; Chicago Park District, engineers; welded-steel girder; award of merit, 1961.

   Dearborn Street bridge over main river, 1959–63; Department of Public Works, engineers; bascule Pratt truss; award of merit, 1963.

   Pedestrian bridge, 51st Street and South Lake Shore Drive, 1966; Westenhoff and Novick, engineers; welded-steel girder on T-piers; award of merit, 1967.

   In addition to the above the pedestrian bridge over North Lake Shore Drive a little above North Avenue, a three-hinged steel-arch span built in 1939–40 from the designs of Ralph H. Burke, was shown in photographs at the exhibition "Built in USA, 1932–1944," Museum of Modern Art, New York, 1944.

4. The relatively happy outcome of the Oak Street controversy inevitably gave rise to the question why the citizens' voices carried some weight in this case but none whatsoever during the numerous acts of destruction visited upon the south lakeshore. The public bodies were virtually the same in all cases (Chicago Heritage Committee, Chicago chapters of the American Institute of Architects and the American Society of Planning Officials, Northeast Illinois Metropolitan Plan Commission, Metropolitan Housing and Planning Council, and the Department of Urban Planning at IIT). There was the suggestion that the difference lay in the character of the local opposition, a group of upper-income Gold Coast residents, on the one hand, whose favor the Daley administration had been diligently and successfully cultivating, and ghetto residents, university professors, and assorted intellectuals on the other.

5. Service on this line of the North Shore was terminated in 1963, but the right-of-way was acquired by the North Western Railway to provide a better route for an existing freight-transfer line. The two rail lines originally lay on contiguous rights-of-way, so that the expressway bridge had to be long enough to clear both of them.

6. The ancestor of the idea of multitransportation arteries was probably the practice

that originated in Europe in the late nineteenth century of placing streetcar lines in the planted media of broad streets. The only example surviving in the United States in 1970 is the Saint Charles Avenue car line in New Orleans.

7. This generalization applies to all transportation media, including water, highway, and air, which are heavily subsidized by municipal, state, and federal governments through the construction of canals, locks, roads, and airports, and in the case of the last, through mail contracts. Even with these advantages the airline industry as a whole operated at a deficit in 1970.

8. The rise in the basic city fares for rapid transit and surface lines since 1910 is shown in the following table:

1910–22, all fares	5 cents
1922–42, all fares	7 cents
1942–April 1947, all fares	8 cents
April–October 1947, all fares	9 cents
October 1947–May 1948, all fares	10 cents
May–June 1948, surface	11 cents
rapid transit	13 cents
June 1948–October 1949, surface	13 cents
rapid transit	15 cents
October 1949–August 1951, surface	15 cents
rapid transit	17 cents
August 1951–June 1952, surface	17 cents
rapid transit	18 cents
June 1952–July 1957, all fares	20 cents
July 1957–July 1961, all fares	25 cents
July 1961–November 1967, all basic fares	25 cents
transfer fares	30 cents
November 1967–December 1968, all basic fares	30 cents
transfer fares	35 cents
December 1968 et seq., all basic fares	45 cents
transfer fares	50 cents

The fares for rapid transit service to Evanston and Skokie had always been higher than the city fare. By December 1968 these had risen to 60 cents for Evanston and 70 cents for Skokie, levels which meant that rapid transit fares were no longer competitive with those for multiride commutation tickets on standard railroads operating over comparable distances.

For the annual volume of passenger traffic on the CTA, see table 7.

9. The CTA inherited a far from adequate system of block signaling, which was restricted to curves and short distances of the tangent approaches to them, to the approaches to heavily used stations, and to outer tracks north of Wilson Avenue. Although full automatic signaling was introduced in the State Street subway from the beginning, the truncated installation on the elevated lines has never been expanded. All switches and signals at junctions and crossings are operated by electropneumatic interlocking machines with two-light semaphore dwarf signals.

10. Electrodynamic braking on the CTA cars is used in conjunction with the traditional air-brake system, but electrical control is maintained throughout both phases. The great advantage for the motorman is that brakes are operated by the power controller rather than by a brake valve with a separate controlling device.

11. The Chicago, Aurora and Elgin Railroad had completely abandoned service in 1957, leaving only the Chicago, South Shore and South Bend to provide electric interurban service in the Chicago metropolitan area. For the history of these companies, see Carl Condit, *Chicago, 1910–29* (Chicago: University of Chicago Press, 1973), pp. 50–52.

12. Associated with the CTA engineering staff in planning these lines were the consulting engineers De Leuw, Cather and Company.

 The total cost of the three projects was divided between $6,000,000 for the Englewood terminal and $107,000,000 for the two rapid transit lines. The glass-walled terminal and the associated steel-girder bridge were opened in 1969.

13. The record number of passengers to travel on the Century came on 7 January 1929, when the eastbound train (Number 26) was operated in seven sections to accommodate 822 reservations. The occasion, ironically enough, was the opening of the National Automobile Show in New York. The flood of wartime traffic (at the peak 910,000,000 passengers and 95,000,000,000 passenger-miles in 1944) was a different kind from the free-spending tycoons and the movie stars who filled the Century's Pullmans.

14. The distribution of average weekday suburban traffic on the Chicago railroads in 1969 was as follows (figures indicate total of inbound and outbound passengers to the nearest thousand):

North Western (three main lines)	90,000
Illinois Central (main line and two branches)	75,000
Burlington (single main line)	40,000
Milwaukee (two main lines)	40,000
Rock Island (main line and branch)	28,000
South Shore (single main line)	22,000
Gulf, Mobile, and Ohio, Norfolk and Western, Penn-Central (single main line each)	1,500
Total	296,500

15. For the location of Lake Calumet and its relation to the other waterways of the area, see Condit, *Chicago, 1910–29,* fig. 1. Chicago had always enjoyed transoceanic commerce, but the old canals built to bypass the Saint Lawrence rapids limited ships to 1,200 tons maximum.

16. Tonnage of ocean cargo handled at the combined ports of Chicago in the last year before the opening of the Saint Lawrence Seaway, the first year of seaway operation, and the tenth year after the opening is given in the accompanying table.

Ocean Cargo Handled in Chicago

Year	Tons Export	Tons Import	Total
1958	114,834	93,711	208,545
1959	754,272	394,019	1,148,291
1968	2,130,319	2,202,463	4,332,782

The Federal Reserve Bank of Chicago estimated in 1959 that the tonnage would rise to 6,000,000 in 1965, from which we could extrapolate a total of around 8,000,000 tons in 1970, but competitive freight rates on cargo shipped by rail to Gulf Coast and East Coast ports, inadequate publicizing of the port's facilities, and a high rate of loss from thievery prevented the city from drawing the full potential of cargo

from its own agricultural and industrial hinterland as well as from European and
Asiatic shippers.

17. The expansion of the Chicago water supply system after World War II embraced the
following elements:
   I. Water tunnels
      1. 79th Street, 1959. Length 4.8 miles; interior diameter 10, 12, and 16 feet (all
         new tunnels concrete lined).
      2. North Lake Shore, 1962. Connection between Central District Filtration
         Plant and Lake View Pumping Station. Length 5.80 miles; interior diameter
         8 and 16 feet (tunnel laid throughout horizontal run in Niagara dolomite at
         a depth of 160 feet below grade).
      3. Columbus Avenue, 1963. Length 2.85 miles; interior diameter 9 and 12 feet.
   II. Pumping station: Southwest, 8422 South Kedvale Avenue, 1963. Four electri-
       cally driven pumps; capacity 175 mgd.
   Aggregate length of tunnels by district, 1967:

North	16.42 miles
Central	27.10 "
South	31.03 "
Total	74.55 "

   Pumping capacity by district, 1967:

North	560,000,000 gallons per day
Central	1,280,000,000 " " "
South	1,050,000,000 " " "
Total	2,890,000,000 " " "

   Quantities of water pumped, 1965:

Daily average, Chicago	852,539,000 gallons
Daily average, suburbs	138,031,000 "
Total daily average	990,570,000 "
Maximum pumpage (23 July)	1,502,330,000 "

   Daily per capita consumption 200 gallons, constant since 1910 and the highest
   per capita consumption in the world.

   Chemical treatment shown in total quantities of compounds dissolved in water,
   1966:

Aluminum sulfate	6,207 tons
Hydrofluosilicic acid	3,850 tons
Chlorine	2,532 tons
Lime	2,300 tons
Activated carbon	1,547 tons
Aluminum oxide	1,271 tons
Fluorine	701 tons
Ferrous sulfate	226 tons
Anhydrous ammonia	143 tons
Sodium silicate	35 tons

   These various compounds are introduced for the following purposes: chlorine and
   anhydrous ammonia, disinfectants; aluminum sulfate, aluminum oxide, ferrous sulfate, and sodium silicate, coagulants in the filtration process; activated carbon, taste
   and odor inhibitor; lime, softening and anticorrosive agent; hydrofluosilicic acid and
   fluorine, dental-caries inhibitors. (Chief source: Chicago Department of Water and
   Sewers, *The Water Supply System of Chicago* [Chicago, 1966].)

18. The history of the Sanitary District's diversion of water from Lake Michigan has been a continuing national and eventually international controversy since the Sanitary and Ship Canal was placed under construction. The chief events in this history are given in the following table:

    1891–1900.   Chicago Sanitary and Ship Canal constructed.

    1899.   Provisional permit granted by the secretary of war allowing the district to divert 5,000 cubic feet per second (cfs).

    1900.   The state of Missouri filed suit in the United States Supreme Court to enjoin the district from diverting water into the Illinois River as a means of transporting and oxidizing raw sewage. The court denied the injunction in 1901.

    1912.   The Sanitary District petitioned the secretary of war to increase diversion to 10,000 cfs.

    1922.   Wisconsin filed suit in the United States Supreme Court to compel the district to reduce diversion.

    1925.   The secretary of war granted a permit to the district to divert 8,500 cfs. Minnesota, Ohio, and Pennsylvania joined the Wisconsin suit.

    1926.   Michigan and New York filed similar actions against the district. Former Secretary of State Charles Evans Hughes was appointed Special Master in Chancery to hear the combined suits.

    1927.   Hughes recommended dismissal of actions but was reversed by the Supreme Court.

    1928–29.   The Sanitary District allowed diversion to increase to an average of 10,000 cfs.

    1929.   Hughes recommended a timetable for the reduction of diversion.

    1930.   The Supreme Court, following the recommendation of Hughes (appointed chief justice later the same year), decreed the following step-by-step diversion: 6,500 cfs by 1 July 1930; 5,000 cfs by 31 December 1935; 1,500 cfs by 31 December 1938. All direct diversion to be in addition to domestic and industrial pumpage.

    1954–57.   Repeated attempts by the Sanitary District to increase diversion through congressional legislation.

    1958.   The Great Lakes states secured permission from the United States Supreme Court to reopen the 1930 decree and instituted suit to compel the Sanitary District to return all effluent of the sewage treatment plants to the lake.

    1966.   Judge Albert B. Maris, special master appointed to hear the suit, ruled in favor of the Sanitary District and fixed the total maximum diversion for all categories of usage at 3,200 cfs.

    (Source: "Chicago's Lake Diversion Upheld," *Engineering News-Record* 177 [15 December 1966]:64–65.)

19. By 1966 the Metropolitan Sanitary District had expanded to meet the sewage disposal requirements of 858 square miles, embracing Chicago and 114 other municipalities together having a total population of about 5,000,000; its facilities provided secondary treatment for 1,180,000,000 gallons of domestic and industrial sewage per day, a treatment adequate to remove 90 percent of the suspended solids and 91 percent of the biological oxygen demand; its total capital investment was $625,000,000.

    The ultimate solution of the sludge-disposal problem was to transport the material as a slurry by pipe and railroad tank car to areas in central Illinois where it is sprayed on demonstration farms by means of movable nozzles.

20. Quoted in "Committee Report Vindicates Bacon," *Engineering News-Record* 185 (17 September 1970):58–59.

21. The magnitude of the operation makes the achievement all the more impressive: the Alsip tunnel is 18,000 feet long and 16 feet 10 inches in diameter and is situated 220 feet below grade, where the density of the dolomite gives it a compressive strength of 15,000–40,000 pounds per square inch.
22. Burke came close to the target: at the end of 1960 the traffic at O'Hare exceeded that at Midway for the first time, and the combined total was about 13,000,000 passengers for the year.
23. O'Hare Field was incorporated within the city limits of Chicago by the simple device of adding a great saclike embayment to the urban area and was given the official address of 11000 West O'Hare Expressway. The distance of the parking area from the Loop is seventeen miles, and the field proper extends so much farther to the west that a small part of it lies in Du Page County.
24. O'Hare Field is the world's largest and busiest airport, although several were in the planning stage in 1970 that will exceed it in area. Its total area of 6,600 acres is a little more than ten square miles. Drainage of this vast flat surface requires twenty-five miles of storm sewers. The distribution of water and electric power is provided by 102,987 lineal feet of water mains and 12,850 lineal feet of concrete-lined tunnels for pipes and conduits. The water-supply system can deliver 7,000,000 gallons of water per day, and the four main pipelines of the aircraft fuel-delivery system had an original capacity for 2,700,000 gallons of fuel per day. The work force when the field opened numbered 25,000 men and women.
25. The total traffic at O'Hare was very nearly equal to the number of suburban passengers carried by the Chicago and North Western Railway. Reduced to daily averages, the comparison is instructive: the average number of passengers at O'Hare Field was 82,308 in 1968, as against about 86,000 at North Western Station; the air terminal embraces 6,600 acres, as opposed to 43 for the rail terminal and its immediate approaches.

7. The New Chicago Plan

The separation of urban planning from urban renewal and reconstruction ought to be an arbitrary device adopted solely for the convenience of the historian, but in the American city the rebuilding of neighborhoods and core areas is seldom carried out under the terms of a genuine citywide plan, and then only in a sporadic and piece-meal way, so that the separation in question is in fact the pattern that the city customarily follows. The planning legacy of Haussmann and Burnham actually survived with alterations to the time of the Second World War, chiefly through the influence in Europe of Tony Garnier's *Cité Industrielle* and the Congrès Internationaux d'Architecture Moderne (usually designated by the initials CIAM), whose most authoritative spokesman was Le Corbusier. In England and the United States, however, the Garden City concept of Ebenezer Howard proved more congenial, and his leading American apostles, Clarence Stein and Henry Wright, persuaded private developers to build model communities in the extravagant twenties that proved to be forerunners of the more extensive essays undertaken by the Farm Security Administration and the Tennessee Valley Authority during the experimental days of the New Deal and of the planned satellite communities of the fifties and sixties. But the program of the CIAM was made up of dogmas that would have had an inhibiting effect on city life and growth, and the Garden City was an oversimplified idea that aimed to transform cities into cheerful suburbs; neither bore much relation to urban reality. What was more fruitful was the idea of regional planning, which in the United States goes back to Gifford Pinchot and the Inland Waterways Commission of 1907 and was given its demonstration on the grand scale by the TVA before it became a power-generating empire. The concept of the unified development and conservation of resources and its application to metropolitan areas was perhaps the chief stimulus to the theory of organic urban planning that reached the ascendent in the years following World War II.

The history of planning in Chicago after the Burnham phase began in 1925, when the Illinois General Assembly granted a charter to the Chicago Regional Planning Association for the purpose of undertaking a comprehensive survey of resources and needs in a fifteen-county tristate area centered on the mother city. It was a Chicago counterpart to the famous *Regional Survey of New York and Its Environs* that was published in 1928, though far less influential. The next step came with the establishment of the Metropolitan Housing and Planning Council in 1934, which marks the beginning in Chicago of the recognition of building as a social force and of the responsibility of the federal, state, and municipal governments for the crea-tion of a healthy city. The council's six hundred members inaugurated a program of investigating urban problems that led to a series of valuable acts of the state legis-lature in the years following the war of 1941. A preliminary report on the planning needs of the metropolitan area was issued in 1944 and was followed by recommen-dations to the general assembly that bore fruit in the form of the Blighted Areas Redevelopment Act of 1947 and the Urban Community Conservation Act of 1953. The council in 1951 proposed the merger of all the city's agencies having to do with land clearance, planning, conservation, and redevelopment into a single Department of Urban Renewal, a much-needed step that was realized in stages over the years up to 1966. The chief goals of the council throughout the decade of the sixties were a long-term overall plan for lakefront development, the distribution of public hous-ing throughout the city, and the expansion of the city's renewal program.[1] These activities were paralleled on a regional scale by the planning work of the Northeast-ern Illinois Metropolitan Area Planning Commission, established by an act of the Illinois legislature in 1956 and subsequently given the less awkward title of North-eastern Illinois Planning Commission. Its most valuable contribution to area plan-ning was a proposal presented in a series of annual reports for reservation of land in the outer metropolitan area against future public needs and for green corridors extending through the suburban rings, both of them suggested long before in the original Chicago Plan.

Meanwhile, the municpal government began to arouse itself from its planning slumbers by creating in January 1957 the Department of City Planning, which thus took the place of the long-dormant Plan Commission that had been established un-der the Burnham legacy. Under the direction of Ira J. Bach, the new department took its first major step by preparing a development plan for the core area of Chi-cago in 1958. The plan was predicated, quite correctly, on the assumption that the central business district and its neighboring lakefront had constituted Chicago's most distinguishing and most impressive characteristic down through the years, the one that gave the city its particular esprit and placed it in the front rank of world cities. Its revitalization and its maintenance in a flourishing state through all its dimensions were matters of prime importance. As the magazine *Fortune* was later to put it,

Two characteristics . . . are common to all great cities. They all have an exciting downtown filled with a great variety of shops, theatres, museums, and other attrac-tions, and laid out as a place of great beauty—designed, in the words of the architect Louis Kahn, to be "the cathedral of the city." Equally important, they have a large middle-class population residing near downtown, possessing the purchasing power and the tastes to help sustain its activities. . . . Of all our cities, only New York, Chicago, and San Francisco can even claim to be great cities.[2]

Much of what the plan commission proposed was realized in the great building boom of the sixties and would have been realized whether area plans had existed or not. Among the recommendations that were carried out under various public and corporate needs were the Civic Center, the Federal Court House as a first step in the future Federal Center, the parking garages on the periphery of the core area, the connection between the Ryan–Stevenson expressway interchange and Lake Shore Drive, new apartments on the Near North Side within walking distance of the Loop, new apartment and office towers with associated plazas in the Michigan–Wacker area and along the north bank of the river, new cargo-handling facilities at Navy Pier, an exposition hall cold-bloodedly proposed for the lakefront, where it was mistakenly built, the Chicago campus of the University of Illinois, but proposed to be built on vacated rail property rather than in a residential neighborhood, and the industrial redevelopment of the area on the West Side along Canal and Clinton streets. But much remained undone, although some of it was of questionable benefit or need. Among the useful proposals affecting traffic circulation that have yet to pass beyond the planning stage were the relocation of Lake Shore Drive to remove the turns along the river, the extension of Columbus Drive across the river to the Near North Side, the eastward extension of Wacker Drive to Lake Shore, and the concentration of South Side rail passenger traffic in Union Station, erroneously thought to require enlargement for the purpose. The plan for a unified rail-bus-helicopter-ticket office transportation center over the Union Station tracks, although offering the advantages of unification, possessed the obvious disadvantage of being remote from hotels and from the recently completed Union Bus Terminal. The best features of the Central Area Plan, however, came in good part directly from Burnham and Bennett's handiwork of 1909—new parks and beaches along the harsh, stony, unplanted strip of lakefront from Navy Pier to North Avenue, islands, lagoons, and yacht harbors along the south lakeshore below Northerly Island, and a planned apartment enclave over the Illinois Central Railroad property between Randolph Drive and the river.[3]

The Central Area Plan proved to be a preliminary exercise to the primary goal of the commission, which was to prepare a comprehensive plan that was to be a new guide to the city's future growth and was to take the place of the now forgotten Chicago Plan of 1909. The new document was prepared in two stages between 1960 and 1966 by a staff of researchers and theorists working under the direction of Larry Reich, who was the principal author of the Philadelphia Plan of 1960. After a considerable controversy arising from unnecessary secrecy, refusals to keep the public informed of progress, and frequent delays in publication beyond the announced date, the initial document was completed and published in 1964 under the title *Basic Policies for the Comprehensive Plan of Chicago*. The idea was to stimulate popular discussion followed by the public presentation of critical views by community groups and private interests, out of which it was hoped there would arise guidelines and advice for the ultimate plan itself. But since the city did little to realize these aims, and although the newspapers valiantly strove to publicize the document's features along with much cogent criticism, the hoped-for public debate never occurred. The city accordingly went ahead with the preparation of the *Comprehensive Plan of Chicago,* publishing it in 1966, and then, in a veritable frenzy of document production, issued at regular intervals during the following two years a *Summary Report* of the main plan and sixteen detailed reports on the planned renewal and revitalization of sixteen corresponding divisions of the urban area. The ultimate objectives of the Comprehensive Plan and the theoretical means of achieving them (as opposed to the practical exigencies of urban building) are conveniently summarized in the introductory section of the *Summary Report* and indicate immediately the differences in aims, strategies, and concerns between the Burnham Plan and its 1966 counterpart.

The 1966 *Comprehensive Plan of Chicago* provides the means by which citizens, through their elected representatives, can define programs that will effectively move the city toward future goals.

The 1964 *Basic Policies for the Comprehensive Plan of Chicago* set forth the central goal: to improve the quality of life. This means to enlarge human opportunities, to improve the environment, and to strengthen and diversify the economy. . . .

The complete Comprehensive Plan document contains four major parts:

The Quality of Life, the philosophy and strategic objectives of the plan.

The Planning Framework, trends and policies for population, economy, and land use and a statement of principles for metropolitan development.

The Policies Plan, derived largely from the Basic Policies report, with modifications and additions of a number of new subjects.

The Improvement Plan, which identifies methods of implementing the policies. . . .

The Comprehensive Plan . . . deals with things that can be done now to have the greatest beneficial impact on the quality of life in Chicago. . . . Therefore, policies for action are focused on six strategic objectives:

Family Life and Environment. Neighborhoods that are attractive to families with growing children, as well as young unmarried people and older couples, will be created and retained.

Expanded Opportunities for the Disadvantaged.   The city will increase, intensify, and coordinate programs to arrest poverty and improve living conditions for low-income people, through urban opportunity programs, education and job-training, public housing, social services, and other efforts.

Economic Development and Job Opportunities.   Chicago's dynamic industrial and business economy continues to thrive because of the city's location at a focal point of world trade routes and because of its expanding role as a regional capital. The city's programs will select and emphasize the key opportunities to build upon this economic potential.

Moving People and Goods.   Chicago's role as a regional transportation center requires efficient and convenient air, rail, highway, and water routes and terminals. Within the Chicago area a system of high accessibility corridors will provide a logical framework for the development of both major transportation routes and high-intensity land uses.

The Proper Allocation of Land.   The city's basic pattern of land use is logical. In most cases activities are appropriately related to the lakefront, rivers, and major transportation routes. But there are opportunities for improvement in the quality of areas, especially in the central city, while still retaining their present functions.

Unified City Development.   In translating these strategic objectives into tangible progress, the city will continue to work for cooperation and coordination in public and private efforts. The Development Area planning procedure will serve as a means of achieving maximum effectiveness of programs within large areas of the city.[4]

The new master plan sought to guide the city through the year 1981, and realizing its aims for the urban fabric was expected to require a program of public works involving an expenditure of $6,000,000,000 in this fifteen-year period, of which total it was hoped a major proportion would be borne by the federal government. Private investment would at least have to match this figure and preferably exceed it by several times. Although the document is the first plan in the United States to be concerned with social, personal, and economic goals as well as physical structure, the chief respect in which it differs from the Burnham Plan, it nevertheless offers a broad outline of public construction in somewhat similar form though in far less detail than the comparable programs of its predecessor. The closest parallels between the two plans appear in the respective programs for the facilities of recreation and transportation. The *Comprehensive Plan* proposes the addition of 1,800 acres of intracity parks, to be supplemented by two hundred joint school–park sites and 1,200 acres of beach and shore area to be created by lake filling chiefly on the Far North and Far South sides. The standard for the city parks is the small neighborhood area designed for intensive and diversified recreational use, rather than the big scenic spaces of meadow, woodland, and lagoon that Burnham envisioned. In transportation the new plan exhibits striking similarities to its antecedent: major streets are to be widened and rebuilt to speed the flow of traffic, yielding an arterial system laid out at approximately one-mile intervals; little-used streets are to be closed and replaced by pedestrian shopping malls; the expressway system is to be rounded out with the construction of the Crosstown link; and the rapid transit network is to be vastly expanded through the construction of seven new lines, of which only the Ryan and the Kennedy routes have been built (pp. 247–49). Closely associated with rearrangements in the transportation pattern is the clearing of spaces for the establishment of regional business and service centers and the expansion, rearrangement, and concentration of industrial zones.[5]

The characteristics in which the *Comprehensive Plan* differs most profoundly from the Burnham are those having to do with what the new document calls "the quality of life." The improvement of this intangible yet all-important feature of urbanism involves a massive public works program calling for a roughly 15 percent expansion of fire-fighting and police forces, the addition of standard community health centers, clinics, and mental health centers throughout the urban area, the construction of two hundred new elementary schools, fifty high schools, and seventy-five branch libraries, and an expansion of the University of Illinois campus sufficient to double the enrollment of 1967. But the overriding problem, on the solution of which the quality and even the very existence of the city stands or falls, is the provision of adequate housing for low- and middle-income groups. In this respect the plan is none too generous, proposing a total of 235,000 new dwelling units, divided between 35,000 units of public housing and 200,000 units of private, which would presumably leave a net addition of 200,000 dwellings after the necessary demolition of substandard homes and apartments. This volume of construction is to be supplemented by a massive program of conservation and rehabilitation, the various coordinated efforts aimed at providing decent housing for a population expected to increase by 225,000 up to 1981. All this proved to be wildly optimistic and to bear little relation to the realities of the urban economy.

The sheer complexity of public works and residential programs in a city the size of Chicago and the problem of citizen participation in the planning process led the Department of Planning to divide the city into smaller areas for which programs of public construction and development could be worked out in adequate detail and related to the specific needs and varied conditions of individual neighborhoods. The department defined a total of sixteen of these "development areas," ranging in population from 150,000 to 250,000, in size from six to twenty square miles, and in character from airport and rail properties to upper-income residential streets, and issued a corresponding number of planning documents in 1967 and 1968.[6] The primary aims were to initiate a series of meetings between neighborhood organizations and representatives of the municipal government and thus to coordinate public action with private needs, but since the documents contained no proposals for specific action that could be translated into practice, and since city hall had a long history of excluding citizen participation from its municipal undertakings, the microplans, with their prettily colored maps and charts of the kind that planners love, produced no discernible results. The area plans failed for the same reason that the *Comprehensive Plan* failed: the documents are cautious to the point of being innocuous; they show no awareness of the unique assets and powers of the city, which Burnham and Bennett had grasped with remarkable understanding and vision; and they reveal either an incredible ignorance of or a deliberate refusal to see the appalling and steadily deepening social problems of the city.

The aims of all the plans were certainly laudable enough: to encourage all the numerous activities and institutions of the city—residential life and building, industry, commerce, transportation, recreation, education, safety, and health—to develop in a vigorous yet harmonious way in order to achieve three great ends of civic life— a life-enhancing environment, the opportunity for all to participate fully in organized community and political life, and a strong, stable, and diversified economy. The urban geographer Harold Mayer took a hopeful view of the main plan and its possibilities, seeing it as a central switchboard channeling the many forces of the city in such ways as to create order and strength rather than chaos and conflict. The Chicago Chapter of the American Institute of Architects was less cheerful, offering a balanced criticism of both method and aims. The realization of the program places great dependence on autonomous bodies like the board of education and the Chicago Housing Authority, the institute argued, but in no way defines how these bodies are related to the municipal authority and particularly to the planning department. Moreover, the proposed methods of realization are deficient because of the absence of specific programs, of concrete means for their implementation, and of alternative courses of action that would offer neighborhoods a meaningful choice of goals and possibilities of realization. But the most serious inadequacies are, first, the failure to recognize the extent of Chicago's social problems and hence what must be done to initiate solutions, and, second, the failure to understand the extent of the housing crisis and to realize that only radical means can deal with it. Finally, the plan reveals an indifference to the assets that give the city its unique greatness—its ethnic neigh-

borhoods with their clubs and restaurants, its lakefront, riverfront, Loop, forest preserves, expressway-rail corridors, its architectural heritage—and a casual attitude
toward their preservation and enhancement. And one might add, the authors of the
plan did not choose to recognize that the institutions and legal structure of the urban
economy are in great part designed to serve business, not the needs of the people,
and thus maintained complete indifference to the necessity for land-use control, industrial and commercial regulation, and land reservation.

With respect to Chicago's most serious disease, the racial bigotries and fears of
its white population, the planners apparently acted on the asumption that one can
avoid the sickness by not pronouncing its name. Sociologists and urban critics were
quick to point this out, as was done most emphatically by Joseph Black: "[The plan
is] a monumental effort to present a unified vision of the future of the city. But it is
essentially eyewash, its rhetoric reading more like a political document than a philosophy of planning."[7] The most constructive program of action as well as the most
penetrating and detailed criticism was offered at the same time by Edwin C. Berry
and Walter W. Stafford, respectively executive director and research specialist of
the Chicago Urban League.

The Comprehensive Plan poses more questions on racial problems than solutions.
The solutions proposed in the plan will have very little effect upon the conditions of
the ghetto. On the other hand, the questions that arise from an analysis of the plan
are worthy of future investigation. These questions would require both research and
radically different citizen participation processes. . . .

The major research need is to discover the causal relationships between land-use
arrangements and urban racism. The absence of refined research techniques . . .
weaken[s] the proposals for integration in the Comprehensive Plan. . . .

If the Comprehensive Plan had reversed its racial priorities and placed the first
emphasis upon good housing and environments for lower-income Negroes, undoubtedly some racial success could be achieved. At the least, new housing could be created for Negroes. As a long-range process improving the status of lower-income
Negroes could ease racial and class tensions that are now created by placing the
highest priorities on restricting the loss of white families and accommodating the
Negro middle class. . . .

The second step . . . is to involve Negroes and other low-income persons in the
city in the citizens' planning process. It is senseless to expect racial understanding
between whites and Negroes if the citizens' participation process remains segregated.
. . . The civil rights groups will probably first have to transmit their understanding
of physical planning and race relations to grass roots organizations and utilize advo-

cacy planning to involve organizations in developing alternatives. This presupposes that the civil rights organizations will . . . develop a sensitivity to physical planning and that the city will attempt to include the movement in the planning process.

Radically different priorities on the federal, state and local levels are needed to aid cities confronted with racial problems. The first priority would necessitate creation of regional planning agencies with strong statutory regulations which could link the various metropolitan, city and inner-city renewal proposals together and judge their land-use implications upon segregation. Second, federal and city policies are needed which could financially supplement displaced families from renewal and clearance areas wishing to relocate in the suburban ring near industry. . . . The first job priorities should be given to Negroes when renewal and clearance are instituted in ghetto areas. The policies would simultaneously increase the economic and social stability of lower-income Negroes. . . .

The Department of Development and Planning . . . lacks the power to link the [planning] tools to the city's abstract racial goals. The civil rights movement and planners share one common problem: both are limited in their efforts to improve the status of the Negro because Chicago proper lacks the power to enforce equal opportunity for Negroes in the suburbs.[8]

The sociologist Pierre de Vise, a research associate of the Hospital Council for Metropolitan Chicago, saw the plan's failure to attack the problem of segregation as a consequence of the system of interlocking legal and economic devices by means of which the city and the suburbs together preserve segregation, contrary to the fair-housing ordinance that the municipality itself passed. A massive obstacle to change, grown up over the years by design and through inertia, is the splitting of the municipal authority into numerous independent agencies answerable only to themselves. The "political fragmentation and privatization of government," as de Vise called it, is maintained "by delegating powers of education, public housing, and urban renewal to such satellite governments . . . as the Chicago Board of Education, the Chicago Housing Authority," and other public agencies and private institutions.[9] The *Comprehensive Plan* sprang from a political context determined by the municipal establishment, with the consequence that the planners had to placate city hall and the economic powers behind it rather than turn their attention to pressing social problems. In this way they failed to perform the minimal public service that was their responsibility. Jerome L. Kaufman, assistant director of the American Society of Planning Officials, saw this fact as the basis of the plan's innocuous character. "The Chicago Comprehensive Plan, despite its promises and prose, is a cautious document. It calls for few radical departures from existing policy. . . . [The planners] probably reasoned that if their position in city government was to be maintained and their ideas accepted, they would have to stay within the bounds of reason, discretion, and good sense as defined by city hall. This obviously meant that on the race issue, the plan must be 'sensible.' "[10]

Finally, the city's economic position, on which the whole program ultimately rested, was in a precarious state and offered no ground for the planners' confidence in industrial expansion. The Northeastern Illinois Planning Commission in 1965 estimated that over the thirty-year period from 1955 to 1985 the city's share of manufacturing employment in the Standard Metropolitan Area would drop from 70 percent to 45 percent. At the halfway point all the trends supported this prediction. And there was a more ominous fact that made the planners' concern with "the quality of life" sound like pure dramatic irony: between the censuses of 1960 and 1970 the city lost 485,000 whites to the suburbs, and there is no question that an equal number of blacks, Latin Americans, and Indians would have followed them if they could have escaped from their ghetto prisons. The *Comprehensive Plan* offered pious sentences as a means of stemming the steady and inexorable drift toward a polarized society.

Meanwhile, the federal government offered the cities the means for still another renewal plan in the increasingly tiresome round of abortive liberal panaceas. In 1966 Congress passed the necessary legislation to establish the Demonstration Cities and Metropolitan Development programs. The laudable aim was to end the bulldozer technique of urban rebuilding, to concentrate on the rehabilitation of existing housing, and in recognition of the fact that the complex of urban activities constitutes an organic unity, to make a thoroughly planned approach toward revitalizing the whole spectrum of community services and economic opportunities along with improving the physical fabric. Schools, health centers, recreational facilities, welfare services, local businesses, job training, police and fire protection, and transportation were to be simultaneously and radically upgraded in selected neighborhoods marked by the severest forms of urban pathology. Supplemented by the National Housing Act of 1968, which differs from its predecessors chiefly in its provisions for rental and mortgage subsidies, the so-called Model Cities program was regarded as the implanting of grafts in the most diseased areas in the hope that healthy tissue would spread outward through the urban body. Chicago designated four neighborhoods as most desperately in need of immediate treatment and submitted an application for funds to undertake a multiple program of community renewal and revitalization. The four areas had long been in need of serious attention: Uptown, centered at Wilson Avenue (4600W) and Broadway, the city's major enclave of Appalachian and Indian migrants; Lawndale, the chief West Side ghetto, spreading widely around the intersection of Madison Street and Lawndale Avenue (3700W); and the ghetto areas of the South Side, one in the neighborhood of 55th and State Street, and the other Woodlawn, extending along both sides of the east stretch of 63rd Street.

The goals of Chicago's Model Cities program bordered on the utopian—to achieve a level of income and education adequate for all to command the necessities and to enjoy the amenities of middle-class life, to coordinate all community services ministering to health, safety, and well-being of the citizens and to make them easily available to all, to build an attractive life-enhancing and life-protecting physical environment for all. The means by which these ends were to be achieved had all been employed before; what was unique about the new program was that they were to be brought together in a massive coordinated assault. Housing was to be expanded and its availability increased by construction over expressways and on vacant or derelict land, through the rehabilitation of existing housing, and by means of private loan pools supplemented by rental and mortgage subsidies. Public facilities other than schools were to include park malls, renewed and landscaped commercial areas, and Headstart and kindergarten facilities as well as the usual recreational spaces and cultural institutions. In addition to the construction of new schools, existing schools were to be kept open day and evening throughout the year and used for tutoring, adult education, and job training, and as neighborhood assembly centers. Teachers were to be recruited for teaching in low-income ghetto areas by means of special incentives and prepared for their tasks by special training. By raising the employment level, providing day-care centers for the children of working mothers, expanding local industries, and ending the indignities of the iniquitous welfare system the planners hoped to improve the economic level of the neighborhood to the point where self-sufficiency would not be a chimerical dream. Crime was to be reduced by means of greater numbers of better trained police and an improvement in the relations between the police and private citizens, which are marked in the ghetto by the bitterest kind of animosity.

No one would quarrel with these aims, and some start was made toward reaching them, but they went largely unrealized because of underlying social, economic, and moral defects that the most affluent society in the world had rendered itself powerless to correct even if it had the will to do so. By the mid-twentieth century it seemed clear that the American system in its traditional form could no longer produce a livable urban environment. In 1939 the United States was rescued from the depression by the military expenditures of the Second World War, and in the years that followed the military establishment, aided by its industrial allies, the political directorate of the federal government, and Congress, expanded its power until it finally exercised the controlling voice in the national economy.

The National Advisory Commission on Civil Disorders issued an exhaustive report in 1968 making it obvious that the chief causes of urban violence were gross economic inequalities and white racism, yet politicians found it expedient to respond only to the fears of their white constituents rather than to recognize the truth and to act upon it. Their chief concern, indeed, seemed to be the encouragement of a steady drift toward a police state through the secret and unchecked powers of the Department of Justice and the Central Intelligence Agency.

With a high proportion of its resources sapped by the military behemoth, the industrial machine concentrated the remainder of its power on producing an ever expanding volume of consumer goods, in the process corrupting the environment and filling the cities with the shoddiest examples of bad workmanship, cheap materials, and tasteless design, including the architecture of much of the metropolitan milieu. The United States was rapidly becoming the City of the Apocalypse, and no amount of democratic actions, liberal programs, common causes, urban coalitions, and metaphors like the greening of America could deflect it from its course. If Chicago seemed to be a more malignant cancer than other cities, it was partly because it represented its own special mixture of the American diseases and partly because of the incredible contrast between its evils and its unparalleled artistic, architectural, structural, and planning achievements. Only a radical program of physical and moral reconstruction initiated by the people themselves could restore the promise of an earlier day.

NOTES TO CHAPTER 7

1. For the implementation of these various programs, see chaps. 4 and 5.
2. Edmund K. Faltermayer, "What It Takes to Make Great Cities," *Fortune* 75(January 1967):118.
3. As of 1970 it appeared that the magnificent potentialities of the Illinois Central's land, no longer needed for freight operations, would be used entirely for a forest of skyscrapers.
4. Department of Development and Planning, *The Comprehensive Plan of Chicago: Summary Report* (Chicago: Department of Development and Planning, 1967), p. 2.
5. The main arteries in the street improvement program are arranged by area as follows:
    Chief north–south arteries: Torrence (2634E), Cottage Grove (200–1100E), Michigan (100E), LaSalle (150W), Halsted (800W), Western (2400W,) Pulaski (4000W), Central (5600W), Harlem (7200W).
    Chief east–west arteries on the North Side: Lake (200N), North (1600N), Irving Park (4000N), Foster (5200N), Devon (6400N).
    Chief east–west arteries on the South Side: Roosevelt (1200S), Cermak (2200S), Pershing (3900S), 55th, 87th, 107th, 111th, 127th, 130th, 134th.

Intermediate streets to be widened: Madison (east–west); Racine (1200W), Ashland (1600W), Damen (2000W), all north–south.

The seven rapid transit lines are the following: Ryan Expressway, Kennedy Expressway, Crosstown Expressway (median), Stevenson Expressway (median), Western Avenue (subway), east–west crosstown line on Far North Side to connect new and existing north–south lines (subway, structure, and fill), a similar line on the Far South Side.

6. For the specific titles and dates of these documents, see the Bibliography.
7. W. Joseph Black, "The Renewed Negro and Urban Renewal," *Architectural Forum* 128(June 1968):65.
8. Edwin C. Berry and Walter W. Stafford, "The Critique," in *The Racial Aspects of Urban Planning,* ed. Harold M. Baron (Chicago: Urban League, 1968), pp. 31–32.
9. Pierre de Vise, in Baron, *Racial Aspects of Urban Planning,* p. 52.
10. Jerome L. Kaufman, in Baron, *Racial Aspects of Urban Planning,* p. 45.

Tables

TABLE 1

POPULATION, AREA, AND DENSITY OF CHICAGO

Year	Population of City	Population of Metropolitan Area[a]	Area of City in Square Miles	Density per Square Mile
1830	ca. 100		0.417	240
1840	4,470		10.186	439
1850	29,963		9.311	3,218
1860	109,260		17.492	6,246
1870	298,977		35.152	8,505
1880	505,185		35.152	14,371
1890	1,099,850		178.052	6,177
1900	1,698,575		189.517	8,963
1910	2,185,283	2,805,869	190.204	11,489
1920	2,701,705	3,575,209	198.270	13,626
1930	3,376,438	4,733,777	207.204	15,862
1940	3,396,808	4,890,674	212.863	15,958
1950	3,620,962	5,586,096	212.863	17,011
1960	3,550,404	6,794,453	212.863	16,679
1970	3,366,951	6,892,509	227.251	14,816

SOURCES: United States Census; Frank A. Randall, *History of the Development of Building Construction in Chicago* (Urbana: University of Illinois Press, 1949), p. 4; Municipal Reference Library of Chicago.
[a] The Standard Metropolitan Area of Chicago includes Cook, Du Page, Kane, Lake, and Will counties in Illinois, and Lake and Porter counties in Indiana.

TABLE 2

OFFICE SPACE CONSTRUCTED IN THE CENTRAL BUSINESS DISTRICT
OF CHICAGO, 1872 TO THE PRESENT

Year	Net Area in Square Feet (area added less demolished space)	Continuing Total	Year	Net Area in Square Feet (area added less demolished space)	Continuing Total
1872	322,007	322,007	1912	1,884,780	12,605,638
1873	—a	—	1913	1,280,265	13,885,903
1874	—	—	1914	1,278,914	15,164,817
1875	49,550	371,557	1915	211,020	15,375,837
1876	—	—	1916	293,479	15,669,316
1877	—	—	1917	171,053	15,840,369
1878	—	—	1918	73,651	15,914,020
1879	—	—	1919	150,916	16,064,936
1880	—	—	1920	233,471	16,298,407
1881	—	—	1921	—	
1882	88,430	459,987	1922	151,687	16,450,094
1883	—	—	1923	2,018,792	18,468,886
1884	92,266	552,253	1924	1,110,345	19,579,231
1885	319,560	871,813	1925	447,510	20,026,741
1886	418,480	1,290,293	1926	1,044,953	21,071,694
1887	17,953	1,308,246	1927	3,017,778	24,089,472
1888	303,703	1,611,949	1928	2,072,474	26,161,946
1889	45,901	1,657,850	1929	2,890,594	29,052,540
1890	335,046	1,992,896	1930	1,674,555	30,727,095
1891	189,923	2,182,819	1931	−119,177	30,607,918
1892	957,615	3,140,434	1932	78,853	30,686,771
1893	730,046	3,870,480	1933	49,392	30,736,163
1894	288,270	4,158,750	1934	383,868	31,120,031
1895	499,037	4,657,787	1935	13,569	31,133,600
1896	216,776	4,874,563	1936	—	—
1897	125,250	4,999,813	1937	—	—
1898	89,025	5,088,838	1938	−17,953	31,115,647
1899	22,664	5,111,502	1939	−193,724	30,921,923
1900	334,039	5,445,541	1940	−33,678	30,888,245
1901	—	—	1941	−157,643	30,730,602
1902	359,323	5,804,864	1942	—	—
1903	463,319	6,273,183	1943	—	—
1904	513,739	6,786,922	1944	—	—
1905	480,388	7,267,310	1945	—	—
1906	431,365	7,698,675	1946	517,709	31,248,311
1907	591,646	8,290,321	1947	523,205	31,771,516
1908	211,523	8,501,844	1948	—	—
1909	—	—	1949	940,000	32,711,516
1910	1,208,614	9,710,458	1950	526,052	33,237,568
1911	1,010,400	10,720,858	1951	296,287	33,533,855

SOURCE: Building Managers Association of Chicago.
a A dash indicates that no figures were available.

TABLE 2—*Continued*

Year	Net Area in Square Feet (area added less demolished space)	Continuing Total	Year	Net Area in Square Feet (area added less demolished space)	Continuing Total
1952	14,000	33,547,855	1962	187,369	38,045,782
1953	—	—	1963	1,034,000	39,079,782
1954	202,500	33,750,355	1964	150,000	39,229,782
1955	45,766	33,796,121	1965	2,227,066	41,456,848
1956	665,734	34,461,855	1966	280,000	41,736,848
1957	888,085	35,349,940	1967	1,269,093	43,005,941
1958	1,029,186	36,379,126	1968	1,056,207	44,062,148
1959	−78,782	36,300,344	1969	890,206	44,952,354
1960	492,986	36,793,330	1970	2,385,412	47,337,766
1961	1,065,083	37,858,413			

TABLE 3

DWELLING UNITS CONSTRUCTED ANNUALLY, CITY OF CHICAGO AND
CHICAGO METROPOLITAN AREA, 1904 TO 1970

	City of Chicago			Chicago Metropolitan Area[a]		
Year	Homes	Apartment Units	Total Residential Units	Homes	Apartment Units	Total Residential Units
1904			13,185			
1905	3,609	12,437	16,046			
1906	3,905	11,205	15,110			
1907	3,605	11,276	14,881			
1908	3,271	15,894	19,165			
1909	3,261	16,801	20,062			
1910	3,387	14,131	17,518			
1911						
1912	3,827					
1913	3,745	15,105	18,850			
1914	3,846	16,577	20,423			
1915	3,995	19,925	23,920			
1916	3,887	20,525	24,412			
1917	2,033	5,491	7,524			
1918	916	1,030	1,946			
1919	4,222	4,758	8,980			
1920	1,826	1,091	2,917			
1921	4,608	6,708	11,316			
1922	6,390	18,125	24,515			
1923	7,851	25,918	33,769			
1924	8,579	28,503	37,082			
1925	9,412	32,107	41,519			
1926	7,564	35,368	42,932			
1927	5,762	36,875	42,637			
1928	4,381	29,945	34,326			
1929	2,973	13,146	16,119			
1930	1,088	1,487	2,575			
1931	603	372	975			
1932	178	44	222			
1933	116	21	137			
1934	136	63	199			
1935	332	1,118	1,450			
1936	810	1,463	2,273			
1937	975	109	1,084			
1938	1,366	472	1,838			
1939	2,282	2,515	4,797			
1940	3,123	255	3,378	10,684		
1941	4,431	514	4,945	15,873		

SOURCES: Randall, *History of the Development of Building Construction in Chicago*, p. 298; Bell Savings and Loan Association, *Bell Survey of New Building in the Chicago Region, Annual Review*.
a Chicago Metropolitan Area (outside of Chicago) as used here excludes Porter County, Indiana, up to 1966.

TABLE 3—*Continued*

Year	City of Chicago			Chicago Metropolitan Area		
	Homes	Apartment Units	Total Residential Units	Homes	Apartment Units	Total Residential Units
1942	1,870	2,649	4,519	7,810		
1943	1,276	3,158	4,434	4,342		
1944	2,610	2,480	5,090	6,087	2,557	8,644
1945	3,672	1,687	5,359	8,940	2,190	11,130
1946	4,283	1,532	5,815	16,068	1,980	18,048
1947	3,986	1,982	5,968	18,431	6,313	24,744
1948	4,425	1,654	6,079	19,929	2,727	22,656
1949	4,944	4,869	9,813	21,532	6,244	27,776
1950	8,498	9,109	17,607	32,656	10,697	43,353
1951	6,640	4,698	11,338	27,378	5,560	32,938
1952	6,552	4,181	10,733	28,932	5,115	34,047
1953	8,682	3,165	11,847	36,486	4,096	40,582
1954	8,201	4,819	13,020	41,430	5,749	47,179
1955	9,278	6,797	16,075	44,529	8,341	52,870
1956	6,971	6,654	13,625	39,919	8,713	48,632
1957	4,937	5,632	10,569	30,884	8,694	39,578
1958	4,117	4,675	8,792	31,135	9,452	40,587
1959	5,237	4,616	9,853	35,432	12,177	47,609
1960	4,016	10,344	14,360	26,113	17,760	43,873
1961	3,430	10,829	14,259	24,415	20,549	44,964
1962	3,110	9,394	12,504	22,037	20,765	42,802
1963	2,663	6,308	8,971	19,737	19,777	39,514
1964	2,438	7,588	10,026	18,866	18,620	37,486
1965	2,620	7,071	9,691	20,897	19,405	40,302
1966	2,063	9,083	11,146	16,332	11,076	27,408
1967	1,714	9,966	11,680	20,165	16,371	36,536
1968	1,546	14,194	15,740	22,133	20,331	42,464
1969	869	10,245	11,114	17,527	22,790	40,317
1970	1,188	6,677	7,865	13,282	17,055	30,337

TABLE 4

ANNUAL AMOUNT OF NEW CONSTRUCTION IN CHICAGO, 1854 TO 1970

Year	Amount	Cost Index (1913 = 100)	Adjusted Amount (millions) (1913 = 100)	Population Ratio
1854	$ 2,438,910	62	$ 3.9	2.80
1855	3,735,254	53	7.0	3.40
1856	5,708,624	54	10.6	3.57
1857	6,423,518	58	11.1	3.72
1858	3,246,400	53	6.1	3.82
1859	2,044,000	54	3.8	3.95
1860	1,188,300	57	2.1	4.64
1861	797,800	58	1.4	5.10
1862	525,000	61	0.9	5.87
1863	2,500,000	75	3.3	6.37
1864	4,700,000	86	5.5	7.19
1865	6,950,000	92	7.6	7.58
1866	11,000,000	95	11.6	8.57
1867	8,500,000	96	8.9	9.56
1868	14,000,000	96	14.6	10.71
1869	11,000,000	96	11.5	11.89
1870	20,000,000	89	22.5	12.70
1871–72[a]	40,133,600	92	43.6	15.60
1873	25,500,000	92	27.7	16.14
1874	5,785,541	87	6.7	16.79
1875	9,778,080	77	12.7	17.01
1876	8,270,300	76	10.9	17.31
1877	9,071,050	70	13.0	18.26
1878	7,419,100	67	11.1	18.55
1879	6,745,000	64	10.5	20.88
1880	9,071,850	68	13.3	21.37
1881	8,832,305	71	12.4	22.93
1882	16,286,700	77	21.2	23.81
1883	22,162,000	75	29.5	24.63
1884	20,857,300	68	30.7	26.75
1885	19,624,100	68	28.9	28.24
1886	21,324,400	71	30.0	29.89
1887	19,778,100	71	27.9	32.28
1888	20,350,800	70	29.1	34.09
1889	25,065,500	69	36.3	39.71
1890	47,322,100	68	69.6	46.71
1891	54,001,800	66	81.8	48.79
1892	63,463,400	66	96.2	50.95
1893	28,517,700	65	43.9	53.22

SOURCES: Randall, *History of the Development of Building Construction in Chicago*, pp. 294–95; Bell Savings and Loan Association, *Survey of New Building in Chicago, Annual Review;* American Appraisal Company and *Engineering News-Record* (cost index); United States Census; Standard Rate and Data Service, Incorporated (population ratio).

[a] Period of 9 October 1871 to 9 October 1872.

TABLE 4—*Continued*

Year	Amount	Cost Index (1913 = 100)	Adjusted Amount (millions) (1913 = 100)	Population Ratio
1894	33,805,565	65	52.0	55.58
1895	34,920,643	64	54.6	58.05
1896	22,711,115	63	36.0	60.63
1897	21,690,030	61	35.6	63.32
1898	21,294,325	62	34.3	66.13
1899	20,857,570	68	30.7	69.07
1900	19,100,050	74	25.8	72.14
1901	34,911,755	77	45.3	74.21
1902	48,070,390	80	60.1	76.27
1903	33,645,025	82	41.0	77.92
1904	44,724,790	84	53.2	80.41
1905	63,455,020	87	72.9	82.47
1906	64,298,330	95	67.7	84.54
1907	54,093,080	96	56.3	86.61
1908	68,204,080	91	74.9	88.67
1909	90,558,580	94	96.3	90.74
1910	96,932,700	96	101.0	92.81
1911	105,269,700	97	108.5	95.53
1912	88,786,960	99	89.7	97.77
1913	89,668,427	100	89.7	100.00
1914	83,261,710	97	85.8	102.39
1915	97,291,480	100	97.3	104.66
1916	112,835,150	116	97.3	106.91
1917	64,244,450	141	45.6	109.14
1918	34,792,200	170	20.5	111.37
1919	104,198,850	224	46.5	113.61
1920	79,102,650	294	26.9	114.75
1921	125,004,510	226	55.3	120.28
1922	227,742,010	202	112.7	123.06
1923	329,604,312	228	144.6	125.91
1924	296,893,990	225	132.0	128.74
1925	360,794,250	224	161.1	131.51
1926	366,586,400	219	167.4	134.30
1927	352,936,400	222	159.0	137.14
1928	315,800,000	222	142.3	139.94
1929	202,286,800	222	91.1	142.71
1930	79,613,400	205	38.8	143.40
1931	46,440,130	185	25.1	143.47
1932	3,824,500	162	2.4	143.55
1933	3,683,960	156	2.4	143.63
1934	7,898,435	166	4.8	143.72
1935	17,120,947	169	10.1	143.81
1936	25,031,933	179	14.0	143.89
1937	28,806,443	204	14.1	143.98
1938	21,258,299	205	10.4	144.06
1939	41,597,282	205	20.3	144.15

TABLE 4—*Continued*

Year	Amount	Cost Index (1913 = 100)	Adjusted Amount (millions) (1913 = 100)	Population Ratio
1940	39,928,096	207	19.3	144.27
1941	49,151,997	216	22.8	144.40
1942	37,647,648	235	16.0	144.50
1943	15,607,975	244	6.4	144.59
1944	31,648,547	250	12.7	144.67
1945	61,495,655	260	23.7	152.68
1946	116,382,777	303	38.4	152.90
1947	113,431,800	404	28.1	153.32
1948	147,942,400	456	32.4	154.96
1949	141,872,200	452	31.4	155.60
1950	245,665,500	467	52.6	153.79
1951	205,062,583	503	40.8	153.48
1952	166,490,900	525	31.7	154.87
1953	226,548,200	539	42.0	156.58
1954	237,136,480	550	43.1	158.29
1955	285,365,302	569	50.2	160.96
1956	329,637,404	595	55.4	162.50
1957	346,129,984	614	56.4	164.21
1958	373,633,769	626	59.7	162.26
1959	287,413,202	643	44.7	164.17
1960	424,930,631	658	64.6	150.79
1961	409,365,008	671	61.0	150.86
1962	316,984,982	684	46.3	151.07
1963	338,360,257	709	47.7	150.56
1964	373,590,787	726	51.1	150.33
1965	294,225,216	747	39.4	150.56
1966	506,826,336	765	66.3	149.05[b]
1967	299,354,275	785	38.1	147.54[b]
1968	523,688,216	813	64.4	146.03[b]
1969	560,434,015	852	65.8	144.52[b]
1970	395,062,294	946	41.9	142.99

[b] Estimated by extrapolation.

TABLE 5

<small>SCHOOLS BUILT BY THE CHICAGO BOARD OF EDUCATION,
1872 TO 1970, BY DISTRICT</small>

I. Schools Built before 1900

District 1 (Far Northwest)
    None
District 2 (Far North)
    Field, 1890
District 3 (Upper North)
    McPherson, 1888
    Blaine, 1893
    Greeley, 1893
    Nettelhorst, 1893
    Ravenswood, 1893
    Audubon, 1894
    Burley, 1896
    Morris, 1896
    Lakeview High School, 1898
District 4 (Far Northwest)
    Byford, 1892
    Howe, 1896
    Nash, 1896
District 5 (Middle Northwest)
    Brentano, 1893
    Avondale, 1895
    Linne, 1895
    Funston, 1896
    Nixon, 1896
District 6 (Near Northwest)
    Otis, 1879
    Von Humboldt, 1885
    Prosser, Logan Branch, 1889
    Mitchell, 1892
    Anderson, 1893
    Drummond, 1893
    Lafayette, 1893
    Chase, 1894
    Motley, 1894
    Goethe, 1895
    Peabody, 1895
    Talcott, 1895
    Yates, 1896
    Burr, 1897
    Schley, 1899
District 7 (Middle North)
    Schiller, first, 1873
    Headley, 1875
    Sexton, 1883
    Headley, Thomas Branch, 1890

    Mulligan, 1890
    Lincoln, 1894
    Franklin, 1896
    Schneider, 1896
District 8 (Middle West)
    Calhoun South, 1881
    Sumner, 1894
    Marshall Upper Grade, 1895
District 9 (Near West)
    King, 1873
    Gladstone, 1884
    Irving, 1884
    Jefferson, 1884
    McKinley, Emerson Branch, 1884
    Brainard, 1885
    McLaren, 1886
    Jackson, 1894
    Medill Intermediate, 1895
    Smyth, 1897
    Jirka, 1899
District 10 (Middle Far West)
    Bryant, 1894
    Farragut High School, 1894
District 11 (Near South)
    Ward, 1874
    Doolittle Intermediate and Upper, 1881
    Haven, 1885
    Haines, 1886
    Douglas, 1889
    Abbott, 1890
District 12 (Near Southwest)
    Longfellow, 1881
    Everett, 1892
    Burroughs, 1893
    Greene, 1895
District 13 (Middle South)
    Vincennes Upper Grade, 1884
    Farren, 1898
    Willard, 1898
District 14 (Middle South Hyde Park)
    Ray, 1894
    Scott, 1896
    Kozminski, 1897
District 15 (Far Southwest)
    Fulton, 1895
    Earle, 1896

SOURCE: Chicago Board of Education, Office of Operation Services. The table shows schools in existence in 1968 and those added up to 1970, other than mobile and portable units.

TABLE 5—*Continued*

District 16 (Far South)
  Westcott, 1880
  Gresham, 1895
  Burnside, 1898
District 17 (Far South Shore)
  Sheridan, Phil, 1888
  Thorp, 1893
  Gallistel, 1898
District 18 (Far South)
  Esmond, 1891
  Van Vlissingen, 1893
  West Pullman, 1894
  Scanlan, 1897
District 19 (Middle West Southwest)
  Harrison High School, Froebel Branch, 1885
  Cooper Primary and Intermediate, 1885
  Walsh, 1886
  Komensky, 1891
  Howland, 1893
  Whittier, 1893
  Lawson, 1896
  Pickard, 1896
  Spry Primary and Intermediate, 1899
District 20 (Middle Far South)
  Wentworth, 1890
  Kershaw, 1893
  Bass, 1895
  Parker Elementary, 1899
District 21 (Middle South)
  Englewood High School, 1887
  Beale Upper Grade, 1892
  Ross, 1894
  McCosh Intermediate and Upper, 1895
District 22 (South Shore)
  Bradwell, 1895
District 23 (Near South)
  Forrestville Upper Grade, 1892
  Shakespeare, 1893
District 24 (Far North)
  None
District 25 (West)
  Beidler, 1881
  Ryerson, 1891
  Lowell, 1894
  Tennyson Upper Grade, 1896
  Cameron, 1897
District 26 (Near Southwest)
  McClellan, 1881
  Sheridan, Mark, 1881
  Flower Vocational High School, Richards
    Branch, 1885

  Holden, 1893
  Seward, 1894
  Hamline, 1898
District 27 (South)
  Cornell, 1896
Total built up to 1900 and retained   117
Total built and razed   52
Grand Total   169

II. Schools Built 1900-1910
District 1
  Chicago Parental, 1902
  Henry, 1904
  Cleveland, 1910
District 2
  None
District 3
  Coonley, 1902
  Hamilton, 1903
  Budlong, 1907
  Jahn, 1908
District 4
  Spencer, 1904
  May, 1905
  Key, 1907
District 5
  Darwin, 1900
  Belding, 1901
  Stowe, 1903
  Beaubien, 1905
  Monroe, 1905
  Lloyd, 1907
  Schurz High School, 1910
District 6
  Kosciuszko, 1906
  Moos, 1907
District 7
  Prescott, 1900
  Waller High School, 1901
  Cooley Vocational High School, 1908
  Jenner, 1908
District 8
  Marshall High School, 1902
District 9
  Crane High School, 1903
  McKinley Upper Grade, 1904
  Garfield, 1910
District 10
  Burns, 1903
  Whitney, 1905
  Penn, 1907

TABLE 5—*Continued*

Magellan, 1909
District 11
  Drake, 1900
  Oakland, 1903
  Phillips High School, 1904
District 12
  Sawyer, 1901
  Shields, 1902
  Davis, 1905
  Hedges, 1906
District 13
  None
District 14
  Fiske, 1905
District 15
  Libby, 1902
  Altgeld, 1905
  Copernicus, 1905
  Eberhart, 1906
  Raster, 1910
District 16
  Fernwood, 1901
  Oglesby, 1907
District 17
  Warren, 1907
  Bowen High School, 1910
  Marsh, 1910
District 18
  Poe, 1905
  Fenger High School, Curtis Branch, 1906
  Pullman, 1907
District 19
  Jungman, 1903
  Plamondon, 1903
  McCormick, 1905
  Washburne, 1909
District 20
  Harvard, 1905
District 21
  Goethals, 1902
District 22
  Sullivan, 1902
  Bryn Mawr, 1903
District 23
  Felsenthal, 1901
District 24
  Hayt, 1906
  Stewart, 1906
  Trumbull, 1909
District 25
  Morse, 1904

Tilton, 1909
Nobel, 1910
District 26
  Dewey, 1900
  Armour, 1901
  Graham, 1905
  Tilden High School, 1905
District 27
  Revere, 1903
Total built 1900–1910   72

III. Schools Built 1911-20
District 1
  Haugan, 1911
  Hibbard, 1916
  Norwood Park, 1916
District 2
  Armstrong, 1912
District 3
  Waters, 1911
  Bell, 1916
  Le Moyne, 1916
District 4
  Emmet, 1913
  Thorp, 1918
District 5
  Gray, 1911
  Irving Park, 1911
  Mozart, 1911
  Reilly, 1914
  Portage Park, 1915
  Kelvyn Park High School, 1918
  Prosser Vocational High School, 1918
  Falconer, 1919
District 6
  Columbus, 1911
  Sabin, 1915
  Chopin Primary and Intermediate, 1917
  Tuley High School, 1918
District 7
  Agassiz, 1912
District 8
  Roentgen Educational and Vocational Guid-
    ance Center, 1913
District 9
  McLaren, 1911
  Birney, 1915
  Cregier Vocational High School, 1915
  Riis, 1915
District 10
  Corkery, 1911

TABLE 5—*Continued*

District 10 Continued
  Gary, 1911
  Herzl, 1916
District 11
  None
District 12
  Gage Park High School, Maplewood Avenue
    Branch, 1917
District 13
  Parkman, 1911
  Burke, 1912
District 14
  Hyde Park High School, 1911
  Kenwood High School, 1912
  Wadsworth Primary and Intermediate, 1920
District 15
  Harper High School, 1911
  Lindblom Technical High School, 1919
District 16
  Ryder, 1913
  Perry, 1920
District 17
  Clay, 1917
District 18
  Kohn, 1911
  Vanderpoel, 1912
  Morgan Park High School, 1914
District 19
  Hammond, 1912
  Harrison High School, 1912
  Shepard, 1914
  Pope, 1918
District 20
  Guggenheim, 1912
District 21
  Carter, 1913
  Sexton, 1915
  Lewis-Champlin, 1916
District 22
  Parkside, 1917
District 23
  None
District 24
  Senn High School, 1912
  Swift, 1914
  Peirce, 1915
District 25
  Delano, 1913
  Madison-Kildare Upper Grade Center, 1917
  Orr High School, 1919

District 26
  None
District 27
  Park Manor, 1913
  Avalon Park, 1917
Total Built 1911–20   61

IV. Schools Built 1921-30
District 1
  Bateman, 1921
  Farnsworth, 1925
  Peterson, 1925
  Hitch, 1926
  Ebinger, 1927
  Roosevelt High School, 1927
  Onahan, 1928
  Von Steuben High School, 1930
District 2
  Gale, 1922
  Clinton, 1926
  Sullivan High School, 1926
  Boone, 1928
District 3
  Amundsen High School, 1930
  Hawthorne, 1930
District 4
  Hay, 1921
  Young, 1924
  Bridge, 1926
  Lewis, 1926
  Lyon, 1926
  Key, Clark Branch, 1927
  Locke, 1927
  Lovett, 1927
  Burbank, 1929
  Austin High School, 1930
  Sayre, 1930
District 5
  Murphy, 1924
  Palmer, 1926
  Scammon, 1926
  Barry, 1927
  Prussing, 1927
  Foreman High School, 1928
  Reinberg, 1928
  Schubert, 1930
District 6
  None
District 7
  None

TABLE 5—*Continued*

District 8
Gregory, 1923
West Garfield Park Upper Grade, 1926
Manley Primary and Intermediate, 1928
District 9
Grant, 1925
Spalding High School, 1928
District 10
Mason Upper Grade, 1922
District 11
None
District 12
Gunsaulus, 1924
Edwards, 1925
Nightingale, 1926
Peck, 1926
Christopher, 1927
Pasteur, 1927
Twain, 1927
Kelly High School, 1928
Tonti, 1928
District 13
Colman, 1922
Horner, 1922
District 14
None
District 15
Henderson, 1923
Marquette, 1926
Morrill, 1926
O'Toole, 1927
McKay, 1928
Hubbard High School, 1929
District 16
Cook, 1925
Calumet High School, 1926
Barton, 1928
Bennett, 1928
Cook, Foster Park Church Branch, 1928
Fort Dearborn, 1928
Hookway, 1928
Simeon Vocational High School, 1928
District 17
Bright, 1922
Taylor, 1923
District 18
Brenan, 1925
Fenger High School, 1926
Gompers, 1926
Shoop, 1926
Sutherland, 1926

Mount Vernon, 1928
Barnard, 1929
Clissold, 1930
District 19
Hess Upper Grade, 1922
District 20
Bond Upper Grade, 1926
Parker High School, 1930
District 21
None
District 22
O'Keefe, 1925
Coles, 1926
Mann, 1926
District 23
None
District 24
Stockton, 1925
Stone, 1928
District 25
Delano, West Branch, 1922
Westinghouse Vocational High School, 1922
Flower Vocational High School, 1927
District 26
None
District 27
Ruggles, 1925
Hirsch High School, 1926
Dixon, 1929
Total Built 1921–30   88

V. Schools Built 1931-40
District 1
Volta, 1931
Garvy, 1936
Sauganash, 1936
Edgebrook, 1939
Taft High School, 1939
District 2
Kilmer, 1931
Jamieson, 1937
Rogers, 1937
District 3
Lane Technical High School, 1934
Chappell, 1937
District 4
Smyser, 1932
Steinmetz High School, 1934
Dever, 1935
Canty, 1936

TABLE 5—*Continued*

District 5
    None
District 6
    Wells High School, 1935
District 7
    Alcott, 1937
    Newberry, 1937
District 8
    None
District 9
    None
District 10
    None
District 11
    None
District 12
    Byrne, Michael, 1936
    Gage Park High School, 1939
District 13
    Du Sable High School, 1935
District 14
    Harte, 1931
District 15
    None
District 16
    Gillespie Primary and Intermediate, 1937
    Kellogg, Foster Park Branch, 1937
District 17
    Caldwell, 1936
District 18
    Mount Greenwood, 1936
    Kellogg, 1937
    Scanlan, Riverdale Branch, 1937
District 19
    None
District 20
    None
District 21
    None
District 22
    South Shore High School, 1940
District 23
    Doniat, 1935
    Oakenwald North Primary Grade, 1935
    Forrestville High School, 1938
District 24
    Goudy, 1937
District 25
    None
District 26
    Sherman, 1937

District 27
    Madison, 1939
Total Built 1931–40   34

VI. Schools Built 1941-50
District 1
    Oriole Park, 1943
    Wildwood, 1944
    Edison, 1945
District 2
    None
District 3
    Berteau-Hermitage, 1948
District 4
    None
District 5
    None
District 6
    Pulaski, 1949
District 7
    Manierre, 1947
District 8
    Marshall High School, Dante Branch, 1948
District 9
    None
District 10
    None
District 11
    Raymond, 1944
    Abbott, 1949
District 12
    None
District 13
    None
District 14
    None
District 15
    Owen, 1949
District 16
    Perry, Schmid Branch, 1948
District 17
    Chicago Vocational High School, 1941
    Luella, 1945
    Addams, 1948
District 18
    Carver Primary Grade, 1945
    Carver Upper Grade, 1946
    Carver High School, 1950
District 19
    None

TABLE 5—*Continued*

District 20
  None
District 21
  None
District 22
  Black, 1948
District 23
  Fuller, 1942
District 24
  None
District 25
  Goldblatt, 1941
District 26
  None
District 27
  None
Total Built 1941–50   20

VII. Schools Built 1951-60
District 1
  Solomon, 1953
  Ebinger, Stock Branch 1955
  Beard, 1958
  Sauganash, Thoreau Branch, 1959
  Beard, Perkins Branch, 1960
District 2
  Green, William, 1954
  Armstrong, Bartelme Branch, 1957
  Decatur, 1958
  Mather High School, 1959
District 3
  None
District 4
  None
District 5
  Reinberg, Hanson Branch, 1959
District 6
  Andersen, 1955
  Carpenter, 1957
District 7
  Ogden, 1953
  Cooley Upper Grade, 1958
  Mayer, 1959
  Byrd, 1960
District 8
  King Elementary, 1959
District 9
  Skinner, 1954
  Brown, 1956
  Gladstone, Allen Branch, 1958
  Skinner, Sousa Branch, 1958

  Medill Primary Grade, 1959
  Suder, 1959
  Birney, 1960
  Montefiore Social Adjustment, 1960
District 10
  Mason Primary Grades, 1958
  Hughes, 1960
District 11
  Williams, 1952
  Dunbar Vocational High School, 1956
  Attucks, 1957
  Pershing, 1958
  Einstein, 1960
District 12
  Heart, 1952
  Grimes, 1953
  Hale, 1953
  Dore, 1957
  Kinzie, 1957
  Peck, Nelson Branch, 1958
District 13
  None
District 14
  Murray, Philip, 1954
  Carnegie, 1957
  Reavis, 1958
  Fermi, 1959
  Tesla, 1960
District 15
  Dawes, 1954
  Hurley, 1954
  Stevenson, 1954
  Carroll, Rosenwald Branch, 1955
  Pasteur, Lee Branch, 1956
  Carroll, 1958
  Hancock, 1958
  Bogan High School, 1959
  Hurley, Tarkington Branch, 1960
District 16
  Fernwood, Wacker Branch, 1954
  Drew, 1957
  Harlan High School, 1958
District 17
  Burnham, 1954
  Burnham, Goldsmith Branch, 1954
  Caldwell, McDowell Branch, 1954
  Hoyne, 1955
  Burnham, Anthony Branch, 1957
  Washington High School, 1957
  Hoyne, Earhart Branch, 1958

TABLE 5—*Continued*

District 18
  Nansen, 1953
  Mount Vernon, Dunne Branch, 1954
  Newton, 1955
  Cassell, Keller Branch, 1956
  Clissold, Sheldon Branch, 1957
  Whistler, 1958
  Aldridge, 1960
  Cassell, 1960
District 19
  Chalmers, 1959
District 20
  Yale Primary and Intermediate, 1951
  Deneen, 1955
District 21
  Beale Primary and Intermediate, 1958
  Moseley Social Adjustment, 1959
  McCosh Primary Grade, 1960
District 22
  None
District 23
  Oakenwald South Intermediate and Upper,
    1955
  Judd, 1959
District 24
  None
District 25
  None
District 26
  Sherwood, 1951
  Hendricks, 1954
  Holmes, 1960
District 27
  Neil, 1953
Total Built 1951–60   82

VIII. Schools Built 1961-70
District 1
  None
District 2
  None
District 3
  None
District 4
  Spencer, 1968
District 5
  None
District 6
  Wicker, 1961
  Yates Upper Grade, 1962

District 7
  LaSalle, 1961
  Schiller, 1961
  Arnold Upper Grade, 1962
  Jones Commercial High School, 1967
District 8
  Calhoun, North, 1961
  Hefferan, 1961
  Ericson, 1962
  Jensen, 1962
  Marconi, 1962
  Webster, 1962
  Faraday, 1964
  Melody, 1965
  Marshall High School, Dante Branch, 1968
  Bethune, 1969
  Frazier, 1970
District 9
  Dodge, 1961
  Herbert, 1961
  Dett, 1963
District 10
  Crown, 1961
  Henson, 1961
  Dvorak, 1963
  Mason Intermediate Grade, 1964
  Paderewski, 1964
District 11
  Drake, 1961
  Mayo, 1961
  Doolittle Primary Grade, 1962
  Donoghue, 1963
District 12
  Dore, Blair Branch, 1961
  Grimes, Fleming Branch, 1961
  Twain, Baum Branch, 1961
  Kennedy High School, 1965
District 13
  Hartigan, 1961
  Beethoven, 1962
  Du Sable Upper Grade, 1962
  McCorkly, 1963
  Overton, 1963
  Terrell, 1963
District 14
  Shoesmith, 1961
  Dumas, 1963
  Wadsworth Upper Grade, 1963
  Hyde Park High School, Phase I, 1969
  Kenwood High School, 1969

TABLE 5—*Continued*

District 15
    Dawes, Michelson Branch, 1961
    Hancock, Crerar Branch, 1961
    Altgeld, 1968
District 16
    Bennett, Shedd Branch, 1961
    Gillespie Upper Grade, 1961
    Kipling, 1961
    McDade, 1961
    Gresham, 1968
    Ryder, 1968
    Evers, 1969
District 17
    Thorp, J. N., 1961
    Warren, Buckingham Branch, 1962
    Bowen High School, 1969
    Grissom, 1970
District 18
    Bates, 1961
    Mount Greenwood, Wiggin Branch, 1961
    Higgins, 1965
    Mount Greenwood, Duffy Branch, 1965
    Du Bois, 1969
District 19
    Cooper Upper Grade, 1962
    Johnson, 1963
    Lathrop, 1963
District 20
    Brownell, 1961
    Low Upper Grade, 1961
    Yale Upper Grade, 1963

    Banneker, 1963
    Hinton, 1965
    Stagg, 1967
District 21
    Dulles, 1962
    Reed, 1963
    Gershwin, 1965
District 22
    South Shore High School II, 1970
District 23
    Mollison, 1962
    Price, 1964
    Woodson, North, 1965
    Woodson, South, 1966
District 24
    Brennemann, 1963
    McCutcheon, 1964
District 25
    Cather, 1963
    Morton Upper Grade, 1964
District 26
    Healy, 1962
    Holmes, 1968
District 27
    Pirie, 1962
    Sbarbaro, 1963
    Tanner, 1963
Total Built 1961–70   90
Grand Total 1872–1970   616
Total Less Number Razed   564

TABLE 6

RAILROADS OF THE CHICAGO SWITCHING DISTRICT, 1910 TO 1970

I. **Passenger-carrying Steam Railroads by Station**
    Central (Michigan Avenue at 11th Place; 1892–93)
    1. Illinois Central (owner)
    2. Chesapeake and Ohio (tenant; abandoned passenger service on the Chicago Division west of Hammond, Indiana, 1932)[a]
    3. Cleveland, Cincinnati, Chicago and Saint Louis (Big Four; tenant; leased to and merged with the New York Central 1930)
    4. Michigan Central (tenant; leased to and merged with the New York Central 1930; operations progressively transferred to LaSalle Street Station 1934 et seq., then to Union Station 1969)
    Dearborn (Polk and Dearborn streets; 1883–85)
    1. Chicago and Western Indiana (terminal company and owner; abandoned passenger service 1965)[b]
    2. Atchison, Topeka and Santa Fe (Santa Fe; transferred operations to Union Station 1971)
    3. Chicago and Eastern Illinois (Evansville line acquired by the Louisville and Nashville 1969; remainder of property controlled by the Missouri Pacific; abandoned passenger service 1971)
    4. Chicago, Indianapolis and Louisville (Monon; abandoned passenger service 1967)
    5. Erie (merged with the Delaware, Lackawanna and Western to form the Erie-Lackawanna, 1960; abandoned passenger service 1970)[c]
    6. Grand Trunk Western (abandoned passenger service 1971)
    7. Wabash (leased to and merged with the Norfolk and Western 1964)
    Grand Central (Harrison and Wells streets; 1889–90; demolished 1971)
    1. Baltimore and Ohio (owner; see under terminal companies; transferred operations to North Western Station 1969; abandoned passenger service 1971)
    2. Chicago Great Western (Great Western or Corn Belt Route; abandoned passenger service 1956; merged with the Chicago and North Western 1968)
    3. Pere Marquette (merged with the Chesapeake and Ohio 1947; latter company abandoned passenger service 1971)
    4. Wisconsin Central (merged with the Minneapolis, Saint Paul and Sault Sainte Marie [Soo Line] 1961; abandoned passenger service in 1965)[d]
    Illinois Central Suburban (Michigan Avenue and Randolph Street; 1930–31)
      Illinois Central
    LaSalle Street (Van Buren at LaSalle Street; 1901–3)
    1. Chicago, Rock Island and Pacific (Rock Island; joint owner)
    2. New York Central (joint owner; merged with the Pennsylvania to form the Penn Central, 1968; transferred operations to Union Station 1969)[e]
    3. New York, Chicago and Saint Louis (Nickel Plate Road; tenant; merged with the Norfolk and Western and abandoned passenger service 1964)
    North Western (Canal and Madison streets; 1906–11)
      Chicago and North Western (North Western)
    Union (Canal Street between Adams Street and Jackson Boulevard; 1916–25)
    1. Chicago, Burlington and Quincy (Burlington; joint owner)

---

[a] Before July 1910 the Chicago Division of the C. and O. was a separate company, the Chicago, Cincinnati and Louisville Railroad.
[b] All railroads using Dearborn Station except the Chicago and Western Indiana were tenant companies.
[c] Before 1960 the Erie main line between Chicago and Marion, Ohio, was a separate but controlled and merged subsidiary company, the Chicago and Erie Railroad.
[d] All railroads using Grand Central Station except the B. and O. were tenant companies.
[e] Before 1914 the lines of the New York Central terminating at Chicago were divided between the Lake Shore and Michigan Southern and the Chicago, Indiana and Southern railroads.

TABLE 6—*Continued*

2. Chicago, Milwaukee, Saint Paul and Pacific (Milwaukee Road; joint owner)[f]
3. Pittsburgh, Cincinnati, Chicago and Saint Louis (joint owner; leased to the Pennsylvania 1921; latter company merged with the New York Central to form the Penn Central, 1968)
4. Pittsburgh, Fort Wayne and Chicago (joint owner; same history as the P.C.C. and St. L. except that present lease dates from 1918)
5. Chicago and Alton (tenant; merged with the Gulf, Mobile and Ohio 1947)[g]

II. **Switching, Belt, Transfer, and Line-haul Freight-carrying Railroads**
1. Baltimore and Ohio Chicago Terminal (owned by the B. and O.)
2. Belt Railway Company of Chicago (jointly owned by the A. T. and S. F., C. B. and Q., C. and O., C. and E. I., C. I. and L., C. R. I. and P., Erie, G. T. W., I. C., M. St. P. and S. Ste. M., Penna., P. M., and Wabash, and by the various later successors of these companies)
3. Chicago Junction (leased to the Chicago River and Indiana and operated by the New York Central)
4. Chicago River and Indiana (controlled and operated by the New York Central)
5. Elgin, Joliet and Eastern (line-haul carrier; owned by the United States Steel Corporation)
6. Indiana Harbor Belt (jointly owned by the Milwaukee and the New York Central)

III. **Industrial Switching Railroads**
1. Chicago and Calumet River
2. Chicago and Illinois Western
3. Chicago Short Line
4. Chicago, West Pullman and Southern
5. Illinois Northern
6. Manufacturers Junction
7. Pullman

IV. **Terminal Railroads**
1. Baltimore and Ohio Chicago Terminal (proprietary company of Grand Central Station and a switching and transfer line; owned by the B. and O.)
2. Chicago and Western Indiana (proprietary company of Dearborn Station and a switching and transfer line; owned by the Dearborn tenant companies)

V. **Electric Interurban Railroads**
1. Chicago, Aurora and Elgin; terminal at Quincy and Wells streets (operated by trackage rights over the Chicago Rapid Transit and the Chicago Transit Authority, city limits to Market Street [Wacker Drive]; passenger carrier only; abandoned service 1957)
2. Chicago, North Shore and Milwaukee; terminal at Roosevelt Road elevated station (operated by trackage rights over the Chicago Rapid Transit and the Chicago Transit Authority, south city limit of Wilmette to terminal; freight and passenger carrier; abandoned service on the Shore Line 1955, and on the remainder of trackage 1963)
3. Chicago, South Shore and South Bend; tenant company in the Illinois Central Suburban Station, Michigan Avenue and Randolph Street (operated by trackage rights over the Illinois Central from 115th Street to terminal; freight and passenger carrier; controlled by the Chesapeake and Ohio Railway since 1967)

---

[f] Before 1927 the corporate title of the Milwaukee was Chicago, Milwaukee and Saint Paul Railroad.
[g] All tenant companies of the various stations operated their trains by trackage rights over the lines of the proprietary companies for varying distances within the Chicago Switching District with the following exceptions: the Big Four operated trains by trackage rights over the Illinois Central Railroad from Kankakee, Illinois, to Central Station, a distance of fifty-four miles, and the Pere Marquette operated in similar fashion over the New York Central, Baltimore and Ohio, Rock Island, and Baltimore and Ohio Chicago Terminal railroads, in succession, from Porter, Indiana, to Grand Central Station, a distance of forty-eight miles.

TABLE 7

Revenue Passengers Carried by Chicago Transit Authority and Predecessor Companies, 1906 to 1970

Year	Chicago Surface Lines[a]	Chicago Rapid Transit Company	Chicago Motor Coach Company	Combined	Population of Chicago	Rides per Capita	Passenger Automobile Registration (Chicago)	Population per Passenger Automobile
1906	373,900,000	131,958,605		505,858,605	1,990,600	254		
1907	372,123,199	147,263,985		519,387,184	2,039,271	255		
1908	396,073,965	150,371,374		546,445,339	2,087,942	262	5,475b	381.4
1909	442,511,273	152,423,961		594,935,234	2,136,613	278	7,110	300.5
1910	481,822,110	164,875,974		646,698,084	2,185,283	296	9,963	219.3
1911	561,517,222	162,866,136		724,383,358	2,236,926	324	11,876	188.4
1912	589,178,708	164,314,524		753,493,232	2,288,568	329	16,857	135.7
1913	634,026,040	164,164,225		798,190,265	2,340,210	341	22,136	105.7
1914	629,931,909	165,770,135		795,702,044	2,391,852	333	26,814	89.2
1915	619,547,956	164,678,900		784,226,856	2,443,494	321	34,441	70.9
1916	681,583,470	180,649,694		862,233,164	2,495,136	346	48,358	51.6
1917	700,462,712	193,119,829	3,077,558	896,660,099	2,546,778	352	59,382	42.9
1918	676,263,883	197,436,736	4,571,374	878,271,993	2,598,420	338	58,505	44.4
1919	741,252,551	184,667,604	6,060,365	931,980,520	2,650,063	352	75,241	35.2
1920	768,042,418	190,636,873	6,395,472	965,074,763	2,701,705	357	106,500c	25.4
1921	750,386,454	180,626,990	7,774,953	938,788,397	2,769,178	339	137,750	20.1
1922	758,040,458	181,283,785	9,619,558	948,943,801	2,836,652	335	172,655	16.4
1923	821,409,074	203,943,551	21,916,485	1,047,269,110	2,904,126	361	218,991	13.3
1924	829,700,944	213,006,798	49,268,427	1,091,976,169	2,971,599	367	260,887	11.4
1925	840,972,623	216,045,575	57,492,529	1,114,510,727	3,039,072	367	289,948	10.5
1926	874,242,057	228,812,766	55,838,927	1,158,893,750	3,106,545	373	317,433	9.8
1927	881,948,268	226,212,172	59,270,849	1,167,431,289	3,174,018	368	335,263	9.5
1928	890,960,073	207,864,238	61,836,233	1,160,660,544	3,241,490	358	360,985	9.0
1929	899,878,161	196,774,395	69,001,990	1,165,654,546	3,308,962	352	402,078	8.2
1930	821,166,771	182,954,846	58,310,208	1,062,431,825	3,376,438	315	406,916	8.3
1931	739,903,327	152,414,248	49,571,371	941,888,946	3,378,475	279	423,786	8.0
1932	641,101,119	126,989,541	40,799,663	808,890,323	3,380,512	239	396,783	8.5
1933	645,576,749	124,855,354	49,298,578	819,730,681	3,382,549	242	367,402	9.2
1934	676,906,698	127,276,803	43,698,473	847,881,974	3,384,586	251	368,585	9.2
1935	664,742,602	123,497,788	40,019,162	828,259,552	3,386,623	245	397,023	8.5
1936	706,631,957	129,578,269	47,827,417	884,037,643	3,388,660	261	461,527	7.3

SOURCE: Public Information Department, Chicago Transit Authority.

a Chicago Surface Lines includes former Chicago Motor Coach Company passengers for 1953 et seq.

b Automobile registration based on fiscal years ending 30 April of the following year.

c Figure for 1920 estimated by averaging registrations for the fiscal year ended 30 April 1920 and the calendar year of 1921.

TABLE 7—Continued

REVENUE PASSENGERS CARRIED BY CHICAGO TRANSIT AUTHORITY AND PREDECESSOR COMPANIES, 1906 TO 1970

Year	Chicago Surface Lines	Chicago Rapid Transit Company	Chicago Motor Coach Company	Combined	Population of Chicago	Rides per Capita	Passenger Automobile Registration (Chicago)	Population per Passenger Automobile
1937	709,304,031	128,005,374	55,618,162	892,927,567	3,390,697	263	504,207	6.7
1938	663,673,976	121,702,897	54,812,976	840,189,849	3,392,734	248	506,071	6.7
1939	660,324,561	121,426,629	55,386,336	837,137,526	3,394,771	247	516,128	6.6
1940	672,205,539	123,704,810	57,410,265	853,320,614	3,396,808	251	549,537	6.2
1941	690,592,406	127,133,614	60,304,813	878,030,833	3,419,224	257	585,219	5.8
1942	747,407,420	133,208,577	69,189,952	949,805,949	3,441,638	276	545,777	6.3
1943	818,117,640	140,905,171	67,835,380	1,026,858,191	3,464,054	296	467,423	7.4
1944	842,862,953	151,062,563	70,986,197	1,064,911,713	3,486,468	305	433,880	8.0
1945	844,844,660	157,344,085	75,018,686	1,077,207,431	3,508,884	307	427,779	8.2
1946	917,002,050	157,876,421	72,732,022	1,147,610,493	3,531,298	325	461,721	7.6
1947	888,533,148	145,755,514	85,835,806	1,120,124,468	3,553,714	315	512,810	6.4
1948	825,379,675	137,621,520	89,210,955	1,052,212,150	3,576,128	294	567,726	6.3
1949	724,851,315	122,259,827	82,841,920	929,953,062	3,598,543	258	634,352	5.7
1950	641,597,249	110,603,719	80,911,483	833,112,451	3,620,962	230	705,197	5.1
1951	584,141,163	112,807,016	82,297,751	779,245,930	3,613,907	216	734,785	4.9
1952	525,415,421	112,687,227	82,796,043	720,898,691	3,606,851	200	725,746	5.0
1953	574,821,563	111,738,503		686,560,066	3,599,795	191	764,942	4.7
1954	529,934,199	111,232,302		641,166,501	3,592,740	178	792,940	4.5
1955	510,603,672	112,889,976		623,493,648	3,585,684	174	831,418	4.3
1956	505,623,461	115,659,105		621,282,566	3,578,628	174	870,487	4.1
1957	469,785,257	112,280,610		582,065,867	3,571,572	163	874,797	4.1
1958	426,226,629	107,067,414		533,294,043	3,564,516	150	856,443	4.2
1959	432,684,329	113,330,994		546,015,323	3,557,460	153	857,547	4.1
1960	421,832,145	112,924,491		534,756,636	3,550,404	151	854,572	4.2
1961	395,405,445	110,126,318		505,531,763	3,540,000	143	851,073	4.2
1962	390,842,961	114,068,016		504,910,977	3,534,000	143	859,096	4.1
1963	381,166,527	111,065,005		492,231,532	3,534,000	139	861,702	4.1
1964	379,251,204	111,218,011		490,469,215	3,534,000	139	867,399	4.1
1965	388,076,702	114,597,086		502,673,788	3,534,000	142	888,969	4.0
1966	405,728,973	117,562,012		523,290,985	3,466,000	151	913,939	3.8
1967	389,770,830	120,792,566		510,508,396	3,466,000	147	927,210	3.7
1968	346,976,958	110,792,832		457,769,790	3,520,000	130	942,959	3.7
1969	317,024,210	103,071,290		420,095,500	3,470,000	121	957,212	3.6
1970	296,176,300	105,598,382		401,774,682	3,366,951	119	972,000d	3.5

d Estimate.

Bibliography

General Works

Abbott, Edith. *The Tenements of Chicago, 1908–1935*. Chicago: University of Chicago Press, 1936.

Andrews, Wayne. *Architecture in Chicago and Mid-America: A Photographic Essay*. New York: Atheneum, 1968.

Bach, Ira J. *Chicago on Foot*. Chicago and New York: Follett Publishing Company, 1969.

Banham, Reyner. *The Architecture of the Well-Tempered Environment*. London: Architectural Press, 1969.

Brooks, H. Allen. *The Prairie School: Frank Lloyd Wright and His Midwest Contemporaries*. Toronto: University of Toronto Press, 1972.

Burchard, John, and Bush-Brown, Albert. *The Architecture of America: A Social and Cultural History*. Boston: Little, Brown and Company, 1961.

Butler, Rush C., Jr. *Chicago*. Chicago: American Publishers Corporation, 1929.

Condit, Carl W. *American Building Art: The Twentieth Century*. New York: Oxford University Press, 1961.

————. *American Building: Materials and Techniques from the Beginning of the Colonial Settlements to the Present*. Chicago: University of Chicago Press, 1968.

————. *The Chicago School of Architecture: A History of Commercial and Public Building in the Chicago Area, 1875–1925*. Chicago: University of Chicago Press, 1964.

Corplan Associates, IIT Research Institute. *Technological Change: Its Impact on Industry in Metropolitan Chicago*. 8 vols. Chicago: IIT Research Institute, 1964.

Cutler, Irving. *The Chicago-Milwaukee Corridor: A Geographic Study of Intermetropolitan Coalescence*. Northwestern University Studies in Geography, no. 9. Evanston, Ill.: Northwestern University, 1965.

Ericsson, Henry, and Myers, Lewis E. *Sixty Years a Builder*. Chicago: A. Kroch and Son, 1942.

Giedion, Sigfried. *Space, Time and Architecture*, 3d ed. Cambridge, Mass.: Harvard University Press, 1954.

Gilbert, Paul, and Bryson, Charles Lee. *Chicago and Its Makers*. Chicago: Felix Mendelsohn, 1929.

Hitchcock, Henry-Russell. *In the Nature of Materials, 1887–1941: The Buildings of Frank Lloyd Wright*. New York: Duell, Sloan and Pearce, 1942.

Hoyt, Homer. *One Hundred Years of Land Values in Chicago*. Chicago: University of Chicago Press, 1933.

Jones, Cranston. *Architecture Today and Tomorrow*. New York: McGraw-Hill Book Company, 1961.

Jordy, William H. "The Commercial and the 'Chicago School.' " In *Perspectives in American History* (Cambridge, Mass.: Charles Warren Center for Studies in American History, 1967), 1:390–400.

Kranzberg, Melvin, and Pursell, Carroll W., Jr., eds. *Technology in Western Civilization*. 2 vols. New York: Oxford University Press, 1967.

Manson, Grant Carpenter. *Frank Lloyd Wright to 1910: The First Golden Age*. New York: Reinhold Publishing Corporation, 1958.

Mayer, Harold, and Wade, Richard. *Chicago: Growth of a Metropolis*. Chicago: University of Chicago Press, 1969.

Mendelsohn, Felix. *Chicago: Yesterday and Today*. Chicago: Felix Mendelsohn, 1932.

Merriam, Charles Edward. *Chicago: A More Intimate View of Urban Politics*. New York: Macmillan Company, 1929.

"Metals Review." *Progressive Architecture* 50 (October 1969):132–204.

Mujica, Francisco. *The History of the Skyscraper*. New York: Archaeology and Architecture Press, 1930.

Museum of Modern Art. *Built in USA, 1932–1944*. New York: Museum of Modern Art, 1944.

———. *Built in USA: Post-War Architecture*. New York: Museum of Modern Art, 1952.

One Hundred and Twenty Five Photographic Views of Chicago. Chicago and New York: Rand McNally and Company, 1902.

Ousley, Steve. "Engineering Chicago's Buildings." *Actual Specifying Engineer* 13 (January 1965):86–87, 134–38.

Peisch, Mark L. *The Chicago School of Architecture*. New York: Random House, 1964.

Pierce, Bessie Louise. *A History of Chicago*. 3 vols. New York: Alfred A. Knopf, 1937–57.

Randall, Frank A. *History of the Development of Building Construction in Chicago*. Urbana: University of Illinois Press, 1949.

Royko, Mike. *Boss: Richard J. Daley of Chicago*. New York: E. P. Dutton and Company, 1971.

Scully, Vincent. *American Architecture and Urbanism*. New York: Frederick A. Praeger, 1969.

Sexton, R. W. *American Apartment Houses, Hotels, and Apartment Hotels of Today*. New York: Architectural Book Publishing Company, 1929.

Short, James F., Jr. *The Social Fabric of the Metropolis: Contributions of the "Chicago School of Urban Sociology."* Chicago: University of Chicago Press, 1971.

Siegel, Arthur, ed. *Chicago's Famous Buildings*. Chicago: University of Chicago Press, 1969.

Spear, Allan H. *Black Chicago: The Making of a Negro Ghetto, 1890–1920*. Chicago: University of Chicago Press, 1967.

Taylor, Nicholas. "Chicago: America's German Miracle." *Sunday Times Magazine* (London), 1 September 1968, pp. 24–29.

"The Ups and Downs of Chicago Real Estate." *Architectural Forum* 59 (August 1933):141–43, 149.

Chapter 1. Century of Progress Exposition

"A Century of Progress Paradox." *Architectural Forum* 61(November 1934): 374–79.

"Century of Progress, Second Edition. . . ." *Architectural Forum* 61(July 1934): 1–32.

"Concrete Shell Roof Used on World's Fair Building." *Engineering News-Record* 112(14 June 1934):775–76.

Corbett, Harvey Wiley. "The Significance of the Exposition." *Architectural Forum* 59(July 1933):1.

Cram, Ralph Adams. "Retrogression, Ugliness." *Architectural Forum* 59(July 1933):24–25.

Cret, Paul Philippe. "The Festive Stage Setting." *Architectural Forum* 59(July 1933):4–5.

"Exhibition Buildings of Various Countries and Corporations." *Architectural Forum* 59(July 1933):33–46.

Fuller, R. Buckminster. "Profit Control and the Pseudo-Scientific." *Architectural Forum* 59(July 1933):26–27.

Kahn, Albert. "A Pageant of Beauty." *Architectural Forum* 59(July 1933):26.

Kahn, Ely Jacques. "Close-up Comments on the Fair." *Architectural Forum* 59 (July 1933):23–24.

Lohr, Lenox R. *Fair Management: The Story of A Century of Progress Exposition*. Chicago: Cuneo Press, 1952.

"The Modern Houses of the Century of Progress Exposition." *Architectural Forum* 59(July 1933):51–62.

Muschenheim, William. "The Color of the Exposition." *Architectural Forum* 59 (July 1933):2–4.

"Nine Major Buildings. . . ." *Architectural Forum* 59(July 1933):7–22.

Ryan, Walter D'Arcy. "Lighting the Exposition." *Architectural Forum* 59(July 1933):47–50.

Skidmore, Louis. "Planning and Planners." *Architectural Forum* 59(July 1933): 29–32.

Thorud, Bert M. "Engineering Research and Building Construction." *Architectural Forum* 59(July 1933):65–69.

"Transport Building at Chicago's World's Fair." *Engineering News-Record* 106(7 May 1931):766–67.

"The Travel and Transport Building." *Architectural Forum* 55(October 1931): 449–56, 501–6.

Wright, Frank Lloyd. "Another 'Pseudo.' " *Architectural Forum* 59(July 1933):25.

Chapter 2. Building under the New Deal

"American Medical Association Building." *American Architect and Architecture* 150(January 1937):37–38.

Chicago Housing Authority. *Annual Report*. Chicago: Chicago Housing Authority, 1938 et seq.

"Chicago's South District Filtration Plant Near Completion." *Journal of the Western Society of Engineers* 51(September 1946):120–34.

"Chicago's $24 Million Filtration Plant Placed in Partial Operation." *Engineering News-Record* 135(27 September 1945):7.

"Crow Island School, Winnetka, Ill." *Architectural Forum* 75(August 1941): 79–92.

"Filtered Water for Chicago Consumers." *Midwest Engineer* 1(May 1949):12–17.

International Amphitheatre, Chicago: Photo Book and Fact File. Chicago: International Amphitheatre, [1968].

"The Lake County Tuberculosis Sanatorium, Waukegan, Ill." *Architectural Forum* 73(September 1940):146–58.

Nelson, George. *Industrial Architecture of Albert Kahn, Inc.* New York: Architectural Book Publishing Company, 1939.

"Proposed International Amphitheatre for the Chicago Stock Yards." *Architecture* 70(December 1934):316.

Short, C. W. and Stanley-Brown, R. *Public Buildings: A Survey of Architecture of Projects Constructed by Federal and Other Governmental Bodies*. Washington: Government Printing Office, 1939.

"Steel Forms Speed Concrete Washwater Trough Construction." *Engineering News-Record* 134(28 June 1945):76–79.

"Water Filtration Plant, Chicago, Illinois." *Progressive Architecture* 31(March 1950):74–84.

Chapter 3. Residential and Commercial Building after World War II

"Apartment Houses." *Architectural Record* 120(August 1956):171–75.

"Architect Goldberg's Marina City Concept." *Architectural Record* 134(September 1963):214–16.

"Architect Mies: Forty-Eight Years in the Vanguard." *Engineering News-Record* 178(29 June 1967):30–32.

Banham, Reyner. "A Walk in the Loop." *Chicago* 2(Spring 1956):24–27.

"Bell-Bottomed Caissons Will Carry Tower." *Engineering News-Record* 168(28 June 1962):23.

Blake, Peter. *Mies van der Rohe: Architecture and Structure.* Baltimore: Penguin Books, 1964.

Blaser, Werner. *Mies van der Rohe: The Art of Structure.* New York: Frederick A. Praeger, 1965.

Bowen, William. "Chicago: They Didn't Have to Burn It down after All." *Fortune* 71(January 1965):142–51, 231–34.

Brubaker, Charles William. "Planning the First National Bank of Chicago." *Inland Architect* 9(February 1965):13–15.

"Caisson Trouble Hits Chicago." *Engineering News-Record* 177(29 September 1966):14–15.

"Chicago." *Architectural Forum* 116(May 1962):83–142.

"Chicago Reaches for the Sky." *Engineering News-Record* 168(26 April 1962): 59–60.

"Chicago Skyscraper." *Engineering News-Record* 154(17 March 1955):24.

"Chicago's Apartment Developments." *Architectural Forum* 92(January 1950): 69–86.

"Chicago's Prudential Building." *Architectural Forum* 97(August 1952):90–99.

"Chicago's Tallest and Finest." *Engineering News-Record* 153(16 December 1954):35–40.

"Concrete Girder Carries Skyscraper." *Engineering News-Record* 174(17 June 1965):62.

"Concrete Technology in the U.S.A." *Progressive Architecture* 41(October 1960): 158–75.

Condit, Carl W. "Is There a Chicago Style?" *Chicago* 2(Spring 1965):22–23.

———. "The New Architecture of Chicago." *Chicago Review* 17(Winter 1964): 107–19.

———. "The Rise of the New Chicago." *Chicago Tribune Sunday Magazine,* 27 March 1966, pp. 34–53.

"Crane Climbs to Cast Sixty-Story Building Core." *Engineering News-Record* 167 (14 September 1961):26.

"Creepers Hoist Hancock Steel." *Engineering News-Record* 178(22 June 1967):15.

Cuscaden, Rob. "That Anti-Chicago Obelisk." *Chicago Sun-Times Showcase,* 11 October 1970, p. 2.

Darby, Edwin. "New Method Spurs Co-op Buildings." *Chicago Sun-Times,* 20 January 1963, p. 51.

Darby, Edwin, and Clark, William N. "Chicago, the Living City." *Fortune* 66(July 1962):62–106.

"De Witt–Chestnut Apartment, Chicago." *Architectural Record* 139(January 1966):160–61.

Dillman, William. "Chicago's Industrial Profile Changing." *Chicago Sun-Times,* 17 June 1962, p. 57.

———. "Industrial Parks Fit the New Era." *Chicago Sun-Times,* 18 June 1962, p. 45.

———. "Industrial Parks Ignore Traditions." *Chicago Sun-Times,* 19 June 1962, p. 52.

"Dirt in the Caissons." *Engineering News-Record* 177(13 October 1966):238.

Dixon, John Morris. "John Hancock Center." *Architectural Forum* 133(July–August 1970):36–45.

———. "Marina City: Outer Space Image and Inner-Space Reality." *Architectural Forum* 122(April 1965):68–77.

———. "Thirty-Story Slab of Ingenuity." *Architectural Forum* 133(September 1970):20–27.

Drexler, Arthur. *Ludwig Mies van der Rohe.* New York: George Braziller, 1960.

"Equitable Building a Chicago; Skidmore, Owings and Merrill." *Architettura* 12 (June 1966):104–5.

"The Evolution of a Special Form to Meet Its Program." *Architectural Record* 145 (April 1969):192–96.

"Factory Complex." *Progressive Architecture* 37(July 1956):108–10.

"The First National Bank of Chicago." *Architectural Record* 148(September 1970):137–40.

"A Flexible Research Laboratory Complex for Inland Steel." *Architectural Record* 146(July 1969):114–18.

"Forty-One Stories in Steel." *Engineering News-Record* 153(18 November 1954): 22.

Gapp, Paul. "How Future of Industry Looks Here." *Chicago Daily News,* 15 October 1965, p. 1.

"Garden Living Units at Apartment Tower Base Give Scale and Variety." *Architectural Record* 144(September 1968):149–52.

Geyer, Georgie Anne. "Make No Little Buildings!" *Chicago* 2(Spring 1965):46–51.

"Giant Panels Cut Field Installation Costs." *Engineering News-Record* 182(22 May 1969):84–86.

Gorlick, Arthur. "City Growth Rate Slips." *Chicago Daily News,* 12 January 1967, pp. 3–4.

Hanson, Donald D. "Structuring the Loop." *Progressive Architecture* 47(August 1966):194–97.

Haydon, Harold. "Sculpture and Architecture." *Chicago* 2(Spring 1965):44–45.

"Height Record Recipe: Ice Mixed Plastic Forms, Climbing Cranes." *Engineering News-Record* 168(22 February 1962):30–37.

"High vs. Low Apartments." *Architectural Forum* 96(January 1952):100–106.

Hilberseimer, Ludwig. *Mies van der Rohe.* Chicago: Paul Theobald and Company, 1956.

Hornbeck, James S. "Chicago's Multi-Use Giant." *Architectural Record* 141(January 1967):137–44.

Hough, Hugh. "Equitable's Skyscraper Dedicated at Historic Site." *Chicago Sun-Times,* 24 June 1965, pp. 2, 42.

Hunt, Ridgely. "The New Bank on Old Dearborn Street." *Chicago Tribune Sunday Magazine,* 17 March 1968, pp. 28–31, 76–80.

Huxtable, Ada Louise. "Mies: Lessons from the Master." *New York Times,* 6 February 1966, pp. 24–25.

"Immeubles d'appartement: Promontory, 1948, . . . : L. Mies van der Rohe, architecte." *Architecture d'Aujourd'hui* 29(September 1958):50–53, 60–65, 80–86.

"In the Spirit of the 'Chicago School': An Apartment Designed for Light, Air and Views." *Architectural Record* 144(July 1968):109–12.

"Inland Steel." *Architectural Record* 123(April 1958):169–78.

"Inland Steel Builds a New Home." *Engineering News-Record* 158(10 January 1957):43–48.

"Innovation in Chicago: United States Gypsum's Headquarters." *Architectural Record* 135(January 1964):133–38.

"Insulated Aluminum Covers Sheathe John Hancock Building." *Architectural Record* 145(March 1969):168–70.

Jedlicka, Albert. " 'Bargain' Rental Skyscraper Unit." *Chicago Daily News,* 6 January 1967, p. 19.

———. "New 'Bargain' Rental Project." *Chicago Daily News,* 17 February 1967, p. 33.

———. "New Second City Boom West of Loop." *Chicago Daily News,* 26 June 1970, p. 31.

"Job-Built Rig Speeds Fireproofing of Chicago Skyscraper's Columns." *Engineering News-Record* 179(7 December 1967):28–29.

Johnson, Philip C. *Mies van der Rohe*. New York: Museum of Modern Art, 1947.

Jones, Cranston. "Up, up and up in Busy Chicago." *Life* 52(23 February 1962): 28–37.

Karlen, Arno. "The New Chicago." *Holiday* 41(March 1967):46, 152, 155, 157–60.

Khan, Fazlur. "The John Hancock Center." *Civil Engineering* 37(October 1967): 38–42.

Kurtz, Stephen A. "Mies van der Rohe (1886–1969)." *Progressive Architecture* 50 (November 1969):8–11.

"Lake Point Tower: The First Skyscraper with an Undulating Wall." *Architectural Record* 146(October 1969):123–30.

"This Lake Shore Facade Takes a Try at a Balcony Pattern." *Architectural Forum* 103(November 1955):146.

"Landscapes for Work." *Architectural Record* 144(October 1968):145–48.

"Lead Armor Soundproofs New Art Center." *Engineering News-Record* 179 (21 September 1967):82–83.

"The Legacy of Mies van der Rohe." *Inland Architect* 14(August 1970):10, 12–21, 24–25.

"Mies van der Rohe." *Architectural Forum* 97(November 1952):93–103.

Miller, Henry. "Chicago's Thirty-Nine Story R/C Executive House." *Journal of the American Concrete Institute* 31(September 1959):215–22.

Moore, Ruth. "Chicago's Most Towering Triumph." *Chicago Sun-Times,* 24 January 1965, sect. 2, pp. 1, 3.

———. "City Central Area: Big Progress, but Much to Do." *Chicago Sun-Times,* 9 August 1964, p. 36.

———. "Introducing Our New City of Towers." *Chicago Sun-Times,* 30 May 1968, p. 4.

———. "Merits, Flaws Analyzed in Ten Chicago Apartment Groups." *Chicago Sun-Times,* 29 December 1963, p. 43.

———. "A River Site for Fifty-Five-Story IBM Building." *Chicago Sun-Times,* 19 June 1968, pp. 1, 8.

Newman, M. W. "Chicago: City of Tombstones." *Chicago Daily News Panorama,* 24 January 1970, pp. 4–5.

———. "Giantism in the City: Its Triumphs, Its Dangers." *Inland Architect* 13 (January 1969), pp. 8–13.

———. "Is Seventy-Story Tower Too Big for Lakefront?" *Chicago Daily News,* 22 October 1965, p. 5.

———. "Mies: Design as Truth, Clarity and Order." *Chicago Daily News Panorama,* 5 November 1966, pp. 2–3.

———. "A New Giant on the River Offers Lessons for the Future." *Chicago Daily News Panorama,* 17 July 1965, p. 1.

————. "Our Super City in the Sky." *Chicago Daily News,* 9 August 1966, p. 38.

————. "Who Cares about Our Landmarks?" *Chicago Daily News Panorama,* 3 October 1970, pp. 4–5.

"Nineten Glass Tiers Sitting on a Cantilever." *Architectural Forum* 103(November 1955):149.

"Operation Bootstrap: Creepers Erect Steel." *Engineering News-Record* 177(13 October 1966):118–19.

"Return of the Atrium." *Architectural Forum* 116(March 1962):86–88.

Root, Susan. "A Glass House Is a Home." *Chicago Daily News,* 12 October 1968, p. 36.

Schulze, Franz. "The New Chicago Architecture." *Art in America* 56(May–June 1968):60–70.

Schwartz, Donald M. "Marina City: Color It Upper Middle Class." *Chicago Sun-Times,* 9 June 1963, pp. 1, 28, 30.

"Select Bridge Beam Method to Repair Chicago Caisson." *Engineering News-Record* 177(20 October 1966):17.

"Seventy-Story Tower Will Set Concrete Height Record." *Engineering News-Record* 175(4 November 1965):26.

"Shoe Plant: Light Industry Takes a New Stand in the Center of Chicago." *Architectural Forum* 91(December 1949):90–91.

"Skyscraper Is a Living Lab." *Engineering News-Record* 179(10 August 1967): 22–23.

"Skyscraper to Top Chicago Depot." *Engineering News-Record* 151(6 August 1953):26.

"Small Office Building, New Approach." *Architectural Record* 105(January 1949): 112–16.

Stern, Richard G. "A City Forever on the Rebound." *Chicago Sun-Times,* 18 February 1962, sect. 2, pp. 1–3.

"Strength and Cohesiveness for a Crowded Block in Chicago." *Architectural Record* 148(July 1970):122–25.

"A Tale of Two Towers." *Architectural Forum* 124(April 1966):28–37.

"Three Houses . . . A Romantic Solution." *Progressive Architecture* 48(November 1967):112–17.

Van der Rohe, Ludwig Mies. "Where Do We Go from Here?" *Chicago* 2(Spring 1965):52.

"Warehouse and Distribution Centers." *Progressive Architecture* 140(December 1966):121–23.

"Welding Cost Halved by Semiautomatic Process." *Engineering News-Record* 182 (24 April 1969):38–40.

Williams, Michaela. "A Bit of Charm Is Being Erased." *Chicago Daily News Panorama,* 18 February 1967, p. 3.

"X-Braces Trim Steel Tonnage." *Engineering News-Record* 175(23 September 1965):42–43.

Chapter 4. Public Buildings

"Administration and Research Buildings." *Architectural Record* 120(July 1956): 206.

"Administration Building for Child Welfare." *Progressive Architecture* 34(April 1953):80–83.

"Big Steel: Chicago's Civic Center Complete." *Architectural Forum* 125(October 1966):32–37.

Blake, Peter. "A Modern Church for a Modern Faith." *Architectural Forum* 110 (May 1959):130–35.

"Campus City, Chicago." *Architectural Forum* 123(September 1965):21–45.

Cappo, Joe. "Expert Charges High Costs, Poor Management in CHA." *Chicago Daily News,* 13 November 1967, p. 13.

Chandler, Christopher. "CHA Cites Role of City Council in Housing Sites." *Chicago Sun-Times,* 28 March 1968, pp. 6–7.

"Changing High Schools: Chicago's Program for Improvement." *Architectural Forum* 113(November 1960):110–14, 204.

"Chicago Civic Center: Dignity and Continuity." *Progressive Architecture* 47(October 1966):244–47.

Chicago Dwellings Association. *Annual Report.* Chicago: Chicago Dwellings Association, 1948 et seq.

Chicago Housing Authority. *Annual Report.* Chicago: Chicago Housing Authority, 1938 et seq.

"Chicago Teachers College North: Undergraduate Catalogue, 1963–65." *Chicago Teachers College North Bulletin* 3(September 1963):13–15.

Condit, Carl W. "[McCormick Place]: A Special Kind of Building." *Chicago Tribune Magazine,* 14 February 1971, pp. 58–62.

Cuscaden, Rob. "McCormick Place II: Colossal, but Comforting." *Chicago Sun-Times Midwest Magazine,* 17 January 1971, pp. 9–16.

Dierks, Donald. "A Key Milestone for TV Education." *Chicago Sun-Times,* 31 October 1965, sect. 3, p. 1.

Dillman, William. "Chicago Housing Called Midwest's Most Segregated." *Chicago Sun-Times,* 7 December 1962, p. 38.

Dixon, John Morris. "Campus City Continued." *Architectural Forum* 129(December 1968):28–43.

———. "Church in a Grove of Skyscrapers." *Architectural Forum* 130(June 1969):42–45.

————. "Goldberg's Variations on Chicago Public Housing." *Architectural Forum* 125(November 1966):25–33.

————. "New Galaxies at Chicago Circle." *Architectural Forum* 133(November 1970):24–33.

"Exhibition Hall Fire Singes Building Codes." *Engineering News-Record* 178(26 January 1967):52–53.

"First Universalist Church, Chicago." *Architectural Record* 119(June 1956): 190–94.

"Fortunate School: New Trier West H.S." *Progressive Architecture* 48(September 1967):108–17.

"From Roads to Lockers: SOM Designs New Campus for Illinois University." *Interiors* 125(May 1966):130–41.

"Glass Fails, Thick Panes Hardest Hit." *Engineering News-Record* 177(20 October 1966):18.

Golden, Harry, Jr. "OK One-Building McCormick Place." *Chicago Sun-Times,* 17 October 1967, p. 3.

————. "Unveil a New McCormick Place: Hall on Two Levels." *Chicago Sun-Times,* 2 December 1967, p. 3.

Greenberg, Sue. "Northwestern's Chicago Campus. . . ." *Daily Northwestern,* 18 April 1969, pp. 2–3.

Grigg, Steven. "Chicago Circle Campus: A Student's Questioning View." *Inland Architect* 13(April 1969):18–21.

Haas, Joseph. "A Library Programmed for People." *Chicago Daily News Panorama,* 10 January 1970, pp. 4–5.

————. "On the Midway, a Library for All Seasons." *Chicago Daily News Panorama,* 24 October 1970, p. 6.

"IIT Builds Vast New Campus." *Engineering News-Record* 140(1 January 1948): 19.

"Illinois Institute of Technology." *Architectural Record* 117(January 1955): 126–31.

"Industrial Roof Tops a Phoenix." *Engineering News-Record* 183(2 October 1969):28, 33.

"Interiors for the Federal Government." *Progressive Architecture* 46(July 1965): 170–77.

Jarik, George J. "Chicago Civic Center's Mechanical/Electrical Systems." *Actual Specifying Engineer* 13(January 1965):88–100, 114.

Jedlicka, Albert. "New and Green Eden." *Chicago Daily News,* 9 August 1968, p. 15.

"Law School Center, University of Chicago." *Architectural Record* 128(November 1960):132–35.

Logan, Donald-David. "Rest Stop." *Architectural Forum* 129(September 1968): 76–79.

"Long-Span Restaurant Straddles Tollway." *Engineering News-Record* 179(13 July 1967):44.

McCormick Place-on-the-Lake. Chicago: Chicago Convention Bureau, n.d.

McMullen, Jay. "CHA Project: $27 Million Renewal Set." *Chicago Daily News*, 17 May 1968, pp. 1, 7.

Mayer, Albert. "Public Housing Architecture." *Journal of Housing* 19(15 October 1962):446–56.

———. "Public Housing as Community." *Architectural Record* 135(April 1964): 169–78.

"Metals and Minerals Research Building, Illinois Institute of Technology." *Architectural Forum* 79(November 1943):88–90.

"Mies' Enormous Room." *Architectural Forum* 105(August 1956):104–11.

Moore, Ruth. "CHA Contracts for Eighteen Buildings in Lawndale Area." *Chicago Sun-Times*, 26 January 1968, p. 23.

———. "CHA Raises Tenant Income Limits." *Chicago Sun-Times*, 29 March 1968, p. 44.

———. "CHA Selling 122 Racine Court Units to Tenants." *Chicago Sun-Times*, 8 February 1968, p. 24.

———. "Civic Center Details: To Be City's Tallest." *Chicago Sun-Times*, 14 March 1962, pp. 1, 5.

———. "A Dramatic Focus for the City's Heart." *Chicago Sun-Times Midwest Magazine*, 6 May 1962, pp. 4–7.

———. "Former Housing Aid Denounces CHA Policy." *Chicago Sun-Times*, 3 March 1964, p. 14.

———. "Lawndale Gets 'Interim Homes' for Remodeling." *Chicago Sun-Times*, 1 February 1968, p. 88.

———. "New South Shore High School: Design for Learning." *Chicago Sun-Times*, 6 February 1966, p. 54.

———. "Open House Set at CHA Facility in Hyde Park." *Chicago Sun-Times*, 23 June 1967, p. 67.

———. "Prefab Houses Win City's OK." *Chicago Sun-Times* 14 June 1968, p. 3.

———. "Revive Old Mies Design for Vast Convention Hall." *Chicago Sun-Times*, 22 January 1967, pp. 4, 48.

———. "Study of Civic Center Plans Affords a Bold Concept for Its Extension." *Chicago Sun-Times*, 29 April 1962, p. 56.

———. "Thirty Interim Homes Set in Lawndale during Renewal." *Chicago Sun-Times*, 12 January 1968, p. 62.

————. "Upgrading of Old Housing for the Lower-Income Family." *Chicago Sun-Times,* 12 April 1965, pp. 10, 54.

————. "What It Takes to Buy Home Here." *Chicago Sun-Times,* 12 April 1970, pp. 3, 42.

"New Dimensions in Housing Design." *Progressive Architecture* 32(April 1951): 57–68.

"A New Multi-Use Gymnasium for IIT." *Architectural Record* 146(July 1969): 111–13.

Newman, M. W. "Academe in Metropolis." *Chicago Daily News Panorama,* 2 October 1965, pp. 2–3.

————. "Chicago's $70 Million Ghetto." *Chicago Daily News,* 10 April 1965, pp. 1, 4.

————. "The Civic Center: An Eye-Popper of a Skyscraper." *Chicago Daily News,* 18 April 1964, sect. 2, p. 17.

————. "The Colossus of 23rd Street and What May Come Next." *Inland Architect* 14(November 1970):12–17.

————. "Fear, Violence in High-rise Negro Ghetto." *Chicago Daily News,* 12 April 1965, p. 10.

————. "The Ghetto Struggle for Livability." *Chicago Daily News,* 16 April 1965, p. 31.

————. "Ghetto's Teens: A Tragedy of Wasted Lives." *Chicago Daily News,* 14 April 1965, p. 42.

————. "Half-Circle at Heald Square: A Modern Downtown Church." *Inland Architect* 13(March 1969):44–46.

————. "The Hunt for Solutions to High-rise Ghetto." *Chicago Daily News,* 17 April 1965, p. 14.

————. "Irony of the Taylor Homes Mess: It Was Planned." *Chicago Daily News,* 15 April 1965, p. 11.

————. "Our New McCormick Place." *Chicago Daily News,* 17 May 1968, pp. 3–4.

————. "Poor Man's Marina City." *Chicago Daily News,* 12 November 1966, p. 3.

————. "Trouble Boils over in Ghetto Oven." *Chicago Daily News,* 13 April 1965, p. 10.

"Reinterpreting an Ancient Liturgy: A Greek Orthodox Church in the Chicago Suburbs." *Progressive Architecture* 47(March 1966):141–45.

"Reports Housing Segregation Here Is Highest in Fifty Years." *Chicago Sun-Times,* 14 December 1962, p. 32.

"A Research Library for Northwestern University," *Architectural Record* 148(July 1970):89–96.

Schnedler, Jack. "New Trier West: The $10,000,000 High School." *Chicago Daily News,* 14 October 1962, p. 42.

Schoenwetter, Paul. "Chicago a Challenge to Winning Architect." *Chicago Sun-Times,* 18 April 1965, sect. 4, p. 18.

"Sophisticated Technology for a Lutheran Seminary." *Architectural Record* 144 (September 1968):174–79.

Sorkin, Michael, et al. "The Grey City." *Chicago Maroon,* 8 March 1968, pp. 2–17.

"The Stock Exchange and the LaSalle Street Canyon." *Inland Architect* 14(July 1970):18–19.

"Student Commons, Illinois Institute of Technology." *Progressive Architecture* 36 (July 1955):104–6.

Sullivan, Frank. "CDA Is One of the Most Active Home Builders in Chicago." *Chicago Sun-Times,* 31 October 1966, p. 28.

Swibel, Charles R. "The CHA in a Changing City." *Chicago Sun-Times,* 28 November 1965, sect. 2, pp. 3, 8.

"A Synagogue by Yamasaki." *Architectural Record* 136(September 1964):176–77, 191–96.

"Tragic Conflict: Schools vs. Parks in the Inner City." *Inland Architect* 14(July 1970):23.

"Two Campus Religious and Social Centers." *Architectural Record* 113(June 1953):140–42.

"Two Lakefront Policies Issues Raised: Eight Conditions Offered for Rebuilding McCormick Place." *Chicago Sun-Times,* 13 November 1967, pp. 3, 26.

"Union to Build Prefab Housing." *Engineering News-Record* 180(27 June 1968): 11.

"University of Illinois, Chicago Campus." *Progressive Architecture* 46(October 1965):222–31.

"The University of Illinois Serves Chicago, Serves the State." *Chicago Daily News,* 25 September 1965, special supplement.

Von Eckardt, Wolf. "Mies System at Least Turns out Craftsmen." *Washington Post,* 11 December 1966, p. G7.

"William C. Jones Commercial High School." *Architectural and Engineering News,* vol. 7(February 1965).

Chapter 5. Renewal and Reconstruction

Adams, John Kay, and Cohen, Jerry. "Englewood: A Bright New Future for South Siders?" *Chicago Sun-Times,* 21 June 1959, sect. 2, pp. 1–3.

———. "Englewood Gets a New Civic Team." *Chicago Sun-Times,* 25 June 1959, pp. 36–37.

————. "Englewood Working for Harmony." *Chicago Sun-Times,* 22 June 1959, pp. 24–25.

————. "Realty Tricksters Hurt Englewood." *Chicago Sun-Times,* 23 June 1959, pp. 22–23.

————. "Where Englewood's Strength Lies." *Chicago Sun-Times,* 24 June 1959, pp. 24–25.

Beadle, Muriel. *The Hyde Park–Kenwood Urban Renewal Years.* Chicago: Muriel Beadle, 1967.

Berkeley, Ellen Perry. "Woodlawn Gardens." *Architectural Forum* 131 (July–August 1969):72–77.

Black, W. Joseph. "A Far-sighted Study and Some Blind Spots: A Critique of the Park-Mall Lawndale Study." *Architectural Forum* 129 (December 1968):44–49.

————. "The Renewed Negro and Urban Renewal." *Architectural Forum* 128 (June 1968):60–67.

"Bold Plans for Chicago." *Architectural Forum* 101 (November 1954):123–30.

Braden, William, and Petacque, Art. "The Parks: Are They Safe Now?" *Chicago Sun-Times,* 5 June 1963, pp. 3, 30.

Chicago Community Renewal Program. *Community Renewal Program Report.* Chicago: Community Renewal Program, 1964.

————. *Community Renewal Program Report: Proposals for Discussion.* Chicago: Community Renewal Program, 1964.

————. *Housing and Urban Renewal Progress Report, December 31, 1964.* Chicago: Community Renewal Program, [1965].

Chicago Department of Urban Renewal. *Annual Report.* Chicago: Department of Urban Renewal and predecessors, 1962 et seq.

————. *Twenty Years of Progress: Annual Report, 1966.* Chicago: Department of Urban Renewal, 1967.

"Chicago Redevelops." *Architectural Forum* 93 (August 1950):98–104.

De Zutter, Henry. "Lawndale Demands a Part in Renewal Plans." *Chicago Daily News,* 8 June 1967, p. 26.

Dishon, Robert. "City Park Crisis Feared." *Chicago Daily News,* 9 December 1967, p. 10.

————. "Lawndale 'New City' Plan Told." *Chicago Daily News,* 13 June 1967, p. 26.

Eaton, William J. "City's Self-Portrait of Four Worst Areas." *Chicago Daily News,* 28 July 1967, p. 6.

Gapp, Paul. "Lakefront Plans: City's Big Zigzag." *Chicago Daily News,* 7 August 1965, p. 19.

————. "Our Vanishing Open Land." *Chicago Daily News,* 10 July 1965, sect. 2, p. 17.

————. "The Untold Story of Jackson Park Battle." *Chicago Daily News,* 25 September 1965, p. 3.

Golden, Harry, Jr. " 'Piecemealism' Threatens Dead-end for Open-Space Planning Concept." *Chicago Sun-Times,* 21 August 1966, sect. 2, pp. 1–4.

Gorlick, Arthur. "City's Growth Rate Slips." *Chicago Daily News,* 12 January 1967, pp. 3–4.

"How to Keep Your Landmarks and Have Them Too." *Progressive Architecture* 47(October 1966):89–90.

"Huge Air Rights Apartment Rises over Chicago Tracks." *Engineering News-Record* 172(27 February 1964):23.

Hunt, Ridgely. "Resurrection of a Masterpiece." *Chicago Tribune Sunday Magazine,* 29 October 1967, pp. 26–40.

Jacobi, Peter P. "The Awakening Auditorium." *Chicago* 2(Spring 1965):32–38.

Littlewood, Tom. "Model Cities: Chicago, Gary to Get Neighborhood Cash." *Chicago Sun-Times,* 17 November 1967, pp. 3, 22.

McMullen, Jay. "Twenty Years of City Renewal." *Chicago Daily News,* 15 April 1967, pp. 3, 10.

Mark, Norman. "Auditorium Angels Come Through." *Chicago Daily News,* 29 June 1967, p. 3.

Martin, John Bartlow. "My Chicago." *Holiday* 41(March 1967):54, 94, 98, 100, 102.

Miller, John J. B. *Open Land in Metropolitan Chicago.* Chicago: Midwest Open Land Association, 1962.

Moore, Ruth. "Chicago's Plan: Big Changes for Industry, Breadwinners." *Chicago Sun-Times,* 9 September 1964, p. 30.

————. "City Guidelines Set for IC Air Complex." *Chicago Sun-Times,* 24 May 1968, pp. 1, 38.

————. "A City Reborn." *Chicago Sun-Times:* 12 October 1958, sect. 2, pp. 1–3; 13 October 1958, pp. 1 ff.; 14 October 1958, pp. 3 ff.; 15 October 1958, pp. 3 ff.; 16 October 1958, pp. 3 ff.; 17 October 1958, pp. 3 ff.; 18 October 1958, pp. 3 ff.; 19 October 1958, sect. 2, pp. 1–3; 20 October 1958, pp. 3 ff.; 21 October 1958, pp. 3 ff.

————. "The Cost of Urban Renewal? It's Paying off for Chicago." *Chicago Sun-Times,* 14 May 1964, p. 42.

————. "How Good Urban Design Gives Lift to Some City Areas." *Chicago Sun-Times,* 22 December 1963, p. 30.

————. "The Lakefront's Future: Its Ownership, Its Planning." *Chicago Sun-Times,* 27 January 1963, sect. 2, pp. 1–3.

————. "Near South Side: An Area of Transition and Boom." *Chicago Sun-Times,* 25 January 1968, p. 28.

————. "A New Look on City's Lakefront." *Chicago Sun-Times,* 22 October 1961, pp. 3, 18.

————. "New Methods in Chicago Model City Aid Proposals." *Chicago Sun-Times,* 4 May 1967, p. 26.

————. "Offer Legislation to Save Buildings and Landmarks." *Chicago Sun-Times,* 27 November 1967, p. 28.

————. "$100-Million Rehabilitation for Lawndale." *Chicago Sun-Times,* 17 September 1967, pp. 1, 72.

————. "Park District Is Challenged on Grant Park Bowl Plans." *Chicago Sun-Times,* 21 May 1963, pp. 1, 22.

————. "Propose Revamp of Jackson Park." *Chicago Sun-Times,* 30 June 1966, p. 2.

————. "Reese Area Slum Conversion Report Becomes U.S. Model." *Chicago Sun-Times,* 16 July 1962, p. 29.

————. "Remaking a City: Foundation Rescues Slums." *Chicago Sun-Times,* 11 April 1965, pp. 12, 50.

————. "Renewal Projects Alter Face of Old Town." *Chicago Sun-Times,* 13 August 1967, p. 5.

————. "Restoration of Madlener House a National Demonstration." *Chicago Sun-Times,* 13 February 1964, p. 24.

————. "Second Lives for Landmarks." *Chicago* 2(Spring 1965):28–31.

————. "Slum to Model: Transition in Lawndale." *Chicago Sun-Times,* 1 March 1968, p. 35.

————. "A Street Blossoms on the West Side." *Chicago Sun-Times Midwest Magazine,* 7 September 1969, pp. 30–32.

————. "Study Urges Twenty-Six-Mile Lakefront Park." *Chicago Sun-Times,* 28 February 1968, p. 5.

————. "Uptown Area Gets Full-Scale Plan for Urban Renewal." *Chicago Sun-Times,* 17 May 1962, p. 32.

————. "West Side: A Dream Coming True." *Chicago Sun-Times,* 26 February 1961, p. 26.

————. "Woodlawn Plan: 'Total' Renewal." *Chicago Sun-Times,* 16 March 1962, p. 3.

————. "Zoning Group Director Quits, Office Closed." *Chicago Sun-Times,* 23 January 1968, pp. 1, 14.

Newman, M. W. "The Auditorium Returns to Life." *Chicago Daily News Panorama,* 7 August 1965, p. 3.

————. "The Behind-Scenes Battling over IC 'Skyscraper City.' " *Chicago Daily News,* 24 January 1967, p. 31.

———. "The City House: Urbane Renewal in a Vintage Neighborhood." *Inland Architect* 13(February 1969):14–17.

———. "City of Skyscrapers to Tower over IC." *Chicago Daily News,* 23 January 1967, pp. 1, 50.

———. "City Parks Put in Bad Light." *Chicago Daily News,* 2 November 1965, p. 10.

———. "Four-Level City Due below IC Tracks." *Chicago Daily News,* 27 February 1968, p. 40.

———. " 'High-rise Calcutta' on IC a Crucial Question for City." *Chicago Daily News,* 25 January 1967, p. 6.

———. "How Creeping 'Non-Green' Takes over Our Parks." *Chicago Daily News,* 30 October 1965, sect. 2, pp. 17–24.

———. "Lake View Fighting Spread of Four-plus-ones." *Chicago Daily News,* 23 March 1968, p. 5.

———. "The $156,000,000 Charade of Jackson Park." *Chicago Daily News,* 3 November 1965, p. 23.

Newman, M. W., and Sons, Ray. "Our Parks Groaning at Seams." *Chicago Daily News,* 4 November 1965, p. 20.

Northeastern Illinois Planning Commission. *Annual Report.* Chicago: Northeastern Illinois Planning Commission, 1958 et seq.

O'Faolain, Sean. "The Three Chicagos." *Holiday* 28(December 1960):74–87, 180–89.

Real Estate Research Corporation. *Economic Analysis of Housing and Commercial Property in the City of Chicago, 1960–1975.* [Chicago: Community Renewal Program, 1963.]

Rossi, Peter H., and Dentler, Robert A. *The Politics of Urban Renewal: The Chicago Findings.* New York: Free Press of Glencoe, 1961.

Solomon, Ezra, and Bilbija, Zarko G. *Metropolitan Chicago: An Economic Analysis.* Glencoe: Free Press, 1959.

Sons, Ray. "City's Parks: Beauty Spots—and Eyesores." *Chicago Daily News,* 5 November 1965, p. 11.

Sullivan, Frank. "Funds OKd for Lawndale Renewal." *Chicago Sun-Times,* 29 September 1967, pp. 3, 28.

———. "Plans for $500 Million 'City' over the IC Told." *Chicago Sun-Times,* 30 September 1966, pp. 1, 46.

Talbott, Basil, Jr. "Ripon Society Debuts Here by Attacking Park District." *Chicago Sun-Times,* 27 June 1968, p. 38.

Welfare Council of Metropolitan Chicago, Open Lands Committee. *Open Lands Project.* Publication no. 3500. Chicago: Welfare Council of Metropolitan Chicago, 1964.

Wise, Malcolm. "High Bidder Offers Unique North Side Dwelling Project." *Chicago Sun-Times,* 12 May 1961, pp. 1, 4.

———. "Sandburg Village, a Bold New Concept." *Chicago Sun-Times,* 18 October 1962, p. 56.

Chapter 6. The New Transportation Pattern

American Institute of Steel Construction. *Prize Bridges, 1928–1956; Prize Bridges, 1961; Prize Bridges, 1963–1964; Prize Bridges, 1966.* New York: American Institute of Steel Construction, 1958, [1962], [1965], [1967].

American Trucking Association, Department of Research. *Trends.* Washington: American Trucking Association, 1947.

Boyd, H. T. *More Median Transit for Chicago.* Chicago: De Leuw, Cather and Company, [1970].

"Burlington Buys Gallery Suburban Cars." *Railway Age* 129(21 October 1950): 20–23.

"C & N W Unveils Push-Pull Trains." *Railway Age* 147(19 October 1959):16–17.

Chicago Area Transportation Study. *Final Report.* 3 vols. Chicago: Chicago Area Transportation Study, 1962.

Chicago Department of the Port. *The Seaport of Chicago.* Chicago: Department of the Port, [1961].

"Chicago Getting Two More Median Strip Transit Lines." *Railway Age* 163(4 December 1967):28, 30, 45.

"Chicago Ships Its Sludge to the Farmland." *Engineering News-Record* 186(4 February 1971):22–23.

"Chicago Strains for Waste Treatment." *Engineering News-Record* 183(16 October 1969):34–35.

Chicago Transit Authority. *Chicago's Mass Transportation System.* Chicago: Chicago Transit Authority, 1959.

———. *New Horizons for the Chicago Metropolitan Area.* Chicago: Chicago Transit Authority, 1958.

"Chicago Transit Authority's New Elevated-Subway Cars Feature All-Electric Operation, Including Braking." *Storage Battery Power* 21(July 1951):7–9.

"Chicago's Lake Diversion Upheld." *Engineering News-Record* 177(15 December 1966):64–65.

"Committee Report Vindicates Bacon." *Engineering News-Record* 185(17 September 1970):58–59.

De Leuw, Cather and Company, and Sanderson and Porter. *Passenger Terminal Consolidation Study, Chicago.* Chicago: Chicago Railroad Terminal Authority, 1959.

De Zutter, Henry. "Chicago's Inland Waterways: Where Pollution Ruins Fun." *Chicago Daily News,* 20 August 1966, p. 4.

————. "Crisis on the Lake." *Chicago Daily News,* 16 August 1966, pp. 1, 4; 17 August 1966, pp. 1, 56; 18 August 1966, pp. 3, 4.

Dishon, Robert. "Seven Rails Win Fight for Port Access." *Chicago Daily News,* 14 November 1966, p. 57.

An Era of Excellence: The History of Greyhound. Chicago: Greyhound Corporation, [1966?].

Forsythe, S. D. "Rapid Transit Is Expanding in Chicago." *Transactions of the American Institute of Electrical Engineers,* vol. 78, part 2 (*Applications and Industry*), no. 46 (January 1960), pp. 474–76.

Gapp, Paul. "Facts Explode the Myths about Our Expressways." *Chicago Daily News,* 2 February 1965, p. 16.

————. "How Expressway Lobbyists Barricade CTA." *Chicago Daily News,* 1 February 1965, p. 5.

————. "Superhighways vs. Mass Transit." *Chicago Daily News,* 11 January 1965, pp. 1, 9.

————. "Super-Road Foes Starting to Make a Serious Impact." *Chicago Daily News,* 30 January 1965, p. 5.

Heinecke, Burnell. "1962 Year of Decision for Chicago Port." *Chicago Sun-Times,* 12 August 1962, p. 49.

Hoge, James. "New O'Hare: Giant Step into Jet Age." *Chicago Sun-Times,* 17 December 1961, p. 61.

Jedlicka, Albert. "Land Values Rise in O'Hare Area." *Chicago Daily News,* 20 December 1967, p. 36.

Kandlik, Ed. "Dearborn Street Bridge: Its History." *Chicago Daily News,* 26 March 1963, p. 44.

Kaufmann, Edgar, Jr. "O'Hare International Airport." *Progressive Architecture* 44 (August 1963):102–11.

Lewis, Richard W. "U.S. Report Calls Waterway 'One of Most Polluted.' " *Chicago Sun-Times,* 12 April 1963, p. 2.

————. "Waterway Sludge Peril Is Abated, Bacon Assures Legislators." *Chicago Sun-Times,* 7 April 1963, p. 12.

Lipson, Jerry. "Is Bacon's Clean-River Plan Feasible?" *Chicago Daily News,* 15 April 1967, p. 12.

McGaffin, William. "City Lake Diversion Upheld." *Chicago Daily News,* 8 December 1966, pp. 1, 11.

McMullen, Jay. "The Skyway: High-speed Road to Fiscal Ruin." *Chicago Daily News,* 28 August 1965, sect. 2, p. 19.

Mayer, Harold M. *The Port of Chicago and the St. Lawrence Seaway.* Research Paper no. 49. Chicago: University of Chicago Department of Geography, 1957.

"Midway Airport Gets a Face-lifting." *Engineering News-Record* 180(2 May 1968):48–53.

Moore, Ruth. "Chicago Plans a Future Transit System." *Chicago Sun-Times,* 10 September 1964, p. 38.

———. "Congress: The City's New Grand Axis." *Chicago Sun-Times,* 2 May 1963, p. 36.

———. "$18 Million Plan Offered for Building Jackson Park 'Balanced' Road System." *Chicago Sun-Times,* 29 March 1968, p. 2.

———. "New, Elegant Look for Chicago Subway." *Chicago Sun-Times,* 26 October 1969, pp. 4, 38.

———. "New Expressway System Opposed by City Planners." *Chicago Sun-Times,* 8 September 1962, p. 58.

Motor Truck Facts. New York: Automobile Manufacturers Association, 1935 et seq.

Newman, M. W., and Warden, Rob. "Here's How to Save Lake Michigan." *Chicago Daily News,* 17 November 1967, pp. 1, 50.

Northcutt, James P. "Chicago's New Congress Street Rapid Transit." *Revue de l'Union Internationale de Transport Public* 8(August 1959):157–69.

"Report on Expressways." *Chicago Sun-Times:* 15 June 1959, pp. 29–32; 16 June 1959, pp. 25–28; 17 June 1959, pp. 33–36; 18 June 1959, pp. 39–41.

Schiller, Andrew. "Chicago's Commuter Railroad Miracle." *Harper's Magazine* 232 (January 1966):65–76.

Schwartz, Donald M. "Roads without End: Vital Arteries or Varicose Veins?" *Chicago Sun-Times,* 16 September 1962, pp. 1, 3.

South Side Planning Board. *Proposal on Railroad Consolidation.* Chicago: South Side Planning Board, 1949.

Sullivan, Frank. "Two New Central Subways Proposed." *Chicago Sun-Times,* 20 May 1967, pp. 3, 26.

United States Department of Health, Education and Welfare. *Report on Pollution of the Waters of the Grand Calumet River, Little Calumet River, Calumet River, Lake Michigan, Wolf Lake and Their Tributaries, Illinois–Indiana.* Chicago: U.S. Department of Health, Education and Welfare, Public Health Service, Region V, February 1965.

"Urbane Freeway." *Architectural Forum* 129(September 1968):68–73.

"Vinton W. Bacon: Construction's Man of the Year." *Engineering News-Record* 178(16 February 1967):20–24, 108.

Wilson, Fletcher. "Cal-Sag: All-American Ditch." *Chicago Sun-Times,* 19 July 1959, sect. 2, pp. 1–4.

———. "$2.2 Billion Transit Plan for 1980s Proposes CTA–Railroad Hookups." *Chicago Sun-Times,* 7 July 1967, p. 3.

Wise, Malcolm. "Jet Age Chaos." *Chicago Sun-Times,* 13 November 1960, sect. 2, pp. 1–5.

———. "Oak Street Interchange Stirs Storm." *Chicago Sun-Times,* 29 January 1962, pp. 1, 8, 9.

———. "Present $158 Million Plan for Rail Terminal Merger." *Chicago Sun-Times,* 26 March 1959, pp. 1, 4, 28.

Chapter 7. The New Chicago Plan

Baron, Harold M., ed. *The Racial Aspects of Urban Planning: Critique on the Comprehensive Plan of the City of Chicago.* Chicago: Urban League Research Department, 1968.

Burnham, Daniel H., Jr., and Kingery, Robert. *Planning the Region of Chicago.* Chicago: Chicago Regional Planning Association, 1956.

Chicago Department of City Planning. *Annual Report.* Chicago: Department of City Planning, 1957 et seq.

———. *Basic Policies for the Comprehensive Plan of Chicago.* Chicago: Department of City Planning, 1964.

Chicago Department of Development and Planning. *The Comprehensive Plan of Chicago.* Chicago: Department of Development and Planning, 1966.

———. *The Comprehensive Plan of Chicago: Summary Report.* Chicago: Department of Development and Planning, 1967.

———. Area Plans. Chicago: Department of Development and Planning, as follows:

Far North Development Area, 1968.

Far Northwest Development Area, 1968.

Far South Development Area, 1968.

Far Southeast Development Area, 1968.

Far Southwest Development Area, 1968.

Far West Development Area, 1968.

Illinois Central Air Rights Development, 1968.

Mid-South Development Area, 1968.

Mid-West Development Area, 1967.

Near South Development Area, 1967.

Near West Development Area, 1967.

North Development Area, 1967.

Northwest Development Area, 1968.

O'Hare Development Area, 1968.

Southeast Development Area, 1968.

Southwest Development Area, 1968.

Chicago Plan Commission. *Building New Neighborhoods: Subdivision Design and Standards.* Chicago: Chicago Plan Commission, 1943.

Dishon, Robert. "$6 Billion Plan for Chicago." *Chicago Daily News,* 13 December 1966, pp. 1, 3, 4.

Gapp, Paul. "Architects Find Flaws in City's Master Plan." *Chicago Daily News,* 24 January 1966, p. 9.

———. "The Future Chicago." *Chicago Daily News,* 19 August 1964, pp. 1, 46.

Huxtable, Ada Louise. "A New Plan for Chicago's South Side." *Museum of Modern Art Bulletin* 14(June 1947):12–18.

Moore, Ruth. "New Chicago Plan: More than a Vision." *Chicago Sun-Times,* 12 March 1967, sect. 2, p. 4.

———. "Unveil Future Chicago Plan." *Chicago Sun-Times,* 20 August 1964, pp. 1, 42.

Von Hoffman, Nicholas. "City's Master Plan: Some Questions." *Chicago Daily News,* 20 August 1964, pp. 1, 6.

———. "How Chicago Will Change: A Profile of the City in 1975." *Chicago Daily News,* 2 January 1964, p. 50.

Credits for Illustrations

1. Painting by H. M. Pettit for Rand McNally Company; courtesy Chicago Historical Society.
2. Courtesy Chicago Historical Society.
3. Photo by Chicago Park District.
4. Photo by Chicago Park District.
5. *Chicago Water System* (Chicago: Department of Water and Sewers, 1966).
6. Photo by Metro News; courtesy Chicago Department of Water and Sewers.
7. *Progressive Architecture.*
8. *Progressive Architecture.*
9. Courtesy the Perkins and Will Partnership.
10. Courtesy the Perkins and Will Partnership.
11. Photo by Mart Studios, Incorporated; courtesy Chicago Housing Authority.
12. Photo by Bill Hedrich, Hedrich-Blessing.
13. Photo by Hedrich-Blessing.
14. Photo by Richard Nickel.
15. Courtesy Ludwig Mies van der Rohe.
16. Photo by Hube Henry, Hedrich-Blessing; courtesy Ludwig Mies van der Rohe.
17. Photo by George H. Steuer; courtesy Ludwig Mies van der Rohe.
18. Courtesy Ludwig Mies van der Rohe.
19. Photo by Hube Henry, Hedrich-Blessing; courtesy Metropolitan Structures, Incorporated.
20. Photo by Bill Engdahl, Hedrich-Blessing; courtesy Ludwig Mies van der Rohe.
21. Courtesy Ludwig Mies van der Rohe.
22. Photo by Bill Engdahl, Hedrich-Blessing.
23. Photo by Evanston Photographic Service; courtesy J. Marion Gutnayer.
24. Courtesy J. Marion Gutnayer.
25. Courtesy Loewenberg and Loewenberg.
26. Photo by Bill Engdahl, Hedrich-Blessing; courtesy Harry Weese and Associates.
27. Photo by Bill Engdahl, Hedrich-Blessing; courtesy Harry Weese and Associates.
28. Courtesy Harry Weese and Associates.
29. Photo by Orlando R. Cabanban; courtesy Harry Weese and Associates.
30. Courtesy Harry Weese and Associates.
31. Photo by Harr, Hedrich-Blessing.
32. Photo by Richard Nickel.
33. Photo by and courtesy Portland Cement Association.
34. *Architectural Forum.*
35. *Architectural Forum.*
36. Photo by Hedrich-Blessing; courtesy Schipporeit-Heinrich.
37. Courtesy Schipporeit-Heinrich.
38. Photo by Baltazar Korab; courtesy Edward Dart.
39. Photo by Kaufmann and Fabry Company.
40. Photo by Bill Engdahl, Hedrich-Blessing; courtesy the Perkins and Will Partnership.
41. Photo by Richard Nickel.
42. Photo by Bill Engdahl, Hedrich-Blessing.
43. Photo by Hedrich-Blessing.
44. Photo by Richard Nickel.
45. Photo by Bill Engdahl, Hedrich-Blessing; courtesy the Perkins and Will Partnership.
46. Photo by Ezra Stoller Associates; courtesy Skidmore, Owings and Merrill.
47. Photo by Dorman Anderson; courtesy Skidmore, Owings and Merrill.

48. Photo by Bill Hedrich, Hedrich-Blessing; courtesy Skidmore, Owings and Merrill.
49. Photo by Richard Nickel.
50. Courtesy Skidmore, Owings and Merrill.
51. *The First National Bank Building*, First National Bank of Chicago.
52. Photo by Richard Nickel.
53. Photo by Richard Nickel; courtesy Department of Architecture, Illinois Institute of Technology.
54. Photo by Bill Hedrich, Hedrich-Blessing; courtesy the Perkins and Will Partnership.
55. Photo by Bill Engdahl, Hedrich-Blessing; courtesy the Perkins and Will Partnership.
56. Photo by Bill Engdahl, Hedrich-Blessing; courtesy the Perkins and Will Partnership.
57. Photo by Hedrich-Blessing; courtesy Ludwig Mies van der Rohe.
58. Photo by Hedrich-Blessing; courtesy Ludwig Mies van der Rohe.
59. *Progressive Architecture*.
60. Photo by Hedrich-Blessing.
61. *Progressive Architecture*.
62. Photo by Richard Nickel.
63. Rendering by and courtesy C. F. Murphy Associates.
64. Photo by Idaka; courtesy Chicago Housing Authority.
65. Photo by Hedrich-Blessing; courtesy Chicago Housing Authority.
66. Photo by Hedrich-Blessing; courtesy Chicago Housing Authority.
67. Photo by Chicago Photographers; courtesy Chicago Housing Authority.
68. Courtesy Chicago Housing Authority.
69. Photo by Mart Studios; courtesy Chicago Housing Authority.
70. Photo by Gates Priest; courtesy Chicago Housing Authority.
71. Photo by Mart Studios; courtesy Chicago Housing Authority.
72. *Architectural Forum*.
73. *Architectural Forum*.
74. Photo by Suter, Hedrich-Blessing; courtesy the Perkins and Will Partnership.
75. *Chicago Teachers College North Bulletin*.
76. Photo by Bill Engdahl, Hedrich-Blessing; courtesy the Perkins and Will Partnership.
77. Courtesy the Perkins and Will Partnership.
78. Photo by Baltazar Korab; courtesy Harry Weese and Associates.
79. Photo by Arthur Siegel; courtesy University of Chicago Press.
80. Photo by Baltazar Korab; courtesy Skidmore, Owings and Merrill.
81. Photo by Hedrich-Blessing; courtesy University of Chicago.
82. Photo by Bill Engdahl, Hedrich-Blessing; courtesy University of Chicago.
83. Photo by Richard Nickel.
84. Courtesy Ludwig Mies van der Rohe.
85. Photo by Hube Henry, Hedrich-Blessing; courtesy Ludwig Mies van der Rohe.
86. Photo by Orlando R. Cabanban; courtesy the Perkins and Will Partnership.
87. Courtesy the Perkins and Will Partnership.
88. Photo by Orlando R. Cabanban; courtesy Skidmore, Owings and Merrill.
89. Photo by Orlando R. Cabanban; courtesy Skidmore, Owings and Merrill.
90. Photo by Orlando R. Cabanban; courtesy Skidmore, Owings and Merrill.
91. Photo by Orlando R. Cabanban; courtesy Skidmore, Owings and Merrill.
92. Courtesy Skidmore, Owings and Merrill.
93. Photo by Photography Unlimited; courtesy Mittelbusher and Tourtelot.
94. Photo by Harr, Hedrich-Blessing;

courtesy the Perkins and Will
Partnership.
95. Photo by Philip A. Turner; courtesy
Harry Weese and Associates.
96. Courtesy I. W. Colburn.
97. Photo by Hube Henry,
Hedrich-Blessing; courtesy Edward
Dart.
98. Photo by Llewellyn Studio; courtesy
Skidmore, Owings and Merrill.
99. Photo by Chicago Architectural
Photographing Company; courtesy
Loebl, Schlossman and Bennett.
100. Photo by Orlando R. Cabanban;
courtesy Ezra Gordon, Jack M.
Levin and Associates.
101. Courtesy Louis R. Solomon, John D.
Cordwell and Associates.
102. Courtesy Louis R. Solomon, John D.
Cordwell and Associates.
103. Photo by Richard Nickel.
104. Photo by Richard Nickel.
105. Photo by Richard Nickel.

106. Photo by Richard Nickel.
107. Photo by Richard Nickel.
108. Chicago Department of
Development and Planning,
*Community Renewal Program
Report,* 1964.
109. Photo by Chicago Department of
Public Works.
110. Photo by Chicago Department of
Public Works.
111. Photo by William J. Boyd; courtesy
United States Steel Corporation.
112. Photo by Chicago Transit Authority;
courtesy George Krambles, Chicago
Transit Authority.
113. Photo by Chicago Transit Authority;
courtesy George Krambles, Chicago
Transit Authority.
114. Photo by Chicago Department of
Water and Sewers.
115. Photo by Chicago Aerial Survey;
courtesy C. F. Murphy Associates.

Index

Abbott, Edith, 42, 47
Addams, Jane, 148
Adler, Max, Planetarium, 231
Adler and Sullivan, 121, 149, 199, 264
Airports
  Maywood, 33
  Meigs, 182, 203, 258
  Michigan, Lake, proposed, 263
  Midway, 33–34, 46, 258, 259, 263, 269
  O'Harc, 34, 46, 242, 249, 258–60,
    262–63, 269, fig. 115
Air-rights construction, 84, 120
Akers, Milburn, 166, 201
American Bridge Division, United States
  Steel Company, 140
American Civil Liberties Union, 166, 201
American Federation of Labor (AFL), 206
American Institute of Architects, 80, 128–
  29, 130, 134, 139, 229, 230, 264, 276
American Institute of Planners, 230
American Institute of Steel Construction,
  139, 233–34, 243, 264
American Public Health Association, 165
American Society of Civil Engineers, 120
American Society of Planning Officials,
  264, 278
Ammann and Whitney, 123
Anderson and Battles, 80
Anemometer, 76–77, 119
Archdiocesan Conservation Council,
  Roman Catholic Church, 218
Architects Collaborative, The, 193
Architectural Forum, 4, 52, 139, 175
Architectural Record, 65
Armour Institute, 52, 173
Armstrong, John A., 47
Art Institute of Chicago, 126, 231
Associated Housing Architects, 48
Atomic Energy Commission, 176
Auditorium Theater Council, 149
Austin, Richard B., 166, 202
Austin Engineering Company, 36

Bach, Ira J., 271
Bacon, Edmund N., 43–44, 48

Bacon, Vinton W., 254, 256–57
Bandel, Hanskarl, 73
Band Shell, Grant Park, 231
Banham, Reyner, 139, 198
Baron, Harold M., 282
Barton-Ashman Associates, 227
*Basic Policies for the Comprehensive Plan
  of Chicago,* 273
Bauhaus, Dessau, Germany, 173
Bavaria, kingdom of, 87
Baylis, John R., 26
Bennett, Edward H., 6, 11, 19, 182, 235,
  243, 263, 272, 276
Berry, Edwin C., 277, 282
Black, W. Joseph, 160, 200, 277, 282
Blighted Areas Redevelopment Act, 205,
  271
Bogardus, James, 11
Bolt, Beranek and Newman, 123
Bonwit-Teller Store, 123
Booth and Nagle, 80
Boston, Massachusetts, 228
Brass-button reference point, 76–77, 119
Brazier, Arthur M., 214
Brice, Fanny, 18
Bridges
  Bataan-Corregidor Memorial (State
    Street), 233, 264
  cantilever, 237
  Chicago Skyway, 237
  Damen Avenue, 234
  Dearborn Street, 234, 264
  Eisenhower (Congress) Expressway, 236
  girder, box, 242
  girder, continuous, 242
  lift, vertical, 108
  Link, 23–24, 45
  Milwaukee Avenue, 242
  Ontario Street, 242
  pedestrian, Lake Shore Drive at North
    Avenue Beach, 24, 26, 264
  Pennsylvania Railroad, South Branch
    Chicago River, 108
  Ryan Expressway, 242
  Sky Ride, Century of Progress
    Exposition, 11, 19